Brexit and Energy Law

Bringing together leading experts from across the UK and Europe, this book provides a comprehensive analysis of the impact of Brexit on the energy sector in the UK and in the European Union and its Member States. In recent decades, the trend within the EU has been towards greater integration and liberalisation of energy markets. Through the development of the Union's internal energy market and the funding of cross-border energy infrastructure, EU membership facilitates cross-border trade in energy, promotes security of energy supply, and, via the European Atomic Energy Community (Euratom), allows EU Member States to trade in nuclear material for energy production. Brexit changes all of this. The significant level of integration and interdependence in EU energy policy means that the UK's departure from the Union poses many challenges for the UK, the EU, and EU Member States. While certain energy-related arrangements have been addressed, the relationship between the UK and EU in the energy sector has been changed fundamentally. In this context, important and interrelated questions arise, such as the following: Under what terms will energy trading between the EU and UK now take place? What access will the UK have to EU energy markets? What does Brexit mean for the security of energy supply? What does the UK's departure from Euratom mean for nuclear research? Can the cross-border single energy market (SEM) on the island of Ireland continue following Brexit? What implications does Brexit have for renewables, the environment, and climate change? Brexit comes at a time when the European energy sector is undergoing the processes of decarbonisation and energy transition. This book offers researchers, legal practitioners, and policy advisers in-depth understanding of the interplay between these challenges and Brexit.

Ana Stanič is the director and founder of E&A Law, London. She is an English solicitor advocate admitted in Australia, England, and Ireland with over 25 years' experience advising states, energy companies, and international institutions on the transactional, regulatory, and dispute resolution aspects of energy projects.

Silke Goldberg is a partner at Herbert Smith Freehills LLP. She has over 20 years' experience in the energy sector and is a visiting professor at the Energy Law Institute at Queen Mary University, London, and visiting professor at the University of Groningen, the Netherlands. She is a solicitor admitted to practice in Germany, England, and France as well as a member of the Irish Law Society.

Legal Perspectives on Brexit

'Legal Perspectives on Brexit' is a peer-reviewed series of books which goes beyond responding to public curiosity aroused by the triggering of Article 50 to recognize the ongoing legal and political disputes Brexit has prompted. Aimed at academics and professionals it provides expert commentary on and predictions about the possible legislative and judicial implications of Brexit for each of the different sectors of regulation which have for so long been dominated by EU Law, creating a valuable one stop resource which exposes, explores and perhaps even resolves legal problems stemming from the separation of UK and EU legal systems.

Brexit and the Car Industry
Matthew Humphreys and Doug Munro

Brexit and Competition Law
Andreas Stephan and Barry Rodger

Brexit and Agriculture
Ludivine Petetin and Mary Dobbs

Brexit and Intellectual Property Law
Janice Denoncourt

Fisheries and the Law in Europe
Regulation After Brexit
Edited by Jonatan Echebarria Fernández, Tafsir Matin Johansson, Jon A. Skinner and Mitchell Lennan

Brexit and Energy Law
Implications and Opportunities
Edited by Ana Stanič and Silke Goldberg

<https://www.routledge.com/law/series/BREXIT>

Brexit and Energy Law

Implications and Opportunities

Edited by Ana Stanič and Silke Goldberg

Routledge
Taylor & Francis Group
LONDON AND NEW YORK

First published 2023
by Routledge
4 Park Square, Milton Park, Abingdon, Oxon OX14 4RN

and by Routledge
605 Third Avenue, New York, NY 10158

Routledge is an imprint of the Taylor & Francis Group, an informa business

ISBN: 978-1-032-41489-8 (hbk)
ISBN: 978-1-032-42771-3 (pbk)
ISBN: 978-1-003-36433-7 (ebk)

DOI: 10.4324/9781003364337

Typeset in Times New Roman
by Deanta Global Publishing Services, Chennai, India

Dedicated to Pax Europaea

Contents

Contributors

Julian Bowden worked for BP on downstream oil and international gas, mainly in planning, strategy, and business development roles. His career in BP included postings to company offices in Moscow and Brussels. On gas, he was heavily involved in marketing and transportation aspects of the southern gas corridor project bringing gas from Azerbaijan to Europe. He is currently a senior visiting research fellow at the Oxford Institute for Energy Studies.

Owen Collins is a senior associate in the Energy Group in Matheson LLP. He has particular experience in the renewables sphere, having advised on the development, sale, acquisition, and financing of over 1GW of renewable energy projects in Ireland. He specialises in electricity and gas market regulation and has particular expertise in the drafting and negotiation of power purchase agreements (PPAs), advising on all types of PPAs including REFIT, RESS, merchant, and corporate PPAs.

Garret Farrelly is a partner and head of Matheson's LLP Energy and Projects and Infrastructure Groups. He is also chair of Matheson's ESG Advisory Group. He advises on all aspects of Mergers & Acquisitions (M&A) projects and project financing, from Public Private Partnerships (PPPs) to privately financed electricity, oil, and gas field developments and privatisations as well as electricity, gas, and telecommunications network infrastructure. He practice over the past 9 years has focused particularly on electricity and gas market regulation and trading.

Jean-Christophe Füeg is an ambassador and head of International Energy Affairs at the Swiss Federal Office of Energy since 2001, responsible for electricity agreement negotiations with the EU. He is a member of the Governing Board of International Energy Agency (IEA), the Energy Charter Treaty and International Renewable Energy Agency (IRENA). Ambassador Füeg gave evidence to the House of Lords' EU Energy and Environment Sub-Committee on what Brexit lessons UK can learn from Switzerland's energy relationship with the EU in 2017.

Silke Goldberg is a partner at Herbert Smith Freehills LLP. She has over 20 years' experience in the energy sector and is visiting professor with the Energy Law Institute at Queen Mary University, London, and visiting professor at the University of Groningen, the Netherlands. Silke is also an associate professor II at the University of Oslo. She is a solicitor admitted to practice in Germany, England, and France as well as a member of the Irish Law Society.

Paul Hallas, an economist by training, has almost 40 years of energy sector experience in commercial, strategic, regulation/policy, and business leadership roles. He led Centrica's team preparing for the impact of Brexit on the company, its markets, and its customers from 2016 to 2019. Since then, Paul has developed a portfolio of non-executive director and other independent advisory positions. He recently delivered a series of UK training courses on energy trading post-Brexit.

Sir Philip Lowe KCMG is a partner in Oxera Consulting. He graduated from St John's College, Oxford and London Business School. Following a period in industry, he joined the European Commission in 1973 where he was director-general for Development (1997–2000), for Competition (2002–2010), and for Energy (2010–2014). He was a non-executive director of the UK Competition and Markets Authority (2013–2016) and is currently chair of the EUI Competition Law Workshop and of the World Energy Council's Trilemma Initiative.

Wendy Miles is a specialist in international arbitration and dispute resolution with a focus on private and public international law. She brings 25+ years of experience, with particular expertise in energy and climate change disputes. She has considerable experience in the fields of oil and gas, renewables, natural resources, infrastructure, and finance, focusing on transition post-Paris Agreement. Since 2015, Wendy has participated in the UN Framework Convention on Climate Change Conferences of the Parties (COPs).

Jana Nysten works as a senior researcher at the German Stiftung Umweltenergierecht (Foundation for Environmentail Energy Law). Her work focusses on the European Electricity Market and international and European CO2-pricing. She studied law at the University of Maastricht and PennState University in Pennsylvania, USA, after which she worked in Brussels and Berlin as an energy lawyer in private practice before joining the Stiftung in 2019.

Fabian Pause has been a researcher and head of department for European and International Environmental Energy Law and Comparative Law at the German Stiftung Umweltenergierecht (Foundation for Environmental Energy Law), Würzburg, Germany, since 2011. In his research, he focuses on European Environmental Energy Law and Comparative Law aspects that are related to national support schemes for renewable energies and energy efficiency. Further, he is an expert on the EU Governance of the energy union and climate action.

George Peretz KC BL is a barrister at Monckton Chambers in London and the Law Library in Dublin, and has a wide practice in EU and regulatory law, with a particular focus on subsidy control and state aid, in which area he advises and represents public and private sector clients. Recent litigation in the area includes *Credit Suisse v HMRC* (2019), in which he successfully resisted a state aid challenge in the English High Court to the bankers' bonus tax. George is UK correspondent of the *European State Aid Law Quarterly*, and wrote the Chapter on state aid in McCrudden, *Law and Practice of the Ireland/Northern Ireland Protocol* (2021).

Eleanor Reeves is a partner at Ashurst LLP and leads the London Environment and Safety practice. Eleanor specialises in environmental and health and safety law with a particular focus on sustainability. She advises clients on environmental and safety matters across projects, transactions, and litigation. Eleanor is a member of the UK Environmental Law Association and the UK Health and Safety Lawyers' Association.

Maurice Sheridan is a barrister, now retired. After a *stage* with the European Commission, and as assistant to the President of the Italian Constitutional Court and Italian Minister for European Policies, Maurice commenced practice as a barrister in London. He appeared before all levels of the English Court system and the European Court of Justice (ECJ)/Court of Justice of the European Union (CJEU). He acted for States, local government, corporates, and non-governmental organisations (NGOs) and for International Financial Institutions (IFIs). He was a specialist practitioner in EU commercial and environmental law.

Dorothy Smith is stakeholder partner at The Infrastructure Forum in London. Until June 2012 she was director of Public Policy at BT Group. She was director of European Affairs for BT Group, Centrica, and British Gas in Brussels between 1994 and 2005. In the 1980s she was assistant secretary to the British Coal Corporation and the private secretary to Lord Lever of Manchester, Chancellor of the Duchy of Lancaster, in the Cabinet Office, from 1977 to 1979.

Ana Stanič is the Director of E&A Law, London, and visiting professor at Technische Universität in Berlin and UIBE in China. She is an English solicitor advocate admitted in Australia, England, and Ireland with over 25 years' experience advising states, energy companies, and international institutions on the transactional, regulatory, and dispute resolution aspects of energy projects.

Ian Truman is a partner in the nuclear law team at UK law firm Burges Salmon LLP. Ian advises project sponsors, developers, technology vendors, operators, insurers, government departments, funders, and contractors on all aspects of international and UK nuclear law, nuclear new build, and other nuclear projects. Ian is a member of the Nuclear Industry Association, the Nuclear Institute, the International Nuclear Law Association, and the World Nuclear Association.

Eric White is a UK-trained lawyer who has spent most of his career in the Legal Service of the European Commission working on internal market and international law matters. In particular, he led the Trade Policy and WTO team before turning to advising the Commission on climate change. He now works as a consultant in the Competition, Regulation and Trade group of Herbert Smith Freehills LLP in Brussels, focusing on WTO law and the EU's rules governing trade with non-EU countries, including Brexit-related matters.

Preface

In 2016, the year of the referendum vote in favour of UK's withdrawal from the European Union, UK and EU energy policies and regulations were arguably never so closely aligned.

Both the UK and the EU as a whole had binding obligations under international agreements on nuclear energy under the auspices of the International Atomic Energy Agency (IAEA) and on climate change following the COP21 Agreement in 2015. At the same time, the UK had been in the vanguard of initiatives within the EU to create a European-wide, integrated, interconnected, and competitive energy market. The vision of that market was progressively becoming a reality, with stronger interconnections, European-wide codes for managing electricity and gas networks, and the extension of day-ahead electricity market coupling to countries from the West to the East of Europe.

After some years of hesitation in the early 2000s, successive UK governments also recognised that strengthening the gas and electricity connections with European neighbours (including the Republic of Ireland) could significantly enhance the UK's security of supply and the resilience of its domestic energy networks. At the same time, this has allowed UK producers to exploit opportunities to export renewable energy to neighbouring European markets.

In the meantime, the market for gas has become global, covering liquefied natural gas (LNG) and gas delivered by pipeline. In principle, the quantities of gas supplied to the UK from Russia under contract have been very low. But the European gas market is increasingly interconnected and integrated so that it is difficult to tell exactly where your gas supplies from outside Europe originated. Demand in China and India for gas has also been increasing substantially as these countries try to reduce air pollution by decreasing their use of coal. The war in the Ukraine has put further pressure on supplies to Europe and to the UK, which use large quantities of gas both for electricity and for residential heating.

With such common objectives and common challenges, one can only hope that the Energy Chapter of the EU–UK Trade and Cooperation Agreement will be used as a basis for restoring a close level of cooperation between the UK and EU governments and regulators in their efforts to provide secure and sustainable supplies of energy to businesses and households at competitive and affordable prices. An Agreement on Nuclear Cooperation is thankfully already in place, but abandoning the long-fought-for prize of an integrated and competitive European-wide market would surely be seen as throwing away something of real value to all European countries. In a time of transition to a net zero carbon world, energy systems need to be smart, flexible, diverse in primary sources, and resilient. Being part of, or connected to, a large market with different patterns of supply and demand makes the task of meeting medium- and long-term energy objectives easier and more affordable. No wonder so many eastern and south-eastern countries in Europe, including the Ukraine, are anxious to join the EU's single energy market.

Against this background, energy cooperation between the UK and the EU has taken a step backwards since Brexit. Both sides continue to hold to their international nuclear and climate change commitments, but in other respects there is a stand-off. In institutional and regulatory terms, the UK is no longer part of the single European energy market. It is not taking part in further regulatory convergence in energy, nor in the moves towards European-wide Network Codes, covering in particular the management of interconnections. The UK has left the day-ahead coupling arrangements in the EU electricity market and is not taking part in any of the European-wide initiatives to ensure security of supply, especially as far as gas is concerned. It has set up its own emissions trading system with so far no sign of any link between it and the larger market for emission certificates which exists in the EU ETS. Like any other 'third country' to the EU, its trade with the EU could well be faced with the further restrictions implied by any EU carbon border adjustment mechanism.

Leading legal and energy experts in this book analyse the implications of Brexit for both the UK and the EU energy sectors from the perspectives of the World Trade Organization (WTO), trading, market design, energy security, institutional, state aid, and dispute resolution as well as environmental and renewable energy. In addition, the Chapter on the Irish energy market highlights the specific challenges facing the island of Ireland with its integrated electricity market post-Brexit, whereas the Chapter discussing the Swiss experience provides insight into the difficulties faced by a European energy market outside the EU internal energy market but surrounded by the EU. Helpfully, the authors also explore possible ways ahead in EU–UK energy cooperation.

This book is a timely endeavour as pragmatic solutions are needed to meet the current and future challenges of the energy sector. With Switzerland and now also the UK outside the EU, attitudes on both the UK and Swiss sides and at EU level should not cause governments to make the historic mistake of preferring institutional purity to plain simple economic advantage and prosperity for people in Europe.

Sir Philip Lowe KCMG

Abbreviations

ACER	Agency for the Cooperation of Energy Regulators
AP	Additional Protocol
AEC	Atomic Energy Commission
BBL	Balgzand Bacton Line pipeline
BITs	bilateral investment treaties
Brexit	the withdrawal of the UK from the EU and the Euratom on 31 January 2020
Brexit Referendum	referendum held in the UK on 23 June 2016 on United Kingdom's membership of the EU
CACM	capacity allocation and congestion management
CAM	Competition and Markets Authority
CAT	Competition Appeal Tribunal
CB	carbon budget
CBA	cost benefit analysis
CBAM	carbon border adjustment mechanism
CCC	Climate Change Committee
CCR	capacity calculation regions
CCS	carbon capture and storage
CEE	Central Eastern Europe
CEPA	Center for European Policy Analysis
CfD	contracts for difference
Clean Energy Package	Directive (EU) 2019/944 of the European Parliament and of the Council of 5 June 2019 on common rules for the internal market for electricity and amending Directive 2012/27/EU; Regulation (EU) 2019/943 of the European Parliament and of the Council of 5 June 2019 on the internal market for electricity; Regulation (EU) 2019/941 of the European Parliament and of the Council of 5 June 2019 on risk-preparedness in the electricity sector and repealing Directive 2005/89/EC; and Regulation (EU)

	2019/942 of the European Parliament and of the Council of 5 June 2019 establishing a European Union Agency for the Cooperation of Energy Regulators
COP26	2021 United Nations Climate Change Conference
Commission	European Commission
CJEU	Court of Justice of the European Union
CRU	Commission for Regulation of Utilities
CWE	Central Western European Region
DAH	day-ahead
DAMC	day-ahead market coupling
Defra	Department for Environment, Food & Rural Affairs
DG Energy	Directorate-General for Energy
DSO	distribution system operator
EBGL	Electricity Balancing Guideline
EC	European Commission
ECJ	European Court of Justice
ECT	Energy Charter Treaty 1994
ECHR	European Convention on Human Rights 1950
ECtHR	European Court of Human Rights
ECSC	European Coal and Steel Community
ECURIE	European Community Urgent Radiological Information Exchange
EEA	European Economic Area
EEC	European Economic Community
EEPR	European Energy Programme for Recovery
EFET	European Federation of Energy Traders
EFTA	European Free Trade Association
ENC	European Network Code
Energy Charter	European Energy Charter signed on 17 December 1991
Energy Community Treaty	Treaty establishing the Energy Community of 25 October 2005
End of Transition Date	31 December 2020, being the date that the Transition Period, during which the legal status quo was maintained after the UK left the EU, came to an end
ENTSO	European Network of Transmission System Operators
ENTSO-E	European Network of Transmission System Operators for Electricity
ENTSO-G	European Network of Transmission System Operators for Gas

EPA	EU–Japan Economic Partnership Agreement 2019
ESA	EFTA Surveillance Authority
ETS	emissions trading system
EU	European Union
EUA	EU emission allowance
Euratom	European Atomic Energy Community
Euratom Treaty	Treaty establishing the European Atomic Energy Community of 25 March 1957
EU ETS	EU Emissions Trading System
EU Member States	State members of the European Union
EU Exit Date	the date the UK left the EU, 31 January 2020
EUR	Euro
EURDEP	European Radiological Data Exchange Platform
EWIC	East West Interconnector
FBMC	flow-based market coupling
FCR	frequency containment reserves
FDI	foreign direct investment
FES	Future Energy Scenarios
FET	fair and equitable treatment
FMV	fair market value
FTA	free trade agreement
GATS	General Agreement on Services
GATT	General Agreement on Tariffs and Trade
GB	Great Britain
GBP	pounds sterling
General Court	General Court of the CJEU
GHG	greenhouse gas
GNI	Gas Networks Ireland
GO	guarantee of origin
GoOs	guarantees of origin
IAA	Singapore International Arbitration Act 1994 as revised 2002
IAEA	International Atomic Energy Agency
ICC	International Court of Arbitration of the International Chamber of Commerce
ICS	Investment Court System
ICSID	International Centre for Settlement of Investment Disputes
ICSID Convention	Convention on the Settlement of Investment Disputes between States and Nationals of Other States 1966
IEA	International Energy Agency
IEM	internal energy market
IFA	institutional framework agreement

IGCC	International Grid Control Cooperation
IIA	international investment agreement
ILC	International Law Commission
Intra-EU BITs	BITs entered into between two EU Member States
Intra-EU Dispute	disputes between two EU Member States
IPCC	International Panel on Climate Change
ISDS	investor–state dispute settlement
ITER	International Thermonuclear Experimental Reactor
ITRE Committee	European Parliament's Committee on Industry, Research, Telecoms and Energy
Kyoto Protocol	Protocol to the UNFCCC concluded in Kyoto in 1997
LNG	liquified natural gas
m	million
MCO	market coupling operation
MFN	most favoured nation
MIC	Multilateral Investment Court
MPI	multipurpose interconnectors
MRLVC	Multi Region Loose Volume Coupling
NAFTA	North American Free Trade Agreement 1994
NBP	national balancing point
NC	network code
NCA	Nuclear Co-operation Agreement between the UK and Euratom
NECP	national energy and climate plans
NEMO	nominated electricity market operators
Net Zero Target	target set for net zero greenhouse gas emissions by 2050
New York Convention	Convention on the Recognition and Enforcement of Foreign Arbitral Awards 1959
NGO	non-governmental organisation
Northern Ireland Protocol	Protocol on Ireland/Northern Ireland to the Withdrawal Agreement
NPP	nuclear power plant
NRA	national regulatory authority
NREAP	National Renewable Energy Action Plan
NSL	North Sea link
NTC	net transfer capacity
OECD	Organisation for Economic Co-operation and Development
OJEU	Official Journal of the European Union
OFTO	offshore transmission owner
ONR	Office for Nuclear Regulation

OTC	over-the-counter
PA	Paris Agreement
PCA	Permanent Court of Arbitration
PCI	Project of Common Interest
PCR	price coupling of regions
PPA	power purchase agreement
PSO	public service obligation
RCC	regional coordination centre
REGO	renewable energy guarantee of origin scheme
REMIT	Regulation (EU) No 1227/2011 on wholesale energy market integrity and transparency
RERA	renewable energy resource areas
RES	renewable energy sources
RES-E	renewable energy sources for electricity
RES-T	renewable energy sources in transport
REU	renewable energy unit
RSC	regional security coordinators
RTE	Réseau de Transport d'Électricité
SCE	Specialised Committee on Energy
SDAC	single day-ahead coupling
SEM	single energy market
SEMC	SEM committee
Second Energy Package	Directive 2003/54/EC of the European Parliament and of the Council of 26 June 2003 concerning common rules for the internal market in electricity and repealing Directive 96/92/EC; Directive 2003/55/EC of the European Parliament and of the Council of 26 June 2003 concerning common rules for the internal market in natural gas and repealing Directive 98/30/EC; and Regulation (EC) No 1228/2003 of the European Parliament and of the Council of 26 June 2003 on conditions for access to the network for cross-border exchanges in electricity
SEP	Second Energy Package
SET Plan	Strategic Energy Technology Plan
SMR	small modular reactor
SOE	state-owned enterprise
SPV	special purpose vehicle
TBT Agreement	Agreement on Technical Barriers to Trade
TCA	Trade and Cooperation Agreement between the European Union and the European Atomic Energy Community, and the United Kingdom

	of Great Britain and Northern Ireland of 30 December 2020
TEN-E	Trans-European Energy Network
TEN-T	Trans-European Transport Networks in Europe
TEP	Third Energy Package
TEU	Treaty on European Union 1992
TFEU	Treaty on the Functioning of the European Union (formerly the EC Treaty, the Treaty of Rome or the Treaty establishing the European Community) 2012, Official Journal C 326, 26/10/2012
The 2018 Act	the European Union (Withdrawal) Act 2018
The 2020 Act	the European Union (Future Relationship) Act 2020
Third Energy Package	Directive 2009/72/EC of the European Parliament and of the Council of 13 July 2009 concerning common rules for the internal market in electricity and repealing Directive 2003/54/EC; Directive 2009/73/EC of the European Parliament and of the Council of 13 July 2009 concerning common rules for the internal market in natural gas and repealing Directive 2003/55/EC; Regulation (EC) No 713/2009 of the European Parliament and of the Council of 13 July 2009 establishing an Agency for the Cooperation of Energy Regulators; Regulation (EC) No 714/2009 of the European Parliament and of the Council of 13 July 2009 on conditions for access to the network for cross-border exchanges in electricity and repealing Regulation; and Regulation (EC) No 715/2009 of the European Parliament and of the Council of 13 July 2009 on conditions for access to the natural gas transmission networks and repealing Regulation (EC) No 1775/2005
TPA	third party access
Transition Period	The period during which the legal status quo was maintained after the UK left the EU
TSO	transmission system operator
TTF	title transfer facility
TYNDP	European Ten-year Network Development Plan
UK	United Kingdom of Great Britain and Northern Ireland (including the devolved administrations of Scotland, Wales, and Northern Ireland)

UK ETS	UK Emissions Trading Scheme
UN	United Nations
UNCITRAL	United Nations Commission on International Trade Law
UNCITRAL Model Law	UNCITRAL Model Law on International Commercial Arbitration 1985, with amendments as adopted in 2006
UNCTAD	United Nations Conference on Trade and Development
UNFCCC	United Nations Framework Convention on Climate Change
UR	utility regulator
USA or US	United States of America
USD	United States Dollars
VCLT	Vienna Convention on the Law of Treaties 1969
VOSA	Voluntary Offer Safeguards Agreement
Withdrawal Agreement/WA	Agreement on the withdrawal of the United Kingdom of Great Britain and Northern Ireland from the European Union and the European Atomic Energy Community of 19 October 2019
WTO	World Trade Organization

Introduction

Ana Stanič and Silke Goldberg

The UK formally left the EU and the European Atomic Energy Community (Euratom) on 31 January 2020. Thereafter, pursuant to the terms of the Withdrawal Agreement agreed between the EU and the UK on 17 October 2019, it was in a transition period until 31 December 2020, during which time it continued to be treated as a Member State of the EU both by the other EU Member States and the EU institutions and by third countries and was subject to EU law and the jurisdiction of the Court of Justice of the European Union. The UK had been a Member State of the EU (and its predecessor, the European Economic Community, since 1 January 1973, and is to date the only country to have left the EU.

On 23 June 2016, a legally non-binding referendum was held in the UK on whether the UK should withdraw from the EU. The question on the referendum ballot paper was 'Should the United Kingdom remain a member of the European Union or leave the European Union?' This was the second time the British people were consulted on the UK's membership in the EU. The first referendum was held in 1975. At that time, 67.2% of the electorate voted to stay in the then European Economic Community.

The outcome of the 2016 referendum was different. More than 30 million people cast their vote on 23 June 2016. The turnout was 71.8% and thus considerably higher than it is for a regular election. Of all those who voted, 51.9% voted for the UK to leave the EU, with 53.4% of the electorate in England voting to leave, 52.5% of the Welsh electorate voting to leave, 62% of the Scottish electorate voting to remain, and 55.8% of the Northern Irish electorate voting to remain.

The term *Brexit*, an abbreviation of the two words *Britain* and *exit*, refers to the process of the UK's withdrawal from the EU. The UK officially notified the EU of its decision to withdraw from the EU and Euratom on 29 March 2017, thereby formally triggering Article 50 of the Treaty on the European Union. Pursuant to paragraph 3 of this article, the UK would automatically cease to be a member of the EU if an agreement was not reached on withdrawal within 2 years of the notification of the decision to withdraw. The EU insisted that the paragraph 2 of Article 50 required two-pronged Brexit negotiations with the terms of a withdrawal agreement to be concluded first, followed by negotiations on the framework of a future relationship. The negotiations were fraught, and the terms of the Withdrawal Agreement were only agreed after the UK and EU Council,

DOI: 10.4324/9781003364337-1

with the agreement of the remaining 27 Member State of the EU, agreed three times[1] to delay the date on which the UK would otherwise have automatically ceased to be a member of the EU as per Article 50(3). The Protocol on Ireland/Northern Ireland and the Protocol relating to the sovereign base areas of the United Kingdom of Great Britain and Northern Ireland in Cyprus form part of the Withdrawal Agreement. At the same time, the political declaration setting out the framework for the future relationship between the European Union and the United Kingdom[2] was signed. With the UK having ratified the Withdrawal Agreement on 29 January and the EU a day later, the Withdrawal Agreement entered into force on 31 January 2020. The UK formally left the EU on 31 January 2020. On that date, the transition period started. During the transition period, the relationship with the EU was governed by the terms of the Withdrawal Agreement. The transition period lasted until 31 December 2020. During this transition period, the terms of the agreement setting out the future relationship were hammered out. Only 7 days before the transition period was due to expire were the terms of the Trade and Cooperation Agreement (TCA) finalised.

Energy was not a high priority area in the Brexit negotiations. Only 16 pages of the TCA are dedicated to energy and climate change. Having been a key shaper of the liberalisation of the EU's energy sector and creation of the internal energy market, post-Brexit, the UK energy sector is no longer legally part of it, despite remaining integrated with it through trade and electricity and gas interconnectors, which has led to trading inefficiencies and higher electricity costs.

The regulatory uncertainty facing the sector has been unprecedented and prolonged. Moreover, as the discussion in this book reveals, the uncertainties triggered by Brexit have not diminished since the end of the transition period.

On the contrary, the energy Chapter of the TCA is – as is the fisheries Chapter – subject to review in 2026, which gives the TCA a temporary character insofar as

1 The first decision on Brexit extension was adopted by the European Council on 22 March 2019, whereby the Brexit date was delayed until 12 April 2019 if the UK House of Commons failed to approve the withdrawal agreement by 29 March 2019. See a letter from the Permanent Representative of the UK to the European Union, Sir Tim Barrow, of 22 March 2019 at <https://www.consilium.europa.eu/en/policies/eu-uk-after-referendum/>. The second decision on the Brexit extension was adopted by the European Council on 13 April 2019 to further extend the Brexit date until 31 October 2019. See COUNCIL DECISION amending Decision (EU) 2019/274 on the signing, on behalf of the European Union and of the European Atomic Energy Community, of the Agreement on the withdrawal of the United Kingdom of Great Britain and Northern Ireland from the European Union and the European Atomic Energy Community, XT/21027/2019/INIT, <https://eur-lex.europa.eu/legal-content/EN/TXT/?uri=CELEX%3A32019D0642>. The third decision on the Brexit extension was adopted by the European Council on 29 October 2019 to extend the period under Article 50(3) until 31 January 2020 to allow more time for the withdrawal agreement to be ratified. See EUROPEAN COUNCIL DECISION taken in agreement with the United Kingdom extending the period under Article 50(3)TEU, XT/20024/2019/REV/2, <https://eur-lex.europa.eu/legal-content/en/TXT/?uri=CELEX:32019D1810>. A helpful timeline of the Brexit negotiations and relevant documents can be found at <https://eur-lex.europa.eu/content/news/Brexit-UK-withdrawal-from-the-eu.html>.

2 <https://eur-lex.europa.eu/legal-content/EN/TXT/HTML/?uri=CELEX:12020W/TXT&from=EN#d1e32-101-1>

the energy sector is concerned and renders the energy sector dependent on the political goodwill of the UK and the EU in relation to other, not-energy-related issues. With the energy sector already facing significant regulatory and other uncertainties connected with the implementation of decarbonisation and energy transition targets and objectives, a perfect storm now faces the UK energy sector as it has to deal with Brexit whilst dealing also with supply chain disruptions due to lockdown and other measures adopted by the UK and EU in response to COVID. The European energy crisis as a result of the Russian invasion of Ukraine puts supply security issues discussed in this book into sharper focus as the UK has dropped out of the relevant EU solidarity mechanism.

To help to unpick and tackle these uncertainties, this book examines the implications and opportunities of Brexit for the energy sectors of both the UK and the EU.

Leading legal and energy sector experts from the world of academia and practice examine in turn the impact of Brexit on (i) energy trade (Chapter 1), (ii) the UK's access to the EU's energy market (Chapter 2), (iii) the EU's and UK's perspectives on security of supply (Chapters 3 and 4), (iv) the UK's state aid rules as they concern the energy sector (Chapter 5), (v) the UK's and EU's renewables and climate change policies (Chapters 6 and 7), (vi) the UK's environmental law and policy (Chapter 8), (vii) the UK's nuclear sector (Chapter 9), (viii) energy disputes and mechanisms to resolve the same (Chapter 10), and (ix) Ireland's energy sector in particular, given its geographical separation from the rest of the EU internal energy market (Chapter 11). The Swiss perspective on Brexit and energy discussed in Chapter 12 provides the reader with insight as to the likely form of the future UK–EU energy relations. The final Chapter (Chapter 13) seeks to provide a compressive overview of the impact Brexit has and will have on the UK and EU energy sectors in the coming years.

Given the challenges of decarbonisation and energy transition, in the conclusion, the editors of this book call for concrete steps to be taken to maintain regulatory alignment in respect of the energy sector going forward as between the UK and the EU and for the depoliticisation of decisions affecting the energy sector, in particular in relation to cross-border infrastructure, energy trade, and security.

Against the backdrop of the new geopolitical realities as a result of the war in Ukraine, a shared regional concern for supply security, and the urgent need to tackle climate change and other environmental challenges, close cooperation between the EU and the UK must be the way ahead.

1 Trade in Energy Products between the UK and EU Post Brexit

Eric White

1.1 Introduction

At the end of the transition period established by the Withdrawal Agreement, the UK not only ceased to be part of the EU but also left the EU Single Market and the Single Energy Market. This means that UK energy markets are no longer integrated with those of the EU. This has profound implications for trade in energy products between the UK and the EU.

The Trade and Cooperation Agreement (TCA) is designed to mitigate this rupture by providing a new trade regime. However, it is fundamentally an agreement about managing progressive divergence and does not promote convergence and market integration. By contrast, convergence and market integration are the primary objectives of the EU. While they are to a lesser extent the objectives of other EU trade agreements, the UK is in a unique position, having been an integral part of the single market, and is intending to diverge from its rules.

To understand this new trade regime and how it might develop, this Chapter examines the relevant agreements concluded under the umbrella of the World Trade Organization (WTO) (collectively, the 'WTO Regime') and the Energy Charter Treaty (ECT) as applicable multilateral agreements that will regulate trade in energy products between the two countries, before commenting on the trade provisions of the TCA itself.

1.2 The WTO Regime

The first set of rules governing trade in energy products between the UK and the EU Member States post Brexit that need to be considered are those set out in the WTO Regime. They need to be considered first because the ECT and TCA rules refer to them and build upon them. The WTO has separate regimes governing goods and services, and we will briefly describe below how they relate to trade in energy goods and services. This Chapter will first examine how WTO rules apply to energy as a good and then how they apply to the services of energy transport and distribution. It will then consider the exceptions to those rules in a separate section since the principles are broadly similar for both goods and services.

DOI: 10.4324/9781003364337-2

Finally, we include some comments on the all-important issue of how WTO obligations are enforced, that is, on the dispute settlement system.

1.2.1 Energy as a good

WTO rules on goods date back to the conclusion of the General Agreement on Tariffs and Trade (GATT) in 1947. Further rules on subsidies and technical regulations have been developed over the years together with the gradual reduction in tariffs and quotas culminating in the founding of the WTO in 1994, which also introduced the rules on services (to be discussed here).

Electricity has always been treated as a good in the GATT and the WTO Regime in order to ensure that trade in electricity is treated in an equivalent manner to trade in other energy goods such as coal, oil and gas. The transport and distribution of energy goods, by contrast, were considered services and only covered by the WTO Regime with the creation of the WTO in 1994.

1.2.1.1 Import regime

All GATT Contracting Parties and WTO Members have been required to submit schedules of customs tariffs that they commit not to exceed in their trade with other Contracting Parties/Members. The UK was a founding Contracting Party to the GATT in 1947, and its tariff schedule was integrated with that of the EU after accession in 1973. Since the UK had been a Contracting Party to the GATT, upon leaving the EU it has been deemed automatically a Member of the WTO and has not had to reapply for membership in the WTO. Following Brexit, the UK schedule[1] has been separated from that of the EU,[2] but these separate schedules have not yet been certified by the Members of the WTO, which includes 164 countries (including the EU) (the 'WTO Membership' and 'Member' is to be construed accordingly). Pending certification, the UK and the EU apply their respective tariff schedules provisionally, although technically the UK is probably still bound by the EU schedule. Further, following Brexit, both the EU and the UK are bound to apply their schedules to each other, except to the extent that they have a qualifying Free Trade Agreement (FTA), as discussed here. The changes to the UK schedule compared to the EU schedule are in principle merely those required by the UK's exit from the EU. As regards energy goods, including electricity, both the EU and the UK are bound to low tariffs and no quotas.

1 The UK tariff schedule largely follows that of the EU, but finalisation (certification) is being held up by disputes with a number of WTO Members on tariff rate quotas for certain agricultural goods. The draft schedule is considered confidential by the WTO but is available from the UK government website at: <https://assets.publishing.service.gov.uk/government/uploads/system/uploads/attachment_data/file/762822/UKs_Goods_Schedule_at_the_WTO.pdf>.

2 The EU schedule bears the number CLXXIII and is subject to a number of ongoing modification procedures.

1.2.1.2 Most Favoured Nation treatment

Most Favoured Nation (MFN) treatment is often considered to be the most fundamental GATT principle and is laid down in Article I of GATT. It is essentially a prohibition on any discrimination between the equivalent goods of different WTO Members. The relevant part reads:

> any advantage, favour, privilege or immunity granted by any contracting party to any product originating in or destined for any other country shall be accorded immediately and unconditionally to the like product originating in or destined for the territories of all other contracting parties.

This principle is very important since it applies not only to tariffs but also to any regulatory measure that affects trade in energy goods. Accordingly, if a UK company is treated by an EU Member State going forward any less favourably as regards, for example, interconnectors, compared to any other WTO Member, the UK could in principle invoke the MFN principle to secure equal treatment.

The application of this principle in the case of EU measures is complex because a major feature of the internal market is of course to facilitate trade between EU Member States and thus to favour trade with them over trade with other countries. There is an exception in the GATT for such arrangements, which we return to below. For now, it is useful to illustrate its application in the energy field with the complaint brought by Russia against the EU in Case DS476.[3] One of the many complaints brought by Russia against the EU's package of energy laws was that the TEN-E Regulation[4] breached the MFN principle by including in the criteria for the approval of a Project of Common Interest (PCI) the diversification of gas supplies, which was found to include the objective of the reduction of reliance on Russian gas. The complaint was upheld, and similar arguments could now also be brought by the UK.

1.2.1.3 Internal taxes and regulatory restrictions

The main GATT discipline on internal measures is the national treatment obligation which is drafted in similar terms to the obligation of MFN treatment. There are specific prohibitions on discrimination in internal taxation and the most general obligation is that expressed in Article III:4 GATT:

> The products of the territory of any contracting party imported into the territory of any other contracting party shall be accorded treatment no less

3 DS476: *European Union and Its Member States – Certain Measures Relating to the Energy Sector*. Details are available here: <https://www.wto.org/english/tratop_e/dispu_e/cases_e/ds476_e.htm>. The Panel Report is unadopted since it was appealed by both parties and is now in limbo due to the current blockage of the work of the Appellate Body.

4 Regulation (EU) No 347/2013 of the European Parliament and of the Council of 17 April 2013 on guidelines for trans-European energy infrastructure (the 'TEN-E Regulation'), OJEU, No. L 115, 25.4.2013, pp. 39–75.

> favourable than that accorded to like products of national origin in respect of all laws, regulations and requirements affecting their internal sale, offering for sale, purchase, transportation, distribution or use.

The TEN-E measure mentioned above was also held to violate this obligation by the panel in Case DS476. Russia had also argued that the unbundling requirement of the EU Third Gas Directive[5] infringed national treatment but did not succeed in demonstrating that it led to less favourable treatment of Russian gas compared to the treatment of like domestic products. Again, the requirement for national treatment relied on by Russia in Case DS476 could also be invoked by the UK should its energy goods be treated less favourably than those applying internally in the EU and vice versa.

There is a complementary discipline to that in Article III:4, which is found in Article XI:1 GATT, and which is more applicable to prohibitions or quantitative limitations that may not be considered 'internal measures' or discriminatory. It reads as follows:

> No prohibitions or restrictions other than duties, taxes or other charges, whether made effective through quotas, import or export licences or other measures, shall be instituted or maintained by any contracting party on the importation of any product of the territory of any other contracting party or on the exportation or sale for export of any product destined for the territory of any other contracting party.

The line between Article III:4 and Article XI:1 GATT is not always clear, and they are often invoked together. An example of the potential applicability of Article XI:1 is provided by the EU's capacity limitations imposed on the Opal Pipeline, which were also contested by Russia in Case DS476 and held to constitute a de facto limitation on the import of Russian natural gas contrary to Article XI:1 GATT.

There are many further disciplines on the regulatory treatment of goods contained in the WTO Regime. The most relevant to energy trade are those in the Agreement on Technical Barriers to Trade (the 'TBT Agreement'). This develops a more proportionality-focussed discipline on technical regulations reminiscent of that developed in respect of measures of equivalent effect to quantitative restrictions in the EU. Article 2.2 TBT Agreement, for example, provides that:

> Members shall ensure that technical regulations are not prepared, adopted or applied with a view to or with the effect of creating unnecessary obstacles to international trade. For this purpose, technical regulations shall not be more

5 Directive 2009/73/EC of the European Parliament and of the Council of 13 July 2009 concerning common rules for the internal market in natural gas and repealing Directive 2003/55/EC ('Third Gas Directive'), OJ L211/94.

> trade-restrictive than necessary to fulfil a legitimate objective, taking account of the risks non-fulfilment would create.

The TBT Agreement also contains important disciplines on the use of standards designed to ensure that these are not used to provide protection[6] and that international standards are preferred.[7]

1.2.1.4 Freedom of transit

Article V GATT is a very widely drafted provision designed to ensure freedom of transit for goods through the territories of WTO Members. Paragraph 2 thereof provides that:

> There shall be freedom of transit through the territory of each contracting party, via the routes most convenient for international transit, for traffic in transit to or from the territory of other contracting parties. No distinction shall be made which is based on the flag of vessels, the place of origin, departure, entry, exit or destination, or on any circumstances relating to the ownership of goods, of vessels or of other means of transport.

Article V GATT has the potential to apply to the transit of energy goods, and in particular gas through pipelines and electricity through interconnectors. Article 20 of the TCA explicitly recognises the applicability of Article V GATT to 'the movement of energy goods via inter alia pipelines or electricity grids'. It was, however, notably not invoked by Russia in case DS476.

1.2.1.5 Trade defence

Trade defence measures, against dumping and subsidies, are rarely invoked against energy goods. Russia did, however, claim in the consultations preceding the establishment of the panel in DS476 that a number of EU measures contained in the Third Energy Package[8] constituted subsidies for EU products, but these claims were not pursued (there being many more promising claims).

1.2.2 Energy transport and distribution as a service

The transport and distribution of energy is a service to which the WTO General Agreement on Services (GATS) applies. The GATS dates from 1994 and is modelled to a large extent on the pre-existing GATT.

6 See Article 4 of the TBT Agreement which refers to a Code of Conduct to be followed by standardising bodies.

7 See Article 2.4 TBT Agreement.

8 This is a term referring to the legislative package comprised of Directive 2009/72/EC, Directive 2009/73/EC, Regulation (EC) No 714/2009, Regulation (EC) No 715/2009, Regulation (EC) No 713/2009.

One aspect of the GATS rules that go further than those applicable to goods under the GATT is that the obligations it contains apply to both the supply of the service and to the treatment of the supplier of the service.

As discussed below, the services commitments of the EU and the UK under the GATS are not significant, and in practice it is likely that only the MFN obligations will be a significant constraint on their respective measures. In this regard, it is important to note that the GATT and the GATS apply in parallel and thus overlap.[9] Compatibility with one agreement can only be a defence against violation of the other agreement if it is impossible to comply with both at once. This will only rarely be the case as few measures are required, and it will normally be possible to secure compatibility with both agreements by revoking the contested measure.

1.2.2.1 The importance of MFN

Just as in the case of the GATT, the most fundamental principle of the GATS is that of non-discrimination between WTO Members – the MFN obligation. In the case of the GATS, it requires equal treatment both of the services of other Members and the service suppliers of other Members.

The GATS contains other disciplines on trade in services but, as will be explained below, it is the MFN obligations – and critically the exceptions to it – that are likely to be the most important in any potential dispute concerning the trade in energy products between the UK and the EU.

1.2.2.2 The other GATS obligations (Market Access, National Treatment, and Domestic Regulation)

1.2.2.2.1 INTRODUCTION

Since duties cannot be applied to services in the same way as they can in the case of goods, the liberalisation of trade in services was sought through the negotiation of commitments to grant market access and national treatment rather than tariff reductions as under GATT. These commitments are listed in schedules of commitments for each WTO Member. A further complication arises from the fact that commitments are listed separately for each 'mode of supply', that is, (1) cross-border, from the territory of the supplying Member into the territory of the consumer; (2) in the territory of the supplying Member; (3) through commercial

9 See case DS31: *Canada – Certain Measures Concerning Periodicals* – especially at page 19 of the Appellate Body Report. The Appellate Body took a rather more nuanced approach in case DS27 *EC – Bananas*, where it held (at page 121) that the GATT would apply to the aspects of the measures that affect the goods, while the GATS would apply to those aspects that affect the supply of the service or the service suppliers.

presence in the territory of the consumer; and (4) by temporary presence of persons in the territory of the consumer.

There are a number of provisions of the GATS that apply only to the sectors covered by specific commitments. One way of understanding how these relate to each other is as follows:

Quantitative restrictions (whether or not discriminatory)	Market Access – Article XVI GATS
Discriminatory qualitative restrictions	National Treatment – Article XVII GATS
Non-discriminatory qualitative restrictions	Domestic Regulation – Article VI GATS

The dividing lines between these obligations are not always easy to discern and are not relevant for the discussion in this Chapter.

1.2.2.2.2 THE SCHEDULES OF SPECIFIC COMMITMENTS

The service sectors for which a WTO Member commits to grant market access or accord national treatment are listed in its schedule, generally by reference to the UN classification of services applicable at the time.[10] Limitations are often added to the commitments. The schedules are positive lists in the sense that only if a commitment is listed is there an obligation to allow market access or to accord national treatment. In the absence of an express mention of a sector, the obligations of national treatment and market access do not apply, and that Member can exclude all trade in the service concerned (although it is not entitled to deny MFN treatment).

The UK[11] and the EU[12] have now separated their schedules of GATS commitments. Just as in the case of goods, these have not yet been agreed with other Members and are applied provisionally.

The EU schedule contains the following entries for pipeline transport and services incidental to energy distribution.

10 That is the UN provisional Central Product Classification, ref. ST/ESA/STAT/SER.M/77, available at <https://unstats.un.org/unsd/classifications/Family/Detail/16>. Not all Members used the Central Product Classification, although the EU did.

11 The UK schedule is available here: <https://assets.publishing.service.gov.uk/government/uploads/system/uploads/attachment_data/file/762808/SCW380_-_UK_GATS_Schedule-FINAL_03_12_2018.pdf>.

12 The latest EU schedule is here: <https://docs.wto.org/dol2fe/Pages/SS/directdoc.aspx?filename=q:/SCHD/GATS-SC/SC157.pdf&Open=True>. This schedule does not take account of commitments applying to Bulgaria, Hungary, and Croatia, which are listed in separate schedules that are not yet consolidated into a single EU Schedule. *A fortiori*, the amended schedule taking account of the withdrawal of the UK is not yet finalised.

Sector or Sub-sector	*Limitations on Market Access*	*Limitations on National Treatment*	*Additional Commitments*
11. TRANSPORT SERVICES … G. Pipeline Transport LT: CPC 713	1) All Member States: Unbound 2) All Member States except HU, LT: Unbound HU, LT: None 3) All Member States except HU, LT: Unbound HU: Services may be provided through a Contract of Concession granted by the state or the local authority LT: None 4) ICT and BV: All Member States except HU, LT: Unbound HU, LT: Unbound except as indicated in the horizontal section CSS All Member States: Unbound	1) All Member States except HU: Unbound HU: None 2) All Member States except HU, LT: Unbound HU, LT: None 3) All Member States except HU, LT: Unbound HU, LT: None 4) ICT and BV: All Member States except HU, LT: Unbound HU, LT: Unbound except as indicated in the horizontal section CSS All Member States: Unbound	
1. BUSINESS SERVICES … F. Other Business Services … j) Services incidental to energy distribution LV: CPC 887. HU: only consultancy services, ex CPC 887. LT: Covers consultancy services related to the transmission and distribution on a fee basis of electricity, gaseous fuels, steam and hot water to household, industrial, commercial and other users-CPC 887 SI: Services Incidental to Energy Distribution – for gas only – part of CPC 887)	1) 2) 3) All Member States except HU, LV, LT, SI: Unbound HU, LV, LT, SI: None 4) ICT and BV: All Member States except HU, LV, LT, SI: Unbound HU, LT, LV, SI: Unbound except as indicated in the horizontal section CSS All Member States: Unbound	1) 2) 3) All Member States except HU, LV, LT, SI: Unbound HU, LV, LT, SI: None 4) ICT and BV: All Member States except HU, LV, LT, SI: Unbound HU, LT and SI: Unbound except as indicated in the horizontal section LV: None CSS All Member States except LV: Unbound LV: None	

42 LT: Service specified constitutes only a part of the total range of activities covered by the CPC concordance.
43 SI: Public utility exists; concession rights can be granted to the private operators established in the Republic of Slovenia.

These entries indicate that the EU as a whole has chosen not to commit through the WTO to any liberalisation of trade in pipeline transport (that is what 'unbound' means) but has taken over some obligations from the WTO schedules of Hungary and Lithuania (commitments made before accession to the EU). The EU has also taken over some obligations from the WTO schedule of Croatia, but those have not yet been consolidated in the EU schedule. Hungary and Lithuania have undertaken obligations in respect of business services related to energy distribution as have Slovenia and Latvia.

The UK GATS schedule is notably silent on the transport and distribution of energy, and thus it is likely to be difficult for EU companies to make market access and national treatment claims based on the current UK schedule.

1.2.2.2.3 DOMESTIC REGULATION

Barriers to trade in services are primarily regulatory in nature. It is, therefore, perfectly possible for market access to be allowed, with no discernible discrimination between WTO Members (i.e. no failure to accord MFN treatment) or discrimination in favour of domestic services and service suppliers (i.e. without breaching national treatment obligation), but for foreign service providers to still find it difficult to provide their services due to the slowness or opaqueness of regulatory procedures. For this reason, the GATS also provides for disciplines on domestic regulation. Article VI:1 GATS provides that:

> In sectors where specific commitments are undertaken, each Member shall ensure that all measures of general application affecting trade in services are administered in a reasonable, objective and impartial manner.

This is a very general obligation which only applies in sectors where commitments are undertaken. Its application in respect of trade in energy services between the EU and the UK is, therefore, very limited. The subsequent paragraphs of Article VI provide more substance, such as obligations to deal with applications for authorisation within a reasonable period of time (paragraph 3) and to provide for judicial or administrative review (paragraph 2). Again, these obligations only apply in sectors where specific commitments have been undertaken and they are therefore unlikely to be of much relevance to trade in energy services between UK and EU post Brexit.

Negotiations on a new agreement between 67 WTO Members, including both the UK and the EU, on Services Domestic Regulation were concluded on 2 December 2021; this agreement is designed to facilitate the licensing and authorisation of services trade and to require the use of international technical standards.[13] They only apply to sectors in respect of which commitments are

13 The declaration concluding the negotiations and containing the text of the disciplines is WTO document WT/L/1129. The disciplines set out in that document are to be incorporated into the schedule of each participating Member within one year.

undertaken, and so it remains to be seen to what extent the UK and the EU include energy-related services going forward.[14]

1.2.2.2.4 CONCLUSION

While the structure of the GATS makes it difficult to discern the precise obligations of the EU and the UK resulting from their schedules, it does not appear that they are significant. In case DS476, Russia could only rely on a few commitments for pipeline transport services in the separate schedules of Hungary, Lithuania, and Croatia in order to be able to claim a violation of market access and national treatment obligations, and the panel, in any event, rejected all these claims. The commitments of Hungary, Lithuania, and Croatia are naturally much less relevant for the UK whose trade in energy products will principally be with its neighbouring EU Member States such as the Netherlands, Belgium, and France. It is therefore the MFN obligation under the GATS that is likely to be the most significant for trade in energy services between the UK and the EU post-Brexit/ going forward.

1.2.3 Exceptions (defences) to WTO obligations

Both the GATT and GATS contain a number of exception clauses that can be invoked by the UK and the EU to exclude the application of the disciplines described above.

1.2.3.1 The general exceptions

The main provisions are Article XX GATT and Article XIV GATS. In both cases, there are exceptions to the rights discussed above with regard to the adoption of measures necessary for the protection of public order, health, and safety, and to secure compliance with other legitimate objectives. In the case of goods, there is a separate exception for measures relating to the conservation of exhaustible natural resources (which has been interpreted as extending to 'clean air'[15]) and essential to the acquisition and distribution of products in short supply. In the case of GATS, there are exceptions for anti-fraud, privacy, and tax measures.

In many cases, it can be difficult to establish the applicability of a justification in Article XX GATT/Article XIV GATS. Necessity appears to be the most rigorous of the various qualifiers in Article XX GATT and Article XIV GATS. Its meaning has been explained by the Appellate Body in a number of cases,[16] and

14 The EU schedule is document INF/SDR/IDS/EU/Rev.1 and the UK schedule is INF/SDR/IDS/GBR/Rev.1. Both are listed as 'restricted' on the WTO website on 3 December 2021.

15 See case DS4: *United States – Standards for Reformulated and Conventional Gasoline.*

16 See Appellate Body Reports in DS161: *Korea – Various Measures on Beef*; DS285: *US – Gambling*; and in DS332 *Brazil – Retreaded Tyres.*

applied by the panel in DS476. An assessment of 'necessity' involves 'weighing and balancing' a number of distinct factors relating both to the measure sought to be justified as 'necessary' and to possible alternative measures that may be reasonably available to the responding Member to achieve its desired objective.

There is a general requirement in both provisions that these exceptions not be invoked as means of arbitrary discrimination or as disguised restrictions on trade, and many measures fail these tests.

Again, Case DS476 illustrates the application of these general exceptions and the limits placed on them by the requirement that they must not constitute arbitrary discrimination or disguised restrictions on trade. The EU invoked the exception for products in short supply to defend some of the measures under attack, but the panel rejected the defence, holding that the EU had not established that gas was in short supply. In the case of the application of the third country certification measure in the implementing legislation of Croatia, Hungary, and Lithuania, where the panel had found a denial of national treatment, the EU had sought to argue that protection from its supply being controlled by foreign transmission system operators was necessary to protect public order. That was accepted by the panel, but it went on to reject the defence on the grounds that such a danger arose also from foreign control of *domestic* transmission system operators (which was not prohibited). For that reason, the measure was found to be an arbitrary or unjustified discrimination and the defence was rejected.

There is a much broader exception in Article XXI GATT/Article XIVbis GATS for measures to protect essential security interests. Some WTO Members, and in particular the United States, consider this exception to be entirely self-judging, so that as soon as it is invoked, all consideration of a possible violation is moot. Recent panels[17] have however held there are limits to this exception – principally that the defending country must define which essential security interest is involved and that the security interest must have a rational relationship with the contested measure. Further clarification of the scope of this exception may be provided if there should ever be adopted Reports in the various pending panel proceedings concerning the US national security duties on aluminium and steel.[18]

1.2.3.2 The FTA/Customs Union exception

The most important exception in practice, because of its wide application, is set out in Article XXIV GATT and the corresponding exception in Article V GATS. These provisions permit otherwise infringing measures, on the grounds

17 See case DS512: *Russia – Measures Concerning Traffic in Transit* and cases DS526-DS528: *United Arab Emirates/Bahrain/Saudi Arabia – Measures Relating to Trade in Goods and Services, and Trade-Related Aspects of Intellectual Property Rights Saudi Arabia – Measures Relating to Trade in Goods and Services, and Trade-Related Aspects of Intellectual Property Rights.*

18 See the series of cases entitled *US – Steel and Aluminium Products* brought against the US measures by a series of countries (DS544, DS547, DS548, DS550, DS551, DS552, DS554, DS556 and DS564).

of the existence of customs unions and/or free trade areas. There are a number of requirements that need to be met for this exception to apply. In particular, that the formation or creation of customs unions and free trade areas must not raise barriers to trade with other WTO Members,[19] that any restrictions must be '*necessary*'[20] for such formation and that the liberalisation of trade brought about by the FTA must be extensive.[21]

On the only occasion that the customs union exception was considered in WTO dispute settlement, the Appellate Body appeared to give a very narrow interpretation of the scope of this exception by indicating that panels must verify whether there really is a qualifying customs union and that measures in question must be necessary for the formation of the customs union.[22]

The EU is itself a customs union and is widely considered to qualify for this exemption, although ever fewer of the measures it adopts will be strictly necessary for the *formation* of the customs union. There is, however, an alternative view that the EU does not need to benefit from this exemption as it is a member of the WTO in its own right. Curiously, the matter was not discussed in Case DS476, which instead focussed on the question of whether the EU could be held responsible for the action of EU Member States.

The problem of applying the MFN principle to the EU is that both the EU and all its Member States are WTO Members. Since there is no provision or declaration regulating whether these obligations are cumulative, whether they are owed by the EU or by the EU Member States, it can be argued that all possible obligations apply. Therefore, unless the exemption can be invoked, every EU Member State is obliged to apply the treatment it accords to the other Member States to all WTO Members – that is, extending the rules which apply in the EU internal market to the whole WTO Membership without reciprocity.

In this regard, it should be noted that most of the complaint in Case DS476 was brought both against the EU and the individual EU Member States. Some of the measures identified as infringing GATS obligations were owed only by Croatia, Lithuania, and Hungary, since only they had made the relevant GATS commitments. Nevertheless, the EU happily accepted responsibility for all measures and defended them. It seems to have been assumed that for the purpose of establishing the scope of non-discrimination obligations, each measure was considered as belonging to the entity that had adopted the measure at issue. Where Member States have discretion as to how to apply a measure, that measure is considered to be a measure of that Member State. Where the EU applies a measure or a Member State applies a measure of the EU where it does not have discretion, the measure is considered to be a measure of the EU. This was most relevant in the case of

19 See Article XXIV:4 GATT.

20 See Article XXIV:5 GATT.

21 An Understanding attached to the WTO Regime specifies that the level of liberalisation must be at least 90%.

22 See case DS34: *Turkey – Restrictions on Imports of Textile and Clothing Products.*

the unbundling requirements where Member States had the discretion to choose between various unbundling models.

Case DS476 suffers from confusion as to exactly which measures were being impugned (EU or Member State measures) and at what level and in respect of whose obligations they should be assessed. In any event, the variable geometry of EU measures – which are often decided in principle at EU level and implemented, often with variations, at Member State level – allows creative formulation of complaints and also (as in Case DS476) creative defences. However, since the panel found no discrimination in respect of unbundling measures and the appeal to the Appellate Body is in abeyance, the matter remains unresolved.

In summary, the extent to which EU Member States may treat trade in energy products with some third countries – and indeed trade between themselves – more favourably than that with other third countries remains open. In this regard, it is instructive to consider the case of the proposed EU Carbon Border Adjustment Mechanism (CBAM), which the EU proposes to apply to imports of certain products, including electricity.

1.2.3.3 Application of WTO Exceptions to the CBAM

Very difficult questions concerning the scope of the exceptions to GATT are likely to arise in the case of the CBAM, which is currently being considered by the EU as part of its climate policy. The EU CBAM is a compensatory charge on imports that is designed to avoid 'carbon leakage', whereby emission-intensive production shifts to another country which does not have the same greenhouse gas emission controls. Other justifications advanced are that it will 'level the playing field' for EU producers and that it will provide a valuable source of revenue that could be spent on climate action.

The GATT has traditionally considered as discriminatory any measure that distinguishes between products based on the way in which they were produced, and that is precisely what the CBAM is designed to do. It will no doubt have to be assessed under the exception provisions relating to health and safety or, more likely, on the wider basis of measures related to the conservation of exhaustible natural resources, i.e., a stable climate. The decision will turn on whether the EU can establish that there is no unjustified or arbitrary discrimination and no disguised restriction on trade (in principle for each product). A major difficulty arises from the fact that the requirement to purchase emission allowances is not the only way of encouraging decarbonisation. Many jurisdictions do so by means of regulation, which also increases costs of production, although this is much less easy to calculate.

1.2.4 Enforceability of WTO rights: Dispute settlement

The enforceability of WTO obligations is of critical importance. Being an international agreement, WTO obligations are owed by and to States and equivalent entities (such as the EU). Private parties have no standing to enforce WTO obligations under the aegis of the WTO Regime. There is, however, a mechanism[23] at EU level for private parties to bring complaints to the European Commission in respect of violations of obligations under the WTO Regime, which requires the latter to issue a reasoned decision as to whether a violation exists and whether the EU will take action. It is, however, not widely used. It is well established that WTO obligations do not have direct effect in the EU, that is, they cannot be relied upon in domestic courts.[24] The UK likewise has no tradition of allowing private parties to invoke international agreements as a basis for commencing proceedings before UK courts.

The WTO dispute settlement system is sophisticated but is unfortunately not currently functioning due to the blockage of appointments to the Appellate Body by the US.[25] Panel proceedings can still be brought, but if the losing party appeals, the appeal cannot be adjudicated and the panel report cannot be adopted.

Another feature of the WTO dispute settlement system is that the remedy which can be awarded is for the losing party to be ordered to bring the measure found to be inconsistent with its obligations into conformity within a reasonable period of time, typically being 6 months after the decision was issued. Compensation for damage suffered cannot be awarded. However, if the losing party fails to comply, the complaining party can be authorised to adopt proportionate countermeasures in order to induce compliance.

1.3 The Energy Charter Treaty (ECT)

The ECT[26] was drawn up by the EU to render applicable certain EU and WTO rules relating to trade and investment in the energy sector to Eastern European states, including former members of the Union of Soviet Socialist Republics, many of which were not WTO Members at the time.

Most of these countries are now Members of the WTO, and therefore the ECT trade rules are now less important. The ECT does, however, remain an important forum for cooperation in energy matters.

23 Regulation (EU) 2015/1843 of the European Parliament and of the Council of 6 October 2015 laying down Union procedures in the field of the common commercial policy in order to ensure the exercise of the Union's rights under international trade rules, in particular those established under the auspices of the World Trade Organization (OJEU No. L272 of 16.10.2015, page 1).

24 See, e.g., Judgment of the Court of 23 November 1999 in Case C-149/96, *Portugal v Council*, ECLI: EU:C:1999:574.

25 See, e.g., Jean Galbraith, 'United States continues to block new appellate body members for the World Trade Organization, risking the collapse of the appellate process' (2019) American Journal of International Law, Volume 113, Issue 4, pp. 822–831.

26 There are in fact a number of separate instruments amending and extending the Energy Charter Treaty that can be found on the website of the Energy Charter Secretariat at: <https://www.energycharter.org/process/energy-charter-treaty-1994/energy-charter-treaty/>. The version of the Energy Charter Treaty concluded by the EU is annexed to Council and Commission Decision of 23 September 1997 on the conclusion by the European Communities of the Energy Charter Treaty and the Energy Charter Protocol on energy efficiency and related environmental aspects, OJ L69/1 of 9 March 1998.

Much trade in energy goods and services is only possible after making significant investments in the necessary infrastructure. Investment protection is therefore an essential part of the liberalisation of trade in energy goods and services and this is expressly recognised in the ECT. These rules on investment have given rise to a large number of disputes. The ECT goes much further than the WTO Regime and, arguably, the TEU/TFEU in protecting investments. In particular, Article 10 of the ECT provides that:

> Each Contracting Party shall, in accordance with the provisions of this Treaty, encourage and create stable, equitable, favourable and transparent conditions for Investors of other Contracting Parties to make Investments in its Area. Such conditions shall include a commitment to accord at all times to Investments of Investors of other Contracting Parties fair and equitable treatment. Such Investments shall also enjoy the most constant protection and security and no Contracting Party shall in any way impair by unreasonable or discriminatory measures their management, maintenance, use, enjoyment or disposal. In no case shall such Investments be accorded treatment less favourable than that required by international law, including treaty obligations. Each Contracting Party shall observe any obligations it has entered into with an Investor or an Investment of an Investor of any other Contracting Party.

Some contracting parties excluded their consent to international arbitration under Article 26 Energy Charter when concluding the ECT, but the EU did not do so. Since the EU Member States were all parties to the ECT alongside the EU itself, a number of proceedings have even been brought by investors in EU Member States against EU Member States, and the admissibility of such actions has been contested.[27] The question of the direct effect of the Energy Charter and in particular of Article 10 is unsettled.[28] It has been raised a number of times, but the CJEU has avoided pronouncing on the subject.[29]

In relation to Brexit, it needs to be noted that the UK was considered to be a Contracting Party to the ECT 'in its own right' and has remained a Contracting Party following withdrawal from the EU.[30]

27 In particular, the Court of Justice ruled in Case C-284/16 *Achmea*, ECLI: EU:C:2018:158 that Articles 267 and 344 TFEU preclude an investor from one Member State from bringing proceedings against another Member State before an arbitral tribunal under a bilateral investment treaty, since this would undermine the autonomy of EU law. It is not certain that a similar incompatibility arises in the case of the ECT since that is an agreement concluded by the EU itself.

28 The issue is examined by Professor Panos Koutrakos in an Article entitled 'The Direct Effect of the Energy Charter Treaty'. He expresses the view that the ECT is capable, in principle, of conferring rights that are enforceable by individuals before domestic courts.

29 See, most recently, the judgment in Case C-798/18 – *Federazione nazionale delle imprese elettrotecniche ed elettroniche (Anie) and Others* ECLI: EU:C:2021:280, at paras 67–71.

30 This is in contrast to the position taken under other EU mixed agreements where the UK participated as a Member State of the Union rather than 'in its own right' (for example, in the case of many free trade agreements). The UK separately ratified the 1998 Trade Amendment to the ECT,

Since the UK, the EU, and most EU Member States are party to the ECT, its provisions can also be invoked in disputes concerning trade in energy products. One great advantage of the ECT over the WTO – and indeed the TCA – is that it would appear to be directly applicable in the EU and can therefore be invoked before EU courts. Another advantage is that it provides for recourse by investors of parties to the ECT to arbitration against the contracting parties in the event of violation of the investment protection provisions (although it is unclear following the *Achmea* case-law whether the CJEU would allow ECT arbitral decisions to be enforced in the EU).[31]

1.4 The key provisions of the TCA

1.4.1 Overall description of the regime

Post Brexit, the relationship between the EU and the UK is governed by the Withdrawal Agreement (whose continuing relevance principally relates to trade with Northern Ireland) and the TCA. It is primarily the TCA that is discussed in this Chapter as Chapter 11 is dedicated to issues concerning Ireland and Northern Ireland.

As discussed in Section 1.2.3.2, for the UK and the EU not to be required pursuant to their WTO MFN obligation to offer the same liberalisation measures to all WTO Members as contained in the TCA the TCA as a whole must liberalise 'substantially all trade' as between them. In other words, the liberalisation of trade under the TCA goes significantly further than what is required under the WTO Regime.

In respect of goods, the approach adopted under the TCA is that all trade is free from tariffs and quotas (except for trade defence measures imposed in accordance with WTO rules). In respect of services, there is extensive liberalisation and a negative list approach is taken – in contrast to the WTO Regime – whereby all restrictions regarding services trade in modes 1, 2, and 3 are listed in schedules of 'non-conforming measures' giving rise to similar issues of lack of clarity as arise with respect to GATS commitments.

When negotiating the TCA, care was taken to ensure its alignment with obligations of the UK and the EU and its Member States under the WTO Regime. Accordingly, the TCA is replete with references to WTO obligations that will continue to apply and statements that its provisions are 'without prejudice to WTO obligations'.

One interesting example is Article 20 of the TCA, entitled 'Freedom of transit' which states as follows:

> Each Party shall accord freedom of transit through its territory, via the routes most convenient for international transit, for traffic in transit to or from the

an amending agreement that had been ratified by the EU alone on 13 July 2001 (deposited on 21 December 2001).

31 See the Chapter on Brexit and energy disputes.

territory of the other Party or of any other third country. To that end, Article V of GATT 1994 and its Notes and Supplementary Provisions are incorporated into and made part of this Agreement, mutatis mutandis. The Parties understand that Article V of GATT 1994 includes the movement of energy goods via inter alia pipelines or electricity grids.

1.4.2 General provisions on the liberalisation of goods and services

Although there are specific provisions on energy in the TCA (Title VII of Part Two – Trade), the general provisions on the liberalisation of goods and services trade also apply. Indeed, Article 301 TCA provides that these general rules prevail in case of conflict. It may well be therefore that the general provisions of the TCA will provide more protections than the energy-specific provisions, especially if the latter are not further implemented.

1.4.3 Reservations in the TCA

The schedules of reservations for so-called 'existing measures' of the EU and the UK are contained in Annex 19 to the TCA. There is a specific reservation (No. 17) for the EU relating to 'energy related activities'. There are a number of reservations that relate to mining and extraction activities, but part (b) of Reservation No. 17 lists some reservations on the production, transmission, and distribution of electricity, gas, steam, and hot water; pipeline transportation of fuels; storage and warehouse of fuels transported through pipelines; and services incidental to energy distribution.

These reservations are listed for each EU Member State to which they apply (Austria, Czech Republic, Denmark, Lithuania, Malta, the Netherlands, and Poland). Most of the restrictions are in the form of licensing requirements and include nationality or residence restrictions. In each case, there is a reference to the national legal instruments that contain the restrictions.

There is a UK reservation on 'energy related activities' (UK Reservation No. 8), but it relates to exploration and extraction rather than to trade in such energy products.

There are however further schedules of reservations in Annex 20 to the TCA for so-called 'future measures'. Reservation No. 22 contains wide-ranging permissions to apply measures for the protection of security of supply, again with significant variations between EU Member States.

1.5 Conclusion

Trade in energy products between the UK and the EU will continue to be important after Brexit. However, the UK's departure from the Single Energy Market and the cessation of the application of the Treaty on European Union (TEU) and the Treaty on the Functioning of the European Union (TFEU) will lead to significant changes in the rules regulating such trade. As discussed in this Chapter, the new legal regime is governed primarily by the provisions of the WTO Regime. The TCA does provide a number of avenues for trade in energy products to be developed and for cooperation to be promoted, and these are the subject of several other Chapters of this book. At the time of writing, whether such cooperation will develop is uncertain and is likely to depend on how the relationship between the UK and the EU develops more broadly.

In the absence of specific measures implementing the cooperation in the field of energy envisaged by the TCA, the rules set out in the WTO Regime will govern trade in energy products between the UK and the EU. As explained in this Chapter, these rules are more extensive in respect of trade in energy goods than for energy services. Trade in energy services between the UK and the EU will be principally governed by the prohibition of discrimination between WTO Members (the MFN principle), which is a very significant constraint on their respective ability to adopt policies to hamper energy services. Should the customs union exception in the WTO Regime be narrowly interpreted to apply only to measures strictly necessary for the operation of the customs union, then the UK may find itself able to require the treatment accorded by EU Member States to each other's companies to be extended also to UK companies.

2 The Impact of Brexit on EU Market Access

Silke Goldberg

2.1 Introduction and scope

This Chapter explores issues relating to the access of UK entities to the EU energy market post-Brexit. The Chapter focuses on the relevant provisions of the Trade and Cooperation Agreement (TCA), which establishes the basis for a relationship between UK and the EU in the energy sector. However, given the broad nature of the TCA, any obligations it imposes on the parties are not as clearly defined as would be expected from fully termed legislation, with many provisions only setting out the applicable principles rather than giving any details as to their practical implementation.

Given the limited provisions of the TCA – compared to the EU regulatory regime applicable to the gas and electricity markets – in relation to the future interaction between the UK and EU energy markets, this Chapter will also explore what the TCA does not stipulate in relation to market access issues and highlights the issues that will need to be addressed by them in due course in order to improve the workings of the energy market post-Brexit.

In this Chapter, two aspects of market access are examined in turn in Sections 2.2 and 2.3:

- the general market design aspect, which pertains to the fundamental principles of regulatory oversight and fundamental principles relating to unbundling and third-party access, and which applies to the UK market as a whole, as well as the EU. This includes issues such as the legal basis for market access, relationships between regulatory authorities, and rules of engagement for the future development of a common regulatory framework for the UK–EU energy market (if any); and
- the specific regulatory regime which governs cross-border infrastructure and access to the EU and UK energy markets, respectively (i.e., the flow of electricity and gas between the UK and EU markets), trading arrangements, and the governance of the physical infrastructure linking the two markets (i.e., current and future electricity and gas interconnectors).

Section 2.4 seeks to draw up a list of issues the UK and the EU ought to consider in order to provide for a functional and reliable market access regime. Section 2.4

DOI: 10.4324/9781003364337-3

will also discuss the implications/consequences for the UK and EU energy sector should they fail to do so.

2.2 General market principles

With effect from 1 January 2021, the entire EU regulatory framework for the energy market fell away in the UK. It was replaced by the TCA and the 'retained EU law', i.e., EU law which has been transposed into UK law and therefore will continue to apply.

Retained EU law remains important for the UK energy sector as it allows for the retention of some key features of the EU's energy market in relation to the energy regulatory framework within Great Britain (GB) (the regulatory settlement for the energy market in Northern Ireland is separate; see also Chapter 11). However, retained EU law's status as such does not equate to it being recognised by the EU as EU acquis or EU-equivalent legislation, not least because it is subject to the UK legislative process only and as such are subject to amendment through that process.

One example of such retained EU law is Regulation (EU) 2019/943[1] (the EU Electricity Regulation), which has been retained in UK national law with certain amendments effected by the Electricity and Gas (Internal Markets and Network Codes) (Amendment etc.) (EU Exit) Regulations 2020/1006 (the EU Exit Regulations, the amended version of the EU Electricity Regulation retained in UK law being the UK Electricity Regulation).

In Section 2.2, I will explore the fundamental market principles which will continue to apply post-Brexit, the role of UK and EU regulatory authorities, and cooperation between transmission system operators (TSOs), as well as post-Brexit market access issues which arise in relation to individual national markets within the EU.

2.2.1 Market principles

Both third-party access (TPA) to the grid and the unbundling of transmission systems from generation and supply of electricity played a key role in the liberalisation of the energy industry, first in the UK and later in the EU. They remain core tenets and hallmarks of liberalised and mature electricity and gas markets and have been anchored in both UK and EU legislation. In this regard, the TCA provides continuity as it retains both concepts and commits the parties to safeguarding the principles of TPA and unbundling, albeit at a high level, and without reference to criteria for the exact practical implementation of the same.

From a market access perspective, adherence to these principles is essential for UK companies, not only in relation to legal compliance with UK legislation, but also in terms of their investments or investment plans in the EU. This is because

1 Regulation (EU) 2019/943 of the European Parliament and of the Council of 5 June 2019 on the internal market for electricity (Text with EEA relevance) [2019] OJ L 158, 14.6.2019, pp. 54–124.

compliance with these principles is expressed in EU legislation as a key criterion for investments, for instance, in grid companies and for the relevant certification of such companies.

2.2.1.1 Third-party access

Article 306 TCA imposes obligations on the UK and the EU to ensure the implementation of a system of TPA to their transmission and distribution networks. The key obligations set out in this Article are essentially equivalent to the TPA principle set out in Article 6 of Directive (EU) 2019/944 (the EU Electricity Directive), save for example to the provision relating to the approval of tariffs. There is therefore little change between the new rules on market access in this regard as compared to the previous EU regime.

2.2.1.2 Unbundling

Article 307 of the TCA imposes a broadly drafted obligation on the parties to implement arrangements to remove conflicts arising as a result of the same person exercising control over a TSO and a producer or supplier. Given the limited detail in the TCA, this obligation appears unlikely to impose restrictions in excess of the provisions set out in the EU Electricity Directive and the UK Electricity Act 1989.

In this area, it is unlikely – at least for the time being – that any access issues will arise for UK companies as there do not seem to be any immediate plans by UK legislators to change the current TPA and unbundling regime. However, given that the TCA does not commit the parties to the EU set of unbundling models (as established by the Electricity and Gas Directives, respectively), it may be possible for divergence to arise in the future.

2.2.2 Regulatory authorities

Article 318 TCA provides that the UK and the EU commit to ensuring that the EU Agency for Cooperation of Energy Regulators (ACER) and the national regulatory authority (NRA) for the UK, Ofgem, develop contacts and enter into administrative arrangements to facilitate meeting the objectives of the TCA.

The working scope of the future arrangements will include access to networks, offshore energy, the efficient use of electricity and gas interconnectors, gas quality and decarbonisation, infrastructure planning, and cooperation between TSOs.[2]

While the cooperation between ACER and Ofgem is helpful, the TCA makes clear that the arrangements are not intended to confer to Ofgem a status comparable to formal participation in ACER.[3]

2 Article 318 Trade and Cooperation Agreement between the European Union and the European Atomic Energy Community, of the one part, and the United Kingdom of Great Britain and Northern Ireland, of the other part [2021] OJ L 149/10 (henceforth TCA).

3 Article 318(2) TCA.

It is understood that Ofgem and ACER are in the process of developing these contacts as well as a memorandum of understanding that would form the basis of their future cooperation.

As the TCA does not provide a time limit for the establishment of the contacts and administrative arrangements, it may be some time before the relevant arrangements are in place. For issues pertaining to market access and, in particular, modalities for the efficient use of existing interconnectors and the planning of future interconnectors, this could imply delays in the decision-making process and therefore delays for the relevant projects.

2.2.3 Cooperation between TSOs

Cooperation between TSOs, in particular in the frameworks of the European Network of Transmission System Operators for Electricity (ENTSO-E) and the European Network of Transmission System Operators for Gas (ENTSO-G), is an important part of the regulatory regime applicable to the EU energy market. The ENTSOs were established pursuant to Regulation (EC) 714/2009 on conditions for access to the network for cross-border exchanges in electricity, and Regulation (EC) 715/2009 of the European Parliament and of the Council of 13 July 2009 on conditions for access to the natural gas transmission networks and repealing Regulation (EC) No 1775/2005, respectively. The two regulations set out the ENTSOs' respective responsibilities in enhancing the cooperation between their TSO members (from within the EU) and observers (from outside the EU). Broadly, these include a mandate to:

- ensure the secure and reliable operation of the increasingly complex cross-border electricity and gas network;
- facilitate cross-border network development;
- develop EU network codes for electricity and gas networks, respectively; and
- in relation to ENTSO-E, the integration of renewable energy sources and work to assist with the completion of the Internal Energy Market (IEM).

In the electricity sector, the tasks of ENTSO-E also encompass work on the Inter-TSO Compensation Mechanism set up pursuant to Regulation (EU) 838/2010 on guidelines relating to the Inter-TSO Compensation Mechanism. This mechanism establishes the methodology for compensation of TSOs when hosting cross-border flows of electricity, with the aim of incentivising the hosting of cross-border electricity.

In addition, ENTSO-E and ENTSO-G also contribute to the process drawing up the list of Projects of Common Interest (PCIs) pursuant to Regulation (EU) 347/2013 on guidelines for trans-European energy infrastructure (the TEN-E Regulation) through the Ten-Year Network Development Plan, which forms the basis for the selection of PCIs and their work on a cost-benefit methodology for the assessment of electricity and gas transmission infrastructure projects, respectively.[4]

4 Article 11 of Regulation (EU) No 347/2013 of the European Parliament and of the Council of 17 April 2013 on guidelines for trans-European energy infrastructure and repealing Decision No

Membership and participation in the ENTSOs is therefore a key mechanism for TSOs to participate in the shaping of the European energy market and to contribute to the development not only of the energy networks, but also of the rules pertaining to the investment in the same.

Post-Brexit, the membership in the ENTSOs ceased for the British TSOs; as such, they are now excluded from the relevant EU decision-making processes. This is relevant as, with the exception of the offshore transmission owners (known as OFTOs), British TSOs will either operate interconnectors or have interconnection points with interconnectors within the area they serve.

The TCA provides for an alternative engagement for British TSOs by obligating the UK and the EU to ensure that their TSOs develop working arrangements that are efficient and inclusive to support the tasks associated with meeting the objectives of the relevant sections of the TCA, 'including, when recommended by the Specialised Committee on Energy, the preparation of technical procedures to implement effectively'.[5]

Such working arrangements are to include frameworks for cooperation between ENTSO-E and the TSOs for electricity in the UK and are to cover a number of areas, including

- the efficient use of electricity interconnectors;[6]
- electricity trading arrangements at all timeframes;[7]
- efficient use of gas interconnectors;[8]
- network development;[9] and
- cooperation on security of supply.[10]

Despite this framework for cooperation between the TSOs, the TCA also makes clear that it shall not involve, or confer a status comparable to, membership in ENTSO-E to UK TSOs.[11]

At the time of writing of this book, the exact scope and modalities of these cooperation arrangements are unclear, as are the details of their implementation. The work undertaken in relation to the relevant arrangements is, however, understood to have commenced.

2.2.4 National-level access issues

Whilst access issues in relation to individual EU Member State energy markets as a consequence of Brexit are beyond the scope of the Chapter, they will be

1364/2006/EC and amending Regulations (EC) No 713/2009, (EC) No 714/2009 and (EC) No 715/2009 [2013] OJ L. 115/39

5 Article 317 TCA.

6 Article 311 TCA.

7 Article 312 TCA.

8 Article 313 TCA.

9 Article 314 TCA.

10 Article 315 TCA.

11 Article 317(1) TCA.

referenced here for completeness. There is no EU-wide licensing regime for energy trading, nor is there a passporting regime comparable to the passporting regime in place for the financial service industry.[12] Any authorisation (to the extent required) for the generation, supply, transmission, or trading of electricity and/or gas is granted by the relevant national regulatory authority or ministry of the EU Member State.

For instance, the French licensing regime contained in Article L333-1 of the Energy Code provides that any supplier of electricity (including entities wishing to sell electricity to consumers or TSOs) must obtain a licence from the relevant French ministry. In some EU Member States, such as in France, a licence can only be granted to companies that are incorporated in the EU or in countries which have an agreement regulating this matter with France. As the UK does not have an agreement with France (or the EU for that purpose), UK companies cannot currently obtain a licence and therefore do not have access to the French electricity market.

2.3 Cross-border infrastructure

Access to the EU energy market requires, apart from the regulatory framework and any necessary authorisations, the necessary cross-border infrastructure (i.e., interconnectors) and reliable rules governing the same.

Electricity and gas are goods for the purposes of the TCA (see Chapter 1), as is equipment necessary to generate, transmit, distribute, and supply electricity and gas. One of the key Brexit concerns in relation to the energy sector was the avoidance of tariffs on these goods. Whilst the TCA avoids these, the early post-Brexit phase has shown that the impact of the new customs formalities at the EU–UK border has cost implications for business generally and, by extension, for energy projects. Specifically, the UK supply chain has struggled with the paperwork arising from the new customs arrangements.[13]

This Section considers the provisions of the TCA which are relevant to the development of new of infrastructure for electricity and gas connecting the UK with EU Member States as well as the governance and management of such existing infrastructure and any access issues arising as a result of Brexit, including the

12 In the Financial Services sector, such passporting rights are available under, for instance, Directive 2013/36/EU of the European Parliament and of the Council of 26 June 2013 on access to the activity of credit institutions and the prudential supervision of credit institutions and investment firms, amending Directive 2002/87/EC and repealing Directives 2006/48/EC and 2006/49/EC [2013] L 176/338 or Directive 2014/65/EU of the European Parliament and of the Council of 15 May 2014 on markets in financial instruments and amending Directive 2002/92/EC and Directive 2011/61/EU [2014] OJ L 173/349. The passporting regime under these directives allows companies which are authorised for financial services purposes in one EU Member State to 'passport' that authorisation and rely on it in another EU Member State to carry out the same activity there.

13 See, for instance, 'Teething Problems Becoming Permanent', *Financial Times*, 30 June 2021, available at: <https://www.ft.com/content/3a4ef128-91e0-4189-abda-db9b54fa8891>.

position in respect of PCIs (for both electricity and gas). It will also focus on the electricity trading arrangements between the UK and the EU.

Article 314 of the TCA provides that the parties are to 'cooperate to facilitate the timely development and interoperability of energy infrastructure connecting their territories'. The term *energy infrastructure* in this context refers in the first instance to electricity and gas interconnectors. The TCA defines an *electricity interconnector* as

> a transmission line: (i) between the Parties, excluding any such line wholly within the single electricity market in Ireland and Northern Ireland; [and] (ii) between Great Britain and the single electricity market in Ireland and Northern Ireland that is outside the scope of point (i),[14]

whereas the definition of *gas interconnector* is a 'transmission line which crosses or spans the border between the Parties'.[15]

The definition of electricity interconnectors under the TCA is wider than the definition of an interconnector in the EU Electricity Regulation (which is limited to a transmission line between EU Member States). Electricity interconnectors take greater prominence and are accorded more detailed provisions in the TCA than gas interconnectors. This is largely due to the fact that the integration of the EU electricity market is further advanced than that of the gas market. Accordingly, the regulation of the EU electricity market is tighter and more complex, not least regarding the coupling of the national electricity markets and the related implicit trading arrangements. By contrast, the EU gas market is somewhat less integrated, and consequently, the TCA dedicates fewer provisions specifically to the post-Brexit governance of gas interconnectors.

2.3.1 PCIs

The importance of cross-border energy infrastructure and the need to support such projects has long been recognised within the EU. The TEN-E Regulation establishes a framework for the identification, planning, and implementation of PCIs, which are required to implement the nine strategic geographical energy infrastructure priority corridors identified in the fields of electricity, gas, and oil, and the three EU-wide energy infrastructure priority areas for smart grids, electricity highways, and carbon dioxide transportation networks.[16]

The TCA is silent as to the treatment of PCIs. Whilst the (now revised) TEN-E Regulation will continue to apply in relation to relevant UK projects. Following

14 Article 300 (f) TCA.

15 Article 300 (i) TCA.

16 For further detail on PCIs, see also <https://www.ec.europa.eu/energy/sites/ener/files/documents/2%20PCI%20main%20act.pdf>.

the entry into force of the revised TEN-E Regulation[17], the new category of 'Project of Mutual Interest' is now more likely to apply to UK- EU projects, as the criteria for PCIs are harder to meet for projects involving third countries.

The reviewed TEN-E Regulation prescribes that projects between a Member State and the UK (as a country that is not an EU Member State or a European Economic Area country) may still be regarded as a PCI project as it 'is located in the territory of one Member State' provided it 'has a significant cross-border impact'.[18] For electricity transmission projects, a significant cross-border impact means that the project increases the grid transfer capacity between that Member State and other Member States by at least 500MW.[19] Alternatively, a project may meet the criteria by involving 'at least two Member States by directly crossing the border between two or more Member States'.[20]

Whilst cross-border projects between the UK and the EU were in principle eligible to be awarded PCI status, all hitherto UK interconnector PCIs lost their PCI status in the fifth PCI list (expected to come into force in spring 2022).[21] As no reasons for the final decision as to whether or not a project is included in the PCI list are published, it is not in all circumstances clear whether this was the case.

While PCIs may – in future PCI lists – exist between Member States and UK, it is not clear how certain provisions of the TEN-E Regulation would be applied in relation to such projects. For example:

1. in accordance with Article 12 of the TEN-E Regulation, a PCI may submit an investment and cross-border cost allocation request. However, in the case of an interconnector PCI between a Member State and a non-Member State, it is not clear how such an application would be decided by the NRA of the non-Member State (which would not be bound by the TEN-E Regulation);
2. Article 12(1) of the TEN-E Regulation suggests that efficiently incurred investment costs not recovered from congestion rents will be paid for through network user tariffs in the relevant Member States, which appears to suggest Member States could subsidise UK costs; and
3. The UK would not be subject to the jurisdiction of ACER, which is to decide on any such investment request where the NRAs are unable to reach agreement (or on referral).

17 Regulation (EU) 2022/869 of 30 May 2022 on guidelines for trans-European energy infrastructure, amending Regulations (EC) No 715/2009, (EU) 2019/942 and (EU) 2019/943 and Directives 2009/73/EC and (EU) 2019/944, and repealing Regulation (EU) No 347/2013 (the "revised TEN-E Regulation").

18 Article 4(1)(c)(ii) revised TEN-E Regulation.

19 Annex IV.1 revised TEN-E Regulation.

20 Article 4(1)(c)(i) revised TEN-E Regulation.

21 Annex to Commission Delegated Regulation EU …/… amending Regulation (EU) No 347/2013 of the European Parliament and of the Council as regards the Union list of projects of common interest {SWD(2021) 335 final}, C(2021) 8409 final, Brussels 19 November 2021. Available at: <https://ec.europa.eu/energy/sites/default/files/fifth_pci_list_19_november_2021_annex.pdf>

The European Commission proposed an amendment to the TEN-E Regulation on 15 December 2020.[22] This proposal includes a new category of projects of 'mutual' interest for projects between a Member State and a third country (such as the UK) which (i) increase the grid transfer capacity with other Member States and (ii) contribute significantly to sustainability and either market integration or security of supply.

Should the EC's proposal be adopted, the threshold for inclusion of a project as a 'project of mutual interest' will, therefore, be lower than that for PCIs under the existing regulation. This should make it easier for UK–EU interconnectors to meet the criteria for this new category. However, it is not clear as yet whether the status of 'project of mutual interest' will provide project sponsors with access to the same permitting advantages and funding opportunities as the PCI status. The revised TEN-E Regulation is likely to apply from 2023, and the sixth list of PCIs will probably be decided in autumn 2023.

2.3.2 New exemptions for interconnectors

Annex 28 TCA effectively introduces a new exemption regime in relation to UK–EU interconnectors. . The UK or the EU may decide not to apply Article 306 (third-party access) and/or Article 307 (system operation and unbundling of transmission network operators) to (i) emergent or isolated markets or systems or (ii) infrastructure which meet the conditions set out in Annex 28 TCA.[23]

This new 'exemption' regime only applies in respect of the TPA and unbundling provisions in the TCA, and it is therefore narrower than the existing exemption regime in the EU Electricity Regulation (which may also apply in respect of regulations relating to use of congestion revenues and the approval of charging methodologies and access rules).

The conditions for the grant of a new 'exemption' under Annex 28 TCA are similar to, but less onerous than, those in Article 63 of the EU Electricity Regulation. Conditions relating to charging have been removed, and a project is now only required to enhance competition or security of supply, instead of enhancing competition being an absolute condition.

It remains to be seen how (and whether) this will be implemented in UK and EU law and also how this provision might interact with the existing regulations. Article 63 of the UK Electricity Regulation already provides an exemption regime for new interconnectors between GB and another country. However, Article 63 of the EU Electricity Regulation presently only applies to new interconnectors

22 European Commission, Proposal for a regulation of the European Parliament and of the Council on guidelines for trans-European energy infrastructure and repealing Regulation (EU) No 347/2013, COM(2020) 824, 15 December 2020, available from: <https://ec.europa.eu/energy/sites/ener/files/revised_ten-e_regulation_.pdf> with annexes available from: <https://ec.europa.eu/energy/sites/ener/files/annexes_to_the_revised_ten-e_regulation.pdf>.

23 Article 308 TCA.

between EU Member States. Consequently, the UKEU interconnectors do not fall within the scope of this exemption.

As the TCA exemption regime pursuant to Annex 28 applies in respect of the obligations under the TCA only, it cannot grant exemptions from restrictions in EU and English or Scottish law unless such an effect is specifically provided therein (which is currently not the case).

2.3.3 Existing exemptions

Article 309 of the TCA requires the UK and the EU to ensure that existing exemptions granted to UK–EU interconnectors continue to apply.

The energy-related provisions of the TCA are time-limited and will cease to apply on 30 June 2026 unless otherwise determined. The implications on UK–EU interconnectors which have been granted an exemption, either pre-TCA under the EU exemption regime or pursuant to the TCA of the TCA ceasing to be in force, will depend on how Articles 309 and 310 of the TCA are implemented in practice by the EU and the UK regulatory authorities. This uncertainty itself is likely to render the planning of UK–EU infrastructure more difficult going forward.

2.3.4 Market coupling and electricity trading arrangements

Market coupling is a mechanism intended to harmonise different systems of electricity exchanges and reduce price differences between so coupled markets.

The EU has adopted a target model for the day-ahead timeframe on the basis of a price coupling mechanism (European Price Coupling, or EPC), which simultaneously determines volumes and prices in all relevant zones. EPC works on the basis of implicit auctions in which each TSO sends their cross-border transport capacities to a Market Coupling Operator (MCO), which is the interface between the TSOs and the power exchanges.

The MCO operates centrally and independently; its function is 'the task of matching orders from the day ahead and intraday markets for different bidding zones and simultaneously allocating cross-zonal capacities.'[24] The actual coupling takes place on the relevant electricity exchanges, where supply and demand is settled using an algorithm. All TSOs then need to compare their capacity values once again before publication.[25] In the EU, Nominated Electricity Market Operators (NEMOs) carry out the MCO function. According to ACER, progress in the integration of the European electricity market has been significant as 'the development and introduction of market coupling ensures that the available cross-zonal

24 ENTSO-E, 'Governance of the Market Coupling Operation Functions: Transmission System Operators' Perspective' Policy Paper (July 2016), available at: <https://eepublicdownloads.entsoe.eu/clean-documents/Publications/Position%20papers%20and%20reports/entsoe_pp_MCO_web%20(002).pdf>.

25 Next Kraftwerke, 'Market Coupling: How the European electricity market is linked', available at: <https://www.next-kraftwerke.com/knowledge/market-coupling>.

capacities, as calculated by transmission system operators (TSOs), are allocated in the most efficient manner'.[26]

Since 1 January 2021, the UK market has been de-coupled from the EPC and has reverted to the situation which existed prior to the EU's market coupling efforts in 2014.[27] This means, amongst other things, moving to new access rules and losing access to the Joint Allocation Office,[28] the single platform for allocation of long-term electricity transmission capacity to TSOs, and short notice electricity balancing. It also means that interconnection capacities are allocated explicitly rather than implicitly, making it less efficient, as market participants have to first buy transmission capacity from interconnector operators. Then, in a separate process, they have to secure the quantities of electricity they wish to dispatch over the interconnectors. Broadly, this means moving from the implicit day-ahead allocation under the EPC mechanism to explicit day-ahead allocation under the revised (no-deal) access rules of the relevant interconnector. As a result, cross-border capacity will not be optimally used as it will be priced too high or too low.

In order for cross-border electricity trade to continue between the UK and the EU post-Brexit, new access rules for all interconnectors had to be approved by the UK and the relevant EU Member State authorities. In preparation for this, all operational interconnectors between the UK and continental Europe (France, Belgium, and the Netherlands) published their modified access rules in case of a no-deal scenario, and Ofgem approved the proposed modifications in each case.[29]

26 ACER. 'Report on the result of monitoring the margin available for cross-zonal electricity trade in the EU in the second semester of 2020' (2 June 2021), available at: <https://documents.acer.europa.eu/Official_documents/Acts_of_the_Agency/Publication/ACER%20MACZT%20Report%20S2%202020.pdf>, p.13.

27 For more information on market coupling, see ENTSO-E, 'Single Day-ahead Coupling (SDAC)', available at: <https://www.entsoe.eu/network_codes/cacm/implementation/sadc/>.

28 For more information, see: <https://www.jao.eu/aboutus/aboutus/overview>.

29 Ofgem has approved 'No Deal' access rules separately for each interconnector: For IFA, see Ofgem, 'Approval of the updated Access Rules and Charging Methodology for the IFA interconnector to apply in case the UK leaves the EU without a deal' (18 October 2019), available at: <https://www.ofgem.gov.uk/publications-and-updates/approval-updated-access-rules-and-charging-methodology-ifa-interconnector-apply-case-uk-leaves-eu-without-deal>; for Eleclink, see Ofgem, 'Approval of the modified Access Rules and the modified Charging Methodology for the ElecLink interconnector to apply in case the UK leaves the EU without a deal' (13 December 2019), available at: <https://www.ofgem.gov.uk/publications-and-updates/approval-modified-access-rules-and-modified-charging-methodology-eleclink-interconnector-apply-case-uk-leaves-eu-without-deal>; for BritNed, see Ofgem, 'Approval of modified Access Rules for the BritNed interconnector to apply in the event that the UK leaves the EU without a deal' (15 March 2019), available at: <https://www.ofgem.gov.uk/publications-and-updates/approval-modified-access-rules-britned-interconnector-apply-event-uk-leaves-eu-without-deal>; for Nemo, see Ofgem, 'Approval of modified Access Rules for the Nemo Link interconnector to apply in the event that the UK leaves the EU without a deal' (15 March 2019), available at: <https://www.ofgem.gov.uk/publications-and-updates/approval-modified-access-rules-nemo-link-interconnector-apply-event-uk-leaves-eu-without-deal>.

According to the European Federation of Energy Traders (EFET), the return to explicit capacity auctions has led to increased costs of electricity trading. Post-Brexit, EFET argues that 'cross-border capacity may not be optimally used because it will be priced too high or too low' on either side of the border between the UK and the EU.[30] On a practical level, the UK's exit from market coupling arrangements has had the following consequences for the European electricity markets: from 31 December 2020, Nord Pool's day-ahead auction has a new gate closure time of 09:50 GMT with results available no later than 10:00 GMT; in Ireland, the SEM-GB intraday auctions (IDA1 & IDA2) continue to operate with shared order books between power exchanges, offering implicit capacity between the island of Ireland and GB. Explicit capacity auctions will be staggered throughout the morning, starting with the BritNed interconnector, followed by IFA, IFA2, and finally Nemo Link as shown in the illustration.[31]

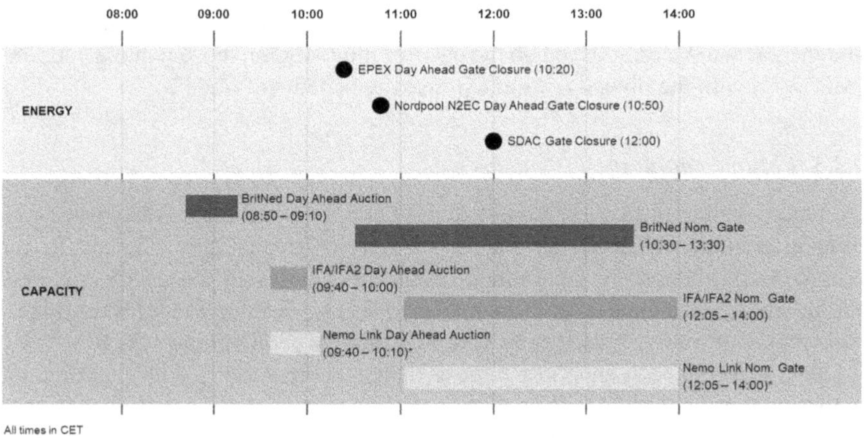

Annex ENER-4 to the Joint Declaration by the EU and the UK,[32] which accompanies the TCA, specifically provides that arrangements for electricity trading should be 'as efficient as possible and should, under normal circumstances, result in flows across electricity interconnectors being consistent with the prices in the Parties' day-ahead markets'.[33]

The Specialised Committee on Energy (SCE), established under the TCA, has been tasked to ensure that TSOs develop arrangements for the necessary technical

30 Frédéric Simon, 'Power flows with UK "less efficient" since Brexit, EU says' *Euractiv* (7 January 2021) <https://www.euractiv.com/section/energy/news/power-flows-with-uk-less-efficient-since-brexit-eu-says/

31 Source: BritNed, <https://www.britned.com/brexit/auctions/> accessed 25 October 2021.

32 Draft EU-UK Declarations, 'Joint declaration by the Union and the United Kingdom on Annex ENER-4', available at: <https://ec.europa.eu/info/sites/info/files/draft_eu-uk_declarations.pdf>, p.7 (henceforth Joint Declaration on Annex ENER-4).

33 Ibid.

procedures.[34] Pursuant to Article 312 of the TCA, the SCE will keep the arrangements under review and, if not satisfied with the arrangements, can take decisions and make recommendations as necessary for each party to request its TSOs to prepare technical procedures in line with the following timeframes (each from the coming into force of the TCA):

(A) within 3 months, the TSOs need to prepare the cost-benefit analysis and outline of proposals for technical procedures;
(B) within 10 months, the TSOs need to make a proposal for technical procedures;
(C) within 15 months, the relevant arrangements will enter into force.

Practically, this means that the technical procedures must enter into force in early 2022, which has not occurred.

Annex 29 of the TCA provides that the new trading arrangements between the UK and the EU will be established on the basis of multi-region loose volume coupling (MRLVC) with the objective to 'maximise the benefits of trade'.

2.3.5 Volume coupling

Volume coupling is an alternative system of coupling to the integrated price coupling used in the EU electricity market.[35] It is a two-step process whereby, firstly, cross-zonal volumes are determined using energy bids in the energy markets. These are then matched with those energy markets, forming the relevant price.[36] This makes it more operationally complex than price coupling, which involves a single step, since it involves three separate computations with coordination between them.[37]

Volume coupling can either be tight or loose:

1. Tight volume coupling: In this model, the traded volumes between countries or regions are determined before individual power exchanges calculate their

34 Article 312 TCA
35 Volume coupling has been the basis for previous phases of European market coupling. For more detail on this and the challenges of volume coupling, see also: Tanguy Janssen, Yann Rebours, Yann and Philippe Dessante, *Tight Volume Coupling: Analytical model, adverse flow causality and potential improvements*, EUI RSCAS, 2012/09, Loyola de Palacio Programme on Energy Policy, [Florence School of Regulation], [Energy] (henceforth 'Janssen, Yann and Dessante, *Tight Volume Coupling*'). retrieved from Cadmus, European University Institute Research Repository, at: <http://hdl.handle.net/1814/21296>.
36 The EU and UK TSOs MRLVC group, 'Cost Benefit Analysis of Multi-Region Loose Volume Coupling (MRLVC)', available at: <https://consultations.entsoe.eu/markets/cost-benefit-analysis-of-multi-region-loose- volume/supporting_documents/MRLVC_CBA_analytical%20results_April_2021_final_publication.pdf>, slide 23 (henceforth EU and UK TSOs MRLVC group, 'Cost Benefit Analysis of MRLVC').
37 Ibid, slide 102.

own prices,[38] which means that the prices are calculated on the basis of all relevant information.
2. Loose volume coupling: In this model, the volume traded between the different countries or regions is determined and the prices are calculated separately.

Tight volume coupling is thought to offer a better degree of full price convergence and is therefore seen as better for capacity optimisation.[39]

The main advantage of volume coupling over price coupling is that it allows the linkage of electricity markets with different regulatory regimes and governance provisions without requiring the harmonisation of products and price determination rules which are needed for price coupling, whilst also avoiding the inefficiencies of explicit allocation. As such, it may offer a solution for cross-border trades at the GB–EU border.

2.3.6 MRLVC at the GB–EU border

The establishment of MRLVC arrangements will effectively involve the development of a market coupling function to determine the net energy positions (implicit allocation) between:

1. bidding zones established in accordance with the EU Electricity Regulation which are directly connected to the UK by an electricity interconnector; and
2. the UK.

The net energy positions over electricity interconnectors will then be calculated via an implicit allocation process by applying a specific algorithm to:

1. commercial bids and offers for the day-ahead market timeframe from the bidding zones established in accordance with Regulation (EU) 2019/943 which are directly connected to the UK by an electricity interconnector;
2. commercial bids and offers for the day-ahead market timeframe from relevant day-ahead markets in the UK;
3. network capacity data and system capabilities determined in accordance with the procedures agreed between transmission system operators; and
4. data on expected commercial flows of electricity interconnections between bidding zones connected to the UK and other bidding zones in the EU, as determined by EU transmission system operators using robust methodologies.

However, the envisaged changes to the arrangements in place do not mean that the GB electricity market will return to being part of the EU internal energy market. The TCA is clear that whilst the MRLVC process needs to produce results

38 Janssen, Rebours and Dessante, *Tight Volume Coupling* (n 33).

39 EU and UK TSOs MRLVC group, 'Cost Benefit Analysis of MRLVC' (n 35) 101.

sufficiently in advance of the operation of the EU and GB respective day-ahead markets (for the EU, this is single day-ahead coupling established in accordance with Commission Regulation (EU) 2015/1222) in order that the relevant outcomes may be used as inputs into the processes which determine the results in those markets. The GB market will remain distinct from the EU electricity market. Annex 29 of the TCA specifically provides that the envisaged algorithm will be distinct and separate from that used in single day-ahead coupling established in accordance with Regulation (EU) 2015/1222.

The UK Secretary of State issued guidance[40] on the post-Brexit electricity trading arrangements in January 2021. At a high level, it covers the expected roles and responsibilities of UK TSOs during the development process, the cooperation of relevant electricity market operators with one another and with TSOs for the purpose of enabling TSOs to develop the arrangements, and the issue of cost sharing, allocation, and recovery for the plans. As expected, Ofgem was granted the regulatory powers to make decisions on the allocation, recovery, and assessment of costs through Electricity Trading Statutory Instruments. It has already been granted the power to determine cost mechanisms relating to the development and implementation of the technical procedures.[41] Further legislation is expected to include the scope of regulatory powers for Ofgem in relation to the operation of the mechanisms.

On 26 May 2021, Ofgem published a consultation on the proposed approach to the allocation, recovery, and assessment of both development and operational costs for the MRLVC trading arrangements.[42] The deadline for this was 24 June 2021, with a report expected in due course, which was not yet available at the time of writing.

2.3.7 A single GB clearing price and two MRLVC options

In the early part of 2021, the UK and EU TSOs worked on the technical aspects of MRLVC. This included a cost-benefit analysis carried out by CEPA on behalf of the UK and EU TSO group, the results of which were published in April (the CBA).[43] The CBA considers two MRLVC options, a 'common order books' option and a 'preliminary order books option'.

40 UK Department for Business, Energy & Industrial Strategy, "Electricity trading arrangements: Guidance from the Secretary of State for Business, Energy and Industrial Strategy to transmission system operators and relevant electricity market operators" (January 2021), available at <https://assets.publishing.service.gov.uk/government/uploads/system/uploads/attachment_data/file/958195/secretary-of-state-electricity-trading-arrangements-guidance.pdf>.

41 The Electricity Trading (Development of Technical Procedures) (Day-Ahead Market Timeframe) Regulations 2021.

42 Ofgem, 'Consultation on the proposed approach to costs for the multi-region loose volume coupling trading arrangements under the EU–UK TCA' (26 May 2021), available at consultation_on_the_proposed_approach_to_costs_for_the_multi-region_loose_volume_coupling_trading_arrangements_under_the_eu-uk_tca_0.pdf

43 EU and UK TSOs MRLVC group, 'Cost Benefit Analysis of MRLVC' (n 35).

For the common order books option,[44] the EU and GB market participants submit their orders prior to gate closure. Then follows a simultaneous process whereby the NEMOs and the GB power exchanges lace the order books into the MRLVC system and into the MCO calculation. The algorithm makes the calculation, which is then validated.

In the preliminary order books option,[45] the MRLVC system will start earlier using whatever order books it has received by 11.45 am (an indicative time, which will depend on the processing time and speed with which results can be transferred to the SDAC MCO). This option would require a GB gate closure at 11.45, and a later SDAC gate closure, e.g., at 12.00 noon. As this option would operate on incomplete order books, there is a risk that it may lead to price distortions and therefore market inefficiencies.

The CBA recommends that MRLVC should be as tight as possible, as, in its view, loose coupling can lead to adverse flows and transmission capacity not being fully utilised, even though price differences between the two markets would be supportive of better utilisation of transmission capacity.[46] The CBA also considers detailed design options for the development of MRLVC.[47]

The GB electricity market currently has no single clearing price. In this regard, the CBA noted that a single GB clearing price would be highly desirable for the effective implementation of MRLVC. The CBA further recommended a single GB clearing price as a common feature in all MRLVC design options.[48]

A consultation to implement a single GB clearing price by the UK Department of Business, Enterprise and Industrial Strategy was held (with a closing date of 28 October 2021) to support the efforts to create the MRLVC mechanism.[49] Results of the consultation are expected in due course.

On the basis of the CBA, it can be said that implementation of MRLVC might not be straightforward, at least within the timeframe stipulated in the TCA, both from an economic and a legal perspective:

- From an economic perspective, as noted above, MRLVC might not be immune to market inefficiencies, which might lead to a loss of socio-economic welfare[50] and high price discrepancies.

44 EU and UK TSOs MRLVC group, 'Cost Benefit Analysis of MRLVC' (n 35) 9.

45 EU and UK TSOs MRLVC group, 'Cost Benefit Analysis of MRLVC' (n 35) 101.

46 EU and UK TSOs MRLVC group, 'Cost Benefit Analysis of MRLVC' (n 35).

47 EU and UK TSOs MRLVC group, 'Cost Benefit Analysis of MRLVC' (n 35) 86.

48 EU and UK TSOs MRLVC group, 'Cost Benefit Analysis of MRLVC' (n 35) 30.

49 UK Department for Business, Energy and Industrial Strategy, 'GB Wholesale Electricity Market Arrangements Re-coupling GB auctions for cross-border trade with the EU at the day-ahead timeframe', (September 2021), available at: <https://assets.publishing.service.gov.uk/government/uploads/system/uploads/attachment_data/file/1022065/power-exchange-consultation-gb-wholesale-electricity-market-arrangements.pdf>.

50 The socio-economic welfare of interconnectors relates to their wider societal impact, such as their contribution to the improvement of supply security, the cost to meet electricity demand, or improvements in which electricity from renewable sources is integrated into the overall energy system. For

- From a legal perspective, the CBA highlights a potential need to amend the gate closure times for the SDAC process in order to fully realise the benefits of low volume coupling. This might be quite complex as SDAC gate closures are codified by the Commission Regulation (EU) 2015/1222 of 24 July 2015 establishing a guideline on capacity allocation and congestion management,[51] the amendment of which is a long and drawn process which would be difficult to achieve by the TCA deadline of April 2022. Apart from the timing difficulties, such an amendment would also require the political support to change an EU Regulation in order to accommodate a third country. Against the backdrop of the continued war of words on the Northern Ireland Protocol,[52] political will to do so might be hard to come by.

Until the MRLVC mechanism is implemented, electricity will be traded between the GB and EU markets on the basis of the current no-deal access rules, with all the trading inefficiencies this implies. The impact of the absence of market coupling could be felt particularly keenly during the early autumn of 2021, when Europe as a whole was experiencing high gas prices.[53] Whilst electricity prices spiked as a result in both the EU, prices in the GB market were often significantly higher than on the continent, as shown in the table.[54]

	10 September	*18 September*	*2 October*
GB	£660.53	£153.39	£159.45
Germany	€144.48	€94.10	€40.96
Netherlands	€150.94	€106.10	€111.59
France	€135.33	€98.59	€64.53

According to the power market analyst EnAppSys, high spikes in the GB day-ahead power prices could be observed throughout September. On 6 September,

a detailed discussion of the socio-economic impact of interconnectors, please see: Pyöry, Costs and Benefits of GB Interconnection, A Report to the National Infrastructure Commission, February 2016, available here: <https://assets.publishing.service.gov.uk/government/uploads/system/uploads/attachment_data/file/505222/080_Poyry_CostsAndBenefitsOfGBInterconnection_v500.pdf>

51 Available here: <https://eur-lex.europa.eu/legal-content/EN/TXT/?uri=CELEX%3A02015R1222-20210315>

52 For more detail on the Northern Ireland Protocol and the positions of the UK and EU, respectively, see also Jess Sargeant, Joe Marshall, 'Northern Ireland protocol: ongoing UK–EU disagreements' (14 October 2021), available at: <https://www.instituteforgovernment.org.uk/explainers/northern-ireland-protocol-disagreements>.

53 For more background on this, see, for instance, 'The EU's electricity market and why soaring gas prices are driving bills higher', *Financial Times*, 13 October 2021, available at: <https://www.ft.com/content/f37d2a36-4609-4b3e-9795-064b6d459676>.

54 All data in the table taken from Epex day-ahead data, as published on <https://www.epexspot.com/en/market-data>, on the indicated dates.

day-ahead auctions cleared at £731/MWh during the evening peak.[55] For 14 September, day-ahead prices peaked at £1,675.30/MWh on the EPEX power exchange and at £1,750/MWh on the Nordpool power exchange. Previous record prices were £1,500/MWh and £1,499.62/MWh on 14 January 2021 and 13 January 2021 for EPEX and Nordpool, respectively.[56]

There are a number of possible causes for such high prices. A shortage of generation and low wind generation are often being cited, as well as some gas-fired power stations being offline and some generators preferring to trade in the high-priced GB balancing mechanism (where prices reached a record £4,037.80/MWh on 9 September and the baseload imbalance price reached £960/MWh on the same day).[57] Notwithstanding, the uncoupled trading arrangements between the GB and EU power markets also played an important role. EnAppSys has gone on record to state that [these] 'high prices are due to the trading arrangements as a result of Brexit'[58] as the previous implicit market coupling arrangements would have softened the GB electricity price significantly. This view is supported by Ofgem data for the year up to September 2021, which also show that GB power prices in the wholesale day-ahead-market have steadily risen since January 2021.[59] It also confirms the view submitted by Energy UK, a trade association for the energy sector, to the House of Lords' EU Committee to the House of Lords that

> [l]eaving the IEM on 1 January … [led] the legislation that supported the coupling of the Day-Ahead market in GB to fall away. This means GB power exchanges no longer share order books to deliver a single day ahead price. This has led to the two day ahead auctions often clearing at different prices, leading to additional risk for market participants (especially renewable generators) and ultimately additional cost for customers.[60]

For completeness, it should be noted that after the Russian invasion of Ukraine on 24 February, electricity prices across Europe have risen due to soaring gas prices. The trading inefficiencies between GB and the EU however remain a significant concern.

55 Molly Lemprire, 'Power prices spike to record highs amidst "perfect shoulder month storm"' Current News (6 September 2021) <https://www.current-news.co.uk/news/the-perfect-shoulder-month-storm-power-prices-spike-to-record-highs> accessed 22 October 2021.

56 Alice Grundy, 'Record-breaking day-ahead power prices shoot to £1,750/MWh' Current News (13 September 2021) <https://www.current-news.co.uk/news/record-breaking-day-ahead-power-prices-shoot-to-1-750-mwh> accessed 5 October 2021.

57 Ibid.

58 Ibid.

59 Ofgem, 'Wholesale market indicators', available at: <https://www.ofgem.gov.uk/energy-data-and-research/data-portal/wholesale-market-indicators>.

60 House of Lords European Union Committee, 22nd Report of Session 2019–2021, 'Beyond Brexit: food, environment, energy and health' (23 March 2021) available at: <https://publications.parliament.uk/pa/ld5801/ldselect/ldeucom/247/247.pdf>.

2.3.8 Congestion management and transmission costs

Consistent with Article 16 of each of the EU Electricity Regulation and the UK Electricity Regulation, Article 311 of the TCA requires the UK and the EU to ensure that capacity allocation and congestion management on electricity interconnectors is market-based, transparent, and non-discriminatory and that the maximum level of capacity of electricity interconnectors is made available to the market.[61]

The TCA does not specify a threshold for the minimum capacity that must be made available to the market (unlike Article 16[8] of the EU Electricity Regulation, which requires that a minimum of 70% of capacity be made available); this discrepancy between the TCA and the EU Electricity Regulation may lead to inefficiencies in the capacity allocation. Article 311(1)(f) of the TCA requires the coordination of capacity allocation and congestion management between EU and UK TSOs, involving the development of arrangements for all relevant timeframes (forward, day-ahead, intraday, and balancing).

Article of 311 the TCA also requires the UK and the EU to ensure that relevant TSOs conclude a multi-party agreement relating to the compensation for the costs of hosting cross-border flows of electricity. Such a multi-party agreement should aim to ensure that UK TSOs are treated on an equivalent basis to a TSO in an EU Member State (which will automatically participate in the inter-transmission system operator compensation mechanism). Until such time as this agreement is concluded, a transmission system use fee may be levied on scheduled imports and exports between the EU and the UK.[62] At the time of writing, the mechanism stipulated in the TCA is not yet in place.

2.3.9 Capacity markets

A capacity market is a mechanism which has been introduced in many power markets to help stabilise power markets as more intermittent renewable energy comes on stream. Whilst the design of such capacity markets varies from jurisdiction to jurisdiction, typically, power generator companies can bid for capacity market contracts, often several years ahead, to offer capacity to the market when it might be needed. In turn, they receive fixed payments based on the amount of MW they offer, again typically by the TSO.

Article 304 of the TCA provides that neither the UK nor the EU are required to permit capacity located in the territory of the other to participate in its capacity mechanisms.[63] This has the effect of limiting the access of companies on both sides of the Channel to such capacity markets. This provision will impact the possibility of overseas generation using interconnectors to bid into capacity markets, which in turn will likely impact GB power prices further.

61 Article 311 TCA.
62 Article 311(3), 311(4) and 311(5) TCA.
63 Article 304(3) TCA.

2.4 Conclusion

By way of conclusion, it can be said that access to the EU energy market for UK companies (and, conversely, access to the UK market by EU companies) has, post-Brexit, become – for the time being – both more complex and less efficient as well as more politicised, more short-term focused, and less predictable .

It is more complex as new rules need to be created to replace the previously applicable tightly woven EU regime of regulations, directives, and network codes. It will take time for these new rules to be drawn up. In contrast to the EU regime, the TCA does not come with the 'administrative scaffolding' of the established legal processes of EU regulations and directives, which in turn means that the implementation of the TCA will be a slow and tentative process.

It is less efficient especially as concerns cross-border trading of electricity since it currently operates on a no-deal basis until such time as the MRLVC is implemented. The system will remain less efficient even after the proposed coupling mechanism is put in place compared to the price coupling applicable in the EU. This has already been shown to have contributed to higher electricity prices in the UK.

It is more politicised as the implementation of the TCA is dependent on the political will and therefore less predictable than the EU directives and regulations which are implemented on the basis of established legal rules.

Given that the energy provisions in the TCA could cease to be in force after 30 June 2026 (unless the UK and EU agree to an extension), the new regime for cross-border energy market has a more short-term outlook, which in turn makes long-term investment decisions, including whether or not to construct new interconnectors, more difficult and costly.

3 The Impact of Brexit on the EU's Supply Security

Silke Goldberg

3.1 Introduction and scope

This article explores the impact of Brexit on the EU's energy supply security by analysing the prevalent elements of 'availability' and 'deliverability' used in the definition of supply security in the relevant EU legislation.

Section 2 of this Chapter briefly defines both of these elements, Section 3 summaries the physical reality of the EU's import dependency and the growth in renewable energy sources ("RES"), and Section 4 addresses the availability aspects of supply security in the EU post-Brexit, first by setting out the details of the EU's import dependency as regards fossil fuels and ambitions to increase the share of RES in its overall energy mix as part of its decarbonisation strategy, and second by providing a brief overview of the relevant EU legislation and TCA provisions and an appraisal of the likely impact of the TCA arrangements. Section 5 discusses aspects of deliverability, starting with a brief overview as to the many layers of both the concept and its application in EU law, followed by an examination of the relevant provisions of the TCA and an impact assessment of the same. Section 6 concludes and considers the future of supply security-related issues in the EU.

It comes as no surprise that the EU Member State most affected by Brexit is Ireland, due both to the fact that it is the only EU Member State to share a border with the UK and the particular constitutional arrangements in relation to Northern Ireland. There are additional specific, energy-related issues as well: the electricity market on the island of Ireland encompasses both Ireland and Northern Ireland, Ireland is dependent on the UK for its gas supply, and the UK is the only country to which Ireland is connected in terms of both electricity and gas interconnectors. Post-Brexit energy supply security is therefore a particular concern for Ireland. The specific post-Brexit considerations in relation to the Irish energy sector are discussed in detail in Chapter 11 of this book. Certain aspects of energy security linked to market access issues are addressed in Chapter 2. In order to avoid duplication, cross references are made to these Chapters where appropriate.

DOI: 10.4324/9781003364337-4

3.2 What is supply security?

At the outset of this Chapter, it is opportune to clarify what is meant by the term *energy security*. As Paul Hallas points out in Chapter 4 of this book, there are many different definitions of energy security. Most of them contain at least two constitutive elements, the first of which refers to the physical availability of 'sufficient energy to meet all reasonable demands for it' and the second of which relates to the affordability of energy supply as expressed in energy price levels both in the wholesale and retail market.

In the context of the EU, given the import dependency of the EU, it is perhaps unsurprising that the EU's energy security is perceived from a *supply* security point of view.[1]

The EU does not have a uniform definition of energy or supply security in its relevant regulations or directives. In relation to electricity, the current EU definition of 'security of electricity supply' refers to 'the ability of an electricity system to guarantee the supply of electricity to customers with a clearly established level of performance, as determined by the Member States concerned'.[2] In relation to gas, the most recent definition of *security* refers to 'both security of supply of natural gas and technical safety' without defining either concept.[3] Given these definitions, it is appropriate to examine the impact of Brexit on the EU's supply security through the lens of *availability*, meaning the physical availability of energy; and *deliverability*, meaning the ability to ensure the delivery of energy through relevant infrastructure.

3.3 The physical reality: import dependency and renewable expansion

3.3.1 The EU's fossil fuel import dependency

In relation to fossil fuels, the energy import dependency of the European Union is well documented.

According to Eurostat, in 2019, almost two-thirds of the extra-EU's crude oil imports came from Russia (27%), Iraq (9%), Nigeria and Saudi Arabia (both 8%), and Kazakhstan and Norway (both 7%). A similar analysis shows that almost three-quarters of the EU's imports of natural gas came from Russia

1 Dicle Korkmaz, 'Internal and external dynamics of European energy security' [2010] 5th Pan-European Conference on EU Politics 2015.

2 Regulation (EU) 2019/941 of the European Parliament and of the Council of 5 June 2019 on risk-preparedness in the electricity sector and repealing Directive 2005/89/EC [2019] OJ L158/1, art 2(10) (Risk Preparedness Regulation).

3 Regulation (EU) 2017/1938 of the European Parliament and of the Council of 25 October 2017 concerning measures to safeguard the security of gas supply and repealing Regulation (EU) No 994/2010 [2017] OJ L280/1. Definition of *security* by reference to Directive 2009/73/EC of the European Parliament and of the Council of 13 July 2009 concerning common rules for the internal market in natural gas and repealing Directive 2003/55/EC [2009] OJ L211/94, art 2(32).

(41%), Norway (16%), Algeria (8%), and Qatar (5%), while over threequarters of solid-fuel (mostly coal) imports originated from Russia (47%), the United States (18%), and Australia (14%).[4]

These trends continued in 2020 and in the first trimester of 2021, the latest period for which figures were available at the time of writing, with Russia being the largest supplier of natural gas to the EU (46.8%) both in 2020 and in the first semester of 2021.[5] The only other partners with a significant share in total extra-EU imports were Norway (26.5%) and, at some distance, Algeria (11.6%).[6] In the same period, gas imports from the UK into the EU amounted to 3.7% of the total import value of gas into the EU.

The EU import dependency for oil and gas is, however, unevenly distributed among the EU's Member States. In the first semester of 2021, more than 75% of imports of petroleum oils of Bulgaria, Slovakia, Hungary, and Finland came from Russia. During the same time, Bulgaria, Czechia, Estonia, Latvia, Hungary, Austria, Romania, Slovenia, Slovakia and Finland imported more than 75% of their natural gas imports from Russia.

3.3.2 Expansion of RES in the EU

It would be wrong to limit an assessment of energy security to fossil fuel availability. Given the EU's climate and decarbonisation objectives,[7] its energy mix and associated electricity generation profile is undergoing a major structural shift towards energy from RES.[8]

In 2020, the share of RES in the EU's gross final energy consumption was 22.1%; this is just over 2 percentage points above the 20% target set out in the 2009 Renewable Energy Directive,[9] compared with 9.6% in 2004.

According to Eurostat, Sweden (60%) had by far the highest share among the EU Member States in 2020, ahead of Finland (44%) and Latvia (42%). At the

4 Eurostat, 'From where do we import energy?' (*Eurostat*) <https://ec.europa.eu/eurostat/cache/infographs/energy/bloc-2c.html#:~:text=Russia%20is%20the%20main%20EU,gas%20and%20solid%20fossil%20fuels&text=In%202019%2C%20almost%20two%20thirds,and%20Norway%20(both%207%20%25)> accessed 1 March 2022.

5 Eurostat, 'EU imports of energy products – recent developments' (*Eurostat*, October 2021) <https://ec.europa.eu/eurostat/statistics-explained/index.php?title=EU_imports_of_energy_products_-_recent_developments#Main_suppliers_of_natural_gas_and_petroleum_oils_to_the_EU> accessed 1 March 2022.

6 Ibid.

7 Commission, '"Fit for 55": delivering the EU's 2030 Climate Target on the way to climate neutrality' (Communication) COM (2021) 550 final.

8 IEA, 'Energy security: Reliable, affordable access to all fuels and energy sources' (*IEA*) <https://www.iea.org/topics/energy-security> accessed 1 March 2022 (IEA Energy security).

9 Directive 2009/28/EC of the European Parliament and of the Council of 23 April 2009 on the promotion of the use of energy from renewable sources and amending and subsequently repealing Directives 2001/77/EC and 2003/30/EC, [2009] OJ L140/39.

opposite end of the scale, the lowest proportions of renewables were registered in Malta (11%), followed by Luxembourg (12%) and Belgium (13%).[10]

As such, conventional power plants' share of the generation landscape in the EU is declining and with it the reliance on fossil fuels. This shift in the generation profile brings its own supply security challenges, such as the intermittent and often decentralised nature of RES increases, as well as increased risks to the energy system through cyberattacks and the reliance on 'metals and minerals that are in tight supply or whose production is dominated by a limited number of nations'.[11]

As part of the proposals[12] to amend the recently recast Renewable Energy Directive[13] in the context of the Fit for 55 Package tabled by the European Commission in July 2021, the overall minimum renewable energy target is proposed to be increased to 40% from the previous 32%.

Specific sub-targets aim to replace 50% of grey hydrogen (produced from natural gas) used in the EU with green hydrogen (produced from renewables) by 2030, and aim for 2.6% of the energy demand from the transport sector (which will not only include road and rail but also maritime and aviation) to be covered by RES. These two targets alone require 500 TWh of renewable energy generation,[14] which is more than the entire electricity consumption of France in 2020 (at 449.51 TWh).[15]

Coupled together, these targets will have a noticeable impact on renewable power demand, raising questions over the possible effect on energy prices over the coming years.

3.4 Availability in EU legislation

It is useful to briefly set out and summarise the EU legislation in relation to supply security in order to then contrast it with the provisions of the TCA and the consequences of the latter. Energy security as a policy aim is anchored in Article 194(1) TFEU which provides that '[EU] policy on energy shall aim, in a spirit of solidarity

10 Eurostat, 'Renewable energy statistics' (*Eurostat*, January 2022) <https://ec.europa.eu/eurostat/statistics-explained/index.php?title=Renewable_energy_statistics#:~:text=In%202020%2C%20renewable%20energy%20sources,and%2033%20%25%2C%20respectively> accessed 1 March 2022.

11 IEA Energy security (n 10).

12 Commission, 'Proposal for a Directive of the European Parliament and of the Council amending Directive (EU) 2018/2001 of the European Parliament and of the Council, Regulation (EU) 2018/1999 of the European Parliament and of the Council and Directive 98/70/EC of the European Parliament and of the Council as regards the promotion of energy from renewable sources, and repealing Council Directive (EU) 2015/652' COM (2021) 557 final.

13 Directive (EU) 2018/2001 of the European Parliament and of the Council of 11 December 2018 on the promotion of the use of energy from renewable sources [2018] OJ L328/82.

14 Transport & Environment, 'A clean shift for EU transport fuels?' (*T&E,* November 2021) <https://www.transportenvironment.org/wp-content/uploads/2021/11/TE-Briefing-RED-II-review-Autumn-2021-Final-22.11.2021.pdf> accessed 1 March 2022.

15 IEA, 'France Key energy statistics 2020' (*IEA*) <https://www.iea.org/countries/france> accessed 1 March 2022.

between Member States, to: … (b) ensure security of energy supply in the Union'.[16] As such, supply security is a major theme that runs through the EU's energy policy; however, there is no single legislative framework for it. Instead, security of supply features directly or indirectly in most EU energy directives and regulations. Below is a brief summary of those EU legislative acts which specifically address the availability (or otherwise) of energy in the EU and measures to counteract acute shortages.

3.4.1 Electricity

The 2019 Risk Preparedness Regulation[17]

> sets out a common framework of rules on how to prevent, prepare for and manage electricity crises, bringing more transparency in the preparation phase and during an electricity crisis, and ensuring that measures are taken in a coordinated and effective manner.[18]

It establishes a regime for the identification of regional and national crisis scenarios,[19] requires Member States to prepare risk-preparedness plans and detail their contents,[20] and sets out exactly what is required of Member States should a connected Member State request assistance (to cooperate in a spirit of solidarity in order to prevent electricity crises).[21]

It also requires that Member States 'act and cooperate in a spirit of solidarity in order to prevent or manage electricity crises', implying a more proactive approach and cooperation between Member States without specifying how such an approach might look in practice. Arguably, to some extent, this cooperation takes place in EU fora such as the ENTSO-E whose Steering Group on Operational Frameworks counts 'ensuring supply security' amongst its tasks;[22] however, the 2019 Risk Preparedness Regulation also assigns monitoring tasks to the electricity coordination group established by a Commission decision in 2012.[23]

3.4.2 Gas

The 2017 Gas Supply Regulation[24] seeks to ensure the continued security of gas supply during a crisis, its objective being 'to ensure that all the necessary

16 Consolidated version of the Treaty on the Functioning of the European Union [2012] OJ C326/47, art 194.

17 Risk Preparedness Regulation (n 2).

18 Ibid recital 6.

19 Risk Preparedness Regulation (n 2) arts 6–7.

20 Ibid arts 10–13.

21 Ibid arts 15–16.

22 For more detail on the Steering Group, see ENTSO-E, 'System Operations Committee' (*ENTSO-E*) <https://www.entsoe.eu/about/system-operations/> accessed 1 March 2022.

23 Commission Decision of 15 November 2012 setting up the Electricity Coordination Group [2012] OJ C353/2.

24 Regulation (EU) 2017/1938 of the European Parliament and of the Council of 25 October 2017 concerning measures to safeguard the security of gas supply and repealing Regulation (EU) No 994/2010 [2017] OJ L280/1 (Gas Regulation).

measures are taken to safeguard an uninterrupted supply of gas throughout the Union, in particular to protected customers in the event of difficult climatic conditions or disruptions of the gas supply'.[25]

To this end, as with the 2019 Risk Preparedness Regulation, the 2017 Gas Supply Regulation sets out when a crisis may be declared,[26] mandates preventive action plans and emergency plans,[27] and prescribes the contents of the plans in detail.[28] The solidarity mechanism contained within the regulation, however, is somewhat more explicit than the 2019 Risk Preparedness Regulation which reflects the function of gas as a primary fuel, i.e. a fuel that is 'found in nature and can be extracted, captured, cleaned, or graded without any sort of energy conversion or transformation process'.[29]

Pursuant to the 2017 Gas Supply Regulation, a Member State called to assist another has to 'take the necessary measures to ensure that the gas supply to customers other than solidarity protected customers in its territory is reduced or does not continue to the extent necessary'.[30]

Article 13(2) specifically provides that a Member State has to provide solidarity measures for 'another Member State to which it is connected via a third country unless flows are restricted through the third country', subject to an agreement to that effect between the relevant Member States and, to the extent appropriate, the relevant third country.

In addition, the Gas Coordination Group created by Article 4 of the 2017 Gas Supply Regulation provides for a coordination forum for ACER, ENTSO-G, industry, and customer groups to assist the Commission in relation to questions of gas supply, specifically in an emergency, and in information gathering as to the security of gas supply at national, regional, and EU level.

3.4.3 Oil

The 2009 Stockpiling Directive[31] is the only piece of EU legislation that directly addresses the physical availability of fuel stock in the EU. It stipulates that Member States have to ensure sufficient accessible oil/petroleum reserves equal to at least 90 days of net imports or 61 days of consumption, whichever is higher.[32] While the 2009 Stockpiling Directive recognises that indigenous production can

25 Ibid recital 3.

26 Ibid art 11.

27 Ibid art 8.

28 Ibid art 9–10.

29 Energy Education, 'Primary Fuel' (*University of Calgary*, 27 September 2021) <https://energyeducation.ca/encyclopedia/Primary_fuel#:~:text=Primary%20fuels%20are%20fuels%20that,energy%20conversion%20or%20transformation%20process.&text=Primary%20fuels%20such%20as%20coal,like%20wind%20and%20solar%20power> accessed 1 March 2022.

30 Gas Regulation (n 27) art 13.

31 Council Directive 2009/119/EC of 14 September 2009 imposing an obligation on Member States to maintain minimum stocks of crude oil and/or petroleum products [2009] OJ L265/9.

32 Ibid art 3.

offset the need to stockpile somewhat, Member States with indigenous oil production still have to comply with a 61-day stockpiling requirement.[33] Importantly, such stocks need to be maintained at all times in the EU.[34]

Member States must send the European Commission a statistical summary of their stocks at the end of each month, setting out the number of days of net imports or consumption that the stocks represent.[35] In case of a supply crisis, the Commission is to arrange for a consultation between Member States. Generally, no withdrawals from the stockpiled reserves may be made prior to this consultation, except in a very urgent situation.[36]

Article 17 sets up a Coordination Group for oil and petroleum products to assist with the analysis of the supply security situation in as far as oil and petroleum products are concerned. This group also facilitates the coordination and implementation of any relevant measures.

3.4.4 Non-fuel-specific provisions

In addition to the provisions of the fuel-specific EU legislation set out above, the Energy Union Governance Regulation[37] contains general provisions pertaining to energy security in the EU. As supply security constitutes one of the pillars of the EU's Energy Union strategy, the Energy Union Governance Regulation obligates Member States to report on energy security as part of their integrated national energy and climate progress reports, including information on the implementation of:

> (a) national objectives for the diversification of energy sources and supply; (b) where applicable, national objectives with regard to reducing energy import dependency from third countries; (c) national objectives for the development of the ability to cope with constrained or interrupted supply of an energy source, including gas and electricity; (d) national objectives with regard to increasing the flexibility of the national energy system, in particular by means of deploying domestic energy sources, demand response and energy storage [and..] (f) regional cooperation in support of supply security as well as any relevant financing measures.[38]

33 Ibid.
34 Ibid.
35 Ibid art 14.
36 Ibid art 20.
37 Regulation (EU) 2018/1999 of the European Parliament and of the Council of 11 December 2018 on the Governance of the Energy Union and Climate Action, amending Regulations (EC) No 663/2009 and (EC) No 715/2009 of the European Parliament and of the Council, Directives 94/22/EC, 98/70/EC, 2009/31/EC, 2009/73/EC, 2010/31/EU, 2012/27/EU and 2013/30/EU of the European Parliament and of the Council, Council Directives 2009/119/EC and (EU) 2015/652 and repealing Regulation (EU) No 525/2013 of the European Parliament and of the Council [2018] OJ L328/1 (Energy Union Regulation).
38 Energy Union Regulation (n 37) art 22.

This provision adds further to the tightly woven framework of reporting and coordination of EU Member States in relation to supply security measures and the fuel-specific measures sketched out in Sections 3.3.1–3.3.3 above.

3.4.5 Availability in the TCA

Section 3 of Chapter 2 of the TCA sets out provisions concerning the cooperation of the EU and the UK in relation to supply security.

Article 315 contains a commitment that the UK and the EU 'shall cooperate with respect to the security of supply of electricity and natural gas'.[39] To underscore this commitment, through Article 315 both the UK and the EU undertake to 'develop appropriate frameworks for cooperation with respect to the security of supply of electricity and natural gas',[40] to 'inform each other without undue delay where there is reliable information that a disruption or other crisis relating to the security of electricity or natural gas may occur and on measures planned or taken',[41] or (if the disruption or other crisis has already occurred) seek to enable the coordination of possible mitigation and restoration measures.[42]

Article 315 is a clear attempt to both pre-empt possible supply emergency situations, while also creating minimum requirements for how to act if such an emergency is foreseen or actually occurs.

Article 316 builds on it further by requiring each party to be proactive in setting out a commitment to 'assess risks affecting the security of supply of electricity or natural gas, including the likelihood and impact of such risks, and including cross-border risks'.[43]

These assessments are to take the form of regularly updated plans, which shall contain 'measures needed to remove or mitigate the likelihood and impact of any risk identified ... and the measures needed to prepare for, and mitigate the impact of, an electricity or natural gas crisis'.[44] Moreover, each party has committed to share these plans with one another,[45] exchanging information on any potential risks to security of supply 'in a timely manner'.[46] Importantly, Article 316 contains a commitment from each party not to plan any measures that would 'endanger the security of supply of electricity or natural gas of the other Party'.[47]

39 Trade and Cooperation Agreement between the European Union and the European Atomic Energy Community, of the one part, and the United Kingdom of Great Britain and Northern Ireland, of the other part [2021] OJ L149/10, art 315(1) (TCA).

40 Ibid art 315(7).

41 Ibid art 315(4).

42 Ibid art 315(5).

43 Ibid art 316(1).

44 Ibid art 316(2).

45 Ibid art 315(3).

46 Ibid art 315(2).

47 Ibid art 316(3)(c).

Whilst these provisions paint a picture of close cooperation between the EU and the UK, this cooperation is largely limited to the exchange of information in various forms. The TCA does not replicate the solidarity mechanisms of the 2017 Gas Regulation or the 2019 Risk Preparedness Regulation, neither does it create other forms of mutual assistance, nor does it address minimum stockpiling obligations in either jurisdiction.

Instead, Article 302 TCA explicitly provides that the UK and the EU preserve the right to adopt, maintain, and enforce measures necessary to pursue legitimate public policy objectives, such as securing the supply of energy goods and raw materials. Article 340(3) TCA explicitly provides that nothing in the TCA shall prevent a party from developing their own rules pertaining to energy security. This implies that even against a backdrop of cooperation efforts, policy divergence is possible and in fact likely. Given that the TCA contains no minimum stockpiling or other obligations that affect the availability element of supply security directly, it is likely that the UK will develop its own policy in this regard.

3.4.6 Impact of the TCA on availability of energy in the EU

Taking into consideration the UK‘s contribution to the EU‘s energy supply (see Section 3.3.1 above), it is difficult to argue that the UK's departure from the EU's Internal Energy Market has had a material impact on 26 of the 27 EU Member States[48] – though there may be some minor geopolitical ripple effects in the EU as a result of it losing one of its few large-scale gas producing Member States.[49]

In relation to electricity, the direction of flow on GB–EU interconnectors is generally, with few exceptions, from the EU into GB due to price differentials. However, this could change in the future depending on the scale of offshore wind deployment in the North Sea.[50] Whilst the electricity trading arrangements post-Brexit do not, in terms of efficiency, match those of the EU's market coupling arrangements (see Chapter 2 on market access for further details), the Brexit-related changes to interconnector trading have not affected the availability of electricity.[51]

48 Thierry Bros, 'Brexit's impact on gas markets' (*The Oxford Institute for Energy Studies*, January 2017) <https://a9w7k6q9.stackpathcdn.com/wpcms/wp-content/uploads/2017/01/Brexits-impact-on-gas-markets-OIES-Energy-Insight.pdf> accessed 1 March 2022.

49 Aziiz Sutrisno and Floor Alkemade, 'EU gas infrastructure resilience: Competition, internal changes, and renewable energy pressure' [2020] 6 Energy Reports 24, 25.

50 Jonny Bairstow, 'UK could become net exporter of electricity by 2040s' (*Energy Live News*, 14 October 2020) <https://www.energylivenews.com/2020/10/14/uk-could-become-net-exporter-of-electricity-by-2040s/> accessed 1 March 2022 and Rachel Morison 'UK may become net power exporter to Europe in five years' (*Bloomberg*, 3 June 2021) <https://www.bloomberg.com/news/articles/2021-06-03/u-k-could-become-net-power-exporter-to-europe-in-five-years> accessed 1 March 2022.

51 National Grid, 'Why electricity interconnection between Europe and the UK matters' (*National Grid*, 8 September 2021) <https://www.nationalgrid.com/stories/engineering-innovation-stories/why-electricity-interconnection-between-europe-and-uk> accessed 1 March 2022.

The sole exception to this assessment, however, is Ireland, a country which (like the UK) is not currently capable of meeting demand through indigenous supply,[52] whose only gas pipelines come via Great Britain,[53] and which, for EU purposes, is an energy island as it is not interconnected with the electricity system of any other Member State. In addition, Ireland faces a particular geographical challenge in relation to its oil stocks. Chapter 11 discusses the gas availability challenges in Ireland post-Brexit in further detail, including in relation to alternative investments; indigenous gas supply from the Corrib field, which has peaked, with production 'projected to decline throughout the 2020s';[54] and import strategies through the Shannon LNG terminal.

There is currently no biogas production facility in Ireland, despite the country having the highest potential for biogas production per capita among EU Member States.[55] Gas Networks Ireland (GNI) estimates that 'up to 30% of demand could be met by renewable gas by 2040',[56] indicating that renewable gas has potential to improve the long-term gas security of Ireland. This is even more important as there are no public stocks of natural gas in the country, the last storage site having ceased operations in 2017.[57] The GNI and EirGrid joint report (the 'Joint Report') identified that investment in storage capacity in Ireland would raise the country's N-1 position in a 2030 median demand scenario to 68%.[58] The N-1 standard 'describes the ability of the technical capacity of the gas infrastructure to satisfy total gas demand in the calculated area in the event of disruption of the single largest gas infrastructure during a day of exceptionally high gas demand occurring with a statistical probability of once in 20 years'.[59] The Joint Report recommended that 'opportunities for permanent gas storage in Ireland and gas storage operations in the rest of Europe'[60] be monitored.

This will be of particular importance as the UK is no longer legally bound to show solidarity to a connected country such as Ireland that requests gas supplies in an emergency. However, Byrne Ó Cléirigh has argued that Ireland 'may need special arrangements with the UK and, or, other Member States to ensure that it has access to gas supplies during a gas crisis'.[61]

A bilateral agreement between Ireland and the UK in relation to energy matters will undoubtedly raise difficulties under EU law (as individual Member States cannot enter into international treaties in relation to energy matters, such

52 Byrne Ó Cléirigh, 'Energy Security in Ireland: 2020 Report' (*SEAI*, September 2020) 28-29 (SEAI Report).

53 Ibid 29.

54 Ibid 3.

55 IEA Secretariat, *Energy Policies of IEA Countries: Ireland – 2019 Review* (IEA, April 2019) 68–9 (IEA Ireland 2019 Review).

56 GNI and EirGrid, *Long Term Resilience Study: 2018* (GNI, 2018) 28 (GNI and EirGrid).

57 IEA Ireland 2019 Review (n 58) 66.

58 GNI and EirGrid (n 59) 32.

59 Gas Regulation (n 27) Annex II.

60 GNI and EirGrid (n 59) 5.

61 SEAI Report (n 55) 40.

competency sitting solely with the European Commission on behalf of the EU since the entry into force of the Lisbon Treaty) and is therefore unlikely.

Chapter 11 also considers the impact of Brexit on the electricity market on the island of Ireland (I-SEM). From a supply security perspective, it can be added that whilst a 2020 SEAI report identified that Ireland 'currently has significant surplus power generation capacity',[62] it noted that a combination of an increase in electricity demand and planned closures of generation stations will lead to a reversal of this position from 2026.[63] Failing the construction of new infrastructure, Ireland will therefore be reliant on energy imports from the UK to secure an adequate supply of electricity for its population.

Whilst the UK's annual oil production is barely sufficient to meet even its own demand,[64] and as such is unlikely to raise supply security issues for the EU generally, Brexit raises a particular issue for Irish oil stocks from a logistics and access perspective. The IEA noted in 2019 that 'Ireland has been pursuing a policy of rebalancing its emergency oil reserves by maximising stocks stored on the island of Ireland, composed of stocks held in Ireland and Northern Ireland'.[65] As of 2019, Ireland held 59% of its required stocks in country, with the remaining 41% held abroad such that 21% of the country's total stocks were held in the UK (11% in Great Britain, 9% in Northern Ireland), with the remaining 20% of total stocks held in Denmark, Spain, and Sweden.[66]

In the absence of Ireland having sufficient capacity to store reserves locally, practical solutions (including capacity building within Ireland) must be considered to ensure that both EU law is respected (i.e. oil is stored in the EU) and the relevant reserves can be accessed with sufficient speed.

3.5 Deliverability

3.5.1 Deliverability in the EU context

As mentioned in Section 3.2, *deliverability* refers to the ability to ensure the delivery of physically available energy through the relevant infrastructure to the desired destination.

This Section explores the extent to which Brexit has had an impact on the deliverability of energy within the EU. Deliverability of energy post-Brexit generally is of particular importance to Ireland, as Brexit has had little impact on the availability of fossil energy in the EU generally.

In relation to the decarbonisation of the EU's energy supply (see Section 3.2 above), energy infrastructure development, management, and governance (and

62 SEAI Report (n 55) 63.

63 SEAI Report (n 55) 64–65.

64 BEIS, *Energy Trends: UK, April to June 2021* (BEIS, 2021) 6–7.

65 IEA Ireland 2019 Review (n 58) 47.

66 IEA Ireland 2019 Review (n 58) 47.

therefore the regulatory regime) plays an important role due to the special characteristics of renewable energy.

Therefore, this Section focusses on the deliverability of energy in Ireland post-Brexit as well as issues pertaining to the deliverability of energy (specifically electricity) arising out of the shift towards RES in the EU.

Deliverability is not an isolated concept in EU legislation; rather, it is woven through numerous pieces of legislation which frame the Internal Energy Market, including the 2019 Electricity Directive,[67] the 2019 Gas Directive,[68] and the 2019 Electricity Regulation.[69] All impose supply security-related obligations on different market participants, NRAs as well as Member States. The dispersed obligations on different market participants are a reflection of the liberalised nature of the EU energy market in which no single organisation is solely responsible for ensuring supply security standards. Instead, EU legislation has created a complex web of obligations, with national regulatory authorities (NRAs), Transmission System Operators (TSOs), and the EU Agency for Cooperation of Energy Regulators (ACER), as well as the European Network of Transmission System Operators for Electricity (ENTSO-E) and the European Network of Transmission System Operators for Gas (ENTSO-G) (the ENTSOs), playing prominent roles in relation to planning, developing, and maintaining, as well as the governance of, the energy systems which in turn are crucial for the deliverability of energy.

By way of example, Article 1 of the 2019 Electricity Directive provides that Member States, regulatory authorities, and TSOs cooperate in relation to the integration of electricity from renewable sources, free competition, and security of supply. Article 59 of the same provides that NRAs are to monitor investment in generation and storage capacities in relation to security of supply. The ENTSOs are mandated to work closely with TSOs to plan of energy infrastructure on the basis of the Ten-Year Network Development Plans,[70] whereas the network codes and guidelines adopted pursuant to Articles 59, 60, and 61 of the 2019 Electricity Directive govern the trading of electricity, including over interconnection points, in the Internal Energy Market (IEM). Together, all of these measures ensure the appropriate infrastructure and governance for energy deliverability is in place.

However, a detailed overview of the relevant obligations is beyond the scope of this Chapter.

67 Directive (EU) 2019/944 of the European Parliament and of the Council of 5 June 2019 on common rules for the internal market for electricity and amending Directive 2012/27/EU [2019] OJ L158/125.

68 Directive (EU) 2019/692 of the European Parliament and of the Council of 17 April 2019 amending Directive 2009/73/EC concerning common rules for the internal market in natural gas [2019] OJ L117/1.

69 Regulation (EU) 2019/943 of the European Parliament and of the Council of 5 June 2019 on the internal market for electricity [2019] OJ L158/54.

70 Article 51 of Directive (EU) 2019/944.

3.5.2 Energy deliverability in the TCA

The TCA touches, largely indirectly, on a number of concepts important to deliverability, in particular on provisions pertaining to the development and maintenance of energy infrastructure and on the 'regulatory backdrop' or framework that relates to such infrastructure. By its nature, the TCA touches chiefly on cross-border energy infrastructure, i.e. interconnectors between the UK and the EU. In particular, Article 311 TCA mandates that 'the maximum level of capacity of electricity interconnectors is made available', albeit with some minor caveats.[71]

By seeking to maximise available interconnector capacity between the EU and the UK, the EU has ensured the deliverability of electricity from the UK. To enable a more seamless utilisation of interconnectors, Article 311 envisages the UK and the EU ensuring that 'capacity allocation and management across electricity interconnectors is coordinated between concerned [EU] Union transmission system operators and [UK] transmission system operators',[72] and that 'this coordination shall involve the development of arrangements to deliver robust and efficient outcomes for all relevant timeframes, being forward, day-ahead, intraday and balancing'.[73]

Whereas Article 311 commits both parties only to ensure that, in relation to electricity interconnectors, 'capacity allocation and congestion management on electricity interconnectors is market based, transparent and non-discriminatory',[74] Article 313 goes a little further in relation to gas. Beyond the commitment to ensure that 'capacity allocation and congestion management procedures for gas interconnectors are market-based, transparent and non-discriminatory' (seeking to continue the efficient use of pipelines, a keystone in safeguarding regional energy security),[75] there is a specific commitment that each party 'shall take the necessary steps to ensure that: transmission system operators endeavour to offer jointly standard capacity products which consist of corresponding entry and exit capacity at both sides of an interconnection point'.[76]

This commitment to offer jointly standard capacity products (i.e. within-day, daily, monthly, quarterly, and yearly) further facilitates gas trade between the UK and the EU. The issues arising out of the scant trading arrangements over electricity interconnectors are addressed in more detail in Chapter 2 of this book, but suffice to note that the TCA arrangements will require supplementing with detailed arrangements in relation to electricity trading, as all UK–EU electricity interconnectors currently operate on a 'no-deal' basis only.

Article 314 provides for a commitment by the UK and the EU 'to facilitate the timely development and interoperability of energy infrastructure connecting their

71 TCA (n 42) art 311(1)(b).
72 Ibid art 311(1)(f).
73 Ibid art 311(1)(f).
74 Ibid art 311(1)(a).
75 Ibid art 313(1)(b).
76 Ibid art 313(2)(a).

territories'.[77] This will be especially relevant to new electricity interconnectors between the UK and the EU, not least as both jurisdictions have a clear policy aim to increase their respective interconnection capacity: the UK aims for 18 GW of interconnection capacity by 2030[78] (with a current baseline of 6 GW of operational interconnector capacity),[79] and the EU has a target of 15% interconnection capacity of the EU's installed generation capacity.[80]

Article 317 specifically requires UK and EU TSOs to 'develop working arrangements that are efficient and inclusive' and to work with ENTSO-E and ENTSO-G to establish frameworks for cooperation covering *inter alia* access to networks,[81] the security of electricity and gas supply,[82] infrastructure planning,[83] and the efficient use of electricity and gas interconnectors.[84] As explained in further detail in Chapter 2, these working relationships fall short of a status comparable to membership in ENTSO-E or ENTSO-G by UK TSOs,[85] and will establish fora for the exchange of information rather than proactive joint planning and decision making, which in turn may have a negative impact on the development of UK–EU gas and electricity interconnectors.

Cooperation between regulatory authorities is key to establishing the regulatory regime for cross-border energy infrastructure. In this regard, Article 318 provides that ACER and Ofgem are to make administrative arrangements 'as soon as possible in order to facilitate meeting the objectives of this Agreement',[86] covering inter alia access to networks,[87] the security of electricity and gas supply,[88] infrastructure planning,[89] the efficient use of electricity and gas interconnectors,[90] and cooperation between TSOs.[91] This, together with the relevant market access issues arising from this form of cooperation and its limitations, is discussed in further detail in Chapter 2.

In light of the growing importance of renewable energy and particularly offshore wind in the energy mix of both the EU and the UK,[92] Article 321 provides for

77 Ibid art 314(1).

78 Ofgem, 'Interconnector Policy Review: Decision' (*Ofgem*, 13 December 2021) <https://www.ofgem.gov.uk/publications/interconnector-policy-review-decision> accessed 1 March 2022.

79 Ofgem, 'Interconnectors: Gas interconnectors' (*Ofgem*) <https://www.ofgem.gov.uk/energy-policy-and-regulation/policy-and-regulatory-programmes/interconnectors> accessed 1 March 2022.

80 Energy Union Regulation (n 40) art 4(d)(1).

81 TCA (n 42) art 317(1)(b).

82 Ibid art 317(1)(c).

83 Ibid art 317(1)(e).

84 Ibid art 317(1)(f).

85 Ibid art 317(1).

86 Ibid art 318(1).

87 Ibid art 318(1)(b).

88 Ibid art 318(1)(d).

89 Ibid art 318(1)(e).

90 Ibid art 318(1)(g).

91 Ibid art 318(1)(h).

92 Nearly 80% of the global offshore wind capacity (23.1 GW) is situated in Europe, where the UK is the leading market (8 GW capacity), followed by Germany (6.4 GW), followed by Denmark

the cooperation of the parties in the development of offshore renewable energy. Its provisions commit the parties to 'sharing best practices and, where appropriate, by facilitating the development of specific projects'. Article 321 explicitly references the North Seas Energy Cooperation[93] and provides for the creation of a forum for technical discussions between the European Commission, ministries and public authorities of the Member States, UK ministries and public authorities, and TSOs as well as other offshore energy industry bodies and stakeholders. Whilst the language of Article 321 does not directly refer to supply security, its references to offshore grid development and the RES potential of the North Seas region indicate that this cooperation will be important to the deliverability of electricity generated by offshore wind farms. Cooperation pursuant to Article 321 includes, at a minimum, (a) hybrid and joint projects; (b) maritime spatial planning; (c) support framework and finance; (d) best practices on respective onshore and offshore grid planning; (e) the sharing of information on new technologies; and (f) the exchange of best practices in relation to the relevant rules, regulations, and technical standards. As with the cooperation in relation to the ENTSOs, the cooperation pursuant to Article 321 takes the form of information sharing.

3.5.3 Impact of the TCA on deliverability of energy in the EU

3.5.3.1 Ireland

For both gas and electricity, Ireland is only interconnected to the UK, and as such is an energy island with both availability (see Section 3.4 above) and deliverability issues.[94] Ireland's vulnerability from an energy deliverability perspective can be ascertained by reference to N-1 standard. Pre-Brexit, Ireland met the minimum standard to cope with an N-1 disruption on the basis of a joint risk approach between the UK and Ireland, which evaluated the two countries together. Post-Brexit, such a regional approach is no longer an option, and consequently Ireland no longer meets the minimum standard prescribed by the N-1 criteria.[95]

Plans are afoot to reduce the energy dependency of Ireland on the UK and to improve deliverability of electricity from the EU to Ireland through the new subsea 700 MW Celtic interconnector intended to link France with Ireland directly. Chapter 11 discusses the importance of this interconnector for the Irish electricity market in more detail.

(1.3 GW), Belgium (1.2 GW) and the Netherlands (1.1 GW). See also, Alex Wilson, 'Offshore wind energy in Europe' *(European Parliament*, November 2020) <https://www.europarl.europa.eu/RegData/etudes/BRIE/2020/659313/EPRS_BRI(2020)659313_EN.pdf> accessed 1 March 2022.

93 For further details on the North Seas Energy Cooperation see, European Commission, 'The North Seas Energy Cooperation' (*European Commission*) <https://energy.ec.europa.eu/topics/infrastructure/high-level-groups/north-seas-energy-cooperation_en> accessed 1 March 2022.

94 Commission, 'Communication on strengthening Europe's energy networks' COM (2017) 718 final, footnote 18.

95 SEAI Report (n 55) 40.

There have been some reports that a fixed pipeline to northern France may be constructed,[96] but the project does not seem well advanced and would come at significant cost (an estimated €727 million),[97] while only raising the country's N-1 position in a 2030 median demand scenario to 73%.[98]

Much has been made of the potential of the Shannon LNG project[99] for Irish energy security; however, the project is somewhat controversial, with no government support,[100] and Green Party TD Neasa Hourigan has recently proposed banning the construction of LNG infrastructure in Ireland.[101]

3.5.3.2 Deliverability of RES in the EU

The IEA's Stated Policies Scenario (based on existing government policies) estimates that the EU and UK together will account for nearly 40% of the global offshore wind market by 2040, and will increase their installed capacity to almost 130 GW. Offshore wind would then deliver 16% of the UK and EU combined region's electricity supply by 2040 (12% by 2030).[102]

This increase will continue to render the EU's power systems more complex as multiple tools are required to achieve and maintain electricity supply security, in particular to maintain power system adequacy and to address peak capacity requirements. Due to the intermittent nature of RES, a range of tools, including the use of battery storage, capacity markets and demand response providers will be needed to meet this challenge. As Thaler and Hofmann note,[103] the integration of electricity systems and markets with neighbouring jurisdictions will also assist by providing 'access to flexible balancing power and the .levelling of energy demand and supply across larger areas'.[104]

96 Sarah McInerney, 'Ireland aims to go full gas on French pipeline' *Sunday Times* (17 July 2016) <https://www.thetimes.co.uk/article/ireland-aims-to-go-full-gas-on-french-pipeline-jb6rw9rph> accessed 1 March 2022.

97 GNI and EirGrid (n 59) 31.

98 GNI and EirGrid (n 59) 32.

99 European Commission, 'Shannon LNG Terminal and connecting pipeline' (*European Commission*, June 2021) <https://ec.europa.eu/energy/maps/pci_fiches/PciFiche_5.3.pdf> accessed 1 March 2022.

100 Cantillon - Irish Times, 'Government decision on Shannon LNG plant not straightforward' *Irish Times* (24 August 2021) <https://www.irishtimes.com/business/energy-and-resources/government-decision-on-shannon-lng-plant-not-straightforward-1.4654435> accessed 1 March 2022.

101 Cormac McQuinn, 'Law proposed that would see liquefied natural gas terminals banned' *Irish Times* (18 February 2022) <https://www.irishtimes.com/news/politics/law-proposed-that-would-see-liquefied-natural-gas-terminals-banned-1.4806106> accessed 1 March 2022.

102 Alex Wilson, 'Offshore wind energy in Europe' (European Parliament, November 2020) <https://www.europarl.europa.eu/RegData/etudes/BRIE/2020/659313/EPRS_BRI(2020)659313_EN.pdf> accessed 1 March 2022.

103 Philipp Thaler and Benjamin Hofmann, 'The Impossible Energy Trinity: Energy Security, Sustainability, and Sovereignty in Cross-Border Electricity Systems' [2022] 94 Political Geography 102579 <https://doi.org/10.1016/j.polgeo.2021.102579> accessed 1 March 2022.

104 Ibid. See also: Heymi Bahar and Jehan Sauvage, 'Cross-Border Trade in Electricity and the Development of Renewables-Based Electric Power: Lessons from Europe' [2013] OECD Trade and Environment Working Papers <https://doi.org/10.1787/5k4869cdwnzr-en> accessed 1 March 2022.

Offshore projects, such as offshore wind farms or multipurpose interconnectors (MPIs), such as the Kriegers Flak Combined Grid Solution project by 50Hertz and Energinet in the Baltic Sea,[105] are particularly suited to cross-border projects and depend on a seamless regulatory regime. In light of the offshore wind potential in the North Sea region, the provisions of Article 321 TCA are therefore key to the successful expansion of offshore wind projects in the region. The UK currently has a large pipeline of offshore wind projects, and a number of these have the potential to connect to MPIs, which in turn would enhance deliverability security for the connected jurisdictions and also lead to efficiencies as fewer offshore transmission assets would be required.[106]

However, even within the EU, the development of the North Sea offshore potential faces some regulatory and market design issues. For instance, Article 16(8) of the 2019 Electricity Regulation requires that TSOs have to make available a minimum level of 70% of capacity for inter-zonal trading from 1 January 2020. This rule and related issues currently represent an obstacle for offshore grid development and MPIs in the North Sea area, with several sponsors having obtained or applying for (temporary) exemptions pursuant to Article 64 of the 2019 Electricity Regulation.[107] Further uncertainty as to the future regulatory regime for such projects is increased by the fact that the TCA does not replicate this rule and reduces the cooperation between NRAs and TSOs largely to the sharing of information.

3.6 Conclusions

The implications of the UK's departure from the EU on energy security within the EU, are, for 26 of 27 Member States at least, limited in nature in as far as the availability and deliverability of fossil fuels are concerned.

The exception to this is Ireland, which has particular challenges in relation to both availability and deliverability security, as it does not currently seem prepared to deal with a major supply shock on her own in the absence of any solidarity measures from the UK. The speed of investments in the relevant energy infrastructure, whilst forthcoming at least in relation to electricity, seem to suggest

105 For more detail about Krieger's Flak, see 50hertz, 'Kriegers Flak – Combined Grid Solution' (*50hertz*) <https://www.50hertz.com/en/Grid/Griddevelopement/Offshoreprojects/CombinedGridSolution> accessed 1 March 2022.

106 For more details on potential benefits from coordination of offshore transmission infrastructure, see nationalgridESO, 'Offshore Coordination Project' (*nationalgridESO*) <https://www.nationalgrideso.com/future-energy/projects/offshore-coordination-project> accessed 1 March 2022.

107 The Krieger's Flak project benefits from such an exemption: covering the Belgian TSO, Elia (Herman Moestue, 'Belgian TSO wins exemption from 70% cross-border rule' (*montel*, 29 October 2021) <https://www.montelnews.com/news/1268810/belgian-tso-wins-exemption-from-70-cross-border-rule> accessed 1 March 2022), and the Swedish TSO (Wilhelm Zakrisson, 'Swedish TSO seeks exemption from 70% cross-border rule' (*montel*, 7 September 2020) <https://www.montelnews.com/news/1145777/swedish-tso-seeks-exemption-from-70-cross-border-rule> accessed 1 March 2022.

that this situation is likely to persist for several years. Should a supply crisis arise, pragmatic solutions will be required.

Whilst the other Member States may not be materially affected by Brexit, the EU27 has plenty of challenges of its own to address in relation to supply security. In relation to availability, the recent outbreak of war in Ukraine has put the EU's dependence on Russian gas into critical focus. This concern is not new – already in 2014, the European Commission stated that '[i]n the long term, the Union's energy security is inseparable from and significantly fostered by its need to move to a competitive, low-carbon economy which reduces the use of imported fossil fuels'.[108] However, in light of the war in Ukraine, the energy security policies of the EU in relation to gas are likely to undergo a paradigm shift[109] and contribute to the acceleration of investment in renewable energies and the accompanying infrastructure.

From a deliverability perspective, if the ambitious Fit for 55 decarbonisation objectives are to be achieved (see Section 3.2), the EU needs to invest more into RES and, critically, the infrastructure required to deliver renewable energy to the consumer.

In 2016, the Ten-Year Network Development Plan of ENTSO-E noted that '[there is a] need for up to €150 billion investment in electricity infrastructure only, of which 70-80 billion for mid-term and long-term projects (committed in national plans and to be commissioned by 2030)' and that '[i]n its Progress Monitoring Report, ACER estimates the investment costs for electricity transmission Projects of Common Interest (PCIs) reported by project promoters to reach €49.3 billion'.[110] In 2020, ENTSO-E noted that in addition to the '35 GW of new cross-border reinforcements expected to be built by 2025 in addition to the 2020 grid, 50 additional GW of cross-border reinforcements would be cost-efficient to support the electric system in its path towards decarbonisation'.[111] Without such investment, it is difficult to see how the EU will be able to deliver its Energy Union and climate objectives.[112]

Finally, from a deliverability perspective, an increase in RES will also mean greater reliance on interconnectors and therefore a greater need for cooperation between the EU, the UK, and Switzerland. In addition, pragmatic solutions will be required for cross-border projects in the North Sea with the UK, even if these transcend the letter of the TCA.

108 Commission, 'European Energy Strategy' COM (2014) 330 final.

109 Nikolaus J. Kurmayer, 'EU ministers brace for future without Russian energy', Euractiv, 1 March 2022 <https://www.euractiv.com/section/energy/news/eu-ministers-brace-for-future-without-russian-energy/>

110 ENTSO-E, 'A push for Projects of Common Interest' (*ENTSO-E*) <https://tyndp.entsoe.eu/2016/insight-reports/common-projects/#:~:text=ENTSO%2DE's%20TYNDP%202016%20identifies,to%20be%20commissioned%20by%202030> accessed 1 March 2022.

111 ENTSO-E, 'Completing the map – Power system needs in 2030 and 2040' (*ENTSO-E*, November 2020) <https://eepublicdownloads.azureedge.net/tyndp-documents/IoSN2020/200810_IoSN-2020mainreport_beforeconsultation.pdf> accessed 1 March 2022.

112 Adina Valean, 'No chance of meeting EU renewable goals if infrastructure neglected' (*euobserver*, 24 September 2018) <https://euobserver.com/opinion/142922> accessed 1 March 2022.

4 UK Security of Supply Post-Brexit

Paul Hallas

4.1 Introduction

This Chapter reviews the impact of Brexit on UK energy supply security. Section 4.2 explains what is meant by security of supply and Section 4.3 summarises the key provisions of the Trade and Cooperation Agreement (TCA) relevant to security of supply. Section 4.4 examines in detail nine implications of Brexit on the UK's security of supply, some of which were identified before the EU Exit Date as well as others which have emerged subsequently. In Section 4.5, brief conclusions are drawn in the light of the actual impact on the UK's security of supply since the UK left the EU.

4.2 What is meant by *security of energy supply*?

Discussions on energy supply security often conflate two separate but related issues – the physical availability of sufficient energy to meet all reasonable demands for it, and the consequences of reduced (tight) energy supply for wholesale energy price levels and consumer bills. Exceptionally high energy prices can threaten the international competitiveness of energy-intensive industries based in the UK and the budgets of public service organisations such as local authorities, schools, and hospitals, and can lead to fuel poverty among UK households. Both the security of price and the security of physical supply of UK energy have been of material concern from both a policy and a consumer perspective from time to time, as shown by the selected example below.

The winter of 2005–2006 saw an unusually tight UK gas market, reflecting a heavy reliance on under-performing gas imports via the Interconnector UK pipeline as UK gas production declined. There was little risk to physical gas supply security, however, and the UK power sector had considerable flexibility to switch from gas to coal-fired generation. The primary concern was unprecedented wholesale gas prices at the UK National Balancing Point (NBP), going above £2/

DOI: 10.4324/9781003364337-5

therm for a short period during March 2006.[1] The consequences were harsh for household customers who saw a 22% price hike from British Gas[2] in that same month; this was a 'security of price' case.

Towards the end of winter 2017–2018, the 'Beast from the East' brought very cold weather to the UK and the threat of upward pressure on the cost of energy. There was legitimate concern over physical gas supply security (at least among industrial gas customers) and severe wholesale gas price increases at the NBP.[3] Sufficient gas supplies were (just) maintained, but the concerns expressed by National Grid and the cited market analysts had been genuine.

On Friday 9 August 2019, power outages in the UK resulted in over one million consumers having electricity supply interrupted and in rail services and other services being disrupted. The interruptions to supply were not caused by tight underlying market conditions or any material impact on the market price of energy, but by a combination of physical and technical factors, including a lightning strike.[4]

In 2021, the dramatic increase in UK and other European gas and electricity prices again presented concerns over security of supply. Wholesale gas prices at the GB NBP more than doubled between March and September 2021, reaching an unprecedented peak level of just over £3/therm in early October. Whilst National Grid Gas did not foresee a material risk to physical gas supply security for winter 2021–2022,[5] some large energy-intensive industries (such as CF Fertilisers) decided on a temporary halt to UK production that was no longer viable at the prevailing gas prices.[6] Ofgem recently announced a 54% increase in the retail energy price cap from April 2022. This illustrates the principal economic, social, and political concerns around 'security of price'.

4.3 TCA provisions relating to energy supply security

The 'break point' for the UK in its relationship with the EU is considered not to be the EU Exit Date itself, but rather the end of the transition period, i.e.,

1 Ofgem, 'Winter 2005–2006 – an update' (*Ofgem* 26 January 2006) <wintertodatefs.qxp (ofgem.gov.uk)> accessed April 2022

2 BBC news, 'British Gas raises prices by 22%' (17 February 2006)<http://news.bbc.co.uk/1/hi/business/4723648.stm>

3 Adam Vaughan, 'UK running out of gas, warns National Grid' *The Guardian* (1 March 2018) <https://www.theguardian.com/business/2018/mar/01/uk-is-running-out-of-gas-national-grid-warns-freezing-weather>

4 Ofgem, '9 August 2019 power outage report' (3 January 2020) <https://www.ofgem.gov.uk/system/files/docs/2020/01/9_august_2019_power_outage_report.pdf>

5 National Grid Gas Transmission, 'Gas Winter Outlook' (October 2021) <https://www.nationalgrid.com/uk/gas-transmission/document/137156/download>

6 Nathalie Thomas, 'Gas price surge triggers UK fertiliser plant closures' *Financial Times* (16 September 2021) <https://www.ft.com/content/b2e7b6ed-fa14-48e1-a463-4d3b09c654dd>

31 December 2020. After much last-minute uncertainty, the TCA[7] was agreed on 24 December 2020.

The TCA does include an 'Energy Chapter', although several issues relating to energy continued to remain open following the signing of the TCA, such as cross-border electricity trading arrangements from April 2022 onwards and the functioning of a new UK emissions trading scheme (ETS), which held its first UK allowances auction on 19 May 2021. Uncertainty continues about the provisions regulating energy trading and relations as, pursuant to Article 331 of the TCA, the entire Energy Chapter will cease to apply on 30 June 2026 unless an agreement is reached between UK and EU to extend it, on an annual basis or otherwise. From a supply security perspective, the TCA has by no means removed all Brexit-related uncertainty from the UK energy sector.

4.3.1 General provisions

The TCA creates a new governance framework to oversee the implementation of the new UK–EU energy sector relationship, most notably a Specialised Committee on Energy[8] (SCE), which sits beneath the overarching Partnership Council and is intended to replace the previous framework for institutional cooperation which existed under applicable EU energy legislation.[9]

For cross-border electricity trading arrangements, Annex 29 to the TCA provides that a new system must be developed by April 2022 for the implicit allocation of day-ahead (DAH) electricity interconnector capacity – in effect, establishing a Brexit-compatible form of DAH market coupling which is to be based on the concept of multi-region loose volume coupling (MRLVC).[10] This system may be amended by the SCE. For what the scenario may be now that the April 2022 deadline to establish the system has not been met, see Chapter 2 on market access.

The TCA provides for further cooperation between the UK and the EU, in partial replacement for what previously took place within the EU framework. Specifically, Article 317 provides that UK TSOs will cooperate with the EU ENTSOs, but without membership equivalent status. Article 318 stipulates that Ofgem will establish 'administrative arrangements' to cooperate with ACER on a series of matters which include energy supply security, but without participating in ACER's governance structure. The mechanism for cooperation between

7 Trade and Cooperation Agreement between the European Union and the European Energy Community, of the one part, and the United Kingdom of Great Britain and Northern Ireland, of the other [2020] OJ L 149/10

8 TCA. Article INST.2, paragraph 1(l).

9 Decisions in respect of TPA exemptions for electricity interconnectors may be relevant to supply security concerns, a matter which previously fell to Ofgem to co-ordinate with national energy regulators from the relevant EU Member State.

10 For more on the MRLVC (multi-region loose volume coupling), see Section 4.4 [pp.64] on cross-border trading arrangements.

national energy regulators and TSOs has in the past been helpful from a supply security perspective, but this historic level of cooperation is unlikely to be replicated under the post-Brexit arrangements envisaged in the TCA.

Article 7.3[11] recognises that the UK will have its own system of carbon pricing from January 2021. The UK and the EU agreed to the principle of 'non regression' from current levels of environmental protection and to give serious consideration to linking their respective ETS.

4.3.1.1 TCA provisions on the SEM

The TCA contains a stand-alone Chapter on the maintenance of the single electricity market (SEM) on the island of Ireland,[12] which is helpful to electricity supply security in Northern Ireland. As per Article 18 of the Ireland/Northern Ireland Protocol, these provisions are in place until the end of 2024 whereafter they have to be confirmed by the UK seeking Democratic Consent in Northern Ireland, in a manner consistent with the 1998 Good Friday Agreement. The continued uncertainty as to the applicable rules concerning the electricity market in Northern Ireland may investment deter and increase costs of energy projects.

4.3.1.2 TCA and energy – supply security

Articles 315 and 316 of TCA Title VIII relate specifically to energy supply security and therefore merit being quoted *verbatim*.

Article ENER.17: Cooperation on security of supply

1. The Parties shall cooperate with respect to the security of supply of electricity and natural gas.

2. The Parties shall exchange information on any risks identified pursuant to Article ENER.18 [Risk preparedness and emergency plans] in a timely manner.

3. The Parties shall share the plans referred to in Article ENER.18 [Risk preparedness and emergency plans]. For the Union, these plans may be at Member State or regional level.

4. The Parties shall inform each other without undue delay where there is reliable information that a disruption or other crisis relating to the supply of electricity or natural gas may occur and on measures planned or taken.

5. The Parties shall immediately inform each other in the event of an actual disruption or other crisis, in view of possible coordinated mitigation and restoration measures.

6. The Parties shall share best practices regarding short-term and seasonal adequacy assessments.

11 TCA, Title XI.
12 See Chapter 11, 'The Impact of Brexit on Ireland: The Energy Perspective.'

7. The Parties shall develop appropriate frameworks for cooperation with respect to the security of supply of electricity and natural gas.

Article ENER.18: Risk preparedness and emergency plans

1. Each Party shall assess risks affecting the security of supply of electricity or natural gas, including the likelihood and impact of such risks, and including cross-border risks.

2. Each Party shall establish and regularly update plans to address identified risks affecting the security of supply of electricity or natural gas. Such plans shall contain the measures needed to remove or mitigate the likelihood and impact of any risk identified under paragraph 1 and the measures needed to prepare for, and mitigate the impact of, an electricity or natural gas crisis.

3. The measures contained in the plans referred to in paragraph 2 shall:

(a) be clearly defined, transparent, proportionate, non-discriminatory and verifiable;

(b) not significantly distort trade between the Parties; and

(c) not endanger the security of supply of electricity or natural gas of the other Party.

In the event of a crisis, the Parties shall only activate non-market based measures as a last resort.

These enunciated principles of cooperation on supply security, risk preparedness, and emergency plans are clearly helpful, but they are high-level and leave much to further definition and development. The final part of Article 316 also leaves open the possibility of non-market interventions as a last resort in crisis conditions.

Based on the cited TCA text alone, it is difficult to formulate any robust assessment of its likely effect. However, more detailed provisions in the relevant EU legislation on electricity and gas supply security form part of UK retained EU law, including the EU gas security of supply regulation[13] and the EU regulation on risk preparedness in the electricity sector.[14] At least for the present, therefore, UK and EU rules are closely aligned; the role the TCA may play is to deter the parties' willingness to depart from the existing provisions. It is clear, however, that the TCA envisages regulatory divergence between the UK and the EU and simply provides for mechanisms to address such divergence.

4.4 Nine implications of Brexit for the UK's security of supply

4.4.1 Cross-border electricity supplies

Net electricity imports from the EU accounted for 5.4% of total UK electricity supplies in 2020.[15] This figure tends to increase as new cross-border

13 Regulation (EU) 2017/1938 of the European Parliament and of the Council on measures to safeguard the security of gas supply and repealing Regulation (EU) No 994/2010 [2017] OJ L280/1

14 Regulation (EU) 2019/941 of the European Parliament and of the Council on risk-preparedness in the electricity sector and repealing Directive 2005/89/EC [2019] OJ L158/1

15 UK Government, *Digest of UK Energy Statistics, Electricity: Commodity Balances (DUKES 5.1)* (26 July 2021) <https://www.gov.uk/government/statistics/electricity-chapter-5-digest-of-united-kingdom-energy-statistics-dukes>

> electricity interconnectors come onstream. The UK now has over 8GW of cross-border electricity interconnection (see Figure 4.1), equivalent to more than 10% of maximum UK electricity demand. Over 5GW connects the UK to the European continent, whilst two interconnections with the island of Ireland account for 1GW. Brexit notwithstanding, further interconnector projects have been committed since the 2016 referendum, and a total of 3.5GW is under construction to/from France and Scandinavia.[16]

An important feature of interconnector operations under EU rules is day-ahead market coupling (DAMC), which is designed to ensure that electricity flows across borders efficiently, from low-priced to high-priced markets, based on exchange price quotations for the following day. This arrangement applied across UK interconnectors with continental Europe from 2014 and on the two GB–Ireland interconnectors from October 2018. It ended at the end of the Brexit Transition Period on 31 December 2020.

The EU has implemented a similar system for electricity trading across interconnectors within the current trading day, i.e., intra-day market coupling, which is live in substantial parts of the EU, but this had not been applied in the UK before Brexit.

There are also arrangements between EU TSOs to exchange balancing reserves cross-border and thereby manage electricity systems more effectively and cost-efficiently. Project Terre went live[17] in January 2020 and is progressively being extended to further EU Member States. However, it is 'on hold' for the UK – primarily as a result of Brexit.

As the UK has lost access to the EU platform for DAMC[18] (Euphemia), the TCA envisages that a new (and somewhat less efficient) version of DAMC (i.e., MRLVC)[19] will be introduced on UK interconnectors from April 2022. In the meantime, those interconnectors have reverted to still less efficient trading arrangements (see Figure 4.2).

Two cross-border electricity trading arrangements took effect post-Brexit. The 'channel interconnectors' reverted to the former explicit capacity allocation process, whilst market coupling now applies to the Irish Sea interconnectors on an

16 Statnett press statement, 6 December 2021, <https://www.statnett.no/en/about-statnett/news-and-press-releases/news-archive-2021/nsl-interconnector-to-have-reduced-capacity-until-february/>

17 ENTSO-E press release, 'Trans-European Replacement Reserves Exchange (TERRE) project to deliver a European platform for the exchange of balancing energy from replacement reserves based on LIBRA solution live in January 2020' (*ENTSO-E*, 9 January 2020) <https://www.entsoe.eu/news/2020/01/09/trans-european-replacement-reserves-exchange-terre-project-to-deliver-a-european-platform-for-the-exchange-of-balancing-energy-from-replacement-reserves-based-on-libra-solution-live-in-january-2020/>

18 See above Section 4.3.

19 ENSTO-E consultation, 'Cost Benefit Analysis of Multi-Region Loose Volume Coupling (MRLVC) arrangements to apply between the UK and the bidding zones directly connected to the UK' (*ENTSO-E*, April 2021) <https://consultations.entsoe.eu/markets/cost-benefit-analysis-of-multi-region-loose-volume/>

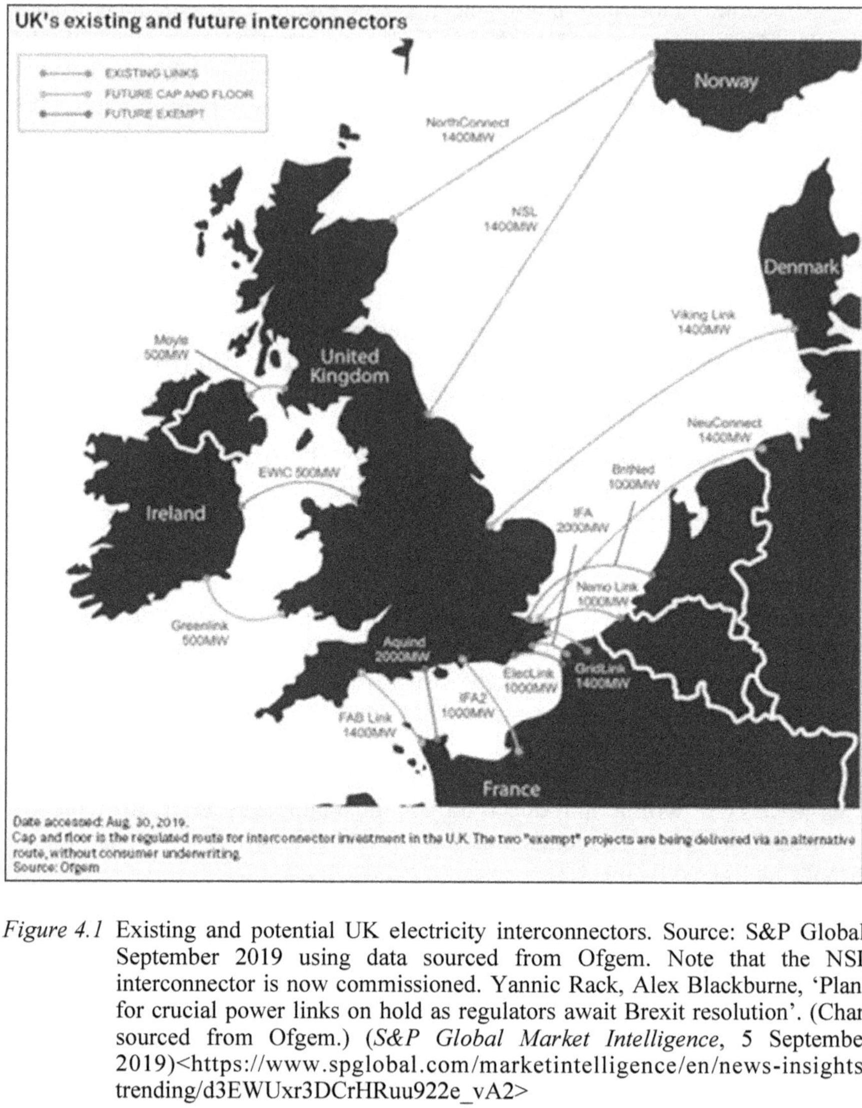

Figure 4.1 Existing and potential UK electricity interconnectors. Source: S&P Global, September 2019 using data sourced from Ofgem. Note that the NSL interconnector is now commissioned. Yannic Rack, Alex Blackburne, 'Plans for crucial power links on hold as regulators await Brexit resolution'. (Chart sourced from Ofgem.) (*S&P Global Market Intelligence*, 5 September 2019)<https://www.spglobal.com/marketintelligence/en/news-insights/trending/d3EWUxr3DCrHRuu922e_vA2>

intra-day basis. The latter arrangement, although maintaining a form of market coupling, is less than ideal because the intra-day spot markets (in both GB and the SEM) are less liquid than those which trade day-ahead.

On 3 February 2021, the House of Lords Select Committee on the EU heard oral evidence on the TCA during which witnesses provided views and insight

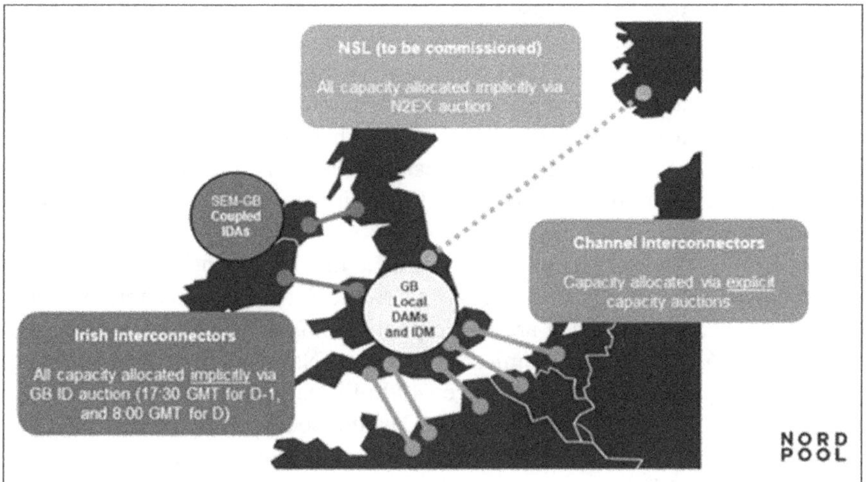

Figure 4.2 Cross-border electricity trading arrangements applicable after 1 January 2021. Source: nordpoolgroup.com.

regarding the post-Brexit electricity trading arrangements.[20] The House heard that the MRLVC version of DAMC envisaged under the TCA would be a welcome improvement on existing post-Brexit arrangements. In addition to the improved efficiency of interconnector capacity use, MRLVC would help to reconnect spot price quotations on the two GB electricity exchanges. The MRLVC would not, however, be as efficient and beneficial as the EU regime for cross-border electricity trading which the UK left on 1 January 2021.

A third cross-border electricity regime applies to the North Sea Link (NSL) interconnector. This is a bespoke form of DAMC between the Nordpool electricity exchange (in the Nordic electricity market) and N2EX, the Nordpool-operated spot electricity exchange platform in the UK. The NSL is expected to operate in a 'GB import mode', and a version of DAMC will allow more efficient use of its 1.4GW total capacity. The reason for this distinct (and more favourable) interconnector trading arrangement may be partly political in that Norway (a European Economic Area [EEA] state) is outside the EU, albeit bound by EU Internal Electricity Market (IEM) rules.

Brexit has also hindered work on new electricity interconnectors, particularly between France and England. Ostensibly for Brexit-related reasons, CRE (the French energy regulator) in 2019 decided not to sanction any new interconnector

20 House of Lords Select Committee on the European Union, Environment Sub-Committee, *Corrected oral evidence: Future UK-EU relations: energy, environment and health* (3 February 2021) <https://committees.parliament.uk/oralevidence/1683/html/>

projects for the foreseeable future. More recently, in January 2022, the CRE declined to approve the proposed Gridlink interconnector, for similar reasons. This post-Brexit investment uncertainty is further illustrated by the finding of Ofgem and CRE in January 2021 that they no longer had the legal powers to determine the Aquind interconnector project's application for an exemption from the TPA.[21] This legal hiatus may be resolved when the SCE foreseen under the TCA becomes operational, but in the meantime (January 2022), the UK government decided to deny the Aquind project planning permission for the necessary onshore works.

Post-Brexit, electricity continues to flow across interconnectors without any import duty, albeit less efficiently.[22] Various studies have quantified this efficiency loss to the UK, two of which are in the public domain. The first was published in March 2016 by Vivid Economics on behalf of National Grid[23] and estimated a potential impact (by mid-2020s) of c.£400 million p.a. At the time of Vivid's analysis, it was not appreciated that DAMC would be disapplied on existing interconnectors post 1 January 2021. Since 2016, on the other hand, two interconnectors that Vivid had assumed would not proceed are under construction. On balance, therefore, £400m/p.a. remains a fair estimate of the efficiency loss.

The second study was published by the Cambridge Energy Policy Research Group in April 2019.[24] Focusing specifically on the loss of market coupling, the authors estimated an economic welfare loss to the UK of €300m/p.a. (£260m/p.a.). Whilst the absolute numbers are material, the estimated economic welfare loss to the UK is only c. 2%–3% of the normal wholesale cost of annual electricity supplies. Losing efficient cross-border electricity trading arrangements is regrettable, but the direct impact on UK electricity supply security is modest.

The proposed move to MRVLC on UK interconnectors is to be welcomed, should it prove achievable. The cost–benefit analysis and consultation on MRLVC was published by ENTSO-E in a timely manner, but complex issues remain to be resolved. One major issue is that the preferred version of MRLVC would require changes to the timing of the EU's single day-ahead coupling (SDAC) process, which now covers most EU Member States. Approval for such changes seems unlikely to be straightforward.

21 Ofgem press release, 'CRE and Ofgem discontinue public consultation on Aquind's exemption request.' (*Ofgem*, 28 January 2021) <https://www.ofgem.gov.uk/publications-and-updates/cre-and-ofgem-discontinue-public-consultation-aquinds-exemption-request>

22 Department for Business, Energy and Industrial Strategy, *Trading Electricity with the EU.* (3 February 2021) <https://www.gov.uk/government/publications/trading-electricity-with-the-eu/trading-electricity-with-the-eu>

23 Vivid Economics Case Study, 'The Impact of Brexit on the UK energy sector'(March 2016) <https://www.vivideconomics.com/casestudy/the-impact-of-brexit-on-the-uk-energy-sector/>

24 Cambridge Energy Research Group, 'Elecxit: The Cost of Bilaterally Uncoupling British–EU Electricity Trade' (*EPRG Working Paper 1916*, May 2019) <https://www.eprg.group.cam.ac.uk/wp-content/uploads/2019/05/1916-Text.pdf>

One indirect impact of Brexit has already been a real concern. Until the end of 2020, the two electricity spot market exchanges in the UK, Nordpool (sometimes known as N2EX) and EPEX Spot, held day-ahead prices on the two platforms in alignment by virtue of their participation in EU market coupling. Since 1 January 2021, the respective market prices have diverged significantly on occasions – usually at peak times of very high spot electricity prices.[25] For one evening peak hour in mid-January 2021, when the electricity spot price went as high as £1,500/MWh, day-ahead spot prices on the two UK exchanges diverged by as much as £500/MWh – something which would have been unthinkable prior to the end of 2020. Such conflicting price signals can only complicate the arrangements for incentivising UK electricity market participants to balance their own commercial portfolios and thus contribute to overall electricity system supply security.

In conclusion, the main impact of Brexit on cross-border electricity trading arrangements on UK energy supply security concerns 'security of price' rather than physical continuity of energy supplies. In all but the most extreme circumstances, electricity is likely to continue to be traded across the interconnectors; however, it is being traded less efficiently, increasing UK market exposure to wholesale electricity price spikes.

4.4.2 Cross-border gas supplies

The UK gas market is strongly interconnected (see Figure 4.3); net gas imports accounted for around half of total UK gas supplies in each year from 2016 to 2020. Cross-border gas flows remain more important for overall UK energy supply security than cross-border electricity supplies, especially as gas-fired plants account for over 35% of total UK power generation and frequently occupy a marginal (electricity price-setting) position in the UK's generation merit order. The impact of extremely tight global gas markets in 2021–2022 in terms of exceptionally high wholesale gas and electricity prices in the UK is evidence of this. As the majority of UK gas imports come from Norway and from liquefied natural gas (LNG) outside the EU, the impact of Brexit on gas supply has been limited.

Typically, the UK is an annual net exporter across the interconnector pipeline links with EU Member States. The Interconnector UK and BBL pipelines typically export gas to the continent in summer and import in the winter peak, whilst the UK exports to Ireland year-round.

The UK/EU wholesale gas price differentials (e.g., the differences between prices quoted at the UK NBP and the Dutch TTF) are generally much narrower than electricity price differentials. As 2021 has shown, the UK gas market is more strongly influenced by global trading patterns than it is by cross-border gas trading with the UK's EU neighbours. In contrast with DAMC in electricity, trade in

25 Tim Dixon, 'Divergent electricity prices in the wake of Brexit' (*Cornwall Energy*, 13 January 2021) <https://www.cornwall-insight.com/divergent-electricity-prices-in-the-wake-of-brexit/>

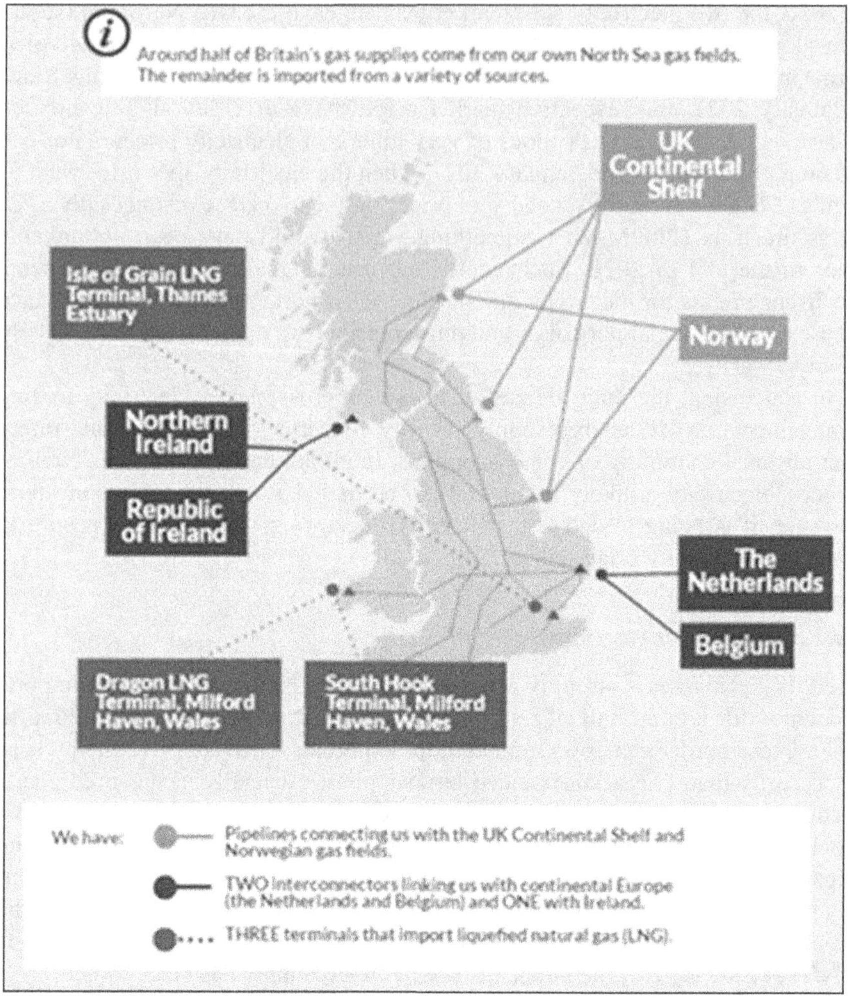

Figure 4.3 UK gas pipeline interconnections and LNG terminals. Source: Ofgem publication, 'Infographic: energy security' (*Ofgem*, 28 May 2020) <https://www.ofgem.gov.uk/publications/infographic-energy-security>

gas across UK–EU interconnectors is more commercially driven and less dependent on the application of EU Internal Energy Market rules. Belgium and the Netherlands have passed legislation providing that they will continue to apply the EU Capacity Allocations Mechanism Code[26] to gas interconnectors with the UK,

26 Commission Regulation (EU) 2017/459 of 16 March 2017 establishing a network code on capacity allocation mechanisms in gas transmission systems and repealing Regulation (EU) No 984/2013

whilst the Irish government confirmed that no further legislation was required. Accordingly, the UK's access to PRISMA, the common European platform for booking cross-border gas transmission capacity, has been maintained in a manner that contrasts with the loss of DAMC in electricity.

For these reasons, Brexit has had little or no impact to date on the level and pattern of gas flows in and out of the UK. This is confirmed in the UK government's 2020 notice on gas trading post-Brexit. [27]

4.4.3 Carbon trading and pricing

The pricing of carbon emissions has an important impact on generation dispatch (as it affects the cost of thermal power generation, from gas or coal) and on many UK energy sector investment decisions, especially those concerning renewables and other lower carbon technologies. Especially with falling subsidies for renewables, a robust carbon price signal is an important element in maintaining supply security and achieving net zero by 2050.[28]

There is some uncertainty around the future of the UK ETS, regarding the robustness of the carbon prices it will produce, the risk of government intervention (via the Cost Containment Mechanism, or CCM[29]) and the question of whether/when it is likely to be linked to the larger EU ETS. Over 40 industry organisations have called for the link to be made,[30] but there are potential political obstacles to be overcome. In the meantime, the UK government declined to intervene in December 2021 or January 2022, despite the CCM conditions being triggered in both those months. This is likely to have given market participants greater confidence in the working of the UK ETS.

UK ETS carbon price uncertainty does not currently constitute a material barrier to low carbon energy investments. This is particularly the case as fixed price Contracts for Difference (CfDs) are now available for both onshore and offshore renewables projects that are successful in GB auction bidding rounds.[31]

OJ L72/1

27 Department for Business, Energy and Industrial Strategy, *Trading Gas with the EU* (31 December 2020) <https://www.gov.uk/government/publications/trading-gas-with-the-eu>

28 For further details of UK's net zero target for 2050, see Section 6.1 [pp.92] of Chapter [Ana Chapter on renewables].

29 Victoria Hatherick, UK ETS CCM trigger level climbs for October', *Argus Media*, 13 July 2021 <https://www.argusmedia.com/en/news/2233757-uk-ets-ccm-trigger-level-climbs-for-october>

30 Open letter to the UK Prime Minister from assortment of organisations, 'The importance of linking the UK ETS with the EU ETS ahead of COP26' 14 April 2021 <https://mcusercontent.com/4ba4a05396f0bf7eac512a9b0/files/d7ef9988-2213-4cf4-a775-9f399e9c0f53/UK_EU_ETS_Linkage_Joint_Letter_UK_.pdf>

31 Department for Business, Energy and Industrial Strategy, *Contracts for Difference (CfD) Allocation Round 4*, (2 March 2020, updated 13 December 2021) <https://www.gov.uk/government/collections/contracts-for-difference-cfd-allocation-round-4>

4.4.4 Cross-border trade in goods

Until the conclusion of the TCA, many businesses had been concerned that a World Trade Organization (WTO) ('no deal') scenario would result in cross-border trade in goods with the EU taking place on a 'third country' basis as from 1 January 2021. The most relevant consideration for UK energy supply security was that customs procedures would lead to transit delays, especially on the main 'Channel Straits' route through Dover, which handles c.10,000 lorries per day.

Many UK businesses, including those in the energy sector, therefore decided to hold additional stocks of imported intermediate goods, raw materials, and other supplies to protect themselves and their customers as far as possible against this logistical risk. This put an additional strain on company balance sheets in the lead up to Brexit, which may have inhibited more productive forms of investment at that time.

Notwithstanding greater bureaucracy affecting post-Brexit trade in goods, the spectre of widespread prolonged delays at ports of entry in a 'no deal' scenario has been avoided. Accordingly, the risk that unplanned outages at UK power stations could take significantly longer than usual to resolve, thus impacting electricity supply security, is no longer a material concern.

4.4.5 Euratom and nuclear energy

The UK's exit from the EU has resulted in the UK exiting the European Atomic Energy Community (Euratom), as discussed in detail in Chapter 9 by Ian Truman. Notwithstanding earlier concerns such as those expressed in evidence to the House of Lords European Union Committee in 2018,[32] departure from Euratom does not now appear to pose a material risk to UK energy supply security. As discussed by Ian Truman, independent nuclear safeguards were put in place in the UK before the end of the Transition Period, and UK nuclear cooperation agreements with four major nuclear states outside the EU (the USA, Canada, Australia, and Japan) were renegotiated or replaced in time for Brexit.

4.4.6 The operation of the SEM and supply security in Northern Ireland

In January 2018, the House of Lords Select Committee *(op. cit.)* identified the preservation of the SEM as one of the principal impacts of Brexit on UK energy security of supply, and in particular on the security of electricity supply in Northern Ireland.

The Northern Irish electricity industry was privatised in 1992–1993 and the all-island SEM was established in 2007. The electricity market was small, isolated, and not very competitive, with only a few large power plants and consumer

32 House of Lords European Union Committee, Brexit: energy security. 10th Report of Session 2017–2019, 29 January 2018. <https://publications.parliament.uk/pa/ld201719/ldselect/ldeucom/63/6302.htm>. See, for example, para 157.

electricity prices higher than in other parts of the UK. As the 500MW Moyle electricity interconnector with the UK only became fully operational in 2002, there was no access to the wholesale electricity market in England and Wales for much of this period.

Northern Ireland became part of a larger, more competitive electricity market with the establishment of the SEM in which wholesale prices were set within an all-island pool, with enhanced supply security and access to a growing amount of onshore wind generation in Ireland.

The 500MW EWIC interconnector between Ireland and North Wales was commissioned in 2012, providing further access to/from a more liquid traded market in the UK. In October 2018, the SEM itself became a more competitive market with the launch of reforms (I-SEM), part of which was the enabling of the efficient DAMC on the two electricity interconnectors with the UK. A third UK interconnector project (Greenlink)[33] – between County Wexford in Ireland and Pembrokeshire in South Wales – was awarded EPC contracts in September 2021 and should further enhance the supply security benefits to Northern Ireland of remaining within the SEM.

The SEM helps to maintain electricity supply security in Northern Ireland with greater supply reliability and more competitive prices. A retail energy market review[34] carried out by the Northern Ireland energy regulator confirms that domestic electricity prices in Northern Ireland during 2017–2019 were below the overall UK average – a considerable improvement on the historic position. Electricity switching rates (an indicator of competition) were modestly below those in the UK and higher than those in the Northern Ireland gas market, which is not itself integrated with that in Ireland.

As discussed in Chapter 11, the Ireland/Northern Ireland Protocol has ensured the continuation of the SEM at least until 2024. Supply security in Northern Ireland should be further reinforced by the proposed 400kV North-South Interconnector project,[35] intended to overcome existing cross-border transmission constraints. Whilst a final investment decision for the project is pending, given a judicial review of Northern Irish planning approvals, the SEM continuity provided by the TCA is helpful in moving it towards a positive outcome, with projected completion by 2025.

Brexit did have one downside for the all-island electricity market; the DAMC on the two UK interconnectors was lost, and the markets are now coupled on an

33 Greenlink had been expected to reach financial close at the end of 2021. See Sean Pollock, 'Greenlink powers ahead with €500m electricity interconnector', *Irish Independent* (28 November 2021) <https://www.independent.ie/business/irish/greenlink-powers-ahead-with-500m-electricity-interconnector-41093170.html>

34 Utility Regulator Electricity Gas Water, *Review of the Northern Ireland Energy Retail Market,* (March 2021) <https://www.uregni.gov.uk/files/uregni/media-files/State%20of%20the%20market%20v1.0.pdf>

35 EIRGRID Group, 'North-South 400 kV Interconnection Development' (*EIRGRID Group*) <http://www.eirgridgroup.com/the-grid/projects/north-south/the-project/>

intra-day basis instead. This is less than ideal as SEM is primarily a day-ahead pool; even in the UK, intra-day trading is less liquid than the day-ahead electricity spot market. Market participants can nevertheless adjust their approach to electricity portfolio management, at least to a degree, such that the risk this poses to electricity supply security in Northern Ireland is not material.

4.4.7 The loss of UK influence in the EU

The loss of UK influence on energy policy and regulation in the EU is an inevitable consequence of Brexit. Prior to leaving the EU, UK energy organisations, principally Ofgem and National Grid (the TSO), were strongly engaged and often highly influential in the development and implementation of EU Internal Energy Market rules.[36]

The text of the TCA confirms that the future role of these organisations within EU bodies will not be what it was prior to Brexit. Its provisions regarding the post-Brexit role of the principal UK TSO (currently National Grid) and the independent regulator (Ofgem) were outlined in Section 4.3.

The historic jurisdictional role and influence of Ofgem no longer applies in several areas.[37] For example, decisions regarding electricity interconnector access regimes previously fell jointly to Ofgem and its counterpart national energy regulators elsewhere in the EU. Within the terms of the TCA, such matters may now fall to the SCE. However, the SCE is not a permanent body with the level of energy-specific resource and expertise to be found at Ofgem. By nature, the SCE's activities and its relationship with EU counterparties are more influenced by wider political factors and priorities. Energy issues, which are important to those of concern but secondary in political terms, are unlikely to get the focus which National Grid and Ofgem could give them during EU membership.

Based on experience with other non-EU Member States such as Switzerland[38] which are not signed up to the EU Internal Energy Market (see Chapter 12), the level of post-Brexit cooperation likely to be forthcoming in practice may depend on the wider state of economic and diplomatic relationships between the parties.[39]

It is difficult, at this point, to reach a firm conclusion regarding the impact which this loss of influence could have on UK energy supply security. The full impact is only likely to become clear over time with the further evolution of energy policy and regulation in the EU and the UK, but experience to date suggests a greater level of political risk than under EU membership.

36 National Grid ESO, 'European Network Codes (ENC)' <https://www.nationalgrideso.com/industry-information/codes/european-network-codes>

37 For further details of market access, see Chapter 2.

38 Norway participates more actively in the relevant EU energy bodies, but this is not comparable with the post-Brexit position of the UK as Norway has agreed to adopt EU Internal Energy Market rules.

39 For further details of Switzerland, see Chapter 12.

4.4.8 UK's macro-economic outlook

Sterling depreciated sharply immediately after the EU Referendum,[40] and its value remained highly sensitive to Brexit news-flow, especially when a 'no deal' exit from the EU seemed likely. It was widely predicted – including by the Bank of England in December 2020[41] – that a 'no deal' Brexit would lead to a further fall in the value of sterling against other major currencies. Pre Brexit, exchange rate risks may have led some businesses to defer energy investments reliant on imported equipment. Energy utilities were worried about the impact of a WTO 'no deal' scenario in which UK interest rates would be lower for longer to support the economy. A combination of low interest rates and higher inflation (due to weaker sterling) was forecast to contribute to higher corporate pensions deficits, thus constraining those companies' ability to fund other investments.

Following the TCA, the value of sterling against the euro did not decline further; however, it remained substantially lower than before the vote to leave the EU. Against the US dollar, sterling has appreciated, especially during late 2020 (see Figure 4.4).

Brexit is likely to lead to a somewhat slower rate of future UK economic growth, as the IMF has previously suggested. The OECD recently warned that 'A worsening trade relationship with the European Union could … weigh on the economic outlook in the medium term'.[42] However, the TCA removed the immediate 'no deal' exchange rate risks to UK energy sector investment.

4.4.9 UK energy sector investment climate

The Government's Net Zero Strategy estimates that an additional investment of £85bn–£98bn will be required between 2020 and 2032 to achieve the net zero targets for 2050,[43] much of which will need to be made within the energy sector. Investment in renewables and other low carbon energy production, electric vehicles, energy storage, carbon capture, and complementary network enhancements are likely to be particularly important. Potential impacts on electricity interconnector investment were discussed earlier in this Chapter.

Post-Brexit supply chain issues have received considerable publicity, and shortages of skilled labour required for all kinds of construction activities are

40 Paolo Monasse, Graziano Moramarco, Giulio Trigilia, 'Political risk and exchange rates: the lessons of Brexit', *VOX^{EU} website*, 17 February 2020. <https://voxeu.org/article/political-risk-and-exchange-rates-lessons-brexit>

41 The Independent, 'No deal Brexit would hit pound sterling, warns Bank of England', *website*, 17 December 2020 <https://www.independent.co.uk/news/business/news/brexit-sterling-bank-of-england-b1775553.html

42 OECD 'United Kingdom Economic Snapshot' *website* December 2021. <https://www.oecd.org/economy/united-kingdom-economic-snapshot/>

43 Department for Business, Energy and Industrial Strategy, *Net Zero Strategy: Build Back Greener*, (Policy paper, October 2021) <https://www.gov.uk/government/publications/net-zero-strategy>

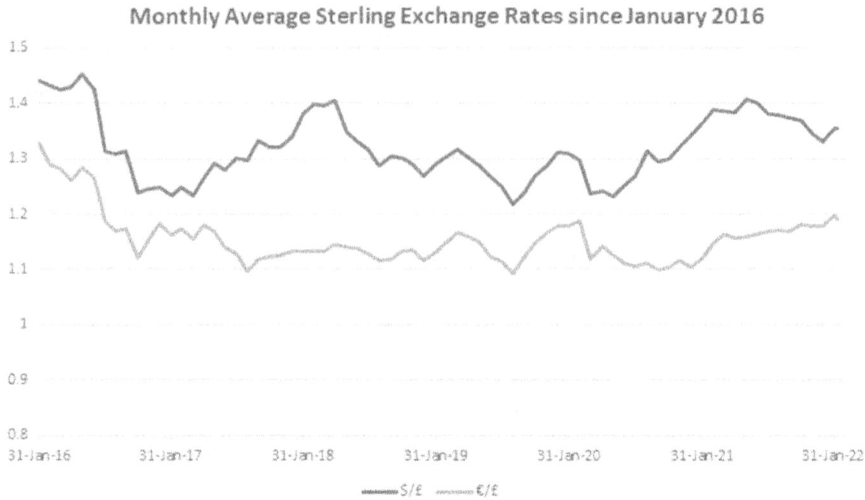

Figure 4.4 Sterling exchange rates since January 2016. Source: OFX website plus author's graphical presentation.

affecting some UK regions.[44] In the energy generation sector, one potential risk is that post-Brexit UK immigration policy might not provide key UK construction projects with access to all the skilled labour they require.

A further consequence of Brexit for the UK energy sector is the likely reduction in access to EU support mechanisms for energy infrastructure investment, including Projects of Common Interest (PCI)[45] and European Investment Bank funding.

Post-Brexit uncertainty adds to the basket of UK investment risks, and this may impact energy sector investment. The future pace of such investment is important to both dimensions of UK energy supply security, i.e., minimising exposure to price spikes and avoiding the risk of unserved energy demand.

4.5 Conclusions

The analysis in this Chapter shows that the direct impact of Brexit on UK energy supply security to date has been detrimental but not yet highly material. It has

44 The Guardian, 'Is Brexit or Covid to blame for Britain's supply chain crisis?' *website*, 24 September 2021. <https://www.theguardian.com/business/2021/sep/24/is-brexit-or-covid-to-blame-for-britains-supply-chain-crisis>

45 European Commission, 'New energy Projects of Common Interest for the European Union built on European solidarity'. *European Commission* (31 October 2019) The PCI mechanism is discussed in further detail in Chapter 2 of this book. <https://ec.europa.eu/commission/presscorner/detail/en/IP_19_6203>

been completely drowned out by the impact of exceptionally tight global gas market conditions in 2021 and 2022 to date, for example. Concerns for the future include a loss of UK influence over European energy policy and regulation, a set of new post-Brexit uncertainties (including the possible expiry of the TCA's energy provisions), and a greater dependence on UK political decision-making, rather than the framework of EU law. Whether these concerns will have a major impact on UK energy supply security in the future still remains to be seen.

5 Brexit and State Aid

The Energy Perspective

George Peretz KC

5.1 Introduction and scope

This Chapter sets out in Section 5.1 the ways in which, under the Withdrawal Agreement and Northern Ireland Protocol, EU State aid rules continue to apply to the UK energy sector after Brexit, and in Section 5.2 describes the UK's proposed new subsidy control regime as it applies to the energy sector.

5.2 The Withdrawal Agreement

The Withdrawal Agreement[1] provides for the continued application of EU State aid rules in the UK after Brexit in three ways: (i) the (now expired) transition period; (ii) the 'run-off' provisions dealing with State aid measures implemented before the end of the transition period and ongoing State aid procedures; and (iii) the Northern Ireland Protocol. Each is examined in turn below. As a matter of UK domestic law, the Withdrawal Agreement has direct effect: Section 7A of the EU Withdrawal Act 2018 (as inserted by the EU Withdrawal Agreement Act 2020).

5.2.1 The transition period

Part 4 of the Withdrawal Agreement provided for a transition period, which lasted from Brexit (31 January 2020) to 31 December 2020. In that period, EU State aid rules continued to apply to the UK as if it were an EU Member State. Over that period, 27 State aid decisions in relation to UK measures were taken by the Commission, many of which concerned COVID-19 related aid measures. All of those decisions were decisions not to raise objections to notified aid measures.

5.2.2 Run-off provisions

Under Article 92(1)(b) and (3)(a) of the Withdrawal Agreement, the Commission remains competent to continue any State aid procedure to which a case number had

1 Agreement on the withdrawal of the United Kingdom of Great Britain and Northern Ireland from the European Union and the European Atomic Energy Community [2019] OJ C 384I/01.

DOI: 10.4324/9781003364337-6

been allocated on or before 31 December 2020. The Commission has, since the end of the transition period, commenced two cases before the Court of Justice alleging infringements by the United Kingdom of EU State aid rules before 31 December 2020.[2] Further, under Article 93(1) of the Withdrawal Agreement, the Commission remains competent until 31 December 2024 to open a State aid investigation in relation to any State aid granted in the UK before the end of the transition period on 31 December 2020 (although, as of 1 March 2022, no such investigation had been made public). That means that, until 31 December 2024, any State aid measure implemented on or before 31 December 2020 could be investigated by the Commission under EU State aid rules, subject only to the general limitation rule in Article 17 of the State aid procedural Regulation[3] to the effect that no order for recovery can be made where 10 years have passed after the grant of unlawful State aid without any action being taken by the Commission. Under Article 95 of the Withdrawal Agreement, decisions adopted in Article 92 or 93 procedures are binding on the UK and on all persons residing or established in the UK.

5.2.3 The Northern Ireland Protocol

Article 10(1) of the Northern Ireland Protocol[4] provides that 'The provisions of Union law listed in Annex 5 to this Protocol shall apply to the United Kingdom … in respect of measures which affect that trade between Northern Ireland and the Union which is subject to this Protocol'.

It is (perhaps intentionally) not immediately clear to a casual reader what this Article does. To understand it, one has to look at Annex 5, which contains the whole corpus of EU State aid law, starting with the basic provisions of the Treaty on the Functioning of the European Union (TEFU) and then running through EU secondary legislation (procedural rules and block exemptions) as well as 'soft legislation' such as Commission communications and guidance on the meaning of key concepts of State aid law and its policy approach to the exercise of its powers under the State aid rules. Moreover, by Articles 13(3) and (4), future EU legislation (including soft legislation) in the field of State aid is imported into Annex 5 and thus incorporated into Article 10.

Article 12(4) of the Protocol provides that, in relation to Article 10, all EU institutions – including the Commission and the Court of Justice of the European

2 One concerns an alleged failure by the United Kingdom to recover State aid given by Gibraltar in the form of a corporate tax exemption: see <https://ec.europa.eu/commission/presscorner/detail/en/ip_21_1266>. The other concerns a judgment of the UK Supreme Court that upheld the enforcement of an arbitral award ordering Romania to compensate investors – an award that that the Commission considers to be State aid. See <https://ec.europa.eu/commission/presscorner/detail/en/ip_22_802>.

3 Council Regulation 2015/1589/EU of 13 July 2015 laying down detailed rules for the application of Article 108 of the Treaty on the Functioning of the EU, [2015] OJ L248/9.

4 Protocol on Ireland/Northern Ireland to the Agreement on the withdrawal of the United Kingdom of Great Britain and Northern Ireland from the European Union and the European Atomic Energy Community [2019] OJ C 384I/01.

Union (CJEU) – have the same powers in relation to the UK and persons within it as they do under EU law, and that under Article 12(5) the exercise of those powers has the same legal effects in the UK (all of it) as it does in the EU (a provision translated into domestic law by Section 7A of the EU Withdrawal Act 2018). In relation to State aid law, those powers are very extensive.

The next point to note is that, subject to the critical final phrase of Article 10(1), its effect is to apply Annex 5 – that is, the whole corpus of EU State aid law – to 'the United Kingdom' (contrast Article 5(3) of the Protocol, which is confined to 'the United Kingdom in respect of Northern Ireland'). In other words, Article 10 potentially applies to any UK measure – that is to say, any measure by the UK government or any UK public authority (even one with no territorial responsibility for Northern Ireland).

Though this may appear surprising, it is less surprising given that the whole purpose of the Protocol is to protect the EU internal market while avoiding any need for checks and controls on the Irish border. Northern Ireland is closely integrated economically with Great Britain, and the Protocol itself refers to it having an 'integral place in the United Kingdom's internal market'. From the point of view of protecting the EU internal market, it would make little sense to limit the scope of the Article to measures taken by the devolved government of Northern Ireland or to measures benefiting businesses 'based in' Northern Ireland (however those might be defined), given the real possibility that subsidies by the UK government or by other public bodies in Great Britain either to Northern Ireland businesses or to businesses in Great Britain that trade with Northern Ireland could have knock-on effects in the EU.

Article 10 is thus very wide; what limits its scope is the last phrase ('in respect of measures which affect that trade between Northern Ireland and the Union which is subject to this Protocol').

There are three concepts in that critical phrase of Article 10(1). The first concept is that of a 'measure'. However, that fails to confine the application of EU State aid rules at all, since a 'measure' is simply anything to which the State aid rules may apply; the wording is used in Article 108(3) of the Treaty on the Functioning of the European Union (TFEU), which prohibits a Member State from putting a 'proposed measure' that falls within the scope of the State aid rules into effect until the Commission has decided whether the measure is compatible with the internal market.

The next concept to consider (in logical order) is the concept of 'that trade between Northern Ireland and the [EU] which is subject to this Protocol'. That raises the question of what trade between Northern Ireland and the EU is subject to the Protocol, to which the answer would appear to lie in those provisions of the Protocol that regulate trade between Northern Ireland and the EU. In that regard, in relation to the energy sector, it is necessary to note that Article 9 of the Protocol applies EU rules on the wholesale electricity market to Northern Ireland, so trade in wholesale electricity would appear to be caught. That conclusion is reinforced by the point that Article 5(5) applies the prohibition (in Article 34 TFEU) on quantitative restrictions on imports and exports to Northern

Ireland;[5] electricity falls within the scope of Article 34[6], as do physical products such as gas and fuels. A measure that affects trade in energy between Northern Ireland and the EU is therefore caught by the Protocol.

The third concept is the meaning of 'affect'. The phrase 'so far as it affects trade between Member States' forms part of the definition of State aid in Article 107(1) TFEU. It is frequently described as a 'low threshold', and in many cases, what appear to be activities of local interest only have been found to give rise to such an effect. A well-known example of such a case (which concerned the question of access by taxi cabs to bus lanes in London) is *Eventech*,[7] where the CJEU at [65]–[69] summarised its case-law, stating that:

> for the purpose of categorising a national measure as State aid, it is necessary, not to establish that the aid has a real effect on trade between member states and that competition is actually being distorted, but only to examine whether that aid is liable to affect such trade and distort competition.

It went on to state in particular that 'when aid granted by an EU Member State strengthens the position of an undertaking compared with other undertakings competing in intra-Community trade, the latter must be regarded as affected by that aid'. It also pointed out that a finding of effect on trade could be made even when the beneficiary of the aid did not itself carry on any intra-Community trade, since the changed pattern of internal trade might affect the ability of suppliers from other EU Member States to penetrate the market. And it emphasised that a finding of effect on trade could be made even if the aid was for a small amount, the beneficiary was small, or the market affected local in character.

If that approach applies to the interpretation of 'affect' in Article 10, then Article 10 potentially applies to a very wide range of UK measures. Indeed, the UK government was so concerned by that possibility that in late 2020 it put legislation before the UK Parliament, in the shape of Part 5 of the UK Internal Market Bill,[8] that would have authorised it to limit the scope of Article 10 even if that meant breaching the terms of the Withdrawal Agreement. The relevant clauses were in the end not proceeded with, in part because the House of Lords rejected them by an overwhelming majority, but also because the UK government secured a declaration from the EU – in the context of the Joint Committee on the Protocol – that the UK government was able to present as a real limitation on the scope of Article 10.

That EU declaration[9] stated that:

5 TFEU Article 34.

6 See Case C-158/94 *Commission v Italy* ECLI:EU:C:1997:500, at [17].

7 Case C-518/13 *Eventech* v *Parking Adjudicator* ECLI:EU:C:2015:9.

8 United Kingdom Internal Market Act 2020.

9 'Unilateral declarations by the European Union and the United Kingdom of Great Britain and Northern Ireland in the Withdrawal Agreement Joint Committee on Article 10(1) of the Protocol', 17 December 2020 <https://assets.publishing.service.gov.uk/government/uploads/system/uploads

> When applying Art. 107 TFEU to situations referred to in Art. 10(1) of the Protocol, the European Commission will have due regard to Northern Ireland's integral place in the United Kingdom's internal market. The European Union underlines that, in any event, an effect on trade between Northern Ireland and the Union which is subject to this Protocol cannot be merely hypothetical, presumed, or without a genuine and direct link to Northern Ireland. It must be established why the measure is liable to have such an effect on trade between Northern Ireland and the Union, based on the real foreseeable effects of the measure.

The difficulty, however, is that subsequent guidance issued by the UK government and by the Commission showed that they interpreted that declaration in rather different ways.

The Commission notice[10] on the issue treats the declaration as re-stating, and adding nothing to, the position in *Eventech.* On that basis, it notes that aid to an undertaking that sells only a small part of its production in the EU may have an effect on trade. Combining that point with the point that where an aid strengthens the position of an undertaking compared with other undertakings competing in intra-Community trade, the latter must be regarded as affected by that aid, the Commission concludes that an aid to a company located in Great Britain may 'notably' meet the 'effect' test if that company 'trades with' Northern Ireland. It also states that aid to a services company could indirectly meet the effect on trade test if it indirectly benefits companies engaged in trade in goods or electricity. It concludes with three examples of where the requisite effect on trade would be 'likely':[11] a tax scheme granting a direct or indirect benefit to any firm trading with Northern Ireland; incentives to the financial services industry that would allow manufacturers or electricity companies engaged in trade between Northern Ireland and the EU to access cheaper credit, thus gaining an advantage over their trading partners; and aid to a manufacturer in difficulty if its goods are available for sale in Northern Ireland.

In contrast, the United Kingdom government's guidance on the point[12] states that 'the starting assumption for subsidies granted to recipients outside of Northern

/attachment_data/file/946286/Unilateral_declarations_by_the_European_Union_and_the_United_Kingdom_of_Great_Britain_and_Northern_Ireland_in_the_Withdrawal_Agreement_Joint_Committee_on_Article_10_1__of_the_Protocol.pdf>

10 Notice to Stakeholders: Withdrawal of the United Kingdom and EU rules in the field of State aid', 18 January 2021 <https://ec.europa.eu/info/sites/default/files/notice-stakeholders-brexit-state-aid_en.pdf>

11 Ibid, para B 1.2. Note that in *R(British Sugar) v Secretary of State for International Trade* [2022] EWHC 393 (Admin), at para.125, Foxton J stated that he was not persuaded that the Notice was admissible as an aid to construction of Art.10.

12 Part 7 of the Department of Business, Energy and Industrial Strategy's 'Technical Guidance on the UK's international subsidy control commitments', updated 24 June 2021 <https://www.gov.uk/government/publications/complying-with-the-uks-international-obligations-on-subsidy-con-

Ireland should be that the NI Protocol does not apply',[13] and though it recognises that it could apply where 'a UK-wide measure benefits NI companies' or a subsidy is given to a company with a subsidiary or branch in Northern Ireland, it considers that it would be 'highly unlikely' to apply to a company in Great Britain that only exports to Northern Ireland. Further, the guidance also states that there is a 'very strong assumption that aid to services cannot be relevant to Article 10', though it goes on to accept that consideration should be given to the application of Article 10 in such cases 'where there is a direct foreseeable link between the subsidy of a service, and the production of goods affecting trade between NI and the EU'.[14]

The difference of view between the UK government and the Commission has both an immediate and a deeper aspect. The immediate aspect is that the UK government treats the EU declaration as substantively affecting the interpretation of Article 10, while the Commission regards it as doing no more than stating and applying established EU law. It is, in fact, hard to see that anything in the EU declaration modifies the application of EU law; unsurprisingly, nothing in the CJEU's case-law expressly allows for a 'hypothetical [or] presumed' effect on trade, or an effect based on anything other than a genuine or direct link to the putatively affected activities (both possibilities ruled out in the EU declaration[15]). Indeed, it is difficult to imagine that the Commission would ever proceed on a basis that openly relied on a hypothetical or presumed effect or on a non-genuine link, or that the CJEU would uphold it if it did. As the Commission notice points out, the effect has to be demonstrated, but the practical point is that the CJEU has accepted as 'demonstration' fairly sparse reasoning that at best shows only that the measure is 'liable to' affect, rather than that it actually has affected, such trade. It is therefore hard to see that the declaration adds anything to, or subtracts anything from, CJEU case-law on 'effect on trade' in Article 107(1) TFEU.

There is, though, a deeper disagreement. The Commission proceeds on the basis that 'affects … trade' means the same thing in Article 10(1) of the Protocol as it does in Article 107(1) TFEU, but the UK government suggests that that critical phrase has to be read differently in the context of the Northern Ireland Protocol. The better view is that the Commission is right. That is because Article 13(2) of the Protocol provides that 'the provisions of this Protocol referring to [EU] law or to concepts or provisions thereof shall in their implementation and application be interpreted in conformity with the relevant case law of the Court of Justice'; given the materially identical wording ('affect that trade between'/'affects trade between') in Article

---

trol-guidance-for-public-authorities/technical-guidance-on-the-uks-international-subsidy-control-commitments>

13 Ibid.

14 Under s.48(4) of the UK Internal Market Act 2020, granting authorities must 'have regard to' the UK government's guidance in exercising their functions, but that obligation would not extend to following it where the authority considers that it is legally incorrect.

15 Note, however, that in *R(British Sugar) v Secretary of State for International Trade* [2022] EWHC 393 (Admin), at para.126, Foxton J accepted that the 'genuine and direct link' wording did to some extent qualify the 'affect' test compared to EU law.

10(1) of the Protocol and Article 107(1) TFEU, it is hard to resist the proposition that Article 10(1) is here referring to a concept of EU law. Further, that reading of the Protocol reflects the overall approach of the Protocol in applying EU law in full to Northern Ireland in the areas of goods and electricity; it is implausible that such a foundational aspect of single market law was intended to apply in any weaker way than it does in the EU. However, that view was rejected by the High Court in *British Sugar*, where Foxton J held that the issue of 'affect' in Article 10 'is not to be approached solely by reference to the general body of EU law'.[16]

Whether, and how, those disagreements will be resolved will become clear over the next few years, though the High Court's judgment in *British Sugar*[17] suggests that the UK courts are likely to treat arguments that Article 10 applies with some scepticism save in obvious cases. In the meantime, however, the UK government, in its Command Paper of July 2021,[18] proposed that the Protocol be amended so as (among other things) to remove Article 10, on the basis that the United Kingdom is in the process of implementing a domestic subsidy control regime (as set out in the following Section) so that Article 10 is, in its view, now unnecessary. The Command Paper did, however, suggest that the UK government would be

> prepared to establish enhanced processes for any subsidies on a significant scale relating directly to Northern Ireland – for example, enhanced referral powers or consultation procedures for subsidies within scope, to enable EU concerns to be properly and swiftly addressed.[19]

In July 2022 the UK Government put the Northern Ireland Protocol Bill before Parliament. If passed in its current form, that Bill would give Ministers wide powers in domestic UK law to disapply large parts of the Protocol, including Article 10. The UK government asserts that the doctrine of "necessity" gives it a basis in international law from departing from the clear terms of the Withdrawal Agreement (which require it to give the Protocol effect in domestic law). At the time of writing, the Bill has completed its stages in the House of Commons, but its fate in the House of Lords, and the result of discussions between the UK government and the EU, remain unclear. The Commission has, to date, not given any indication that the EU is prepared to contemplate any amendment to Article 10.

5.3 The UK domestic subsidy regime

In May 2022 the Subsidy Control Act 2022 received Royal Assent. Its substantive provisions come into force on 4 January 2023. This Section concentrates on the provisions of that Act that affect the energy sector.

16 Ibid, at para.127.

17 *R(British Sugar) v Secretary of State for International Trade* [2022] EWHC 393 (Admin).

18 'Northern Ireland Protocol: the way forward', CP 502, 21 July 2021.

19 Ibid, para 65.

5.3.1 Background

The background to the Act is threefold.

First, after Brexit, the EU State aid rules (apart from Article 10 of the Northern Ireland Protocol, discussed above) ceased to apply to the UK, and the EU State aid rules were removed from 'retained EU law' (EU law given continuing effect in UK law under the EU Withdrawal Act 2018).[20] That left the UK with no domestic restriction on the ability of UK public authorities – some of which, like the Scottish government, are constitutionally and fiscally independent from the UK government – to subsidise in ways that could damage the UK economy as a whole.

Second, the Trade and Cooperation Agreement (TCA) required the UK to implement a domestic subsidy regime. Indeed, Chapter 3 of Title XI of the TCA contains provisions relating to subsidy control that are unprecedented in any previous free trade agreement. Since the requirements of Chapter 3 were already fulfilled on the EU side by the EU State aid regime, the principal effect of that Chapter is on the UK side.

Indeed, until 4 January 2023, much of Chapter 3 had direct legal force in the UK by virtue of Section 29 of the EU (Future Relationship) Act 2020 (passed in the narrow window between agreement of the TCA and the end of the transition period), which had the effect of incorporating into UK law any part of the TCA that required to be implemented, unless and over the period before the Act came into force.[21] However, even Section 29 could not deal with the problem that there was, until the Act came into force, no independent authority (as required by Article 371 of the TCA) with a role in subsidy control procedure.

Third, the UK accepted in its Comprehensive Economic Partnership Agreement with Japan[22] that it would prohibit certain kinds of subsidy; the Act implements that obligation (which is likely to figure in other trade agreements negotiated by the UK).

5.3.2 The central obligations in the Act and key concepts

The central obligations in the Act are the obligations on all public authorities at Sections 12 and 13 to consider, before granting a subsidy, the 'subsidy control principles' (in Schedule 1 to the Act) and the 'energy and environmental principles' (in Schedule 2 to the Act), and to satisfy themselves that the subsidy is consistent with those principles. Those principles are largely, but not entirely, derived

20 See the State Aid (Revocations and Amendments) (EU Exit) Regulations 2020 (SI 2020/1470).

21 For a consideration of how the TCA applied to an alleged subsidy in the form of a tariff quota, see *R(British Sugar) v Secretary of State for International Trade* [2022] EWHC 393 (Admin), at paras 134–151.

22 Agreement between the United Kingdom of Great Britain and Northern Ireland and Japan for a Comprehensive Economic Partnership [2020] CP 311 Volume 1, Article 12.7. See, generally, G. Peretz: 'Subsidy provisions in the UK/Japan Comprehensive Economic Partnership Agreement: what are they, and what do they mean for the UK/EU negotiations?' at <https://uksala.org/subsidy-provisions-in-the-uk-japan-comprehensive-economic-partnership-agreement-what-are-they-and-what-do-they-mean-for-the-uk-eu-negotiations/>.

from, respectively, Articles 366(1) and 367(14) of the TCA, which in turn set out general principles surrounding the circumstances in which subsidies should be permitted that can be derived from the decisional practice of the Commission. The energy and environmental principles in the Act will be discussed in more detail here, but for present purposes it should be noted that the general subsidy control principles in Schedule 1 include, in addition to principles derived from Article 366(1) of the TCA, the principle that subsidies should seek to minimise their negative effect on competition and investment within the United Kingdom – a purely domestic consideration that does not feature in the TCA.

'Public authority' is defined in Section 6[23] so as to include any person exercising functions of a public nature. The term does not, however, cover the UK or devolved Parliaments and so excludes all primary legislation from the scope of the main part of the Act (secondary legislation, which is made by Ministers or other public bodies, is not affected by that point). However, Schedule 3 does bring back within the scope of the Act, with a modified regime, all primary legislation passed by the devolved legislatures (but not, save to a very limited extent, Acts of the UK Parliament).[24]

'Subsidy' is defined along the lines set out in the TCA. By Section 2(1), it means

> financial assistance which
>
> (a) is given, directly or indirectly, from public resources by a public authority;,
> (b) confers an economic advantage on one or more enterprises,
> (c) is specific, that is, is such that it benefits one or more enterprises over one or more other enterprises with respect to the production of goods or the provision of services, and
> (d) has, or is capable of having, an effect on
>
> (i) competition or investment within the United Kingdom,
> (ii) trade between the United Kingdom and a country or territory outside the United Kingdom, or
> (iii) investment as between the United Kingdom and a country or territory outside the United Kingdom.

That definition requires there to be:

- 'financial assistance' (which Section 2(2) makes clear includes assistance given in a wide variety of ways, including foregoing revenue and making purchases);

23 Ibid, cl 6.

24 That Schedule sets out a detailed regime for the application of the subsidy control rules to primary legislation by the devolved parliaments (the Scottish Parliament, Senedd Cymru, and the Northern Ireland Assembly). Essentially, such legislation may be made subject to reports by the CMA and to challenge by third parties in the same way as acts by public authorities, save that the CAT is given no rule on adjudicating such challenges (the CAT's role being taken by the High Court or Court of Session). Primary legislation by the UK parliament is not affected by the Act, save for a provision that permits the promoter of legislation that involves a subsidy to ask the CMA to report on it: see below.

- that confers an 'economic advantage' (which Section 3 makes clear must be over and above what would have been available in the market);
- to an 'enterprise' (which is defined in Section 7 by reference to the concept of 'economic activity', a term which is not further defined);
- that is 'specific' (as to which Section 4 incorporates various principles set out in the TCA and derived from CJEU case-law on when tax measures are to be regarded as 'selective'); and
- which affects or is capable of affecting trade or investment with third countries or competition or investment within the UK (the latter element not being required by the TCA).

Though those concepts – almost all drawn from the TCA – bear a strong resemblance to principles in EU State aid law, the difference in terminology is designed to alert practitioners to the possibility that the EU State aid approach to concepts such as 'selectivity' (that is to say, the extent to which a measure confers advantages on a particular business or businesses, or class of businesses, as opposed to being a general measure, an issue that has generated much case-law in the EU regime) is not necessarily to be followed.[25] (The term *specificity* is also designed to draw a line between general measures not capable of being subsidies and measures of application to a particular business or class of businesses, but may not necessarily draw it in precisely the same place.)

5.3.3 The energy and environment principles

In the case of a 'subsidy in relation to energy and environment', the duty on a public authority under Section 13 is to consider and satisfy itself as to compliance with the 'energy and environmental principles' (Schedule 2), as well as with the general Section 12 duty to consider and satisfy itself as to compliance with 'subsidy control principles' (Schedule 1). The public authority's consideration of the energy and environmental principles in Schedule 2 is enforced in the same way as its consideration of the Schedule 1 issues.

As noted above, the background to Section 13 of, and Schedule 2 to, the Bill is Article 367(14) of the TCA, which requires the parties to ensure that

> subsidies in relation to energy and environment shall be aimed at, and incentivise the beneficiary in, delivering a secure, affordable and sustainable energy system and a well-functioning and competitive energy market or increasing the level of environmental protection compared to the level that would be

25 In *R(British Sugar) v Secretary of State for International Trade* [2022] EWHC 393 (Admin), the question of whether the alleged subsidy was 'specific' was discussed without any reference to EU law, and by reference only to WTO panel decisions; however, that was at least in part because there was no EU jurisprudence on the question of whether the subsidy at issue (a tariff quota) could be 'selective' (because in the EU such decisions are taken at EU level and are outside the scope of the EU State aid rules).

> achieved in absence of the subsidy. Such subsidies shall not relieve the beneficiary from liabilities arising from its responsibilities as a polluter under the law of the relevant Party.

Moreover, Article 301(3) of the TCA requires Annex 27[26] to be applied in relation to subsidies. The energy and environment principles in Schedule 2 essentially set out the matters specified in Article 367(14) and Annex 27 of the TCA.

As to the content of the energy and environmental principles that a public authority must consider when granting a subsidy, Principle A in Schedule 2 states that a subsidy in relation to energy or environment 'shall be aimed at and incentivise the beneficiary in (a) delivering a secure, affordable and sustainable energy system and a well-functioning and competitive energy market, or (b) increasing the level of environmental protection compared to the level that would be achieved in the absence of the subsidy'. Principle B is that a subsidy shall not relieve the polluter of obligations. Principle C is that

> subsidies for electricity generation adequacy, renewable energy or generation (a) shall not undermine the ability of the United Kingdom to meet its obligations under Article 304 of the Trade and Cooperation Agreement (provisions relating to wholesale electricity and gas markets), (b) shall not unnecessarily affect the efficient use of electricity interconnectors provided for under Article 311 of the Trade and Cooperation Agreement (efficient use of electricity interconnectors), and (c) shall be determined by means of a transparent, non-discriminatory and effective competitive process.[27]

Principles D and E provide, respectively, that 'subsidies for electricity generation adequacy may be limited to installations not exceeding specified CO2 emission limits' and that 'subsidies for renewable energy or cogeneration shall not affect beneficiaries' obligations or opportunities to participate in electricity markets'.

Principle F states that 'subsidies in the form of partial exemptions from energy-related taxes and levies in favour of energy-intensive users shall not exceed the total amount of the tax or levy concerned'. Principle G provides that

> subsidies in the form of compensation for electricity-intensive users given in the event of an increase in electricity costs resulting from climate policy instruments shall be restricted to sectors at significant risk of carbon leakage due to the cost increase.

Principle H states that 'subsidies for the decarbonisation of emissions linked to industrial activities in the United Kingdom shall (a) achieve an overall reduction in greenhouse gas emissions, and (b) reduce the emissions directly resulting from

26 The EU–UK Trade and Cooperation Agreement [2021] OJ L 149/10 Annex 27 (Energy and Environmental Subsidies).

27 That last obligation is subject to a carve-out in paragraph (2) where there is insufficient competition, no likely material effect on competition or trade, or in the case of a demonstration project.

the industrial activities'. Finally, Principle I provides that 'subsidies for improvements of the energy efficiency of industrial activities in the United Kingdom shall improve energy efficiency by reducing energy consumption, either directly or per unit of production'.

Importantly, Section 51 excludes subsidies for the nuclear sector from the requirement to consider the Schedule 2 principles just set out; such subsidies need be considered only under the general clause 12 subsidy control principles. It is not explained anywhere in the government's policy papers published at the time of publication of the Bill that became the Act why subsidies to the nuclear industry are to be excluded from the duty to consider the energy and environment principles, and it should be noted that the relevant provisions of the TCA do not exclude the nuclear sector. It may be that the central problem is that, as discussed above, principle B in Schedule 2 provides that enterprises should not be relieved from their obligations as polluters, and that it was felt that subsidies to the nuclear industry could not sensibly be made subject to that principle.

5.3.4 The (general) subsidy control principles

These general principles in Schedule 1 to the Act apply to all sectors including energy. In essence, they require the following: a market failure or equity/distributional rationale; proportionality to the policy objective; an incentive effect; no subsidy where the beneficiary would have funded those costs anyway; minimisation of effects on competition within the UK (that principle, as observed above, not being required by the TCA); and beneficial effects outweighing negative ones.

5.3.5 Exemptions and prohibitions

A number of subsidies are exempt from the regime. Subsidies granted in accordance with Article 10 of the Northern Ireland Protocol (i.e., within its scope and either cleared by the Commission or benefiting from a block exemption) are excluded from the Bill by Section 48(3)(a). Subsidies to compensate for natural disasters and other emergencies are excluded, as are subsidies for economic emergencies. There are further exclusions in relation to national security and Bank of England monetary policy and financial stability, as well as 'large cross border or international cooperation projects' as defined in Section 50.

Section 29 sets out a specific regime, similar to the EU services of general economic interest regime, for subsidies to providers of services of public economic interest, namely enterprises carrying out particular tasks in the public interest.

Section 36 exempts subsidies where the enterprise receives less than £315,000 over its current and previous two financial years; this broadly mirrors EU *de minimis* rules (though, as permitted by the TCA, with a somewhat higher threshold than the current equivalent EU threshold of €200,000 over 3 years).

As for prohibitions, Sections 15–17 prohibit unlimited guarantees and subsidies conditional on exports or on import substitution, implementing requirements in the TCA as well as the agreement with Japan.[28] But neither of those treaties contains Section 18, which prohibits subsidies conditional on relocation within the UK unless certain conditions are satisfied. Sections 19–26 deal with rescue and restructuring subsidies; subsidies to 'ailing or insolvent enterprises' are prohibited unless the enterprise has a credible restructuring plan, the subsidy is in the form of a temporary loan or liquidity support and the subsidy contributes to an objective of public interest by avoiding social hardship or preventing a severe market failure, or if there are other exceptional circumstances. These provisions strongly resemble the equivalent EU rules that govern the rescue or restructuring of 'undertakings in difficulty' and restrict other subsidies to such undertakings.

5.3.6 Enforcement

There are four main aspects to enforcement under the Act.

First, Section 33 requires a granting authority to place information about any subsidy on the public central subsidy database.

Second, the granting authority or the Secretary of State may refer certain subsidies (classes to be set out in regulations[29]) to the Competition and Markets Authority (CMA) for a report on whether the subsidy is consistent with the subsidy control and (where relevant) energy and environment principles. Further types of subsidy (again set out in regulations) must be referred to the CMA for that purpose. The CMA's report does not bind anyone. However, a grant must not be made during the CMA's investigation or for 5 days after publication of the report.

Third, any person whose interests may be affected by the giving of the subsidy (or the Secretary of State)[30] may seek judicial review of the subsidy decision before the Competition Appeal Tribunal (CAT), Section 70. The time limits under Section 71 are somewhat complex, but essentially any such application must be made within one month of either publication of the subsidy on the subsidy database, the applicant's knowledge of the subsidy, or the relevant CMA report.

The CAT applies usual UK public law principles on the judicial review of administrative actions.[31] Time will tell whether the CAT uses the flexibility of those principles to subject granting authorities to more intensive review than

28 Agreement between the United Kingdom of Great Britain and Northern Ireland and Japan for a Comprehensive Economic Partnership [2020] CP 311 Volume 1.

29 See the Subsidy Control (Subsidies and Schemes of Interest or Particular Interest) Regulations 2022.

30 See Section 70(7).

31 Section 70(5).

would be the case of a typical regulatory decision, given that the granting authorities whose decisions are at issue may well be influenced by political pressure to award a subsidy – and it may be especially prepared to do so in cases where the CMA has not been asked to report or where its report has not been accepted.

Finally, even though the question of whether an individual subsidy infringes the subsidy control provisions of the TCA is not subject to dispute resolution,[32] the EU is entitled to take remedial measures under Article 374 of the TCA if it considers that a subsidy has been granted that causes, or seriously risks causing, a significant negative effect on trade or investment between the EU and UK. Such remedial measures shall be restricted to what is strictly necessary and proportionate in order to remedy the significant negative effect caused or to address the serious risk of such an effect.[33]

5.4 Conclusion

Any energy business receiving a subsidy in the UK – a term which, like the EU concept of 'State aid', is broadly defined and includes such measures as tax advantages or waivers, loans, contracts, and investment on favourable terms as well as simple grants – will have to consider two separate regimes. First, it will need to consider the EU State aid rules, as partly maintained in the UK by virtue of Article 10 of the Northern Ireland Protocol; and it will need to consider whether there is a real risk that trade in energy between Northern Ireland and the EU would be affected by the subsidy. If it concludes that that is a real risk, and if no relevant block exemption applies, then it will need to persuade the UK government to notify the subsidy to the EU; if the UK government refuses (as it may do), then the enterprise will have to decide if proceeding without notifying raises a commercially acceptable risk, given that any notifiable State aid received without its having been notified and cleared generates a large recovery risk for the recipient.

In cases where Article 10 does not apply, the new UK regime will have to be considered. That will require checking to see if the measure is a 'subsidy' as defined therein, if so, whether it is exempt or prohibited, and if not exempt or prohibited, ensuring that the granting authority carefully considers the energy and environment and subsidy control principles and places the subsidy on the transparency database.

In some cases, the CMA may become involved and will have to be engaged with as well, given that its reports are likely to be persuasive, if not binding. Finally, in the case of large projects, the risk of the EU taking action under the TCA or exerting diplomatic pressure on the UK has to be evaluated.

In conclusion, albeit post-Brexit the UK may, to a large extent, no longer be bound by the EU State aid rules; its new regime has complexities and difficulties of its own.

32 Article 375(2) TCA.
33 Article 374(8) TCA

6 Brexit and UK's Renewable Energy and Climate Change Policies

Implications and Opportunities

Ana Stanič and Julian Bowden

6.1 Introduction

Following a series of natural disasters in 2021 – floods in Germany,[1] fires in Greece[2] – and a major report by the Intergovernmental Panel on Climate Change (IPCC),[3] global warming became the Top-2 issue on most countries' political and economic agenda last year. Emissions targets have been brought forward as energy transition to a non-fossil future seemingly gathers momentum.

The UK has been at the forefront of setting emissions targets. In June 2019, it was the first major economy in the world to commit to a reduction of greenhouse gas emissions to zero by 2050, compared to 1990 levels.[4] In April 2021, the UK government announced that it would set the 'world's most ambitious climate change target' to reduce emissions by 78% by 2035 as part of its sixth budget (see Figure 6.1), thereby bringing the UK more than three-quarters of the way to net zero by 2050.[5] This new commitment was enshrined into law in June of 2021 with the adoption of the Sixth Carbon Budget. In the lead up to COP26 in Glasgow, UK's Prime Minister Boris Johnson committed to ensuring that all of the UK's

1 See: 'Flood disaster fails to move German voters' *Financial Times* (London,18 September 2021).

2 See: Yanis Varoufakis, 'Greece's deadly wildfires were sparked by 30 years of political failure' *The Guardian* (29 August 2021) <www.theguardian.com/commentisfree/2021/aug/29/greece-wildfires-political-failure-climate-emergency> accessed 6 November 2022.

3 IPCC, 'Climate Change 2021: The Physical Science Basis. Contribution of Working Group I to the Sixth Assessment Report of the Intergovernmental Panel on Climate Change' (Cambridge University Press, August 2021) <www.ipcc.ch/report/sixth-assessment-report-working-group-i/> accessed 6 November 2022.

4 Department for Business, Energy & Industrial Strategy and The Rt Hon Chris Skidmore, 'UK Becomes First Major Economy to Pass Net Zero Emissions Law' (27 June 2019) <www.gov.uk/government/news/uk-becomes-first-major-economy-to-pass-net-zero-emissions-law> accessed 15 December 2022. This commitment was enshrined into law with the adoption of the Climate Change Act 2008 (2050 Target Amendment) Order 2019.

5 Department for Business, Energy & Industrial Strategy, 'Press release: UK enshrines new target in law to slash emissions by 78% by 2035' (20 April 2021) <www.gov.uk/government/news/uk-enshrines-new-target-in-law-to-slash-emissions-by-78-by-2035> accessed 15 December 2022.

DOI: 10.4324/9781003364337-7

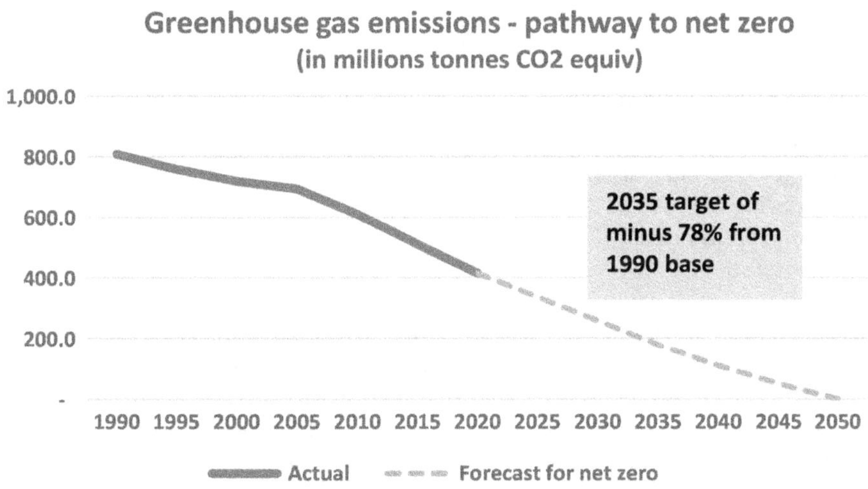

Figure 6.1 Source: Table 1.1 in Final UK greenhouse gas emissions national statistics 1990–2019 available at the website www.gov.uk/government/collections/final-uk-greenhouse-gas-emissions-national-statistics.

electricity was 'to come from clean energy sources by 2035'.[6] A commitment reiterated by Prime Minister Rishi Sunak a year later at COP27 in Egypt.[7]

This Chapter identifies the implications Brexit has had and/or may have on the UK's ability to increase the share of renewables in its energy mix and achieve its ambitious climate change targets. It will do so by first discussing the UK's climate change and renewables targets in Section 6.1. Section 6.2 then explains the fundamentals of the UK energy sector and what these mean for achieving the targets. Section 6.3 outlines the key terms of the Trade and Cooperation Agreement (TCA) concerning renewables and climate change. Section 6.4 identifies the challenges and opportunities that Brexit presents to the UK achieving these targets. Finally, Section 6.5 proposes steps to be taken by the UK government to address and, to the extent possible, minimise the impact of Brexit on the UK's ability to achieve the climate change and renewables targets and policies.

6.2 Key Elements of UK's Renewables and Climate Change Policy

The main elements of UK's renewables and climate change policy can be summarised as follows:

6 'All UK's electricity will come from clean sources, says PM' *BBC* (London, 4 October 2021) <www.bbc.com/news/uk-politics-58792261> accessed 6 November 2022.

7 Prime Minister to travel to Egypt to galvanise action on the climate commitments made at COP26 in Glasgow, <https://www.gov.uk/government/news/pm-pledges-to-make-uk-a-clean-energy-superpower-ahead-of-cop27> accessed 15 December 2022.

(i) net zero greenhouse gas emissions[8] by 2050 and a reduction of greenhouse gas emissions by 78% by 2035;[9]
(ii) no new petrol or diesel cars or vans to be sold after 2030;[10]
(iii) offshore wind capacity to reach 40 GW by 2030 and exceed 100 GW by 2050, with offshore wind becoming the backbone of the UK's power generation;[11]
(iv) large-scale nuclear and small modular nuclear reactors to play a key role in ensuring the robustness and stability of the energy system;
(v) the adoption of a UK emissions trading system (UK ETS) now that the UK has left the EU.

These policies are set out in three key government and near-government documents. All these documents were published in late 2020 whilst the terms of the TCA were being finalised. As such, the policy objectives promulgated in these documents have, or ought to have, taken into account the fact that the UK has now left the EU. These three documents are discussed in turn below.

6.2.1 Ten Point Plan

The first of these documents is the Prime Minister's Ten Point Plan for a Green Industrial Revolution, published in November 2020.[12] Very much a political manifesto, it seeks to marry the Brexit promises of (i) generating new jobs in economically deprived areas and (ii) restoring Great Britain's leadership in the world[13] with climate change policies. This policy paper calls for an increase in offshore wind capacity to 40GW by 2030, up from 10.4 GW as of the end of 2020. The construction of large-scale nuclear power plants as well as research

8 Greenhouse gases include carbon dioxide, methane, nitrous oxide and the 'F' gases. By far the largest contributor is CO_2: in 2019 CO_2 accounted for 80% of greenhouse gas emissions, methane12% and nitrous oxide 5. <https://www.gov.uk/government/collections/final-uk-greenhouse-gas-emissions-national-statistics> accessed 6 November 2022.

9 The Carbon Budget Order 2021, SI 2021/750.

10 Department for Transport, 'Government takes historic step towards net-zero with end of sale of new petrol and diesel cars by 2030' (18 November 2020) <www.gov.uk/government/news/government-takes-historic-step-towards-net-zero-with-end-of-sale-of-new-petrol-and-diesel-cars-by-2030> accessed 6 November 2022.

11 See Aurora Energy Research, 'Reaching the UK Government's target of 40GW of offshore wind by 2030 will require almost £50bn in investment' (6 February 2020) <https://auroraer.com/media/reaching-40gw-offshore-wind> accessed 6 November 2022.

12 Department for Business, Energy & Industrial Strategy, 'Policy paper – The Ten Point Plan for a Green Industrial Revolution' (18 November 2020) <https://assets.publishing.service.gov.uk/government/uploads/system/uploads/attachment_data/file/936567/10_POINT_PLAN_BOOKLET.pdf > accessed 6 November 2022 (Ten Point Plan for a Green Industrial Revolution).

13 'UK is at the forefront of [Green industrial revolution], just as we led the first over 2 centuries ago.' Ministerial forward to the White Paper, see n [13].

into the possibility of using small modular reactors (SMR) is another point of the Plan, albeit lacking concrete details. A commitment to 5 GW of hydrogen production capacity being in place by 2030 is another point of the Plan as is carbon capture storage. The Plan also contains a general commitment to the expansion of the rail network and switching to green electric and hydrogen powered aircraft and shipping.

6.2.2 White Paper: Powering our Net Zero Future14

The second of these documents is the Energy White Paper entitled 'Powering our Net Zero Future', which the UK government presented in December 2020. The White Paper builds on the Ten Point Plan and was meant to provide a roadmap on how to achieve the net zero goal. It acknowledges that achieving the targets set is a 'significant and historic undertaking' which 'means ending [UK's] dependency on oil power[ing] nearly half of our economy' and is likely to require 'the doubling of electricity demand and consequently a fourfold increase in low-carbon electricity generation'.[15] Without setting a specific target for a particular generation mix for 2050, it anticipates that electricity could provide more than half of the final energy demand in 2050 (up from 17% in 2019) and be predominantly generated by wind and solar. Recognising the intermittency of solar and wind, the White Paper envisages complementing these with nuclear, storage, and gas with carbon capture and storage (CCS).

In order to achieve these objectives, the White Paper envisaged the establishment of a new UK Emissions Trading Scheme (ETS) in view of the UK's exit from the EU ETS post-Brexit. Without providing much detail, it provided that the new scheme will need to be aligned to the UK's net zero target, will set a cap on greenhouse gases that businesses can emit (via the total number of allowances in circulation) which will decrease over time, and announced that the scheme will initially apply to energy-intensive industries, electricity generation, and aviation. No express commitment as to timing of the introduction of the UK ETS was given.[16] Instead, reference was made to a willingness to 'consult in due course on how to align the cap with an appropriate net zero trajectory', albeit recognising that unless the cap provides a robust carbon pricing signal, the investors will not have the certainty and confidence to mobilise the scale of capital investment necessary to deploy clean energy technologies. A commitment to 'exploring expanding the UK ETS to the two-thirds of uncovered emissions' is also made, with

14 Department for Business, Energy & Industrial Strategy, 'Energy White Paper: Powering Our Net Zero Future' (18 December 2020) <www.gov.uk/government/publications/energy-white-paper-powering-our-net-zero-future/energy-white-paper-powering-our-net-zero-future-accessible-html-version> accessed 6 November 2022 (White Paper).

15 Ibid., 10.

16 The UK ETS entered into force on 1 January 2021. Department for Business, Energy & Industrial Strategy, 'Guidance: Participating in the UK ETS' (2 August 2021) <www.gov.uk/government/publications/participating-in-the-uk-ets/participating-in-the-uk-ets> accessed 6 November 2022.

more concrete details to be given in the run-up to COP26 in November 2021.[17] The possibility of a link to EU ETS system is contemplated in the White Paper, without expressing preference.

In respect of nuclear energy, the White Paper contained little detail. It simply provided that the UK government 'aim[s] to bring at least one large-scale nuclear project to the point of final investment decision by the end of this Parliament, subject to clear value for money and all relevant approvals' and hopes to build a commercially viable fusion power plant by 2040. It further provided that the UK government's plans are based on an expectation that the cost of nuclear new build projects would fall by 30% by 2030. The setting up of an Advanced Nuclear Fund worth £385 million is envisaged to support innovation in developing advanced nuclear technologies.

The importance of interconnectors to EU and European Free Trade Association (EFTA) countries in enhancing the flexibility of the UK energy system and, in turn, achieving renewables and decarbonisation[18] targets and reducing total system costs is acknowledged in the White Paper. A three-fold increase in interconnector capacity is planned by 2030. The UK government's hope that this will allow it to become a net exporter of excess green energy is noted. The construction and operation of hybrid multi-purpose interconnectors is also mentioned.

The White Paper acknowledges that '[d]elivering this transition will require billions of pounds of investment in clean energy infrastructure or new low-carbon technologies' and that '[t]his challenge is set against the backdrop of an economy which has been hit by the largest recession in 300 years as a result of the COVID-19 pandemic'.

Although it is 160 pages long, the White Paper is largely aspirational in nature and contains very little detail on how the above-mentioned goals will be achieved. The sheer size of the regulatory and legislative challenges to achieving these is clear from the fact that the White Paper does not even contain timeframes for the adoption of the legislation necessary to achieve the set goals. The White Paper merely provides that plans and strategies for *inter alia* transport, hydrogen, and industrial decarbonisation would be drawn up over the 2021–2022 period. In August 2021, the government published a hydrogen strategy which promised 'an integrated and holistic hydrogen economy by the end of the decade'.[19] Rather than setting out a detailed roadmap, the strategy envisages numerous further consultations and publications in the coming 12 months without providing sufficient detail on *inter alia* the hydrogen business model, the low-carbon hydrogen standard, or the Net Zero Hydrogen Fund.

17 White Paper 129.

18 Aurora Energy Research, 'The Impact of Interconnectors on Decarbonisation' (BEIS Research Paper Number 2020/056, 14 December 2020) <www.gov.uk/government/publications/impact-of-interconnectors-on-decarbonisation> accessed 6 November 2022, which was published alongside the White Paper and demonstrates how a higher level of interconnector capacity could decrease cumulative emissions in Great Britain by up to 199 $MtCO_2e$ by 2050, as well as reducing total system costs.

19 HM Government, *UK Hydrogen Strategy* (CP 475, August 2021) <https://assets.publishing.service.gov.uk/government/uploads/system/uploads/attachment_data/file/1011283/UK-Hydrogen-Strategy_web.pdf> accessed 6 November 2022.

In view of this situation, it is fair to say that at the time of writing this Chapter, the UK government is only at the drawing board stage. It will be at least 2–3 years before there is any clarity on what the legislative and regulatory framework will look like. This in itself gives rise to significant legal uncertainty, which in turn makes it very difficult for business to commit the capital needed for new energy infrastructure and low-carbon technologies.

6.2.3 Climate Change Committee's Sixth Carbon Budget

The third document setting out the climate and renewable targets is the Sixth Carbon Budget UK's Path to Net Zero[20] (CB) which was published by the Climate Change Committee (CCC) in December 2020. The CCC is an independent statutory body set up under the Climate Change Act 2008 to advise the UK central and devolved governments on achieving climate change and renewables targets. The CB contains CCS's 'recommendations for the UK's Sixth Carbon Budget, which will run from 2033 to 2037', provides the UK 'Government and Parliament the route map to meeting those statutory obligations'.[21] In particular, it recommends that the 'UK sets a Sixth Carbon Budget to require a reduction in UK greenhouse gas territorial emissions of 78% by 2035'.[22] This in turn means that well over half of the required emissions reduction to 2050 need to be achieved in the next 15 years.

Given that emissions reductions to date were primarily achieved by eliminating coal from the energy mix, the CCC notes that 'future reductions must come from transport, industry, buildings and agriculture, as well as phasing out gas-fired power'.[23] The CB for the first time is extended to international aviation and shipping.

It describes four scenarios for achieving net zero, leaving it up to the government to select between them. The main components of the Balanced Pathway, the central scenario, as concerns renewables include increasing offshore wind capacity from 10 GW today to 40 GW by 2030 and 95 GW by 2050 and hydrogen from 1 TWh as of today to 225 TWh in 2050.[24]

How electricity is generated is of central concern to all four scenarios. As in the case of the White Paper, CCC projects power demand doubling from around 300 TWh today to 610 TWh by 2050 in all the scenarios. With coal phased out completed by 2024, at which point the phase out of unabated gas is planned to start, electricity is expected to be produced from solar, wind, nuclear, and gas with CCS and hydrogen at scale from 2035 onwards. Under all scenarios, offshore wind is to become the backbone of the system by 2050, producing 430 TWh by 2050 and

20 Chris Start and others, 'The Sixth Carbon Budget – The UK's Path to Net Zero' (Committee on Climate Change, 2020) <www.theccc.org.uk/wp-content/uploads/2020/12/The-Sixth-Carbon-Budget-The-UKs-path-to-Net-Zero.pdf> accessed6 November 2022 (CB).

21 Ibid., 6.

22 Ibid., 5.

23 Ibid., 14.

24 Ibid., 68.

representing around two-thirds of UK power generated.[25] In other words, an unprecedented transformation of the UK's power generation system is envisaged in a relatively short time frame. There is much debate on whether this is an achievable goal, especially given the lack of detailed roadmap on how it will be achieved.

Nuclear energy is also key in all four scenarios. With six nuclear power plants (NPPs) expected to be decommissioned before 2030, the CB assumes that nuclear capacity will return to 10 GW by 2035 with the construction of two additional large-scale NPPs in addition to Hinkley C.[26]

The CB also recognises the importance of power interconnector capacity with neighbouring EU countries (plus Norway) in the low-carbon world. It projects an increase from 6 GW today to 18 GW by 2050 to enable power trade.[27]

The colossal size of the investment required to achieve the net zero goal by 2050 is discussed in CB. Low-carbon investment is to increase from around £10 bn per annum in 2020 to around £50 bn per annum by 2030 and then is to continue at that level to 2050.[28] Since CCC expects such investment to be made by the private sector, it emphasises the need for a clear legislative and regulatory framework. In particular, CB calls for 'effective policies [to be] introduced across the economy without delay'. According to the CCC, the

> implication of [the net zero] path is clear: the utmost focus is required from government over the next ten years. If policy is not scaled up across every sector; if business is not encouraged to invest; if the people of the UK are not engaged in this challenge – the UK will not deliver Net Zero by 2050. The 2020s must be the decisive decade of progress and action.[29]

In June 2021, the UK Parliament set the Sixth Carbon Budget for the years from 2033 to 2037 at 965,000,000 tonnes of carbon dioxide equivalent, being the level recommended by the CCC in its CB.[30] Importantly, the government has made clear that 'following the CCC's recommended budget level does not mean [we are] following their specific policy recommendations. Our published analysis is based on the government's own assumptions and does not, for example, assume the CCC's change in people's diet'.[31] Accordingly, in October 2021, in the lead up to COP26 in Glasgow, the government launched its Net Zero Strategy under the title 'Build Back Greener'.[32] It was submitted to the United Nations Framework Convention

25 Ibid., 134–135.
26 Ibid., 135.
27 Ibid., 136.
28 Ibid., 239.
29 Ibid., 5.
30 The Carbon Budget Order 2021, SI 2021/750.
31 Department for Business, Energy & Industrial Strategy, 'Press release: UK enshrines new target in law to slash emissions by 78% by 2035' (20 April 2021) <www.gov.uk/government/news/uk-enshrines-new-target-in-law-to-slash-emissions-by-78-by-2035> accessed 6 November 2022.
32 The government borrows from the slogan Build Back Better from the controversial plan announced by World Economic Forum in July 2020 and video entitled the Great Reset. Peter Bak-

on Climate Change (UNFCCC) as the UK's second Long-Term Greenhouse Gas Emission Development Strategy under the Paris Agreement.

However, the Net Zero Strategy continues to lack the necessary detail on the legislative and regulatory framework for the delivery of UK commitments.[33] The biggest weaknesses are (i) the lack of detail in how the colossal investment will be corralled; (ii) the lack of focus on implementation; (iii) the failure to identify risks that technologies such as CCS and green hydrogen can be delivered at scale, on time, and at reasonable cost; and (iv) limited discussion on risk mitigation. Accordingly, the concern expressed by the Institute of Government in its report of September 2020 that there is 'little evidence that the government … [has] confronted the enormous scale of the task ahead' still remains pertinent.[34]

6.3 UK Energy Fundamentals

The UK's energy fundamentals have evolved over time as a result of a combination of market forces and government policies.

The UK's decarbonisation path towards a net zero position by 2050 is shown in Figure 6.1. At the time of writing this Chapter, the UK is at about the half-way point to net zero, having reduced emissions from 800 million tonnes in CO_2 equivalent in 1990 to just over 400 million tonnes in 2020.[35] This reduction was achieved in two main ways: by significantly reducing the share of coal in the energy mix, and through energy efficiency gains. The extent of the latter achievement is clear from the fact that whilst the economy expanded by 40% over the 2000–2019 period, the UK's energy demand fell by almost 25%.[36] Importantly, the fall in the UK's greenhouse gas emissions per unit of GDP over this period exceeded the EU's average, placing the UK at the very top of the European low emissions league.[37]

---

ker, John Elkington, 'To build back better, we must reinvent capitalism. Here's how' (*World Economic Forum*, 13 July 2020) <www.weforum.org/agenda/2020/07/to-build-back-better-we-must-reinvent-capitalism-heres-how/> accessed 6 November 2022; 'The Great Reset' <www.weforum.org/great-reset> accessed 6 November 2022.

33 Department for Business, Energy & Industrial Strategy, 'Policy paper overview: Net Zero Strategy: Build Back Greener' (19 October 2021) <www.gov.uk/government/publications/net-zero-strategy> accessed 6 November 2022.

34 Tom Sasse, Jill Rutter, Emma Norris and Marcus Shepheard, 'Net Zero – How government can meet its climate change target' (Institute for Government, September 2020) <https://www.instituteforgovernment.org.uk/sites/default/files/publications/net-zero-government-climate-change-target.pdf> accessed 6 November 2022.

35 Greenhouse gas in UK statistics is expressed in terms of CO2 equivalent, and comprises CO2, methane, nitrous oxide, and the fluorinated 'F' gases. Of these in 2019 CO2 was by far the largest component at 80%, followed by methane with 12% and nitrous oxide with 5%. 2020 is estimated from BP Statistical Review of World Energy 2021, and also in UK Energy in Brief 2021, Department for Business, Energy and Industrial Strategy, 'UK Energy in Brief 2021' (29 July 2021) <https://assets.publishing.service.gov.uk/government/uploads/system/uploads/attachment_data/file/1006381/UK_Energy_in_Brief_2021.pdf> accessed 6 November 2022, 15.

36 IEA, 'World Energy Balances, economic and energy indicators', (29 July 2021) <https://wds.iea.org> accessed 6 November 2022.

37 EU Publications Office 2020, 'EU energy in figures - Statistical pocketbook 2020' (15 September 2020) <https://op.europa.eu/en/publication-detail/-/publication/87b16988-f740-11ea-991b

The challenge for the UK is that now that these easier wins have been achieved, the further reductions needed to achieve net zero will be more difficult.

6.3.1 Main changes in UK energy fundamentals over 2000–2019

Three developments have resulted in the composition and size of UK's energy mix changing profoundly over the last 20 years. Firstly, coal has almost been eliminated from the energy mix. By 2000 it was already in decline but still accounted for 16% of total energy use. By 2019, it accounted for less than 3%.[38] Secondly, with the North Sea having entered its decline phase in 2000, UK oil and gas production contracted, and the UK went from being a net energy exporter in 2000 to a net importer of all energy sources by 2019. In particular, around half of the gas is now supplied from imports, with Norway alone supplying one-third of the demand by pipeline.[39] The UK is also a net importer of electricity, supplied via cable interconnectors with France, Belgium, Netherlands, and, since 1 October 2021, with Norway.[40] Thirdly, as noted here, there have been major efficiency gains from lower energy usage.

Figure 6.2 below illustrates both the changes in the composition of the energy mix and also the decline in absolute energy demand over the 2000–2019 period. The mix today is dominated by oil and gas (with 38% share each) with the balance being taken up by nuclear and renewables. The ongoing new dynamic is the growth of renewables, and in particular of offshore wind, which, as discussed in Section 6.1, is seen as key to the UK's progression towards net zero.

6.3.2 Gas and increasing role of interconnectors

The change in the UK's gas demand and supply balance over the same period is significant. Whereas in 2000 the UK was a small net exporter of gas, by 2004 it had become a net importer, and by 2019, imports covered 50% of UK's total gas demand. Gas pipelines with the Netherlands, Belgium, and Norway are key transportation links for managing the gas supply–demand balance and, along with liquefied natural gas (LNG), for covering the UK's gas deficit. In 2019, 36% of the UK's gas demand was met by pipeline imports, principally from Norway, and

-01aa75ed71a1> accessed 6 November 2022, table 4.2.2, 175.

38 All energy mix data is taken from Department for Business, Energy & Industrial Strategy, 'Digest of UK Energy Statistics (DUKES): energy' (26 July 2012, last updated 29 July 2021) <www.gov.uk/government/statistics/energy-chapter-1-digest-of-united-kingdom-energy-statistics-dukes> accessed6 November 202, Chapter 1: statistics on overall energy production and consumption, DUKES 1.1 – 1.3 aggregate energy balances.

39 Department for Business, Energy & Industrial Strategy, 'Digest of UK Energy Statistics (DUKES): foreign trade statistics' (28 March 2014, last updated 29 July 2021) <www.gov.uk/government/statistics/dukes-foreign-trade-statistics> accessed 6 November 2022.

40 National Grid, 'National Grid powers up world's longest subsea interconnector between the UK and Norway' (4 October 2021) <www.northsealink.com/en/news/national-grid-powers-up-world-s-longest-subsea-interconnector-between-the-uk-and-norway> accessed 6 November 2022.

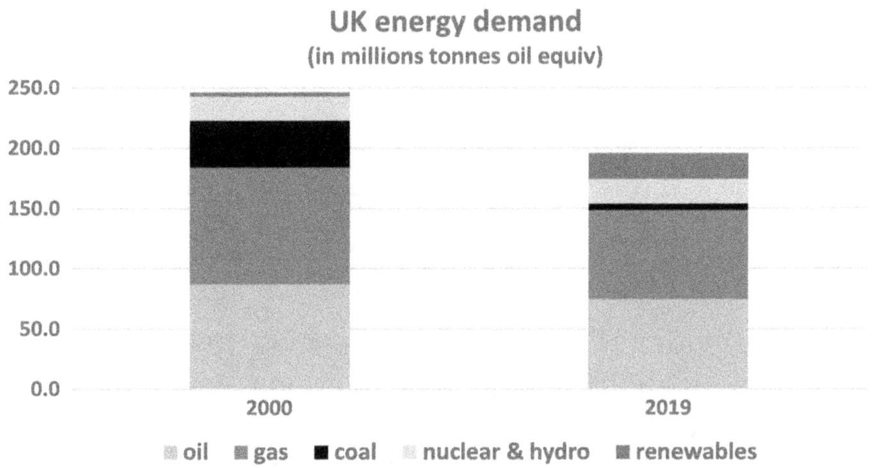

Figure 6.2 Source: Digest of UK Energy Statistics (DUKES) Chapter 1: statistics on overall energy production and consumption, DUKES 1.1 – 1.3 aggregate energy balances at <https://www.gov.uk/government/statistics/energy-chapter-1-digest-of-united-kingdom-energy-statistics-dukes>.

a further 23% of demand was supplied via LNG.[41] Two-thirds of the LNG came into Milford Haven's two terminals (Dragon & South Hook) and one-third into Kent's Isle of Grain. The largest individual source of imports was the Norwegian pipeline, which alone covered 57% of imports.

The share of coal in the energy mix has dropped enormously to just over 3% in 2019. There are now just four coal power plants operating in the UK, and plans are to phase them out by 2025.[42] In the four summer months of 2020 (from mid-April to mid-August), coal-fired generation was used on the grid for just one day.[43] As of today, coal's role in the energy mix is minimal.[44]

6.3.3 Power generation and increasing role of interconnectors

Figure 6.3 illustrates the evolution of UK generation over the last 30 years. It mirrors the afore-mentioned structural changes in the energy market as a whole: the

41 Dept for Business, Energy & Industrial Strategy BEIS energy statistics – the Digest of UK Energy Statistics (DUKES). In particular see Chapter 4 – natural gas, which contains the official balances and trade flows. See www.gov.uk/government/statistics/natural-gas-chapter-4-digest-of-united-kingdom-energy-statistics-dukes.

42 Department for Business, Energy and Industrial Strategy, 'Statistical Release: Energy Trends October to December 2020 and 2020' (25 March 2021) <https://assets.publishing.service.gov.uk/government/uploads/system/uploads/attachment_data/file/976000/Energy_Trends_March_2021.pdf> accessed 6 November 2022, 4.

43 Ibid., 4.

44 Although as discussed below, this proved crucial in September 2021 when winds stopped blowing.

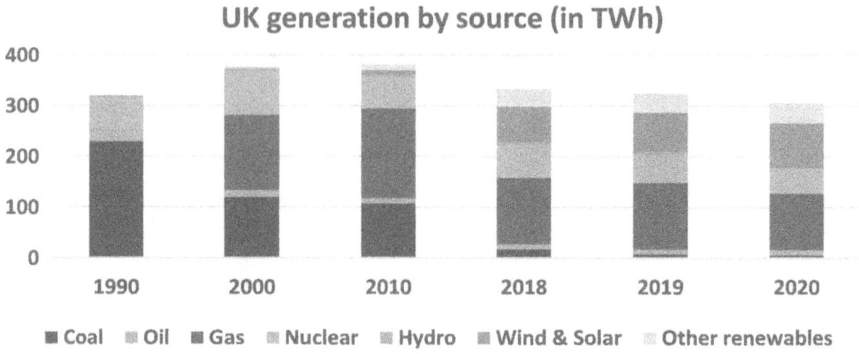

Figure 6.3 Source: Energy in Brief 2021, BEIS July 2021, page 28 at <https://assets.publishing.service.gov.uk/government/uploads/system/uploads/attachment_data/file/1016822/UK_Energy_in_Brief_2021.pdf.

almost complete elimination of coal from power generation, the important role of gas in power generation, and the impressive rise of renewables in recent years.

This chart also reveals the structural problems and challenges facing the UK in reaching net zero and renewable targets. In particular, it reveals that much of the base load capacity has been retired and has been replaced with intermittent renewables. The risks this poses to security of supply and price stability was illustrated by events in the UK power market in September 2021: calm low-wind weather conditions caused wind generation to drop, forcing in turn coal plant capacity to be brought back on at short notice, resulting in wholesale power prices rising to above £400/MWh.[45] Coupled with a big rise in wholesale gas prices, energy supply and prices have suddenly become more important politically.[46]

In aggregate, nuclear capacity from the eight existing NPPs in 2020 was 8.9 GW, representing just under 10% of UK capacity and generating 16% of UK power that year.[47] However, all the NPPs built in the late 1980s–early 1990s are due to close by 2030 (Dungeness B closed earlier than expected in June 2021). By 2030, therefore, only two nuclear power stations, Sizewell B and the new Hinckley C (expected to be commissioned in 2026), will be in operation, taking nuclear capacity down to just 4.4 GW, and thereby reducing the country‘s base load capacity further at a time of build-up of renewables.

45 Widely reported; for example, see Jillian Ambrose, 'Coal power stations to earn record sums to keep lights on' *The Guardian* (London, 14 September 2021) <www.theguardian.com/business/2021/sep/13/britain-last-coal-power-stations-to-be-paid-huge-sums-to-keep-lights-on-record-energy-prices> accessed [6 November 2022].

46 Editorial, 'Gas crisis hits more industries' *Financial Times* (London, 18 Sept 2021).

47 Department for Business, Energy & Industrial Strategy, 'Digest of UK Energy Statistics (DUKES): electricity' (26 July 2012, last updated 28 July 2021) <www.gov.uk/government/statistics/electricity-chapter-5-digest-of-united-kingdom-energy-statistics-dukes> accessed 6 November 2022, Chapter 5 (in particular 5.11).

UK nuclear capacity - all operated by EDF Energy

	type	installed capacity (GW)	start-up date	decommissioning
Dungeness B	AGR	1.09	1983	June 2021
Hartlepool	AGR	1.19	1983	by 2030
Heysham 1	AGR	1.06	1983	by 2030
Heysham 2	AGR	1.24	1988	by 2030
Hinkley Point B	AGR	0.97	1976	2022
Hunterston B	AGR	0.99	1976	2022
Torness	AGR	1.20	1988	by 2030
Sizew ell B	PWR	1.20	1995	2035
Total GW in 2020		**8.9**		
Retirements by 2030		7.7	ie, all the AGRs closed on rolling basis	
Additions		3.2	Hinkley Point C unit 1 on-stream June 2026	
Capacity from 2030		**4.4**		

Uk total generation 2020 (in TWh)	312.8
Nuclear TWh	50.3
Nuclear share	16%

source: DUKES tables 5.11

Electricity imports are much smaller in energy terms compared with gas imports. Nevertheless, as the Chart shows, the gap between generation and demand has widened since the year 2000, and net imports of over 20 TWh in 2019 accounted for 6% of electricity consumption.[48]

The UK imports electricity through several interconnectors with continental Europe. The first interconnector, IFA-1 (Interconnexion France-Angleterre), was commissioned in 1986, and was followed by others with Belgium and Netherlands. A second interconnector with France was commissioned in early 2021, the one with Norway started operating in October 2021, and the one with Denmark is under construction. Once the latter is completed in 2024, total interconnector capacity will be at 7.8 GW. All operational and planned interconnectors are listed in the table below.

Link	*Country*	*National Grid's partner*	*Commissioned/ planned start*	*Kms offshore*	*GW capacity*
IFA-1	France	RTE	1986	45	2
Britned	Netherlands	TenneT	2011	250	1
NEMO	Belgium	Elia	2019	140	1
IFA-2	France	RTE	Jan 2021	200	1
NSL	Norway	Statnett	Oct 2021	730	1.4
Viking	Denmark	Energinet	2023–2024	650	1.4
East West interconnector	Ireland	Owned by EirGrid	2012	186	0.5
Moyle	N Ireland	Mutual energy			0.5

Source: authors' compilation from interconnector websites.

48 Ibid., ch 5.1.

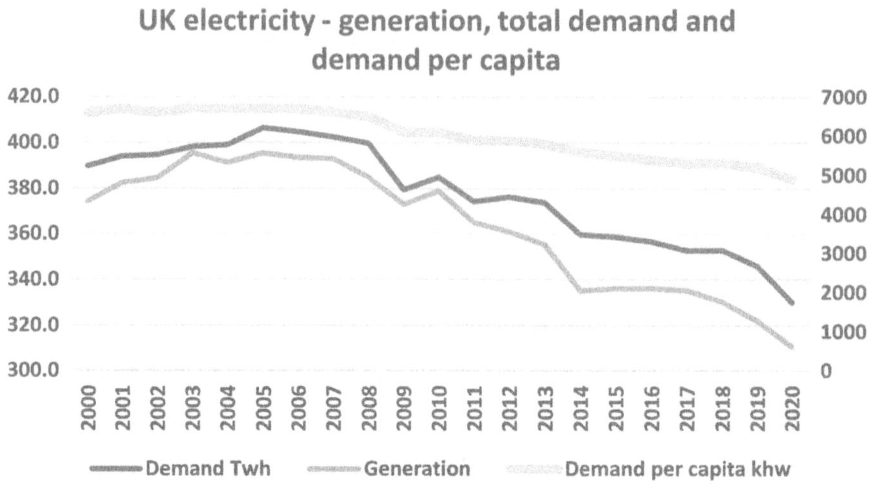

Figure 6.4 Source: DUKES, electricity Chapter 5.1 op cit.

While is it very unlikely that another gas interconnector will be built in the coming years, given the overall declining outlook for gas demand, more electricity interconnectors are planned to be built. The National Grid's latest Future Energy Scenarios (FES) envisages that power interconnector capacity could treble by 2030 to 22 GW, depending on scenario.[49] This increasing use and role of interconnectors between the UK and the EU energy market is evidence of significant level of interdependency between the electricity markets,[50] a topic discussed further in Section 6.4.

6.4 Key Provisions of TCA Concerning Renewables and Climate Change

This Section summarises the key provisions of the TCA relating to renewables and climate change. Although the TCA calls for cooperation between the EU and the UK in these areas, it contains little detail on the framework thereof. Importantly, it does not provide for any mechanism for legislative or regulatory alignment going forward. Instead, an obligation is imposed on both sides not to regress from their respective *inter alia* climate change, renewables, and other targets for 2030 as were in force in their national law at the time the TCA was being negotiated.[51] In other

49 National Grid, 'Future Energy Scenarios (FES) in five minutes' (July 2021) <www.nationalgrideso.com/document/199926/download> accessed [6 November 2022], table at 13.

50 Silke Goldberg, Brexit and Its Impact on the Energy Sector: Pulling the Plug, 12 European Energy Law Report (Martha M. Roggenkamp & Catherine Banet, eds.) 13, 22.

51 Since then, each has set higher targets for 2030. These higher targets, however, do not form part of the non-regression baseline, nor does the net zero target for 2050, which both sides have adopted since then.

words, the TCA acknowledges that there is likely to be a divergence in legislative and regulatory framework between the parties concerning *inter alia* climate change and renewables and provides a mechanism of redress should this happen.

In relation to renewables specifically, there is agreement to promote renewable energy and a reaffirmation of respective 2030 targets in Article 319. There is also an agreement in Article 320 to support the integration of electricity from renewable energy sources in respective electricity markets and an undertaking to provide support for biofuels, bioliquids, and biomass as renewable energy only if they meet robust criteria for sustainability and greenhouse gas emissions saving. In addition, there is an undertaking to ensure that producers of renewable energy are accorded reasonable and non-discriminatory terms in respective markets when procuring products and services pursuant to Article 304. Finally, the creation of a specific forum to discuss cooperation in the development of offshore renewable energy in the North Sea is provided for in Article 321 as a way to share best practices and, 'where appropriate, by facilitating the development of specific projects'.

In relation to climate change, there is a commitment to 'effectively implement ... the Paris Agreement' and an agreement to 'refrain from acts or omissions that would materially defeat the object and purpose of the Paris Agreement' in Articles 401 and 467. Importantly, pursuant to Articles 771 and 772, climate change is elevated to an 'essential element' of the TCA, enabling either party 'to terminate or suspend the operation of [the TCA]' should 'any act or omission' of the other party 'materially defeats the object and purpose of the Paris Agreement ... '. The inclusion of these provisions makes the TCA the first trade agreement in the world which makes climate change a fundamental governance provision.

In respect of carbon pricing, Article 392 obliges the parties to 'have in place an effective system of carbon pricing which covers greenhouse gas emissions from 'electricity generation, heat generation, industry and aviation'.[52] It also requires them to 'give serious thought on linking their respective'[53] ETS systems. As discussed in Chapter 1, no discussions are presently on foot to link the two ETSs.

As noted above, the TCA does not contain any regulatory alignment provisions concerning climate change, renewables, or environmental standards nor indeed any level playing field provisions.[54] Instead, an obligation of non-regression from climate and environmental levels of protection 'below the levels that are in place at the end of the transition period'[55] is set out in Chapter 7. In particular, express reference is made to the 2030 targets as set by the EU and the UK last year in the context of non-regression rather than to the zero carbon targets for 2050.

52 With aviation to be included within ETS scheme no later than two years from the date of TCA entering into force.

53 Article 392 of TCA.

54 Markus W. Gehring, 'Analysis 5 of the Brexit Deal: Environment and Climate Provisions' (22 January 2021) <http://eulawanalysis.blogspot.com/2021/01/analysis-5-of-brexit-deal-environment.htm> accessed 6 November 2022.

55 Articles 390 and 391 of TCA.

In addition, Article 411 gives each party the right to take strictly necessary and proportionate rebalancing measures in circumstances where there is a significant divergence in the parties' future policies and priorities in respect of climate protection and including subsidy control results which materially impact on trade or investment.

Although 'the combination of elevating climate change to an essential element of the treaty, strong non-regression provisions and future balancing measures mean that in this field the TCA is trailblazing',[56] what is key, however, is that at present there is no alignment between the two on how to move to net zero nor much detail on how to ensure that close cooperation on climate is actually achieved. Most importantly, there is no provision on a common rulebook on energy trading, an issue which will be discussed in the following Section.

6.5 Implications of Brexit for UK's Renewables Policies and Climate Change Targets

This Section discusses the implications of the UK's departure from the EU for achieving its renewables policies and climate change targets. In order to appreciate the nature and scope of these implications, it is very important to recall that UK has been at the vanguard of the development of energy and climate policy. In particular, while the UK was part of the EU, UK officials played a key role in designing the liberalisation of the EU energy market. It was also a strong supporter of the EU Energy Union as a means of ensuring security of supply and reducing energy costs to consumers.[57] It was also the first country in the world to introduce the carbon tax, and the Climate Change Act 2008 was the first comprehensive national climate legislation in the world. The UK has over the years also continuously set the bar for greenhouse gas emissions higher than the EU and did so again in 2020.[58]

In other words, its energy and climate change policies have always had an independent pull. In this regard, at least, the departure from the EU will not change matters from the UK's perspective.[59] In fact, being outside the EU may help the UK (i) adopt the necessary legislative and regulatory climate change framework more quickly and (ii) ensure that such framework is more reflective of and aligned with its own energy fundamentals.[60] While it was part of the EU, the UK was

56 Markus W. Gehring, 'Analysis 5 of the Brexit Deal: Environment and Climate Provisions' (22 January 2021) <http://eulawanalysis.blogspot.com/2021/01/analysis-5-of-brexit-deal-environment.htm> accessed 6 November 2022.

57 Thane Gustafson, *The Bridge – Natural Gas in a Divided Europe* (Harvard University Press 2020) chs 6 and 7.

58 For example in 2016 the UK Parliament approved the fifth carbon budget that envisaged a 57% drop in CO_2 emissions from the 1990 levels by the period 2028–2032, thereby setting the bar higher than the EU, which required a 40% cut by 2030.

59 See Chapter 1 for the implications of Brexit regarding renewables from the EU's perspective.

60 Dave Keating, 'U.K. Falls Out of EU Emissions Trading At Midnight Tonight' *Forbes* (Jersey City, 31 December 2020) <www.forbes.com/sites/davekeating/2021/12/31/uk-falls-out-of-eu-emissions-trading-at-midnight-tonight> accessed 6 November 2022.

against prescribing national renewables and other targets and favoured a technology neutral approach to achieving them. In this regard it clashed with Germany and some other EU countries.[61] As discussed in Section 6.1, the White Paper reiterates the UK's technology neutral approach and, unlike the EU Commission's position papers, takes a strong pro-nuclear stance. As the current negotiations on the roadmap to 2050 at EU level reveal, one of the key challenges to EU achieving its climate change targets is the significant divergence in approaches proposed, on the one hand, by EU Member States, where coal or lignite represent a large component in the energy mix (for example Poland and most of south east Europe); and, on the other hand, by the wealthier countries of northwest Europe which are much further down the renewables route. The difference in approach stems from the divergence in their energy fundamentals. Albeit entirely understandable, it makes any consensus on the roadmap for achieving the 2030 and 2050 targets difficult to achieve. There is also a growing schism between anti-nuclear countries led by Germany and Austria and the countries of Central and Eastern Europe (CEE), which see nuclear as key to their decarbonisation.[62] The unfortunate prescriptive approach to legislating at the EU level[63] further exacerbates these differences, since any legislative roadmap agreed by consensus is unlikely to give an individual EU Member State sufficient flexibility to draw up the most optimal decarbonisation approach, in terms of cost and/or best fit, for itself. The inability to obtain EU funding for gas and nuclear projects and the difficulty in getting state aid clearance for nuclear projects are just a few examples of how EU rules limit the choices of EU Member States in devising their individual decarbonisation trajectories.[64]

With the decarbonisation and energy transition trajectory and targets set at the international (rather than EU) level, this new additional flexibility in drawing up the legislative and regulatory framework may prove key to enabling the UK to achieve its renewable and climate change targets – provided, however, that the key implications of Brexit for these targets discussed in turn below can be overcome. At the time of writing this Chapter, this is far from clear.

61 Luigi Serenelli, 'Brexit: A Chance for European Countries to Deepen Cooperation on Renewables?' (Youris, 14 September 2016) <www.youris.com/Energy/Renewables/Brexit-A-Chance-For-European-Countries-To-Deepen-Cooperation-On-Renewables.kl> accessed 6 November 2022.

62 Tim Gosling, 'Energy Transitions Generate Friction in Central Europe' *Reporting Democracy* (Prague, 6 April 2021) <https://balkaninsight.com/2021/04/06/energy-transitions-generate-friction-in-central-europe> accessed 6 November 2022.

63 The prescriptive approach to drafting legislation at the EU level is by no means unavoidable. A non-prescriptive gold standard approach would in fact be better suited to achieving energy transition.

64 See Regulation 2022/869 on guidelines for trans-European energy infrastructure, amending Regulations (EC) No 715/2009, (EU) 2019/942 and (EU) 2019/943 and Directives 2009/73/EC and (EU) 2019/944, and repealing Regulation (EU) No 347/2013, <https://eur-lex.europa.eu/legal-content/EN/TXT/HTML/?uri=CELEX:32022R0869&from=EN, accessed on 15 December 2022.

6.5.1 Implications of UK leaving the EU ETS

In its CB, the CCC identified the UK leaving the EU ETS and having to setup its own ETS as potentially impacting on UK's ability to achieve its climate change targets. It noted that although a standalone scheme 'may offer more policy autonomy' than linking the scheme to the EU ETS, it risked (i) low liquidity in the long term, unless sectoral coverage was expanded; (ii) significant price volatility especially in the early days of the scheme; and (iii) loss of competitiveness of UK industry due to differentiations in regulatory rules.[65]

Although during the Brexit negotiations both the UK and the EU expressed a preference for linked ETSs, a standalone UK ETS was established under the Greenhouse Gas Emissions Trading Scheme Order 2020[66] and the Greenhouse Gas Emissions Trading Scheme (Amendment) Order 2020.[67] It was launched following the end of the Brexit Transition Period on 1 January 2021.[68] As currently adopted, the UK ETS closely follows the EU ETS scheme since its main objective was to provide continuity with the way the EU ETS system regulated greenhouse gas emissions pre Brexit. There are, however, differences between the two. A key difference is that the UK's emissions cap is set at 5% below the cap which was notionally set for Phase IV (2021 to 2030) of the EU ETS.[69] With fewer allowances available, having a lower cap may make it harder for UK participants to be as competitive as their EU counterparts. With little signs of the two systems being linked in the near future, the UK industry may lose competitiveness since the UK ETS market is smaller than the EU ETS one. As discussed in Chapter 1, the 'EU ETS is the largest multi-country and multi sector greenhouse gas emissions trading system in the world covering more than 11,000 power stations and industrial actors … [of which] 1000 … were in the UK' before Brexit.[70] This may also drive the price of carbon in the UK up.

The slow pace in the adoption of regulation and rules governing the UK ETS system has made it very difficult for the participants in the market to fully understand and prepare for the changes. By way of example, the first drafts of the auctioning regulations were only published in February 2021, with further details on the

65 Letter from Lord Deben to Rt Hon. Kwasi Kwarteng MP, Roseanna Cunningham MSP, Lesley Griffiths AM and Dr. Denis McMahon about the future of carbon pricing (7 August 2019) <www.theccc.org.uk/publication/letter-the-future-of-carbon-pricing> accessed 6 November 2022.

66 The Greenhouse Gas Emissions Trading Scheme, Order 2020, SI 2020/1265.

67 The Greenhouse Gas Emissions Trading Scheme (Amendment), Order 2020, SI 2020/1557.

68 As discussed in Chapter 11, Northern Ireland, power generators, as per Article 9 and Annex 4 of the Protocol on Ireland/Northern Ireland, remain part of the EU ETS. The UK remained in the EU ETS during the transition period and operators must therefore comply with obligations relating to the 2020 scheme year, which ended on 30 April 2021.

69 Elena Ares, 'The UK Emissions Trading Scheme' (House of Commons, Briefing Paper Number 9212, 4 May 2021) < https://researchbriefings.files.parliament.uk/documents/CBP-9212/CBP-9212.pdf> accessed 6 November 2022. The 5% lower cap was set in light of UK's commitment to reaching net-zero emissions by 2050.

70 House of Lords, page 2.

scheme provided in the Industrial Decarbonisation Strategy published in March, albeit the first auctions were scheduled for May. Moreover, various aspects of the scheme were still subject to approval and temporary or further guidance a month before participants were required to surrender their EU ETS allowances, adding further uncertainty. This legal uncertainty together with significant additional paperwork have undoubtedly translated into additional costs to companies.

With the TCA committing the UK and the EU only to exploring options of linking the two schemes, there is at present little expectation that such a link will occur in the foreseeable future. Accordingly, these cost and other implications are expected to remain of concern going forward.

6.5.2 Implications of Brexit for the operation and management of gas and power interconnectors

The implications of Brexit for the operation and management of gas and power interconnectors and ensuring the inter-operability of the UK energy system with that of the EU is probably the most important one. In particular, and as discussed in Section 6.2, the UK is at present a net importer of gas and electricity and will very likely remain so beyond 2030. Even in a best-case scenario, where new nuclear capacity comes online by 2030, the role of the gas and power interconnectors with the EU and EFTA countries is and will be key for ensuring the stability and flexibility of a UK energy system largely driven by offshore wind. This is because interconnectors allow the electricity generated to be fully utilised by transferring it to markets in which demand is greatest.[71]

The UK's dependence on interconnectors as a balancing resource for achieving the set targets becomes even greater if new nuclear capacity is not constructed on time. As discussed in Section 6.1, all of the CCC's scenarios for achieving the renewables and decarbonisation targets assume that new nuclear capacity will come on line by the time the existing capacity is decommissioned in 2030 and that capacity on the power interconnectors will more than double to 18 GW by 2050.[72] In particular, the CCC envisages that two large-scale NPPs will be commissioned by then. However, nuclear energy is very controversial due to high costs, long construction time, and environmental implications. There are also geopolitical concerns around Chinese participation in such projects. It is, therefore, very unlikely that the nuclear targets will be achieved. Consequently, the role of power interconnectors in ensuring the stability of the energy system and achieving the renewables and decarbonisation targets for the UK energy system expected to be dominated by intermittent solar and wind will be even more important.

71 Anthony Froggatt and others, *Staying Connected: Key Elements for UK-EU27 Energy Cooperation After Brexit* (Chatham House, 10 May 2017) <www.chathamhouse.org/sites/default/files/publications/research/2017-05-10-staying-connected-energy-cooperation-brexit-froggatt-wright-lockwood.pdf> accessed 6 November 2022, 14.

72 CB (n 19) 136.

And yet, as discussed by Goldberg in Chapter 2, the departure from the EU has made the operation and management of the gas and power interconnectors more complex and costly.[73] This is because the UK market has been decoupled from the European price coupling mechanism. This in turn has meant inter alia loss of access to the joint allocation office, the single platform for allocation of long-term electricity capacity and short notice electricity balancing. The move away from implicit day-ahead allocation under the price-based market coupling mechanism to explicit day-ahead allocation cross border capacity is less efficient and more costly.

As noted in Section 6.3, the TCA does not provide any common rulebook regarding energy nor any mechanism for ensuring regulatory alignment between the UK and EU energy markets. The steps made by the Specialised Committee of Energy, established under the TCA to establish a new trading arrangement on the basis of multi-region loose volume coupling, will not, as explained by Goldberg, come about quickly and even then will not result in trading arrangements between the EU and the UK that will be as seamless and efficient as the price coupling arrangements within the EU electricity market. Moreover, and until then, the trading inefficiency will result in energy prices in the UK being higher as evidenced in Goldberg's Chapter. That this increase in complexity and costs will remain going forward is clear from Chapter 12. As Jean-Christophe Fueeg explains in Chapter 12, a lack of inter-operability between the Swiss and EU electricity markets remains, despite Switzerland transposing all 'main provisions of EU electricity market legislation' (including related EU competition standards and environmental acquis).[74]

Furthermore, as explained by Goldberg in Chapter 2, although the TCA provides for continuity in the regulatory framework for existing interconnectors, the fact that the energy Chapter of the TCA may cease to be in force after 30 June 2026[75] makes planning more difficult and uncertain and consequently also more costly. Goldberg also highlights the uncertainty concerning the ability of UK–EU interconnectors to benefit from the Project of Mutual Interest status including faster permitting and access to EU funding.

6.5.3 Offshore wind

As discussed in Section 6.1, the construction of up to 40 GW of offshore wind capacity by 2030 and around 100 GW by 2050 represents a key supply side element to UK achieving its renewables and climate change targets. Given the enormity of this new capacity creation, which requires the wholesale transformation of

73 For further details of the study by EFET regarding the increased costs of electricity trading, see note 31 in Chapter 2.

74 Commission Regulation (EU) 2015/1222 establishing a guideline on capacity allocation and congestion management' [2015] OJ L 197/24.

75 See Article 33 of TCA.

UK generation from a fossil-fuel and nuclear based system to one predominantly based on renewables, the lack of detail on the legislative and regulatory roadmap is of concern. The permitting, financing, and supply-chain challenges given the relatively short timescale are considerable and haven't been addressed so far in any of the government or CCC documents. Given that the installation of 40 GW of offshore wind will cover the ocean floor the size of Yorkshire, the opposition to its installation on environmental grounds is likely to be considerable. The considerable uncertainty regarding environmental law and standards in post-Brexit UK, discussed by Reeves and Sheridan in Chapter 8, is likely to further amplify the permitting, financing, and supply-chain challenges.

6.5.4 Implications of Brexit for investment

The colossal size of the investment needed in the coming decades to achieve the government's targets was discussed in Section 6.1. The UK government acknowledges in its White Paper that business confidence is key to such investment. Yet, and regrettably, energy had not been a high priority area in the Brexit negotiations. The regulatory uncertainty over the last 5 years across the energy sector has been 'prolonged and unprecedented'.[76] Moreover, as the discussion in this Chapter and elsewhere in this book has revealed, Brexit has caused huge amount of legislative upheaval. The legal uncertainty continues.

The achievement of the decarbonisation goals will require a radical rewrite of legislative and regulatory frameworks for all sectors of the economy. Accordingly, it could be argued that the legislative changes necessitated by Brexit are relatively small compared to these, and that being outside the EU will enable the UK government to more readily address the concerns of business then staying within the EU. With detail frameworks yet to be published, it is too early to say whether the additional flexibility and agility gained from being outside the EU will be used by the UK to provide a more stable and certain legislative and regulatory environment than one which the EU will be adopting as part of its roadmap to achieving its decarbonisation goals. However, things do not look encouraging at the moment. As this book shows, Brexit has undoubtedly added further uncertainty to an energy sector already in transition and facing significant uncertainty.

6.5.5 Increased labour and other costs, access to research and development (R&D)

Brexit has caused a material disruption to the pattern of the UK's trade with the EU, labour movements, and participation in EU research and development

76 See Chapter 2.

programmes.[77] It will take time for trade to rebalance and overall economic issues between the UK and EU to be resolved and relationships restructured. For net zero targets to be achieved, it is critical that there is close and frictionless interaction with EU-based companies and institutions.

One tangible example of the importance of supply chains operating smoothly to achieving net zero targets relates to offshore wind power supply chain. The UK itself manufactures very little offshore wind equipment. The sector is dominated by foreign companies. For example, turbine design and manufacturing are dominated by two companies, Siemens Gamesa (Germany–Spain venture) and Vestas (Denmark). These two companies have supplied over 90% of the offshore capacity installed in Europe to date.[78] General Electric, a US company, will enter the UK turbine market in the coming months with its turbines ordered for what will be the world's largest offshore wind farm, Dogger Bank. A further key component for offshore wind turbines are cables. The inter-array cables linking the individual turbines and the main export cables to bring the power to shore are also predominantly foreign manufactured.

6.6 Possible Steps to Minimise the Impact of Brexit for Achieving Renewable and Climate Change Targets

This Section discusses the steps which the UK government ought to consider taking to minimise the negative impacts of Brexit on its ability to achieve its decarbonisation targets.

The first step would be to remove regulatory and investment uncertainty arising from the fact that energy related provisions in the TCA remain in force only until 2026. Although there is a possibility for the application of these to be rolled over, significant uncertainty at present remains as to the future of UK–EU energy relations. Article 33 of the TCA envisages that more detailed agreement on energy matters will be reached going forward, and steps should be taken in earnest to do so. Only 16 pages of this 1,200-page document are dedicated to energy relations between the UK and EU post-Brexit.

Second, the government should take steps urgently to reduce the uncertainty around the UK's investment and regulatory regimes if it wants to reach net zero by 2050. As discussed in a prior Section, where offshore wind supply chains are dominated by foreign manufacturers of equipment, without a stable framework

77 Office of Budget Responsibility, *Economic and Fiscal Outlook – October 2021* (27 October 2021) <https://obr.uk/efo/economic-and-fiscal-outlook-october-2021> accessed 6 November 2022; Institute for Government, 'Supply Chain Problems' (2021) <https://www.instituteforgovernment.org.uk/publication/supply-chains> accessed 6 November 2022.

78 Wind Europe, 'Offshore Wind in Europe – key trends and statistics 2020' (8 February 2021) <https://windeurope.org/intelligence-platform/product/offshore-wind-in-europe-key-trends-and-statistics-2020> accessed6 November 2022, 24.

the UK is unlikely to attract the needed investment from abroad.[79] The same can be said regarding investments in the nuclear energy. The lack of detail in the government's hydrogen strategy regarding *inter alia* the hydrogen business model, the low-carbon hydrogen standard, and the Net Zero Hydrogen Fund is putting off both local and foreign investors from investing in this new technology.[80]

Third, maintaining and strengthening relations with Norway are essential to the UK's achieving of its goals. With the North Sea Link (NSL) electricity interconnector now online and Norway supplying one-third of the UK's gas needs,[81] the importance of Norway as an energy provider is evident. The September 2021 agreement on electricity goes a considerable way to putting this relationship on a firmer legal footing.[82]

Fourth, steps ought to be taken to shield energy from party politics by creating a cross-party Parliamentary energy body, thereby enabling long-term frameworks to be set beyond the 5-year Parliamentary cycle.

Fifth, and crucially, risk analysis must be conducted in respect of the government's and CCC's proposed routes to achieving 2035 and 2050 targets in particular as concerns hydrogen, CCS, and batteries, and appropriate mitigation measures must be designed which provide for alternatives should those technologies not deliver.

79 Supply chain issues lie outside the scope of this Chapter, but are critical. For some details on supply chain, see ibid.

80 Allen & Overy, 'UK Hydrogen Strategy – Top Ten Takeaways' (8 September 2021) <www.allenovery.com/en-gb/germany/news-and-insights/publications/uk-hydrogen-strategy-top-ten-takeaways> accessed 6 November 2022.

81 Department for Business, Energy & Industrial Strategy, 'Joint statement of Kwarteng and Bru' (28 June 2021) <www.gov.uk/government/news/joint-statement-from-uk-secretary-of-state-kwasi-kwarteng-and-the-norwegian-minister-for-energy-and-petroleum-tina-bru> accessed 6 November 2022.

82 *Agreement between the United Kingdom of Great Britain and Northern Ireland and the Kingdom of Norway on Cross-Border Trade in Electricity and Cooperation on Electricity Interconnection* (Treaty Series No.18, 16 September 2021) <www.gov.uk/government/publications/uknorway-agreement-on-cross-border-trade-in-electricity-and-cooperation-on-electricity-interconnection-ts-no182021> accessed 6 November 2022.

7 The Impact of Brexit on EU Renewable Energy and Climate Change Policy

Jana Nysten and Fabian Pause

7.1 Introduction

With the departure of the UK from the EU at the end of 2020, the EU lost not only one of its members, but also one of the key contributors to its renewable energy and climate goals and policies.[1] This Chapter seeks to explain the impact Brexit has on EU policy regarding the development of renewable energy sources (RES) and its main tool for achieving a reduction in greenhouse gas (GHG) emissions, namely the EU Emissions Trading Scheme (ETS).

7.2 Impact on EU RES policy and objectives post-Brexit

The EU has pursued an ambitious and targeted RES policy for nearly two decades. This policy was first formalised in 2001 with the publication of the original directive on the support to electricity from RES (the RES Directive).[2] Under Art. 3 of the RES Directive, EU Member States were required to 'take appropriate steps to encourage greater consumption of electricity produced from renewable energy sources in conformity with the national indicative targets'. These targets were to be set by each EU Member State for itself and were not binding in nature, albeit they had to take into account certain reference values in the Annex to the RES Directive. These reference values were in turn calculated based on, inter alia, the starting point as well as the potential of the EU Member State for the development of electricity from renewable sources (RES-E).[3] By way of

1 Note that this Chapter does not contain specifics on the isle of Ireland. Northern Ireland is part of the UK and subject to Brexit, although certain special rules apply. Ireland, however, is still a Member State. For more on that, see Chapter 11 in this book.

2 Directive (EU) 2001/77/EC of the European Parliament and of the Council of 27 September 2001 on the promotion of electricity produced from renewable energy sources in the internal electricity market [2001] OJ 2 283/33.

3 Compare: Art. 3 par. 2 RES Directive; see: Maxian Rusche, EU Renewable Electricity Law and Policy (Cambridge 2015) 32; For more general information on EU RES policy development, see: Veum/Pause/Kahles/Wizinger et al., Study on the impact assessment for a new Directive mainstreaming deployment of renewable energy and ensuring that the EU meets its 2030 renewable energy target, Final task 1 & 2 report: 'Mainstreaming RES', Amsterdam, 30 November 2016.

DOI: 10.4324/9781003364337-8

example, as RES-E accounted for 1.7% of the UK's total energy production in 1997, the reference value was set at 10% by 2010 – a target which the UK successfully met.[4]

The system of setting national targets for EU Member States to meet the EU's aggregate RES-E target continued under the regime of the first Renewable Energy Directive (the RE Directive).[5] However, the RE Directive introduced two key changes to the regime. Firstly, national targets were made legally binding and were set by the EU legislature rather than being calculated in accordance with the reference values.[6] Secondly, the RE Directive was no longer restricted to electricity, but pertained to all forms of energy which came from renewable sources. While the aggregate EU target was increased to 20% by 2020, the target for the UK, for example, which had produced only 1.3 % of its energy from RES in 2005, was set at 15% for 2020.[7] The UK achieved this goal in a timely manner and thus contributed to the EU meeting its aggregate target of 20% by 2020.[8]

Recently, under the regime of the 2018 Renewable Energy Directive Recast (the RE Directive II),[9] the EU has committed to increasing the share of energy from RES in final consumption by at least 32% by 2030.[10] The EU introduced a mechanism for energy governance (the Governance Regime) in order to achieve this target.[11] Under the Governance Regime, EU Member States were to develop so-called 'Integrated National Energy and Climate Plans' (NECPs). The NECPs were to contain, inter alia, a national contribution for the development of RES, as well as a brief description of the policies and measures required to achieve it.[12]

4 See Buck, EU-Maßnahmen zum Erreichen des EU-Erneuerbaren-Ziels – Chancen und Herausforderungen, Stiftung Umweltenergierecht, Fachgespräch, Berlin, 14 March 2018.

5 Directive (EU) 2009/28/EC of the European Parliament and of the Council of 23 April 2009 on the promotion of the use of energy from renewable sources and amending and subsequently repealing Directives 2001/77/EC and 2003/30/EC [2009] OJ 2 140/16.

6 Art 3(1); Annex RE Directive. Also: For more information on the history and functioning of the EU renewable energy support policy see: Nysten, The EU Clean Energy Package (ED. 2020), Technical Report, European University Institute, Florence, 17 November 2020; Maxian Rusche, EU Renewable Electricity Law and Policy (Cambridge 2015) 36; *Jensen/Gehring*, Renewable Energy in the Member States of the EU, Chapter 27 – United Kingdom, pp. 1198–1202.

7 Annex I RE Directive.

8 For the latest projections from 2020 see: 'The Commission, Report from the Commission to the European Parliament, the Council, the European Economic and Social Committee and the Committee of the Regions, Renewable Energy Progress Report', COM(2020)925, final, v. 14 October 2020.

9 Directive (EU) 2018/2001 of the European Parliament and of the Council of 11 December 2018 on the promotion of the use of energy from renewable sources [2018] OJ 2 328/82.

10 See: Art. 3 Par. 1 RE Directive II.

11 Regulation (EU) 2018/1999 of the European Parliament and of the Council of 11 December 2018 on the Governance of the Energy Union and Climate Action [2018] OJ 2 328/1.

12 In detail on how the system is set up and supposed to work, see e.g.: Pause/Kahles, Die finalen Rechtsakte des EU-Winterpakets 'Saubere Energie für alle Europäer' – Governance für die Energieunion und Erneuerbare Energien (Teil 1), Zeitschrift für die gesamte Energierechtspraxis (ER), 2019, S. 9-17; Pause, 'Saubere Energie für alle Europäer' – Was bringt das Legislativpaket der EU? Zeitschrift für Umweltrecht (ZUR) 2019, S 387–396.

7.2.1 Separate goals for the EU and the UK

The Trade and Cooperation Agreement (TCA) contains several provisions on renewable energy, but it does not lay down any specific goals for either party in the field of renewable energy, nor does it prescribe any specific mechanisms for achieving these goals. Rather, it stresses that both the UK and the EU will adhere to their renewable energy and climate goals as set out in their respective laws.[13]

The EU's goal of 32% RES by 2030 and the Governance Regime were adopted at a time when the UK had already decided to leave the EU, but had not yet left. Accordingly, and as confirmed by the TCA,[14] the EU's goal remains in place and is to be achieved among the EU 27 Member States without the contribution of the UK. The UK therefore did not submit its final NECP under the Governance Regime.[15]

The Commission's assessment of the final NECPs submitted by the remaining EU Member States concluded that, if fully implemented, they will enable the EU to successfully meet its 2030 goal.[16] Accordingly, if the NECPs are successfully implemented, Brexit will have had little impact on the EU's ability to meet its original 2030 objective. However, it is worth noting that with the recent proposals under the so-called 'Fit for 55' package, the EU is considering raising the RES target to at least 40% in 2030.[17] Still, the corresponding calculations have been made without contribution from the UK, and the relevance of Brexit is thus limited.

7.2.2 Common objectives remain – with some enforcement measures behind them

Although the UK will no longer take part in the Governance Regime, the EU and the UK are still aligned in achieving the objectives of the Paris Agreement (PA).[18] As signatories to the PA, they have committed to limiting global warming

13 Art.319(2) and (3) of the TCA.

14 Art. 319(2) and (3) of the TCA.

15 Although this might constitute a breach of the Withdrawal Agreement, under which the UK had to – for the transitional period until the end of 2020 – abide by the rules of the RED II.

16 See above: Footnote 12. Also: Nysten, EU Law on RES support schemes – Art. 4 RE Directive II vs State Aid Law, Florence School of Regulation, Course EU Clean Energy Package, Florence; Also, see Nysten; The new provisions of the RE Directive II on RES-E support schemes Implementation and interaction with the EEAG, Upcoming revision of the Guidelines on State aid for environmental protection and energy 2014–2020 with regard to renewable electricity, Brussels.

17 See: Proposal for a Directive Of the European Parliament and of the Council amending Directive (2018/2001) of the European Parliament and of the Council Regulation (EU) 2018/1999 of the European Parliament and of the Council and Directive 98/70/EC of the European Parliament and of the Council as regards the promotion of energy from renewable sources, and repealing Council Directive (EU) 2015/652, COM/2021/557 eur-lex.europa.eu/legal-content/EN/TXT/?uri=CELEX%3A52021PC0557accessed 9 November 2021.

18 On the UK policy objectives, see infra, Chapter 6.

to below 2°C, and preferably to below 1.5°C compared to pre-industrial levels, and pledged to make national contributions towards this common objective.[19] Under the United Nations Framework Convention on Climate Change (UNFCCC), of which the aforementioned PA is part,[20] parties to the Convention submit so-called Nationally Determined Contributions estimating the amount of greenhouse gas (GHG) emissions they will be able/intend to save in a given time period. The first 'commitment period' covers the time period from the date of the PA until 2030. Prior to Brexit, the EU in 2016 had originally submitted an undertaking to reduce its GHG emissions by at least 40% by 2030.[21] The EU, this time excluding the UK, then increased its commitment from 40% to 55% in 2020 in line with its updated internal policy.[22] Meanwhile, the UK has committed to reduce its domestic GHG emissions by at least 68% by 2030.[23]

The common objective of achieving the UK and EU's respective commitments of limiting climate change under the international framework, as well as not taking any actions to undermine the pursuit of the objective, has been formalised in the TCA. Further, the EU and the UK included a provision in the TCA triggering its suspension in case either of them breached its commitments under the PA.[24] In other words, their commitments under the PA are now enforceable as between them. The potential suspension of certain provisions of the TCA, such as those relating zero tariffs and zero quotas on traded goods between the parties, may turn into a powerful sanctioning mechanism.

19 Paris Agreement, adopted at the 21st Conference of the Parties, Paris Climate Change Conference – November 2015.

20 Under the United Nations Framework Convention on Climate Change (UNFCCC), which entered into force in 1994, the 197 countries who ratified the convention first officially recognised that there is a problem and consequently agreed to work together on preventing 'dangerous' human interference with the climate system. The UNFCCC framework features several protocols and sets up a comprehensive system for the reporting and monitoring of GHG emissions. More information as well as the texts of the convention and protocols+, see <https://unfccc.int/process-and-meetings/the-convention/what-is-the-united-nations-framework-convention-on-climate-change> accessed 1 December 2021.

21 Submission by Latvia and the Commission on behalf of the Commission and its Member States, Riga, 16 December, 2015, available at: www4.unfccc.int/sites/ndcstaging/PublishedDocuments/European%20Union%20First/LV-03-06-EU%20INDC(Archived).pdf accessed 8 November 2022.

22 Update of the NDC of the European Union and its Member States, Berlin, 17 December 2020 //www4.unfccc.int/sites/ndcstaging/PublishedDocuments/European%20Union%20First/EU_NDC_Submission_December%202020.pdf> accessed 8 February 2022.

23 United Kingdom of Great Britain and Northern Ireland's Nationally Determined Contribution of 12 December 2020 available at: www4.unfccc.int/sites/ndcstaging/PublishedDocuments/United%20Kingdom%20of%20Great%20Britain%20and%20Northern%20Ireland%20First/UK%20Nationally%20Determined%20Contribution.pdf accessed 9 November 2021. For more details on the UK policy, see infra, Chapter 6.

24 Breaches of the commitments with regards to climate change mitigation under those provisions would be subject to a dispute settlement system under the Brexit Agreement – which would allow the other party to suspend its application. For details, see: Part VI Brexit Agreement

7.2.3 RES support schemes in the EU post-Brexit

RES support schemes within the EU are subject to certain legal rules, primarily set out in the RE Directive and the State aid framework. While the latter is also discussed elsewhere in this publication,[25] the following will briefly sketch the content of the provisions as they continue to apply post-Brexit to the EU Member States. As the UK is no longer an EU Member State, the RE Directive will no longer be relevant for the design of its national support schemes. However, some provisions of the Brexit Agreement, in particular the rules on State aid or subsidies, need to be respected and may thus have consequences for the design of the UK's new support scheme for renewable energy sources (RES).

7.2.3.1 National support schemes under the RE Directive II

With regards to the mechanisms required to achieve the goal of increasing the share of RES in the EU, Art. 4 RE Directive II leaves it to each EU Member State to decide how to achieve their contribution to the common EU renewable energy target.[26] Art. 4 RE Directive II outlines key criteria which support schemes need to meet, most of which have been developed in the field of EU State Aid law. Art. 107 par. 1 of the Treaty on the Functioning of the European Union (TFEU) states that State aid measures are illegal, unless they are exempt or can be justified and approved by the Commission.[27] It has turned out to be a powerful provision in the development of RES support schemes in the EU.

Under Art. 4 RE Directive II, support for RES-E shall be granted in an 'open, transparent, competitive, non-discriminatory and cost-effective manner', which is largely understood to pertain to the relevant tendering procedures.[28] However, exceptions may apply for small installations and demonstration projects, and EU

25 See infra Chapter 6.

26 For a detailed assessment, see: Nysten, EU Law on RES support schemes – Art. 4 RED-II vs State Aid Law, Florence School of Regulation, Course EU Clean Energy Package, Florence 12 May 2020; also, see Nysten; The new provisions of the RE Directive-II on RES-E support schemes Implementation and interaction with the EEAG, Upcoming revision of the Guidelines on State aid for environmental protection and energy 2014-–020 with regard to renewable electricity, Brussels, 27 November 2019.

27 *State aid* is defined as 'aid granted by a Member State or through State resources in any form whatsoever which distorts or threatens to distort competition by favouring certain undertakings or the production of certain goods shall, in so far as it affects trade between Member States' and is as a matter of principle declared incompatible with the internal market under Art. 107 par. 1 TFEU. However, exceptions apply – conditional to the approval of the Commission – inter alia for 'aid to facilitate the development of certain economic activities or of certain eco-nomic areas, where such aid does not adversely affect trading conditions to an extent contrary to the common interest' (Art. 107 par. 3 lit. c TFEU) based on which the exceptions and thus national support schemes for RES have evolved.

28 Nysten, Europarechtliche Handlungsspielräume Deutschlands bei der Förderung von Strom aus erneuerbaren Energien, Würzburger Studie zum Umweltenergierecht Nr. 15 vom 09 March 2020.

Member States may consider introducing mechanisms for regional diversification and for cost-efficient system integration. Similarly, Art. 4 par. 5 RE Directive II allows, under certain conditions, for technology-specific support, as opposed to tendering procedures in which all technologies compete against each other.[29]

Since 2014, before the introduction of the RE Directive II, EU Member States' national support schemes were exhibiting a trend towards tendering procedures. Most of those national policy measures have now been classified as State aid under Art. 107 TFEU, and thus subjected to a review and approval procedure by the Commission. Accordingly, the Directorate-General for Competition – the unit responsible for State aid control – has been able to influence their design, notably through the adoption and practice around the Environmental and Energy State Aid Guidelines 2014–2020 (the Guidelines).[30] While the Guidelines are not binding on the EU Member States – and certainly not on the UK or any other non-EU countries – they set out the design features which would, in the view of the Commission, make national support schemes compatible with the rules of the internal market. The Guidelines also introduced a regime of tendering procedures for renewable electricity and required EU Member States to justify any distinctions they wished to make between the different technologies.[31] EU Member States subsequently started experimenting with such systems with mixed results, and by the time the RE Directive II was adopted, most EU Member States had some form of market-orientated focus in their national RES-E support policies.[32]

The TCA does not contain any provisions which amend or otherwise interfere with the application of this regime of the RE Directive II and the State aid rules within the EU. Rather, as the UK is no longer an EU Member State, those provisions will simply no longer apply to the UK. They remain in force with respect to the remaining EU Member States. However, the TCA does contain a Chapter on subsidies in the field of energy and the environment, which will be looked at next.

29 Nysten, Europarechtliche Handlungsspielräume Deutschlands bei der Förderung von Strom aus erneuerbaren Energien, Würzburger Studie zum Umweltenergierecht Nr. 15 vom 09 March 2020, p. 19.

30 The Commission, Communication, Guidelines on State aid for environmental protection and energy 2014–2020, OJ C 200/1, 28 June 2014, as prolonged until the end of 2021 by the Commission, Communication of 08 July 2020, OJ C 224/02; see in general: Maxian Rusche, EU Renewable Electricity Law and Policy (Cambridge, 2015) pp. 193–196.

31 Note that as of 27 January 2022, the new Guidelines 2022–2030 entered into force. Those follow a different system than the one described below; however, they apply the same principles when it comes to support of RES. See, e.g., Kahles/Kamm/Pause, Die neuen Leitlinen für Klima-, Umweltschutz- und Energie-Beihilfen (KUEBLL), Green Deal erklärt Spezial, 09 February 2022, accessible at <https://stiftung-umweltenergierecht.de/wp-content/uploads/2022/02/Stiftung-Umweltenergierecht_Green-Deal-erklaert-SPEZIAL_2022-02-09.pdf> last visited 10 February 2022.

32 For more information, see: Kahles/Pause, The Influence of European State Aid Law on the Design of Support Schemes for Electricity from Renewable Energy Sources in Germany and Other Member States, in: Gawel/Strunz/Lehmann/Purkus (Eds.), The European Dimension of Germany's Energy, Transition – Opportunities and Conflicts, 2019.

7.2.3.2 State aid control in the TCA

Post-Brexit, the criteria of Art. 4 RE Directive II will no longer apply to the UK, and neither will the provisions of Art. 107 TFEU on State aid. The Commission will therefore no longer exercise any supervisory function of the UK's RES support schemes through the provisions on State aid control. However, the parties agreed to a similar regime in the TCA; Annex 27 sets out some principles for energy and environmental subsidies.[33]

While they are significantly less specific than the provisions of the Guidelines, the principles of non-discrimination, transparency, and competitiveness pertaining to subsidies are maintained. While no specific RES regime is introduced, Annex 27 par. 1 of the TCA states that subsidies for adequate electricity production, RES and cogeneration should not unduly interfere with the UK and EU's obligations under the TCA relating to electricity and gas markets, and the efficient use of electricity transmission infrastructure shall be established according to 'transparent, non-discriminatory and effective' mechanisms. The TCA is thereby not intended to amend the not the EU internal State aid regime.[34] In fact, the rules in Annex 27 seem very similar – though less expansive. As with the Guidelines and the RE Directive II, only with the formulation of the exception does it become clear that the 'transparent, non-discriminatory and effective' procedures referred to in Annex 27 par. 1 TCA are meant to refer to 'competitive' procedures, and in particular to tendering procedures. However, as within the EU internal regime, Annex 27 par. 2 TCA envisions possible exceptions to the principle of competitive mechanisms to grant support to RES. Those exceptions shall apply in order to avoid overcompensation, and are allowed in order to (i) support RES or cogeneration, (ii) secure adequate supply, and (iii) ensure competition where the supported capacity is too insignificant to impact the trade and investment between the parties or State aid for demonstration projects.

No explicit mechanism is established under the TCA to review and control the abidance of the UK and the EU by the aforementioned obligations. That being the case, in the course of their cooperation in the field of RES, they will have to inform each other of their actions as discussed in Section 7.4. Even if that is not the case, as subsidies impact trade and thus market participants, it is likely that any violations on either side will be brought to the attention of the other by stakeholders – and might lead to proceedings, not only under the TCA but also potentially even under international settlement mechanisms.[35]

However, as mentioned above, the rules on RES support, and in particular State aid control within the EU Member States, will not be impacted by the UK's exit and the provisions of the TCA.

The TCA only applies to the (external) relationship between the EU and the UK – and not to the internal dealings within the EU. Thus, the provisions of (Art.

33 For more details, see: Chapter 5 on State Aid

34 As mentioned above, the Commission has published new Guidelines since, see fn. 32.

35 See Chapter 10 of this book on dispute settlement

4 of) the Renewable Energy Directive (RED) II and the State aid regime, most notably the European Economic Advisory Group (EEAG) will remain relevant for the design of RES support schemes within the EU.[36] The impact of Brexit on RES support policies within the EU is thus – again – limited.

7.2.4 RES cooperation post-Brexit

While the UK is no longer part of the EU internal market, and thus the provisions on the free movement of goods no longer apply to the UK, the UK and EU have agreed on a customs and tariff-free passage of goods between them. The TCA provides for several sets of rules concerning energy trade and energy in general, which have been discussed elsewhere in this book.[37] However, two aspects pertaining to RES are discussed in turn: First, the issuance, trade, and recognition of Guarantees of Origin under the RE Directive II, which had to be dealt with now that the UK is no longer subject to the provisions of that Directive; and second, the express reference in the TCA to cooperation in the field of offshore RES development.

7.2.4.1 Guarantees of Origin

With the UK no longer being subject to the provisions of the RE Directive II,[38] the question arose of how to allow for the 'green' quality of RES produced in the UK in the EU and vice versa. A system of Guarantees of Origin (GoOs) applies within the EU, according to which suppliers can prove to final customers (i) the percentage of RES comprised in their mix of supplies, and (ii) that a certain electricity product comes from RES. GoOs have to be recognised as between EU Member States, thereby enabling cross-border trade in electricity produced from renewable sources.[39]

These rules now no longer apply to the UK. In its 'Notice to Stakeholders – GoOs',[40] the Commission explained that, after the End of Transition Date, UK

36 Note that the Guidelines are currently undergoing a review process. The Commission has published a proposal for new Guidelines for Climate Environmental and Energy Aid in summer 2021. The new version is supposed to enter into force (2022). For an overview, see: stiftung-umwelt energierecht.de/wp-content/uploads/2021/06/Stiftung_Umweltenergierecht_GD-erklaert_2021-06-29.pdf.

37 See Chapters 1 and 2 of this book

38 See also: The Commission, Communication, Notice to stakeholders – Withdrawal of the United Kingdom and EU rules in the field of Guarantees of Origin of electricity from Renewable Energy Source, of 23 July 2020 (Notice to Stakeholders – GoO).

39 See Art. 15 par. 9 Renewable Energy Directive 2009/28/EG, now Art. 19 par. 9 RED II. For more general information on the system, see: Papke/Kahles, Neue EU-Vorgaben für Herkunftsnachweise und Stromkennzeichnung? – Die Vorschläge im Rahmen des Winterpakets und ihre möglichen Auswirkungen auf das deutsche Recht, Würzburger Berichte zum Umweltenergierecht Nr. 34 vom 30 May 2018.

40 The Commission, Communication, Notice to stakeholders – Withdrawal of the United Kingdom and EU rules in the field of Guarantees of Origin of electricity from Renewable Energy Source, of 23 July 2020 (Notice to Stakeholders – GoO).

producers and UK GoOs will be outside the EU regulatory regime. That being the case, EU Member States are no longer able to accept British GoOs as equal to EU GoOs.[41] Instead, the EU and the UK intend to negotiate a special agreement to enable the trade in GoOs to continue. Such an agreement has, however, not yet been negotiated, and it is not clear from the Commission's communication whether this is planned anytime soon.

For EU suppliers, this means that GoOs from the UK cannot be used to describe their electricity mix to consumers, or as proof of RES in that mix anymore. This is likely to decrease demand for such GoOs and may increase demand for EU GoOs, and IT may result in private parties trying to renegotiate their contracts. Aside from this, the EU internal GoOs system will not be impacted by Brexit.

Similarly, issues arose in respect of qualification schemes for installers of small-scale biomass boilers and stoves, solar photovoltaic and solar thermal systems, shallow geothermal systems, and heat pumps, which are regulated by mutual recognition provisions under the EU legal framework.[42] With Brexit, such recognition is no longer granted to UK companies.[43]

Thus, at least until the UK and EU conclude a special agreement in respect of this matter, when it comes to GoOs for RES (and UK qualified installers' ability to work within the EU), Brexit may well cause some restrictions to trade and the provision of services in the field of RES, which may impact the RES policy of the EU. Looking at the statistics, the number of GoOs from the UK to the EU had already been quite low – and in fact was declining – in the lead up to Brexit, with the overall exports from the UK being at about 7.45 TWh in the 2019–2020 period.[44] The UK did import about 44.5 TWh worth of GoOs, of which 88% were from Norway over the same period, marking a 50% increase in imports. With the new regime coming into force and UK GoOs no longer qualifying under the EU rules, the demand for those is expected to decline even further. Similarly, importing GoOs for use in the UK may face some administrative burden, so that overall trade is likely to slow down even further.[45] For the EU market, however, the impact – due to the limited amount of GoOs imported from the UK before – is likely to be very limited. In the UK, there is still uncertainty about the legal framework and thus viability of using GoOs imported from the EU.[46] However,

41 The Commission, Communication, Notice to stakeholders – Withdrawal of the United Kingdom and EU rules in the field of Guarantees of Origin of electricity from Renewable Energy Source, of 23 July 2020 (Notice to Stakeholders – GoO), p. 2

42 See: Art. 14 par. 3 Renewable Energy Directive 2009/28/EG, Art. 14 par. 3 RE Directive II.

43 The Commission, Communication, Notice to stakeholders – Withdrawal of the United Kingdom and EU rules in the field of Guarantees of Origin of electricity from Renewable Energy Source, of 23 July 2020 (Notice to Stakeholders – GoO), p. 3.

44 Using data from the Association of Issuing Bodies (AIB) which administer the certification and recognition of GoO within the EU, see, e.g., Greenfact, Brexit and the effect on the GO market, <www.greenfact.com/News/1356/Brexit-and-the-effect-on-the-GO-market >, accessed 1 December 2021.

45 Ibid.

46 Ibid.

with a view to keeping trade up, the EU RE Directive II already provides for a potential solution in the form of a special agreement for GoO recognition, which could further limit the impact of Brexit.

7.2.4.2 Cooperation on offshore renewable energy

Under Art. 321 of the TCA, the UK and the EU expressed their intention to cooperate on the development of offshore renewable energy by exchanging best practices, as well as, where appropriate, the development of specific projects. A forum for such exchange between the Commission, the EU Member States, the UK, grid operators, and other stakeholders is envisioned to be set up wherein the development of offshore renewable energy, including grid infrastructures, is to be discussed. Hybrid projects (those connected to more than one country) and common projects,[47] spatial planning, support and financing, grid planning, exchange on technologies, and best practices on regulatory topics are explicitly mentioned as points of discussion, whilst the wording of the Article makes clear that such a platform should cover a broader range of issues relating to offshore RES development.

This provision of the TCA is one of many aimed at mitigating and limiting the impact of Brexit on RES development. As the UK was, and will ideally remain, a partner in most cross-border offshore RES projects which are currently planned, the TCA seeks to provide a framework for the continuance of such cooperation and the requisite stability and legal certainty for those projects to be successfully developed and implemented.

7.3 The EU ETS – with and without the UK

As an EU Member State until end of December 2020, the UK not only contributed to the EU's goals in the field of reducing GHG emissions, but also participated in the EU Emissions Trading Scheme (ETS) system. Post-Brexit, this is no longer the case, necessitating some adaptations on both sides. What is more, the Commission just proposed another reform to the system, including a mechanism applying to third countries, which may encompass the UK as well.

7.3.1 Brief introduction to the EU ETS

In 2005, the EU introduced an EU-wide ETS under which polluters are obliged to purchase emission allowances for the amount of GHGs they emit in excess of

47 Interestingly, the Commission is also already suggesting such 'mutual projects of common interest' to be introduced in the framework for development of essential energy infrastructures. See: The Commission, Proposal for a Regulation of the European Parliament and the Council on Guidelines for trans-European energy infrastructure and repealing Regulation (EU) No 347/2013, COM(2020) 824 final, 15 December 2020.

their permitted cap.[48] The EU ETS, which is now entering its fourth phase, has been subject to continuous expansion and improvement over the years and nowadays applies to most industrial sectors, including EU-wide aviation. For sectors not covered by the ETS, the EU has prescribed certain reduction targets to be implemented by the EU Member States under an 'effort sharing' regime.[49]

The number of emission allowances issued is reduced annually and is intended to allow the EU to reach its GHG emission reduction goals, provided that the EU Member States deliver on their commitments under the 'effort sharing' system. There has been a lot of criticism of the scheme, and the EU has at times struggled to maintain a relevant CO_2-price under the ETS (most notably during the 2008 global financial crisis). Nevertheless, the overall performance of the systems seems to be satisfactory.[50] Indeed, the Commission is considering expanding the scope of the ETS to the transport sector,[51] and could thereby transfer an even larger share of the efforts to reduce GHG emissions into the hands of the EU legislator from that of individual EU Member States.

7.3.2 Impact of Brexit on the EU ETS

As discussed in Section 7.2.2, Brexit does not change the EU's goals to reduce GHG emissions. The new target of reducing emissions by 55% by 2030 was calculated taking the UK's departure from the EU into consideration.

However, one of the consequences of Brexit is that the aggregate volume of emissions will be reduced. Accordingly, the Commission has had to subtract the UK's emissions from the overall target emissions (or allowed emissions) within the EU ETS–covered sectors and adjust the number of allowances accordingly, effectively shrinking the scheme by 11%.[52] In order to do so, the Commission issued a fact sheet on the rules which apply to the ETS post-Brexit.[53]

48 See generally: Fischer, The EU's New Energy and Climate Policy Framework for 2030, SWP Comments, 2014, p. 5; Nysten, Zur Zulässigkeit der Ausweitung des EU-Emissionshandels nach Art. 24 EHS-RL auf die Bereiche Verkehr und Wärme in Deutschland, Würzburger Berichte zum Umweltenergierecht Nr. 43 vom 12 July 2019.

49 See: Art. 1 and 2 Regulation (EU) 2018/842 of 30 May 2018 on binding annual greenhouse gas emission reductions by Member States from 2021 to 2030 contributing to climate action to meet commitments under the Paris Agreement and amending Regulation (EU) No 525/2013, [2018] OJ L 156, pp. 26-42.

50 See the Commission, Impact assessment report, Accompanying the document: Directive amending Directive 2003/87/EC establishing a system for greenhouse gas emission allowance trading within the Union, Decision (EU) 2015/1814 concerning the establishment and operation of a market stability reserve for the Union greenhouse gas emission trading scheme and Regulation (EU) 2015/757, Impact Assessment, SWD(2021) 601 final, Part 1/4, 14 July 2021, pp. 11–14.

51 See, e.g., the Commission, Inception Impact Assessment, Ref. Ares(2020)6081850 of 29 October 2020.

52 See: Bloomberg, EU Carbon Market Has Chance to Link With U.K. After Brexit Deal, <https://www.bloomberg.com/news/articles/2020-12-28/eu-carbon-market-has-chance-to-link-with-u-k-after-brexit-deal>

53 The Commission, Notice to stakeholders – Withdrawal of the United Kingdom and EU Emissions Trading System (EU ETS), 07 July 2020 (Notice to stakeholder – ETS).

From 2021 onwards, stationary installations in the UK are no longer covered by the EU ETS. Similarly, as long as there is no agreement linking the UK ETS with the EU ETS, the EU ETS will not apply to flights to and from the UK.[54] Similarly, the UK authorities can no longer accredit verifiers who confirm the emission reports submitted by the installations covered by the EU ETS system. Moreover, the UK is no longer able to administer any accounts in the EU ETS emissions registry where operators keep account of their emission allowances and is not able to access and use it for reporting under the Kyoto Protocol. UK-based operators and market actors are also be excluded from the allowances for the EU ETS (EUA) auctions, while rules similar to those which relate to the financial markets may apply with regard to trade in emissions allowances. As mentioned, a transitional period, which was introduced in order for UK operators to adjust to the consequences of Brexit, ended on 31 December 2020.

For the obligations arising under the EU ETS for emissions in 2020, operators established in the UK were until April 2021 treated in the same way as operators established within the EU. Their accounts in the EU ETS registry, which are needed to fulfil their obligations under the ETS, remain accessible and will be managed by the UK authorities.[55] Following this transitional period, supervision of the UK's emissions has reverted to the UK's own ETS. Northern Ireland, however, remains part of the EU ETS and is treated as an EU Member State for emissions purposes.[56] With regard to sectors which are not covered by the ETS, no amendments have thus far been made.[57]

The EU ETS is therefore geared to operate without the UK. While the calculations and adjustments of the number of allowances might necessitate some more adjustments in the coming years, the impact of Brexit on the ETS is likely to remain limited. This is particularly apparent when the impact of Brexit is juxtaposed with the significant reforms planned by the EU, in particular the consideration of a so-called Carbon Border Adjustment Mechanism (CBAM).[58] Proposed

54 The Commission, Notice to stakeholders – Withdrawal of the United Kingdom and EU Emissions Trading System (EU ETS), 07 July 2020 (Notice to stakeholder – ETS), p. 3.

55 The Commission, Notice to stakeholders – Withdrawal of the United Kingdom and EU Emissions Trading System (EU ETS), of 07 July 2020 (Notice to stakeholder – ETS), p. 6.

56 The Commission, Notice to stakeholders – Withdrawal of the United Kingdom and EU Emissions Trading System (EU ETS), of 07 July 2020 (Notice to stakeholder – ETS), p. 7.

57 Note that the Commission recently proposed a revision of both the EU ETS and the regime of the EU Effort Sharing regulation, which – in addition to an update on the GHG emission reduction targets – includes an extension of the EU ETS to the buildings and transport sector. See: The Commission, Proposal for a Regulation of the European Parliament and the Council amending Regulation (EU) 2018/842 on binding annual greenhouse gas emission reductions by Member States from 2021 to 2030 contributing to climate action to meet commitments under the Paris Agreement, COM/2021/555 final, eur-lex.europa.eu/legal-content/EN/TXT/?uri=CELEX:52021PC0555 accessed 9 November 2021. For an overview, see: The Commission, Delivering the EU Green Deal ec.europa.eu/info/strategy/priorities-2019-2024/european-green-deal/delivering-european-green-deal_en accessed 9 November 2021.

58 See, e.g., Nysten, Eine EU CO2-Bepreisung für internationale Importe, Würzburger Berichte zum Umweltenergierecht Nr. 52 vom 23 July 2021.

by the Commission in July 2021, such a mechanism – mirroring the EU ETS but without a cap on GHG emissions or imports for that matter – is intended to introduce a system to internalise CO_2 prices for imports into the EU.[59] However, it would credit importers if and insofar that they had already paid such a price within their home country.[60]

The possibility of the EU ETS and the UK ETS being linked is expressly referred to in Article 395 of the TCA.[61] This could be a mutually beneficial development for both the UK and the EU[62] and would be in line with the stated intention to cooperate on climate protection and emissions reduction issues under the Brexit Agreement. It might also allow the UK to 'escape' the EU CBAM.

7.4 Conclusion

Prior to Brexit, the UK was one of the most important and high-profile contributors to the climate and energy goals and policies of the EU. Its departure has left a significant gap and resulted in a realignment of the EU's RES target architecture. Even though the UK and the EU no longer operate under the same regulatory regime, they are still united in their common objective of limiting global warming according to the targets set by the PA.

The present analysis of the impact of Brexit on the EU's RES policy has shown that much of EU RES acquis no longer apply to the UK. Over the past two decades, the EU has developed an elaborate legal framework for the promotion of RES. Its scope has widened from its initial ambit of electricity and now applies to all sectors where the use of fossil fuels can be substituted for RES. Besides setting specific EU and national RES targets for the reference years 2010, 2020, and 2030, the relevant EU law has streamlined the national support schemes which were originally in place. Traditionally, this aspect of national support for RES is not only influenced by EU secondary law, but also by EU State Aid law. The handling of financial subsidies is one of the issues which is explicitly dealt with in the TCA. It provides that subsidies for RES shall be established according to 'transparent, non-discriminatory and effective mechanisms'. It is also apparent that the core principles of the Commission's Guidelines for Environmental and Energy Aid are encapsulated in the TCA.

The exchange of GoOs, and therefore the trade in the green value of RES, is for the moment slowed down whilst the EU and UK figure out whether and to

59 The Commission, Proposal for a Regulation of the European Parliament and the Council establishing a carbon border adjustment mechanism, Brussels, COM (2021) 564 final, <https://ec.europa.eu/info/sites/default/files/carbon_border_adjustment_mechanism_0.pdf> accessed 9 November 2021.

60 For a detailed assessment of the proposal, see, e.g., Marciu et al., Guide to the European Carbon Border Adjustment Mechanism, ECRST, 27 September 2021.

61 Art. 395 of the TCA.

62 See: Bloomberg, EU Carbon Market Has Chance to Link With U.K. After Brexit Deal, www.bloomberg.com/news/articles/2020-12-28/eu-carbon-market-has-chance-to-link-with-u-k-after-brexit-deal accessed 4 February 2021.

what extent they want to allow for their recognition to continue. Given the limited relevance of imported GoOs from the UK for the EU market to date, it may not be the highest item on the agenda for negotiations between them, in particular as the prices for EU GoOs rose at the end of 2021.[63] In view of this, joint development of offshore RES is more likely to be an area of cooperation between the EU and UK going forward. The EU is still working on the improvement of electricity transmission infrastructures in the North Sea, from which joint renewable energy projects between the two countries may benefit. The specific reference in the TCA to cooperation regarding offshore RES, including for the sharing best practices and development in the field of grid infrastructures, is notable. This may allow private project developers to continue working on their business models and thus allow for joint RES projects between the EU and UK.

Another field of potential cooperation between the UK and the EU concerns the potential linking of the EU ETS with the UK ETS. As discussed in Section 7.3.2, the TCA expressly makes reference to it, although it would require a significant amount of political goodwill from both sides for this to actually happen. Given the Commission's plans to introduce the CBAM to deal with CO_2-emissions from imports into the EU, plans to link the EU ETS with the new UK ETS have not materialised yet. It remains to be seen whether the UK will try to 'opt-in' to the EU ETS again, or rather try to get recognition of its national CO_2-prices under the CBAM, or whether a totally different form of cooperation will emerge going forward regarding GHG emissions.[64]

63 See Greenfact, European GoO prices double in the third quarter of 2021 < www.greenfact.com /News/1681/European-GoO-prices-double-in-the-third-quarter-of-2021> accessed 1 December 2021.

64 In this regard, see also the discussion on the formation of a 'climate club' which is particularly strong in German literature and politics, e.g., in *Nysten*, Eine EU CO2-Bepreisung für internationale Importe, Würzburger Berichte zum Umweltenergierecht Nr. 52 vom 23 July 2021, p. 23 (with further references).

8 UK Environmental Law and Policy Post-Brexit

Eleanor Reeves and Maurice Sheridan

8.1 Introduction

The legal framework for environmental law and policy in the UK has been materially and structurally altered since the Brexit Referendum. From being an EU Member State, and so co-maker of and subject to EU environmental law and policy, the UK[1] is now a 'third country', albeit in a quite particular position compared to other third countries.

During the period of its EU membership, there were, of course, areas of environmental law and policy in the UK which were entirely 'domestic'.[2] However, the majority of environmental law and policy in the UK was then, and currently remains, derived from or influenced by EU environmental law and policy.[3] The range and number of EU environmental legislative acts relevant for this purpose

1 The UK comprises for this purpose England, Scotland, Wales, and Northern Ireland, the latter three of which possessed, pre-Brexit, extensive devolved powers to legislate on environmental matters (albeit subject to the obligation not to conflict with EU law). Post-Brexit, the European Union (Withdrawal) Act 2018 (the 2018 Act) re-reserves, by s 12, the equivalent measures to the Westminster Parliament so that the devolved institutions cannot pass post-Brexit legislation inconsistent with inter alia 'retained EU law' on the environment, as to which see further below; and similarly as regards regulations adopted by the devolved institutions in relation to the TCA: see the European Union (Future Relationship) Act 2020 (the 2020 Act), s 38, with sch 5.

2 See, e.g., the broad review in Richard Macrory, 'Environmental law in the United Kingdom post Brexit' (2019) 19 ERA Forum 643, at <https://link.springer.com/article/10.1007/s12027-018-0531-6> accessed 15 February 2022.

3 Some estimates had put the proportion at some 80%: see Environmental Audit Committee, *The Future of the Natural Environment after the EU Referendum* (HC 2016–17, 599–6) at <https://publications.parliament.uk/pa/cm201617/cmselect/cmenvaud/599/599.pdf> accessed 21 January 2021; Ruth Chambers, 'What does Brexit mean for Defra?' (*Insidetrack*, 5 December 2019) at <https://greenallianceblog.org.uk/2019/12/05/what-does-brexit-mean-for-defra/> accessed 21 January 2021. It is, however, difficult to verify the accuracy of such estimates of the 'Europeanisation' of law within the UK: see, e.g., the various approaches to such a task within Vaughne Miller, 'How much legislation comes from Europe?' (Research Paper 10/62, House of Commons Library 2010) at <https://researchbriefings.files.parliament.uk/documents/RP10-62/RP10-62.pdf> accessed 15 February 2022. A useful indication of the scope and scale of EU environmental legislation can be obtained through the European Commission's (the Commission) website for its Directorate General (DG) Environment, in particular through its drop-down options for 'Policies' and 'Legal Com-

DOI: 10.4324/9781003364337-9

are extensive, though precise tallies are not easy to come by. A UK House of Lords EU Committee Report of February 2017, 'Brexit: Environment and climate change',[4] noted that as at 2010 there were within EU environmental legislative acts some 111 Regulations, 256 Directives, and 136 Decisions (addressed to one or more Member States).

Brexit has, of course, provided for change in this position. Early on in the process of exiting the EU, the UK government had signalled that it wished to reset environmental law and regulation in the UK post-Brexit.[5] Even prior to the adoption of the Trade and Cooperation Agreement (TCA), there were indications that in some areas, EU environmental standards were being altered (some in error, some reduced) by the UK Parliament.[6] In that context, it may appear a surprise that, as explained below, the UK has given, in essence, substantively direct effect to the Withdrawal Agreement,[7,8] and likewise to the TCA.[9, 10]

This Chapter traces the scope of this legacy and UK provision for its retention as well as for its alteration in the future.[11] It sets out changes to environmental

---

pliance', at 'Environment' (European Commission) <https://ec.europa.eu/environment/index_en.htm> accessed 15 February 2022.

4 European Union Committee, *Brexit: environment and climate change* (HL 2016–17, 109–12) at <https://publications.parliament.uk/pa/ld201617/ldselect/ldeucom/109/109.pdf> accessed 15 February 2022.

5 See, e.g., 'The Clean Growth Strategy' (HM Government, 2017) (as amended in April 2018) at <https://assets.publishing.service.gov.uk/government/uploads/system/uploads/attachment_data/file/700496/clean-growth-strategy-correction-april-2018.pdf> accessed 27 July 2021. This set proposals for future UK environmental and industrial-related policies, though much still in the context of EU targets and any, then future, EU–UK future relationship agreement. See also Section 8.4.

6 See Alexandra Sinclair and Joe Tomlinson, 'Brexit Delegated Legislation: Problematic Results' (*UK Constitutional Law Association*, 9 January 2020) <https://ukconstitutionallaw.org/2020/01/09/alexandra-sinclair-and-joe-tomlinson-brexit-delegated-legislation-problematic-results/≥ accessed 27 July 2021; Emily Lydgate, Chloe Anthony and Erik Millstone, 'Brexit food safety legislation and potential implications for UK trade: The devil in the details' (Briefing Paper 37, UK Trade and Policy Observatory 2019) at <https://blogs.sussex.ac.uk/uktpo/publications/brexit-food-safety-legislation-and-potential-implications-for-uk-trade-the-devil-in-the-details/> accessed 27 July 2021. The latter claims a reduction in various sectors of food safety law at the time, including, e.g., as regards pesticide controls.

7 2018 Act, s 7A(1)–(3).

8 The Withdrawal Agreement is at <https://eur-lex.europa.eu/legal-content/EN/TXT/PDF/?uri=CELEX:12019W/TXT(02)&from=EN>.

9 2020 Act, s 29. This direct effect potential is expressly acknowledged as regards 'retained EU law' and the Withdrawal Agreement in the 2020 Act, s 38.

10 The TCA is at <https://eur-lex.europa.eu/legal-content/EN/TXT/PDF/?uri=CELEX:22021A0430(01)&from=EN>.

11 UK Government positions in late 2021 and throughout 2022 suggest yet more radical change to current environmental law (in fact all EU law) in the UK which is derived from EU law is to be anticipated: see, e.g., the Statement of Lord Frost, then Minister of State in the Cabinet Office, *Brexit Opportunities: Review of Retained EU Law*, 9 December 2021, at <https://questions-statements.parliament.uk/written-statements/detail/2021-12-09/hlws445> accessed 14 February 2022; and the UK Government publication, *Benefits of Brexit*, of January 2022 at <https://assets.publish-

law in the UK arising from EU membership (Section 8.2); sets out changes under the Withdrawal Agreement and prior to the EU Exit Date (Section 8.3); sets out changes post the EU Exit Date, especially due to the TCA (Section 8.4); and addresses the risks of future divergence between environmental law in the UK and EU law and implications for business (Section 8.5). Such implications for future UK environmental law and policy are potentially significant, as described here, although in the short term, little may alter substantively.

8.2 Environmental law in the UK as a result of UK Membership of the EU prior to Brexit

EU law was brought into force for the UK with effect from 1973 by way of an Act of Parliament,[12] the European Communities Act 1972 (the 1972 Act).[13]

EU Treaty articles and EU Regulations whenever adopted were 'directly applicable' on the UK domestic plane without further legislative action needed by the UK, as they were then 'self executing'.[14]

EU environmental directives, however, required the UK to implement in its domestic law their full spirit and wording[15] (often referred to as their *effet utile*[16]). Reliance on rights intended to be created by directives for companies and individuals could then be placed on the UK implementing legislation (i.e., primary legislation – Acts of Parliament, or secondary legislation – principally, Statutory Instruments SIs), though the legal relevance of the underlying directive remained throughout.[17] The supremacy of EU law further meant that even if the UK failed in its EU Treaty obligations to implement a directive in full or in part, provisions of a directive capable of having direct effect could, in principle, be relied upon

ing.service.gov.uk/government/uploads/system/uploads/attachment_data/file/1052148/benefits-of-brexit-document.pdf> accessed 14 February 2022. In September 2022 the UK Government introduced a Bill, the Retained EU Law (Revocation and Reform) Bill (the Revocation Bill), to provide for "sunset" clauses to effectively remove EU-derived law in the UK from the statute books, currently, by end of 2023. The Bill, as published, is at <https://protect-eu.mimecast.com/s/7P8BCj2ZzCwyVWjsWWVOD>, <https://publications.parliament.uk/pa/bills/cbill/58-03/0156/220156.pdf> accessed 29 November 2022. The Bill is controversial both within and outside Parliament.

12 A necessary step given the UK's dualist nature: see *McWhirter v Attorney General* [1972] CMLR 882.

13 European Communities Act 1972 Act (as amended immediately prior to the EU Exit Date). The 1972 Act was repealed on the EU Exit Date: 2018 Act, s 1.

14 Though Member States would, in furtherance of their EU obligations, often still need to supplement the EU Regulations by way of national legislation providing for, e.g., criminal offences, penalties, and procedural matters for contravention of the same.

15 See by way of illustration Case C-671/13 *IID* [2015] ECLI 418.

16 See further on this concept Case C-503/17 *Commission v UK* [2018] ECLI 831, especially paras 40–47.

17 See, e.g., Case C-62/00 *Marks & Spencers plc v UK Commissioners of Customs and Excise* [2002] ECLI 435, paras 27–28.

against UK public authorities, and enforced through the UK courts.[18] Ultimately, a Member State's failure to ensure EU rights may lead to a claim for damages against the state, under the well-known *Francovich* doctrine.[19]

The UK was, in addition, subject to the regulatory powers of the Commission, the Commission here acting as the 'guardian of the Treaties',[20] and as with other Member States was taken to the Court of Justice of the European Union (CJEU) in infraction/infringement proceedings by it for breaches of EU law on a number of occasions,[21] including notably in environmental cases.[22]

Post-Brexit, one (and potentially more than one) of three legal regimes is potentially applicable to any given legal scenario depending on the subject matter and/or processes involved, and timing of the same. These legal regimes are described below.

8.3 Environmental law in the UK post-Brexit further to the Withdrawal Agreement for matters arising up to the EU Exit Date

This period marks the start of the UK diverging from EU law, including EU environmental law and policy. Although brief, it merits being addressed as (i) as some legal situations arising in this period may be of relevance to subsequent UK government decisions or regulatory or enforcement actions with ongoing relevance and/or legal effect for individuals or companies and (ii) it lays down the framework for the continuity as well as for the amendment of EU law in the UK post-Brexit.

18 As is well known, EU environmental directives are capable of providing directly effective rights for companies and individuals: see, for illustration, Case C-131/88 *Commission v Germany* [1991] ECR I-865, especially paras 6–7 (regarding the then Groundwater Directive 80/68/EEC); Case C-244/12 *Salzburger Flughafen GmbH* [2013] ECLI 203, para 48 (on the direct effect of provisions of the then EIA Directive 85/337/EEC).

19 See Case C-6/90 *Francovich* [1991] ECR I-5403. A more recent exposition of the same was provided in Case C-129/19 *BV* [2020] ECLI 566, para 34.

20 Principally, including for environmental law cases, under Article 17 TEU and Articles 258 and 260(2) TFEU.

21 The EC Report on infringement actions against Member States, including the UK, for the last full year of the UK's participation in the EU is at 'Performance per Member State' (*European Commission*, 2020) at <https://ec.europa.eu/internal_market/scoreboard/performance_by_member_state/uk/index_en.htm#infringements> accessed 21 July 2021. The figures for the Commission's environment department, DG Environment infringements actions against, inter alia, the UK in 2019 is at 'Legal Enforcement' (*European Commission*, 2019) <https://ec.europa.eu/environment/legal/law/statistics.htm≥ accessed on 21 July 2021.

22 See by way only of illustration Case C-669/16 *Commission v UK* [2018] ECLI 844 (on the Habitats Directive 92/43/EEC) and Case C-502/15 *Commission v UK* [2017] ECLI 334 (on the Urban Wastewater Treatment Directive 91/271/EEC). See also Case C-2-1/02 *Wells* [2004] ECLI 12 (providing for Francovich damages in the UK for breaches of environmental directives).

Under the Withdrawal Agreement, the UK agreed to give effect domestically,[23] in principle, to the Withdrawal Agreement and to all EU environmental law as adopted as at the end of the implementation period, as amended or replaced, with the same legal effects as they would produce within the EU and its Member States.[24] That includes upholding domestically the EU doctrines of supremacy and of direct effect in respect also of EU environmental provisions contained in or referred to in the Withdrawal Agreement;[25] disapplying inconsistent or incompatible domestic provisions;[26] and interpreting and applying the relevant provisions of the Withdrawal Agreement and EU environmental law provisions referred to in the Withdrawal Agreement in accordance with the methods and general principles of EU law.[27] Such national conformity in the UK is to be maintained in accordance with the case law of the CJEU handed down before the end of the implementation period,[28] and so would include provision for *Francovich* damages.

For legal continuity (and certainty) purposes, the 2018 Act also makes provision for the continuing effect of the 1972 Act for general purposes, notwithstanding its repeal, prior to the EU Exit Date.[29]

In regulatory terms, during and in respect of the period prior to the EU Exit Date, under the Withdrawal Agreement, the Commission retains its jurisdiction as regards enforcing EU environmental law against the UK,[30] as does the CJEU with respect to ongoing cases.[31] Queries have, however, been raised that infringement

23 Under Article 3(1) of the Withdrawal Agreement, unless the Withdrawal Agreement, or EU law made applicable by the Withdrawal Agreement, provides otherwise, reference to the UK in the Withdrawal Agreement is to be understood as referring to the UK, together with a range of other territories for which the UK has international responsibility and which were within the scope of various acts of the EU. In contrast, the TCA extends only, and to a limited extent, to the Crown Dependencies of the Bailiwick of Guernsey, the Bailiwick of Jersey, and the Isle of Man – TCA, art 774.

24 Withdrawal Agreement, art 4(1), with arts 127(1) and (3). Furthermore, under the Withdrawal Agreement, art 4(1), 2nd indent, individuals can rely directly on provisions contained in or referred to in the Withdrawal Agreement which meet the test for direct effect, including inter alia before UK domestic courts.

25 Withdrawal Agreement, art 4(1), 2nd indent.

26 Ibid, art 4(2).

27 Ibid, art 4(3).

28 Ibid, art 4(4). 'Implementation period' is the terminology from the UK legislation. The end of this 'implementation period' coincides with the deadline noted in this book as the EU Exit Date. The latter term, therefore, is used hereafter.

29 2018 Act, s 1A and s 1B.

30 Withdrawal Agreement, art 87. This is for a period of 4 years after the EU Exit Date (and for an additional four years specifically after any resulting CJEU judgment finding a breach of the same by the UK). See, e.g., 'February infringements package: key decisions' (*European Commission*, 12 February 2020) at <https://ec.europa.eu/commission/presscorner/detail/en/inf_20_202> accessed 12 May 2020 (initiation in February 2020 of the infringement procedure against the UK, here on breaches alleged of the directive on road-charging). The Commission thereby has jurisdiction within 4 years of the EU Exit Date to initiate enforcement action against the UK before the CJEU for any alleged breaches of EU environmental law arising prior to the EU Exit Date.

31 Withdrawal Agreement, art 86(1).

cases against the UK will not in fact be pursued further.[32] The right/duty of UK courts to send a preliminary reference regarding EU environmental law to the CJEU continued during the period prior to the EU Exit Date.[33]

Apart from the Northern Ireland Protocol,[34] however, there are no provisions in the Withdrawal Agreement specifically requiring the UK to respect or maintain EU environmental law in respect of or in the UK post-Brexit or post the EU Exit Date. EU environmental law is therefore to have legal effect post-Brexit and post the EU Exit Date in the UK in common with EU legislation and case law more generally. Such legal effect is as set out in and under the 2018 Act, the details of which are set out below, as generally these provisions apply during and post-EU Exit Date.

8.4 Environmental law in the UK post-Brexit after the EU Exit Date

8.4.1 The 'roll over' of pre-EU Exit Date EU environmental law

Provision is made under the 2018 Act for giving ongoing effect to pre-EU Exit Date EU environmental law in the UK post-EU Exit Date, and so provide for continuity of the prior legal situation. However, EU environmental law is not granted any special status in the UK post-EU Exit Date and is dealt with in the same manner as other EU law generally.

Under UK constitutional law, the repeal of an Act of Parliament would automatically mean the fall in legal terms of secondary legislation passed under its authority.[35] To prevent this occurring (and also provide more generally for legal certainty in the law after the EU Exit Date), the 2018 Act provides in various, somewhat convoluted ways, to 'roll over' or maintain, post-EU Exit Date, the continuing effect in some form of pre-EU Exit Date EU law and case law. The

32 See Emma Howard, 'EU environment cases against UK left in limbo by Brexit' (*Unearthed*, 25 February 2020) <https://unearthed.greenpeace.org/2020/02/25/brexit-court-cases-eu-uk-environment-bog-burning/> accessed 23 July 2021. Some support for such doubts may perhaps be taken from the July 2020 Commission list of infringement actions against the UK, many of which have been closed in late 2020 and 2021 (although with some new cases opened within that period), see 'Infringement Decisions' (*European Commission*) at <https://ec.europa.eu/atwork/applying-eu-law/infringements-proceedings/infringement_decisions/index.cfm?lang_code=EN&typeOfSearch=false&active_only=0&noncom=0&r_dossier=&decision_date_from=&decision_date_to=&EM=UK&title=&submit=Search> accessed 23 July 2021.

33 Withdrawal Agreement, art 86(2).

34 For the Ireland/Northern Ireland Protocol, see <https://assets.publishing.service.gov.uk/government/uploads/system/uploads/attachment_data/file/840230/Revised_Protocol_to_the_Withdrawal_Agreement.pdf>.

35 See *Kay v Goodwin* (1830) 6 Bing. 576. A Commons Briefing Paper in 2017 on the then European Union (Withdrawal) Bill estimated that such effect would impact some 12,000 EU Regulations alone: see Jack Simson Caird, Vaughne Miller and Arabella Lang, 'European Union (Withdrawal) Bill' (Briefing Paper 8079, House of Commons Library 2017) <https://researchbriefings.files.parliament.uk/documents/CBP-8079/CBP-8079.pdf> 9, accessed 27 July 2021.

latter is referred to as 'retained EU law'.[36] However, it is important to note that 'retained EU law' is not 'EU law' in the UK. It is UK domestic law with a particular status,[37] though similar generally in legal effect on the domestic plane as EU law in the UK pre-Brexit.[38]

Under the 2018 Act, retained EU law is:

- EU-derived domestic legislation – s 2;
- Direct EU legislation – s 3;
- Other rights and obligations, etc., arising from the 1972 Act, s 2(1) – s 4.

EU-derived domestic legislation covers (a) Acts of Parliament adopted so as to give effect to EU obligations (other than the 1972 Act itself); (b) secondary legislation adopted under the 1972 Act; (c) secondary legislation adopted under Acts of Parliament passed to implement EU obligations; and (d) primary and secondary legislation of the devolved institutions within their jurisdiction to implement EU obligations. EU directives themselves are not part of retained EU law. Furthermore, although the doctrine of the supremacy of EU law is retained, with slight modification, in respect of pre-EU Exit Date EU law, the doctrine itself was abolished.[39]

Direct EU legislation includes EU Regulations, EU Decisions, and EU tertiary legislation, provided generally that none of this has already been included within EU-derived legislation.

Other rights and obligations, remedies, etc. include directly effective rights arising under provisions of the EU Treaties themselves, and legal principles and interpretative rulings of the CJEU, provided they are not already part of retained direct EU legislation, or arise under an EU directive and are not of a kind recognised by the CJEU or a UK court or tribunal in a case decided before the EU Exit Date.[40] The right to *Francovich* damages against the UK is, however, (subject to

36 2018 Act, s 6(7).

37 Ibid, s 7.

38 Space constraints preclude a detailed discussion on the nature of this new status, nor on how such law is to be interpreted and may be amended, though a helpful guide on the same, as set out then, for immediate purposes may be found in Graeme Cowie, 'The status of 'retained EU law' (Briefing Paper 08375, House of Commons Library 2019) <https://commonslibrary.parliament.uk/research-briefings/cbp-8375/> accessed 15 February 2022.

39 2018 Act, s 5.

40 See further ibid, s 5(6), with sch 1, paras 2 and 3. See, for example, as regards the continuance of EU general principles of law under this provision in English law, *Lipton v BA City Flyer Ltd* [2021] EWCA Civ 454, para 64; note, though, that this was doubted in *Adferiad Recovery Ltd v Aneurin Bevan University Health Board* [2021] EWHC 2049 (TCC), at para 117. See, also, Harris v Environment Agency [2022] EWHC 2264 (Admin), esp paras 89–94, holding that "direct effect" rights under the Habitats Directive were preserved in law in the UK under s 4(2)(b) regardless of the Habitats Regulations 2017.

transitional savings – 2018 Act s 23(7) and Sch 8, para 39(7)) abolished.[41] UK courts and tribunals are not bound by CJEU case law handed down after the EU Exit Date, though they may have regard to such case law insofar as is relevant to any matter before them.[42] The Supreme Court is not bound by any retained EU case law.[43]

The 2018 Act provides authority for the adoption of UK secondary legislation to address 'deficiencies' arising from retained EU legislation.[44] Deficiencies include references in EU law to UK obligations to submit reports to the Commission, references to EU agencies where no provision has been made for an ongoing relationship of the UK with the same, failures in retained EU law to operate effectively, and/or provisions which are otherwise redundant.[45]

It was estimated that some 800–1,000 statutory instruments would be required to deal with such deficiencies.[46] In September 2017, the Secretary of State for Defra told Parliament that there were some 850 pieces of legislation within Defra's remit which would thereby require amendment, with about one quarter relating to the environmental field.[47] An environmental NGO, GreenAlliance, suggested[48] that as at December 2019, some 122 statutory instruments had been passed by Defra for this purpose.[49]

41 Ibid, s5(6), with sch 1, para 4. See, also, *Adferiad Recovery Ltd v Aneurin Bevan University Health Board* [2021] EWHC 2049 (TCC), at paras 118-121.

42 Ibid, s 6(1) and (2). See, for a specific instance of exercise of this facility by the courts, *The Civil Aviation Authority v Ryan Air DAC* [2022] EWCA Civ 76, paras 21–22.

43 Ibid, s 6(4)(a). Nor, under s 6(4)(ba), is a specified court/tribunal as provided for in regulations adopted under s 6(5A), such as the European Union (Withdrawal) Act 2018 (Relevant Court) (Retained EU Case Law) Regulations 2020 (SI 2020/1525), now including the Court of Appeal. In *Tunein Inc v Warner Music UK Ltd and Anor* [2021] EWCA Civ 441, at paras 74–75, the Court of Appeal said that this power to depart from a ruling of the CJEU was only to be on the basis on which the Supreme Court could depart from one of its own decisions or likewise as regards the House of Lords, and that that power was to be exercised with great caution.

44 2018 Act, s 8.

45 A quick guide to the intended operation of s 8 of the 2018 Act may be found in the Explanatory Notes, available at <https://www.legislation.gov.uk/ukpga/2018/16/section/8≥ accessed 26 July 2021.

46 See 'Legislating for the United Kingdom's withdrawal from the European Union' (Department for Exiting the European Union, March 2017) at <https://assets.publishing.service.gov.uk/government/uploads/system/uploads/attachment_data/file/604516/Great_repeal_bill_white_paper_accessible.pdf> p26, para 3.19, accessed 26 July 2021.

47 See as reported in a review in Macrory (n 2). The majority of amendments were to be to legislation on animal and plant health and agriculture. However, there are likely to be additional environmental measures to be addressed where they fall under the competences of other UK ministries.

48 See European Union Committee (n 4).

49 Defra does not appear to have a webpage specifically dedicated to such measures adopted within its competences remit. This contrasts with the Commission, which has provision specifically for environmental matters to address consequences of Brexit, post the EU Exit Date, on its *Readiness* site, at 'Consequences of Brexit' (*European Commission*) <https://ec.europa.eu/info/european-union-and-united-kingdom-forging-new-partnership/future-partnership/getting-ready-end-transition-period_en> accessed 26 July 2021. This links to the earlier Commission 'no-

To put that in context, by July 2021, over 580 statutory instruments were recorded as having been passed under s 8 of the 2018 Act to address 'deficiencies' in retained EU law.[50] However, it has been reported that the 'deficiency' power has been used *inter alia* (a) to make amendments to legislation outside the scope of the statutory authority granted to address 'deficiencies'[51] and (b) to reduce standards, including, in particular, environmental standards.[52] A consequence of the rush to pass the 'transposing' statutory instruments has been that errors were made which required corrections to be passed, for which, in the 2017–2019 Parliamentary Session, Defra was considered significantly responsible.[53] It is unlikely that the repeated revision of the law in the UK will aid clarity as to the law to be applied.[54] It is considered almost inevitable that litigation will arise as a result.

8.4.2 Ongoing effect generally of the Withdrawal Agreement (other than Part Four)

In terms of the ongoing implementation in domestic law of the remainder (i.e., non-Part Four provisions) of the Withdrawal Agreement (also referred to below as WA) from when it came into force, the 2018 Act makes more general provision.

deal' *Preparedness* site, the measures of which are updated to provide for the post-EU Exit Date period.

50 See, by way of illustration, the LexisNexis webpage in July 2021 for the use of s 8 of the 2018 Act for this purpose available at <https://www.lexisnexis.com/uk/legal/results/enhdocview.do?docLinkInd=true&ersKey=23_T277124175&format=GNBFULL&startDocNo=0&resultsUrlKey=0_T277124180&backKey=20_T277124181&csi=274768&docNo=15&scrollToPosition=1340> accessed 26 July 2021. This list incorporates amendments to original s 8 'deficiency' statutory instruments made by subsequent correcting s 8 'deficiency' statutory instruments. The same site lists a total of some 580 pieces of secondary legislation adopted further to the 2018 Act. It is to be noted that such statutory instruments refer to their coming into force as from the EU Exit Date. However, to give effect to the Withdrawal Agreement extension of EU law during the pre-EU Exit Date period as pre-Brexit, the 2020 Act, s 41(4) and sch 5, part 1, para 1 redefines 'exit day' for this purpose in these statutory instruments as the EU Exit Date.

51 See the general criticism of this and other associated matters in Ruth Fox and Bridgid Fowler, 'Brexit delegated legislation: the challenges, and how they should be addressed' (*Hansard Society*, 4 April 2020) <https://www.hansardsociety.org.uk/blog/brexit-delegated-legislation-reform-parliament-scrutiny≥ accessed 26 July 2021 and Lydgate, Anthony and Millstone (n 6).

52 See the review by Sinclair and Tomlinson (n 6). This review noted that as at the date of the review some 620 SIs had been adopted for this purpose. That total would appear to count separately all s 8 'deficiency' statutory instruments, including those 'correcting' earlier deficiency statutory instruments. See also on this point Lydgate, Anthony, and Millstone (n 6).

53 See 'Report of the House of Lords Second Legislation Scrutiny Committee' (UK Parliament, 10 September 2019) <https://publications.parliament.uk/pa/ld201719/ldselect/ldsecleg/420/42003.htm≥, accessed 13 May 2020.

54 A statutory instrument from Defra of June 2020 (the Environment (Amendment, etc) (EU Exit) (Amendment) (England and Wales) Regulations 2020) to amend a prior s 8 2019 'deficiency' statutory instrument illustrates the complexity in identifying which law applied and when and the risk of confusion that might then arise: see the unamended 2019 SI at <https://www.legislation.gov.uk/uksi/2019/458/contents/made> and the amending 2020 SI at <https://www.legislation.gov.uk/uksi/2020/603/contents/made?f00002≥ both as accessed on 27 July 2021.

Thus, s 7A(1) of the 2018 Act provides for the general implementation of the WA in that it provides that all such rights, powers, liabilities, obligations, and restrictions from time to time created or arising by or under the WA, and all such remedies and procedures from time to time created or arising by or under the WA are without further enactment to be given legal effect or used in the UK. Pursuant to s 7A(2), such rights, powers, liabilities, obligations, restrictions, remedies, and procedures are to be recognised and available in domestic law and enforced, allowed and followed accordingly. However, such provisions would not have provided for the ambulatory (i.e., future proofing) effect intended for the future for all such rights, designed to be available through the WA, and in particular, would have left them vulnerable to at least implied repeal.[55] That risk is, at least intended, to be removed by s 7A(3). This provides that every enactment (including an enactment contained in the 2018 Act) is to be read and has effect subject to sub-Section 7A(2).

Section 7A is supplemented by an interpretative obligation arising under s 7C of the 2018 Act. Section 7C(1), as material, provides that any question as to the validity, meaning or effect of any relevant separation agreement law (which expression includes s 7A) is to be decided, so far as they are applicable, in accordance with the WA. However, 'relevant separation agreement law' is such 'as that body of law is added to or otherwise modified by or under the 2018 Act or by other domestic law from time to time' (s 7C[3]).

The combination of the 2018 Act, ss 7A–7C, and associated provisions, as indicated here, suggests that all EU-based environmental law rights, liabilities, remedies, etc. derived from the Withdrawal Agreement are to have such effect post-EU Exit Date as would have arisen had the UK remained an EU Member State (subject to the question of whether s 7C(3) allows for detraction of such effect in the future).

8.4.3 The future EU–UK relationship post-EU Exit Date

By far the most significant potential for change, or for continuity, as regards environmental law in the UK after the EU Exit Date relates to the TCA, the EU–UK future relationship agreement. Set out below are (i) key structural or framework changes, and (ii) the main specific environmental areas affected for the purposes of this Chapter.

55 *Implied repeal* is a UK constitutional court-derived concept, whereby later legislation which is inconsistent with prior legislation is taken, in the absence of express words to this effect, to have impliedly repealed the earlier legislation. However, this does not easily apply to 'constitutional statutes' (such as was the case with the 1972 Act), which may thus prevail over later legislation – see *Thorburn v Sunderland City Council* [2002] EWHC 195 (Admin), especially at [60]–[64]. The question thus arises whether either the 2018 Act (as to the WA, though not Part Four, as given effect in UK law) and/or the 2020 Act (as to the TCA, as given effect in UK law) can constitute 'constitutional statutes' to this effect, a question which has not yet, as far as it has been possible to identify, been addressed by the UK Courts.

Subject to an exception as regards social security, which is not relevant here, Article 16 of the TCA provides that nothing in the TCA shall be construed as (i) conferring rights or imposing obligations on persons other than those created between the UK and the EU under public international law nor (ii) as permitting the TCA to be directly invoked in the domestic legal systems of the UK and the EU.[56] Furthermore, (iii) neither the UK nor the EU shall provide for a right of action under its law against the other on the grounds that the latter has acted in breach of the TCA.

The TCA has been given effect in the UK by way of the 2020 Act. However, the effects prohibited under Article 15 (as outlined at (i) and (ii) above) are in fact currently expressly provided for in UK domestic law.

The key provision for this purpose is Section 29. This sets out a general implementation of agreements provision, as material, at ss (1), as follows:

> Existing domestic law has effect on and after the relevant day with such modifications as are required for the purposes of implementing in that law the Trade and Cooperation Agreement or the Security of Classified Information Agreement so far as the agreement concerned is not otherwise so implemented and so far as such implementation is necessary for the purposes of complying with the international obligations of the United Kingdom under the agreement.

This is therefore an obligation as to 'result or effect',[57] and is subject to such modifications being limited to those 'as far as necessary' (i.e., they are not necessary if a domestic law is already consistent with the TCA), and the modification required is such as best ensures compliance by the UK with its international law obligations (and therefore not just those under the TCA *per se*, but with the international obligations assumed by the UK through the TCA).

Section 30 of the 2020 Act imposes an interpretative obligation on the courts. It compels them to have regard to rules of customary international law, including those codified by the Vienna Convention on the Law of Treaties, and states that neither Party is obliged to interpret the TCA in accordance with the domestic law of either Party.

These provisions may be significant in the event of a challenge to UK environmental law and policy post the TCA as being in breach of either the TCA *per se* or the international agreements incorporated through the TCA.

56 As the UK Court of Appeal has put it again in *Heathrow Airport Ltd and Ors v HMRC and Anor* [2021] EWCA Civ 783, para 224, '*Prima facie*, the TCA does not have direct effect' (emphasis in original). Note that the references to the TCA in cases arising before 1 May 2021 refer to the pre-finalised text of the TCA.

57 See Green LJ in *Lipton v BA City Flyer Ltd* [2021] EWCA Civ 454, para 78. The full judgment of Green LJ merits consideration as the first (and since adopted – see, e.g., within the *Heathrow* case (n 55)) and very clear overview of the effect of the TCA and the 2020 Act in UK domestic law. See, however, subsequent doubts as to aspects of this analysis in the *Adferiad Recovery Ltd* case (n 40).

The TCA seeks to retain the sovereignty of the UK and EU respectively with regard to environmental matters post-EU Exit Date, so that each Party may determine the environmental levels of protection and climate level of protection that it deems appropriate.[58] These provisions fall within Chapter 7 ('Environment and Climate Change') and Title XI of Part Two, 'Level Playing Field for Fair Competition and Sustainable Development'. This is, however, subject to the core 'non-regression' obligation, specifically the commitment not to weaken or reduce levels of environmental or climate protection below the levels in place as at the EU Exit Date 'in a manner affecting trade or investment between the parties'. This includes regression through failing to effectively enforce UK or EU (as applicable) environmental law or 'climate level of protection'. Article 390 of the TCA sets out specific benchmarks as to 'environmental levels of protection' and 'climate level of protection' by reference to a non-exhaustive list of areas including industrial emissions, nature and biodiversity conservation, waste management, and protection and preservation of the marine environment; and including, with respect to greenhouse gases, the EU 40% economy-wide 2030 target,[59] and the UK's share of that, including EU and UK carbon pricing systems. Of particular note is the TCA Article 411, whereby either Party may take 'rebalancing measures' in the event of significant divergences in areas including environment and climate protection.[60]

Given that the UK and the EU share a common biosphere, the UK and the EU commit to respecting international environmental agreements, including the Rio Declaration on Environment and Development, the United Nations Framework Convention on Climate Change (UNFCCC), and the Convention on Biological Diversity.[61] The following non-exhaustive list of internationally recognised environmental principles are specifically referred to in the TCA:[62]

(a) the principle that environmental protection should be integrated into the making of policies, including through impact assessments;
(b) the principle of preventative action to avert environmental damage;
(c) the precautionary approach;[63]

58 TCA, art 391.

59 See n 66 below, though both the UK and the Commission have since announced more ambitious interim emissions reduction targets.

60 A Commons Select Committee on the Future Relationship with the EU noted already in January 2021 the risks the rebalancing provisions pose for future divergences of law and policy in the UK from the base set in the TCA – see Committee on the Future Relationship with the European Union, The Shape of Future Parliamentary Scrutiny of UK–EU Relations (HC 2019–2021, 977), paras 18–21 at <https://committees.parliament.uk/publications/4370/documents/44329/default/> accessed 27 July 2021. The OEP (see Section 8.4.3.4) has called specifically for a "non-regression safeguard" clause in the Revocation Bill - see its Expert Report on the Revocation Bill, p 5, Section 3, <https://www.theoep.org.uk/report/oep-submission-retained-eu-law-bill-committee> accessed 6 December 2022.

61 TCA, art 393.

62 Ibid. Note the risk that these principles are subject to revocation domestically in the UK under the Revocation Bill, clause 5.

63 Specifically noted in the TCA, art 356, fn1, to refer to the precautionary principle as regards implementation in the EU.

(d) the principle that environmental damage should, as a priority, be rectified at source; and
(e) the 'polluter pays' principle.

The UK and the EU also thereby reaffirm their respective commitments to evaluating environmental impacts. Specific reference is made to environmental impact assessments and strategic environmental assessments and the involvement of public participation in accordance with each Party's laws.

Of particular interest are the provisions the TCA makes as regards climate change, carbon pricing, and chemicals.

8.4.3.1 Climate change

The UK and the EU acknowledge the importance of climate change, referring to it as an essential element of the TCA.[64] This status gives either Party the ability to terminate or suspend operation of all or part of the TCA if it considers that there has been a serious and substantial failure by the other to fulfil its climate change obligations.[65] Commitments in the TCA include the effective implementation of the UNFCCC and the Paris Agreement and cooperating on trade-related aspects of climate change policies and measures.

8.4.3.2 Carbon pricing

In respect of carbon pricing, the TCA requires that the UK and EU have an effective system of carbon pricing from 1 January 2021 covering greenhouse gas emissions from electricity generation, heat generation, industry, and aviation.[66] The UK's participation in the EU Emissions Trading System (EUETS) ceased on 31 December 2020, and the UK established a standalone UK Emissions Trading Scheme on 1 January 2021. Under the TCA, the UK and the EU commit to give 'serious consideration' to linking the two systems. One potential advantage for doing so is the Commission's proposal for a carbon border adjustment mechanism for certain carbon intensive goods, which proposes to exclude countries which are fully integrated into, or linked to, the EU ETS.[67]

64 Ibid, preamble, Recital 1, and Part Six, Dispute Settlement and Horizontal Provisions, Title II, Basis for Cooperation, art 771.

65 Ibid, Part Six, Title III, Fulfillment of Obligations and Safeguard Measures, art 772. The TCA sets out that a situation would constitute a serious and substantial failure to fulfil an obligation described as an essential element where its gravity and nature is of an exceptional sort that threatens peace and security or that has international repercussions. The TCA specifically states that an act or omission which materially defeats the object and purpose of the Paris Agreement is a serious and substantial failure.

66 Ibid, art 392.

67 See 'Proposal for a Regulation of the European Parliament and of the Council establishing a Carbon Border Adjustment' (European Commission, 14 July 2021) at <https://ec.europa.eu/info/

8.4.3.3 Chemicals

The provisions on environmental levels of protection relate to the prevention, reduction, and elimination of risks to human health or the environment arising from the production, use, release or disposal of chemical substances. In addition to this, the TCA includes a chemicals annex which addresses registration, evaluation, authorisation, restriction, approval, classification, labelling, and packaging.[68] The annex permits the UK and the EU to set their own priorities on chemicals regulation, including establishing their own levels of protection in respect of the environment.[69] The annex provides for some alignment between the UK and the EU, including an obligation on both the UK and the EU to implement the UN Globally Harmonised System of Classification and Labelling of Chemicals 'as comprehensively as it considers feasible'.[70]

8.4.3.4 Post-EU Exit Date changes to environmental law in the UK

As indicated above, the prospect for change in post-Brexit UK to environmental law has been suggested by the UK government for some time, a prospect that looks more likely in substance in the light of late 2021–late 2022 government publications and policy announcements referred to at the start of this Chapter. Such changes could affect what are referred to as 'horizontal' regulations, such as environmental impact assessments and strategic plan and programme assessments, as well as 'sectoral' areas such as habitats protections, waste management, and air pollution and water and wastewater regulation, alongside further specific areas that have until now been underlain by EU law in great detail. The latter has provided rights for individuals to enforce as black letter personal rights through the courts including in relation to individual regulatory or enforcement actions by domestic regulators or other public bodies, with implementation in practice further enhanced by the possibility of EU enforcement action through infringement proceedings against the UK by the Commission before the CJEU. That 'ecosystem' of legal protections is now open to amendment – and potential reduction in effect in terms of environmental protection – through post-Brexit provisions allowing for their amendment in the UK.

Leaving aside the changes being made to environmental law in the UK through secondary legislation addressing 'deficiencies' in the roll-over of EU environmental law in the UK, major changes are provided for through the Environment Act 2021 (the EA 2021, or the Act in this Section), though how they will be applied in practice is presently quite uncertain as to scope and effect.[71]

---

sites/default/files/carbon_border_adjustment_mechanism_0.pdf> accessed 27 July 2021. See also below ns 93 and 94.

68 TCA, annex 13.

69 Ibid, art 3 of annex 13.

70 Ibid, art 6 of annex 13.

71 Available at <https://www.legislation.gov.uk/ukpga/2021/30/introduction/enacted>.

The Act makes extensive provision for amendments to a range of environmental sectors (including air quality, water resources and wastewater provision, and the promotion of habitats conservation and protection, as well as waste resource protection, collection, and other treatment). Its provisions variously apply to England, England and Wales, and/or Northern Ireland and/or Scotland or the whole of the UK.[72] Four significant governance implications for environmental protection in the UK post-EU Exit Date merit highlighting.

First, in Part 1, Chapter 1, three key new requirements are provided for, potentially extending to England and Wales but currently only apply to England: (i) the setting and reporting of long-term targets for matters relating to the natural environment or people's enjoyment of the natural environment. At least one target for one matter must be set for (a) air quality; (b) water; (c) biodiversity; (d) resource efficiency and waste reduction; and separately (e) annual mean figures for particulate matter ($PM_{2.5}$); and (f) for species abundance; (ii) the adoption of environmental improvement plans (EIPs) for significantly improving the natural environment; and (iii) for implementation of, and effect of some sort (to be elaborated by further regulations under the Act), for a Policy Statement on the key environmental principles derived also from EU law[73] and their incorporation into government policies.

It is unclear what legal or practical effect the setting of the long-term targets or the environmental improvement plans might have.[74] It is also unclear what practical legal effects might arise from the adoption of the Policy Statement of environmental principles, nor how, if at all, they might provide a basis for legal action for their enforcement, other than in relation perhaps to the obligation on Ministers, when making policy, to have 'due regard' to the principles.[75]

72 See 'Explanatory Notes – Environment Act 2021'(The Stationary Office) at <https://www.legislation.gov.uk/ukpga/2021/30/pdfs/ukpgaen_20210030_en.pdf 24–26> accessed 27 July 2021.

73 As to which, see s 17. These replicate the principles set out under the TCA, art 393. Given that, it is unclear why or to what effect the UK chose to insist in the TCA, art 356 to apply the term 'precautionary approach' instead of the EU precautionary principle, nor how that may affect the approach in a specific case under the 2020 Act, ss 29–30.

74 Notwithstanding that s 5 imposes a duty on the Secretary of State to ensure that the targets are met. S 4, however, allows for targets to be reduced or revoked in prescribed circumstances. The UK Government missed its deadline of 31 October 2022 for setting such targets: see <https://questions-statements.parliament.uk/written-statements/detail/2022-10-28/hcws347> accessed 6 December 2022.

75 The duty to have 'due regard', in s 19(1), may of course be used to review public authority policy decisions, but such wording does not in principle set an obligation to achieve a result: see, by way of illustration, *Hotak* [2016] AC 811, especially para 74. More significantly, the UK Government has stated in a draft Environmental Principles Policy Statement that the Policy Statement will not apply to individual regulatory, planning, or licensing decisions: see 'Draft Environmental Principles Policy Statement' (Department for Environment, Food & Rural Affairs, 12 May 2022) <https://protect-eu.mimecast.com/s/D9wjCk58AsRqPxnHVRJNW>, <https://www.gov.uk/government/publications/environmental-principles-policy-statement/draft-environmental-principles-policy-statement> and accessed 29 November 2022

In the draft Policy Statement, the UK government proposes that all referenced environmental principles be applied proportionately. This line of approach has led to concerns that, for example, the precautionary principle would be diluted in effect.[76] Moreover, the draft Policy Statement does not seek to set a formula for how environmental principles should be applied to policy-making. Rather, it seeks to 'empower Ministers ... to think creatively and use environmental principles in an innovative and forward-thinking way to protect and enhance the environment'. Taking each environmental principle in turn, the draft Policy Statement (1) sets out a more detailed description of the principle, (2) explains when it can be used/is relevant, and (3) guides Ministers on its application. For example, for the 'rectification at source principle', the draft Policy Statement says policy makers should 'Consider the feasibility of rectifying the issue at source versus other options, and the costs and benefits of doing so. Efforts should be made to pursue solutions at source, where proportionate'.

It remains to be seen whether the final adopted Policy Statement will be a source of clear guidance which helps Ministers to effectively identify opportunities to protect the environment, or whether in practice it will be regarded as a somewhat 'fuzzy' statement, lacking in detailed and practical application, which Ministers need only consider in a number of limited circumstances.

Further concerns arise in relation to the scope and effect of the duty to have 'due regard' under the EA 2021. (i) In terms of the scope of the statutory duty, it only applies (a) to Ministers and (b) 'when making policy'. It is therefore a relatively limited duty in this way. Importantly, for example, it does not apply to Local Authorities or to other ministerial functions, including individual regulatory, planning or licensing decisions made by Ministers. (ii) The duty to have 'due regard' is qualified by s 19(2), which states that a Minister is not obliged to do anything that would have 'no significant environmental benefit' or would be 'disproportionate to the environmental benefit'. This qualification affords Ministers scope to ignore the principles and could undermine their consistent application. (iii) In addition, under s 19(3), there are a number of exemptions to the statutory duty, including where the policy relates to (a) defence or (b) taxation, spending, or the allocation of resources within government. Exemption (b) appears to largely exempt HM Treasury from the obligation to have 'due regard' to the Policy Statement. Concerns were raised during the Bill's progress through Parliament that these exemptions, in particular (b), undermine the consistent application of the environmental principles across all aspects of government.

76 See one example from industry in a highly critical review addressed to the original 10 March 2021 draft Statement, but which remains applicable to the 12 May 2022 draft Statement: Chartered Institute of Waste Management and the Institute of Materials, Minerals and Mining, 'Joint CIWM and IOM3 response to the Environmental Principles Draft Policy Statement Consultation' <https://www.iom3.org/uploads/assets/b087ced5-b58c-407a-b061bdecc7e0637b/Environmental-Principles-Draft-Policy-Statement-joint-response-CIWM-IOM3.pdf> accessed 27 July 2021.

Second, in Part 1, Chapter 2, extending throughout the UK, whilst mostly leaving intact the devolved administrations powers in respect of the environment,[77] the Act creates an Office for Environmental Protection (OEP). This is intended in some way to replace the oversight and enforcement role of the Commission regarding the UK as an EU Member State.[78, 79]

The OEP is an independent Non-Departmental Public Body.[80] Having existed in an interim capacity since July 2021, the OEP was legally formed on 17 November 2021.[81]

8.4.3.5 The key functions of the OEP

The principal objective of the OEP is to contribute to environmental protection and the improvement of the natural environment.[82]

The EA 2021 gives the OEP the ability to scrutinise and advise on environmental law. The *scrutiny and advice functions* of the OEP can be broken down into three distinct parts:

77 See the interesting high level review by the Centre on Constitutional Change of the implications of Brexit for devolved administrations then considered likely increasingly divergent environmental protection and control policies more generally: 'Devolution and the Environment – now the show begins?' (*Centre on Constitutional Change*, 13 January 2020) <https://www.centreonconstitutionalchange.ac.uk/news-and-opinion/devolution-and-environment> accessed 27 July 2021.

78 See, e.g., this early consideration in the Commons Environment Committee review of the then draft Environment Bill, Chapter 4: 'Pre-legislative scrutiny of the Draft Environment (Principles and Governance) Bill' (UK Parliament, 30 April 2019) at <https://publications.parliament.uk/pa/cm201719/cmselect/cmenvfru/1893/189302.htm> accessed 27 July 2021.

79 Adoption of the Environment Act was so delayed that the UK Government created what was termed an 'Interim OEP' with effect from 1 July 2021. Its Terms of Reference were limited, comprising an oversight and limited advice function: see 'What We Do' (Office for Environmental Protection) at <https://www.theoep.org.uk/what-we-do≥ accessed 27 July 2021. Notwithstanding this, the interim OEP issued a critical report on 6 July 2021 on the then draft Policy Statement, which bears scrutiny also in respect of the 12 May 2022 draft Statement, calling on Defra to look again at its scope and proposed manner of operation: 'Advice on the draft environmental principles policy statement' (Office for Environmental Protection, 16 August 2021)<https://www.theoep.org.uk/news/advice-draft-environmental-principles-policy-statement> accessed 27 July 2021.

80 See its website at <https://protect-eu.mimecast.com/s/rlwPClOxBc3zjQoIy-8iC>, <https://www.theoep.org.uk/what-we-do> accessed 29 November 2022. Illustrating its independence is its 23 November 2022 Expert Opinion on the Revocation Bill suggesting significant amendments to it, at n60.

81 See the Environment Act (Commencement No.1) Regulations 2021.

82 This is not wholly dissimilar to the purpose of the Committee on Climate Change (CCC), which seeks to provide independent advice on setting and meeting carbon budgets and preparing for climate change. Throughout the Parliamentary process, Ministers were alive to the potential for duplication of work by the CCC and OEP. To avoid this, the EA 2021 contains a provision which requires the OEP strategy to set out how it intends to avoid any overlap between the exercise of its functions and those of the CCC.

1. monitoring and reporting on environmental improvement plans (EIPs) and environmental targets;
2. monitoring and reporting on the implementation of environmental law;[83]
3. advising on changes to environmental law or any other environmental matter, where requested by a Minister.

In its role, the OEP must act objectively, impartially, proportionately, and transparently. The OEP is still subject to Parliamentary accountability, as any reports produced, which relate to EIPs, targets, or environmental law, must be laid before Parliament. Advice may also be laid before Parliament, if the OEP thinks fit.

8.4.3.6 OEP investigative powers

The Act gives the OEP the power to investigate *serious breaches* of environmental law by public authorities.[84] The OEP may do this either upon receipt of a complaint, or of its own initiative. In each case, the failure to comply with law must be 'serious', which in practice means that the OEP will only be engaging with significant issues. Further information on how the OEP will interpret whether non-compliance is 'serious' is set out in the OEP's Strategy and Enforcement Policy document.[85]

The Act sets out a number of important points on *process and timing in relation to complaints*. In particular, complaints that a public authority has failed to comply with environmental law must:

- first exhaust any internal complaints procedure; and
- be made within 3 months of the end of the complaints procedure, or 1 year from the date the alleged non-compliance occurred (where there is no complaints procedure).

This suggests that a proportion of complaints will be invalid on the basis that they are either out of time, or that complaints have not first been addressed to the relevant public authority. However, the OEP retains a discretionary power to waive the time limit, in 'exceptional' circumstances.

Having concluded its investigation, the OEP must prepare a report[86] setting out whether the public authority has failed to comply with environmental law, the OEP's reasons for that conclusion, and any recommendations the OEP may have. The OEP has discretion as to whether to publish the report – it is not mandatory. Given the public function which the OEP performs, it is unclear in what circumstances it would not be in the public interest to publish the report.

83 But, to avoid overlap, excluding law within the remit of the CCC.

84 This means that the authority either unlawfully fails to take proper account of environmental law or errs in the performance of its functions under environmental law.

85 <https://protect-eu.mimecast.com/s/MzYZCmwODS7R9O5c9rxNz>, <https://www.theoep.org.uk/strategy-and-enforcement-policy> accessed 29 November 2022

86 Note, however, that the OEP is not required to prepare a report where it has applied for environmental, judicial, or statutory review in relation to the alleged failure.

8.4.3.7 OEP powers of enforcement

The OEP has a variety of enforcement powers. In summary, and in order of escalating effect and urgency, they are:

1. Information notices
2. Decision notices
3. Environmental review
4. Judicial review

8.4.3.8 Information notices

The OEP may serve an information notice on a public authority where it has reasonable grounds for suspecting that a public authority has failed to comply with environmental law. An information notice must set out the alleged failure to comply with environmental law and why the OEP considers it to be 'serious'. The notice of this power is, in most cases, likely to follow a public complaint.

In the information notice, the OEP may also request the public authority to provide information in relation to the alleged breach. The recipient must then respond in writing to the OEP's notice and is under a statutory duty to provide the information requested within 2 months. This enforcement power has the ability to highlight serious breaches of environmental law, and draw the offending public authority into a (potentially public) exchange of information in relation to the breach and the steps which it is going to take to resolve the issue.

8.4.3.9 Decision notices

Following service of an information notice, the OEP may issue a decision notice. The OEP may serve such a notice where it considers that, on the balance of probabilities, the authority has failed to comply with environmental law, and that the failure is serious. The decision notice will describe the breach of law, in effect, 'naming and shaming' the authority. Further, the notice should set out the steps the OEP considers the authority *should* take to address the breach, including to remedy, mitigate, and prevent reoccurrence. Again, the recipient has 2 months to respond.

Many have criticised the fact that the OEP lacks the power to force corrective action in decision notices. The Act only provides that decision notices should set out 'the steps the OEP considers the authority *should* take'. While in this respect, the enforcement powers lack 'teeth', in all likelihood, the process of serving first an information notice, and then a decision notice, will nudge a non-compliant public body into compliance.

8.4.3.10 Environmental review

Where the OEP has served a decision notice and is satisfied that the authority has committed a serious breach of environmental law, it may apply to a court for an environmental review. An environmental review will be undertaken by the High

Court[87] as to the conduct of an authority which has failed to comply with environmental law, applying judicial review principles.

If the Court finds that there has been failure to comply with environmental law, it must issue a statement of non-compliance to the offending authority. Where the Court issues such a statement, it can grant judicial review remedies (other than damages). However, the grant of such remedies is subject to a 'hardship' test.[88]

8.4.3.11 Judicial review

Where there is a serious failure to comply with environmental law, and the matter is urgent, the OEP may apply for judicial review or statutory review in relation to the conduct of a public authority. In this context, urgent means necessary to prevent or mitigate serious damage to the environment or human health.

If, following such judicial or statutory review, the public body is found to have breached environmental law, it is under a statutory duty to publish a statement within 2 months setting out the steps it intends to take in light of the finding.

8.4.3.12 Publicity of remedies

The OEP is generally obliged to publish a public statement where it takes any of the aforementioned steps. However, the OEP can elect to not publish details of its enforcement where it would not be in the public interest to do so. Given the important role to be played by the publicity of such non-compliances, the ability of the OEP to take enforcement 'behind closed doors' has raised concerns. However, it is likely that, in almost all circumstances, it will be in the public interest to disclose the OEP's enforcement action.

There are some significant differences between the OEP and the Commission in terms of the operations and practical effects of their work. The Commission is not constrained by a determination of a severity impact or effect of a breach of EU environmental law by the UK prior to launching investigations or initiating legal proceedings. In addition, the Commission was able to get involved in parallel proceedings (i.e., CJEU preliminary reference cases with an impact on environmental protection) and was not constrained, as is the OEP, with ensuring no overlap with operations by other public authorities with environmental protection responsibilities, nor by a requirement to exhaust all other remedies. In the event of non-compliance by the UK (and its public bodies) with a finding (by the CJEU) that the UK was in breach of its environmental protection obligations under EU law, the Commission could initiate proceedings leading to a financial penalty being imposed on the UK. The OEP has no such powers.

87 In England and Wales.

88 Specifically, the Court can only issue such remedies where they would either (a) not cause substantial hardship or prejudice to a third party or not be detrimental to good administration, or (b) they would cause such hardship/prejudice, but the remedy is necessary to prevent serious environmental damage and there is an exceptional public interest to granting such remedy.

Third, and potentially significant for the operation of the TCA, the EA 2021 provides in s 20 for Ministerial Statements as to whether new draft environmental law would reduce the level of environmental protection provided under existing law.

While it is merely a procedural obligation to report on whether existing environmental law would regress (and not a substantive obligation that environmental law *cannot* regress), the effect of such a Ministerial Statement should not be underestimated. If a Minister has to make a statement that their Bill waters down environmental law, then one can expect Parliamentary and public scrutiny to increase markedly. The existence of this provision should make a Minister think twice about introducing legislation which waters down environmental protections – particularly the *Environment* Minister.

This provision largely aligns with the 'non-regression' principle in the TCA – and could also be used as evidence by the EU in disputes under the TCA.

Debate as to whether a statement has been given correctly can also be expected. The Act provides that the statement given to Parliament should be the 'Minister's view' that a Bill 'will not have the effect of reducing the level of environmental protection'. While this gives the Minister the benefit of the doubt, there will undoubtedly be cases 'close to the line', where the Minister will be challenged about their view and whether a Bill being promoted undermines existing environmental laws.

Furthermore, this provision allows for reduction of environmental protection from the immediate post-Brexit position on an increasing scale, though without constant vigilance with regard to that immediate post-Brexit position as the permanent benchmark. As a result, post-Brexit environmental law may lead in a first instance to an acknowledged reduction, though unstated as to degree, while subsequent environmental law then takes that reduced protection as its next benchmark. As a result, environmental law thereafter may maintain that reduction, though continuing reduction in environmental protection would not require a subsequent Ministerial Statement under s 20 acknowledging that effect.

Fourth, the Act makes provision for a new overarching chemicals regime, though initially more by way of update on/incorporation of the UK equivalent of the EU REACH regime, which was established on 1 January 2021, though with increasing provision for divergence from the EU regime.[89] One example arose in December

89 As to the EU REACH regime, see the website of the European Chemicals Agency (ECHA) at <https://echa.europa.eu/home> accessed 15 May 2020; and, for post-Brexit transition stage operations, its page on UK's EU withdrawal: 'How is the UK withdrawal affecting you?' (*ECHA*) <https://echa.europa.eu/uk-withdrawal-from-the-eu> accessed 15 May 2020. The intended new UK regime has, however, been criticised by industry as not transparent, not workable in practice and costly: see Elizabeth Rough and Georgina Hutton, 'End of Brexit transition: chemicals regulation (REACH)' (Briefing Paper CBP 8403, House of Commons Library 2021) <https://researchbriefings.files.parliament.uk/documents/CBP-8403/CBP-8403.pdf> accessed on 27 July 2021. Note that the UK REACH will not apply to Northern Ireland, as provided for in the Northern Ireland Protocol (n 34) art 5(4) and annex 2, s 23.

2021. Defra published on 9 December 2021[90] a proposal on inclusion of substances of very high concern (SVHC) on what is referred to as 'the candidate list'. This list established a priority for consideration whether a substance should be banned or included on an authorisation list for use only in certain circumstances. Inclusion in the latter list comes with a 'sunset date', after which a specific authorisation for use is required. Companies must inform their regulators and supply chains of inclusion in products they supply of SVHCs, whilst also encouraging the use of alternatives. The Defra proposal differs from the list established by the Commission in 2021, providing for only four of the ten SVHCs presented by the Commission. Significantly, too, the Defra proposal also suggests that there will no longer be an obligation to submit information on SVHCs, but would make that process voluntary. This has led to concerns over potential weakened protections on health and safety grounds as well as regards environmental protection standards.[91] There may also be UK–EU trade flow issues that arise from such differing regimes, including under the TCA.

8.5 Risk of divergence in post-EU Exit Date UK with EU environmental law?

There is clearly a risk of divergence over time, and, as has been indicated here, some alteration of environmental standards is already appearing. In particular, the possibility cannot be ruled out that, in commercial and industrial policy, divergent rules will materialise. It has been the objective of a number of UK government administrations to cut the 'red tape' burden on businesses, specifically including environmental laws, which might be said to contrast with the Commission's agenda of regularly reviewing and expanding the EU's environmental law *acquis*. The UK will, however, continue to be bound by its international commitments, and regulatory divergences which impact placing products on the UK and EU markets may have the effect of *increasing* rather than reducing the burden on businesses. Divergence may also lead to clashes between the UK and the EU under the TCA, and consequent risk of countervailing measures being applied, further increasing uncertainty for businesses.

Whilst the standalone structures established by the UK following the EU Exit Date have been broadly substantively the same as the EU structures they

90 See 'Approach to including substances of very high concern on the UK REACH candidate list' (*Department for Environment, Food & Rural Affairs*, 9 December 2021) <https://www.gov.uk/government/publications/uk-reach-approach-to-including-substances-of-very-high-concern-on-the-candidate-list/approach-to-including-substances-of-very-high-concern-on-the-uk-reach-candidate-list> accessed 16 December 2021.

91 See, e.g., Fiona Harvey, 'Experts warn over post-Brexit UK rule changes on chemicals' (*The Guardian*, 16 December 2021) <https://www.theguardian.com/environment/2021/dec/16/experts-warn-over-post-brexit-uk-rule-changes-on-chemicals> accessed on 16 December 2021. See also concerns of CHEM Trust (an association accredited as a stakeholder to ECHA and concerned with chemicals in the environment) of 3 August 2022 on the new HSE approach to SVHCs at <https://protect-eu.mimecast.com/s/mEzsCnZxEC16k8Gsmrhq3>, <https://chemtrust.org/uk-reach-lacks-capacity/> accessed 29 November 2022.

have replaced,[92] as environmental law and policy continues to evolve at pace in response to the climate and environmental emergencies, it is foreseeable that divergences could start to emerge.

Climate change protection provides an early example. The UK established a net zero emissions target by 2050 in UK law[93] to implement its commitment under the Paris Agreement and subsequently committed to interim targets of a 68% reduction in emissions from 1990 levels by 2030 (its revised Nationally Determined Contribution under the Paris Agreement) and a 78% reduction of the same by 2035.[94] The Commission has since announced a package of measures to meet its interim target of a 55% reduction by 2030 (the 'Fit for 55' policy).[95] If implemented, these measures could create regulatory divergence between the EU and the UK, particularly in relation to emissions trading and carbon pricing. Over time, it is possible that contrariwise more demanding targets are set by the EU than apply within the UK.

If significant divergence does arise in respect of environmental or climate protection, the TCA provides that either Party may take appropriate rebalancing measures to address the situation.[96] This measure is limited to divergence capable of materially impacting trade or investment between the UK and the EU in a manner that changes the circumstances that have formed the basis for concluding the TCA. The measures will be decided either by consultation between the UK and the EU or, if a mutually acceptable solution cannot be found, by an arbitration tribunal. If the rebalancing measures are used frequently or if a measure that has a material impact on trade or investment has been applied for 12 months, a review of the operation of Heading One (Trade), with or without the addition of other headings of the TCA, could be initiated. Either Party may also request a review for the purpose of ensuring that there is an appropriate balance between the UK and the EU's commitments on a more durable basis. This latter review can only be commenced four years after the entry into force of the TCA. A review could result in a modification of the TCA or a termination of the headings that were the subject of the review.

Bespoke enforcement provisions apply to the environment and sustainable development Chapters of the TCA.[97] In the event of a dispute regarding the application of the Chapters, a party may request a consultation with the other party.[98] The purpose of such consultation is to reach a mutually satisfactory resolution. If such

92 See above, however, as regards chemicals regulation under UK REACH, n 90–92 and within their weblinked documents.

93 See the Climate Change Act 2008 (2050 Target Amendment) Order 2019 (SI 2019/1056).

94 See the Carbon Budget Order 2021 (SI 2021/750) (and associated Explanatory Memorandum and Impact Assessment).

95 See the latest approach by the EU to its "Fit for 55" policy, and proposed emission reduction target of 61% by 2030, at <https://protect-eu.mimecast.com/s/NT6BCoYVGI1KQOXsoTFTN>, <https://www.consilium.europa.eu/en/policies/green-deal/fit-for-55-the-eu-plan-for-a-green-transition/ accessed 29 November 2022>.

96 TCA, art 411. The Revocation Bill, if adopted as published, would appear to pose a risk of such re-balancing measures being applied by the EU.

97 Ibid, arts 396 and 407ff.

98 Ibid, art 408.

a resolution is not achieved, either party may request that a panel of independent experts is convened to examine the matter.[99] If the final report of the panel of experts determines that a party has not conformed with its obligation(s), the parties shall discuss appropriate measures to be implemented. In the case of any disagreement on existence of, or the consistency with, the relevant provisions of any measure taken to address the non-conformity, the panel can be called upon. These enforcement provisions are in addition to the dispute settlement provisions set out in Part 6, for example if a party chooses not to take any action to conform with a report from the expert panel, the temporary remedies in Article 749 are still available to the other party.[100]

8.6 Conclusion

Environmental law and policy in the UK is already on a path of divergence from that of the EU. Burdens on businesses exporting to the EU from the UK may increase if they are confronted with differing standards for the two markets which cannot be reconciled. Similar concerns may arise of course as regards imports from the EU for incorporation in goods to be produced as 'Made in Britain'. It is also clear that the legal context for operations within the UK and the EU is becoming more complex.

Given this latter consideration, it may be useful here to recall the cautionary words from the *Lipton* case, cited here, at paragraph 83 (per Green LJ) as to the risk of divergence between the UK and the EU (hence, including in environmental law and policy) and the complexities that may further arise in identifying and addressing the same:

> In this case, the task of the court has been relatively straightforward since as of the date of this judgment the new legal regime has been in place for only a few months and nothing of relevance in the case law of the CJEU has changed. As time moves on, and the case law of the CJEU evolves, then the differences between the current state of EU law and that which the Court is to take account of might become more accentuated. At that stage the analysis might become more complex.

It is considered that the chances of divergence post Withdrawal Agreement and post TCA between environmental law and policy in (and within) the UK and environmental law and policy in the EU remain very much alive, and the work of lawyers in this field will only become much more complex.

99 Ibid, art 409.
100 Ibid, arts 409(19) and 410.

9 Brexit and Euratom

Ian Truman

9.1 The formation of Euratom and the European Community

In Paris, on 18 April 1951, West Germany, France, Italy, Belgium, Luxembourg, and the Netherlands signed the Treaty establishing the European Coal and Steel Community (ECSC).[1] This not only set out to address shortages in the supply of coal and steel after the Second World War but also had the aim of promoting diplomatic and economic stability in Europe.

Whilst the ECSC succeeded in alleviating immediate bottlenecks in the supply of coal and steel, it failed to address lingering concerns that remained about the capacity of European energy production and the potential for dependence to develop on Middle Eastern oil.

In 1955, Louis Armand prepared a report for the Organization for European Economic Cooperation underlining these concerns and proposing a possible solution: nuclear energy. This new technology had enormous potential. However, even then, Armand recognised that it would require a significantly greater degree of international cooperation than any other form of energy.[2]

That same year, the Messina Conference of European Leaders elected the Belgian foreign minister Paul H. Spaak as chairman of a committee charged with the preparation of a report covering the creation of a common European market, investments and social issues, transport, conventional energy, and nuclear energy. The so-called 'Spaak Report', published on 21 April 1956, set out the basis for what later became the European Economic Community and the European Atomic Energy Community (Euratom).[3]

1 Treaty Establishing the European Coal and Steel Community 1951 (Treaty of Paris).

2 Louis Armand, 'Some aspects of the European energy problem – Suggestions for Collective Action' (Organisation for European Cooperation 1955).

3 'The Spaak Report' (Virtual Resource Centre for Knowledge about Europe 2016) <http://www.cvce.eu/obj/the_spaak_report-en-7d169239-fff2-4bcb-b262-8f4d0de4fe0b.html> accessed 2 December 2021.

DOI: 10.4324/9781003364337-10

Following a period of difficult negotiations, on 25 March 1957, the same six States[4] that founded the ECSC signed two further treaties in Rome:

(a) The Treaty Establishing the European Economic Community (EEC),[5] or the 'Common Market', which would later be referred to as 'the Treaty of Rome'; and
(b) The Euratom Treaty.[6]

Although the ECSC, EEC, and Euratom shared certain institutions such as a court of justice and a parliament from the outset, initially they each had separate councils and commissions, meaning they were functionally, as well as legally, separate. On 8 April 1965, the Brussels Merger Treaty unified the executive institutions of the three communities, essentially extending the role of the Council and Commission of the European Economic Community over the Euratom Community and the European Coal and Steel Community. From this point forward, the three communities became known collectively as 'the European Community'. This functional 'intertwining' of the EEC and Euratom was later cited by the UK government as justification for the UK having to leave Euratom as part of the Brexit process, despite the two communities remaining legally separate.

9.2 The Euratom Treaty

The overall task of Euratom, as stated in Article 1 of the Euratom Treaty, is:

> to contribute to the raising of the standard of living in the Member States and to the development of relations with the other countries by creating the conditions necessary for the speedy establishment and growth of nuclear industries.

In Article 2, the scope of the Euratom Treaty is set out as a list of requirements that must be fulfilled by Euratom in order to perform its overall task described in Article 1. These requirements are to:

(a) *promote research and the dissemination of technical information* – which has resulted in the establishment of the Euratom Research and Training Programme, the most recent phase of which has been granted funding of €1.38 billion for the period between 1 January 2021 and 31 December 2025;[7]

4 The UK was invited to participate in the talks that led up to the formation of the ECSC but chose not to participate due to concerns over the supranational elements of the treaties.
5 Codified Version of the Treaty Establishing the European Community [1992] OJ C224/6.
6 Consolidated Version of the Treaty Establishing the European Atomic Energy Community [2012] OJ C327/1 (Euratom Treaty).
7 Directorate-General for Research and Innovation, 'Euratom Research and Training Programme' (European Commission 2021) <https://data.europa.eu/doi/10.2777/200656> accessed 31 January 2022.

(b) *establish uniform safety standards to protect the health of workers and of the general public and ensure that they are applied* – which has led to the adoption of Council Directive 2013/59/Euratom of 5 December 2013.[8] This lays down basic safety standards for protection against the dangers arising from exposure to ionising radiation and implements the IAEA Basic International Safety Standards into EU law.[9] In addition, Article 37 of the Euratom Treaty imposes an obligation on EU Member States to submit 'general data' relating to any plan to dispose of radioactive waste to the Commission, to allow it (acting through a group of experts) to determine whether such plan is liable to result in the radioactive contamination of the water, soil, or airspace of another EU Member State. In the UK (before Brexit), this opinion was required before the UK Environment Agency would issue an environmental permit for the disposal of radioactive waste under the Environmental Permitting (England and Wales) Regulations 2016;

(c) *facilitate investment and ensure the establishment of the basic installations necessary for the development of nuclear energy in the Community* – which has led to the requirement for persons and undertakings engaged in certain industrial activities[10] in Euratom Member States to notify the Commission[11] before commencing certain investment projects[12] relating to new installations, as well as replacements and conversions of existing facilities;[13]

(d) *ensure that all users in the Community receive a regular and equitable supply of ores and nuclear fuels* – which has led to the establishment of the Euratom Supply Agency that has a right of option over ores, source materials, and special fissile materials produced in the territories of Euratom Member States, which it exercises through an exclusive right to conclude contracts relating to the supply of such materials coming from or into Euratom, and the adoption of a common supply policy on the principle of equal access to sources of supply;[14]

(e) *make certain, by appropriate supervision, that nuclear materials are not diverted to non-peaceful purposes* – which has resulted in the establishment of a Euratom nuclear safeguards regime that runs in parallel with the International Atomic Energy Agency (IAEA) nuclear safeguards regime;[15]

8 Council Directive 2013/59/Euratom of 5 December 2013 laying down basic safety standards for protection against the dangers arising from exposure to ionising radiation, and repealing Directives 89/618/Euratom, 90/641Euratom, 96/29/Euratom, 97/43/Euratom and 2003/122/Euratom [2013] OJ L13/1.

9 Euratom Treaty (n 6) art 30.

10 Ibid, annex II.

11 In accordance with Commission Regulation (EC) No 1209/2000 of 8 June 2000 determining procedures for effecting the communications prescribed under Article 41 of the Treaty establishing the European Atomic Energy Community [2000] OJ L138/12.

12 Defined in Council Regulation (Euratom) No 2587/1999 of 2 December 1999 defining the investment projects to be communicated to the Commission in accordance with Article 41 of the Treaty establishing the European Atomic Energy Community [1999] OJ L315/1.

13 Euratom Treaty (n 6) art 41.

14 Ibid Chapter 6.

15 Ibid Chapter 7.

(f) *exercise the right of ownership conferred upon it with respect to special fissile materials* – which has led to a system whereby the Commission countersigns all contracts involving the supply of ores and nuclear fuels to, from, or between Euratom Member States;[16]
(g) *ensure wide commercial outlets and access to the best technical facilities by the creation of a common market in specialised materials and equipment* – which has led to the development of a nuclear common market;[17] and
(h) *establish such relations with other countries and international organisations as will foster progress in the peaceful uses of nuclear energy* – which has led to Euratom concluding Nuclear Cooperation Agreements with 'third states' on behalf of its members.[18]

By the time the UK joined what was then the EEC and Euratom on 1 January 1973, it had already commissioned a fleet of 11 Magnox[19] nuclear reactors. During its membership of Euratom, the UK:

(a) continued the development of its own domestic civil nuclear industry, which included the construction and commissioning of a fleet of advanced gas cooled reactors and (most recently) a pressurised water reactor at Sizewell in Suffolk;[20]
(b) was a net beneficiary of funding under the Euratom Research and Training Programme – in the later stages of its membership, the UK would typically receive around £65 million per year in funding from the Euratom Research and Training Programme for nuclear research activities;[21]
(c) was a member of the EUROfusion consortium, through which it hosted both the Joint European Torus and the Mega Amp Spherical Tokomak at the Culham Centre for Fusion Energy in Oxfordshire; and
(d) participated in the International Thermonuclear Experimental Reactor (ITER) Project in Cadarache in the south of France through the European Joint Undertaking, known as Fusion for Energy.

9.3 Brexit

On 23 June 2016, the UK voted to leave the EU, starting the Brexit process.

16 Ibid Chapters 6, 8.
17 Ibid Chapter 9.
18 Ibid Chapter 10.
19 Named after the magnesium–aluminium alloy used to clad the fuel rods inside the reactor.
20 EDF Energy is currently constructing the UK's first new nuclear power station since Sizewell B at Hinkley Point C in Somerset and has recently secured £700m of government funding to replicate the build at Sizewell C in Suffolk. China General Nuclear had also commenced the development of a UK HPR1000 at Bradwell in Essex but at the time of writing that project is not progressing.
21 Department for Business, Energy & Industrial Strategy, 'Euratom Exit Factsheet, Research and Development' (*GOV.UK*, 18 June 2018) <https://www.gov.uk/government/publications/nuclear-safeguards-bill-factsheets> accessed 2 December 2021.

Although membership of Euratom was not mentioned in the Brexit Referendum or the campaign which preceded it, the Explanatory Notes to the legislation[22] empowering the prime minister to formally trigger the UK's withdrawal from the EU confirmed that the power to withdraw from the EU also included the power to withdraw from Euratom.[23] The reason given by the UK government, in an oral statement to Parliament by the minister for Exiting the European Union, was that in sharing a common institutional framework, Euratom and the EU were 'uniquely legally joined', meaning that in triggering Article 50 of the Treaty on European Union (TEU) to leave the EU, the UK must also leave Euratom.[24] In practical terms, the Lisbon Treaty[25] had inserted a number of provisions of the TEU and the Treaty on the Functioning of the European Union (TFEU) into the Euratom Treaty,[26] including the Article 50 withdrawal mechanism.

Article 106a(2) of the Euratom Treaty incorporated Article 50 of the TEU by reference, stating that references to the 'Union', the TEU, or the TFEU should simply be read as references to Euratom or the Euratom Treaty as the context required. In doing so, Article 106a of the Euratom Treaty created a parallel 'Article 50 mechanism' for leaving Euratom.

As such, when the UK Prime Minister Theresa May gave formal notice to the European Council of the UK's intention to leave the EU on 20 March 2017, she explicitly made such notification in accordance with both Article 50(2) of the TEU and Article 50(2) as applied by Article 106a of the Euratom Treaty.

In accordance with Article 50(2) of the TEU as applied through 106a of the Euratom Treaty, the UK was to leave Euratom at 11pm on 29 March 2019, two years after its Article 50/106a notification was served on the European Council, unless both sides agreed for this period to be extended.

9.4 Brexit negotiations

Once the UK had formally notified the EU of its intention to leave Euratom, it began negotiating the Withdrawal Agreement. Although Euratom issues were never highlighted as a particular problem during the negotiations, it soon became clear that the failure to agree a Withdrawal Agreement for other unrelated reasons[27] – a so-called 'no deal' Brexit – could have particularly significant implications for both the UK and EU nuclear sectors as well as affecting the ability of the UK to continue nuclear trade with its international partners outside the EU.

In the event of a 'no deal' Brexit, the future of the UK's trade with the EU would have defaulted to WTO Rules, subject of course to the requirements of

22 European Union (Notification of Withdrawal) Act 2017.
23 Ibid, Explanatory Notes para 18.
24 HC Deb, 1 February 2017, vol. 620, col 1132.
25 Treaty of Lisbon amending the Treaty on European Union and the Treaty establishing the European Community [2007] OJ C 306/1.
26 Euratom Treaty (n 6) art 106(a).
27 Such as the failure to agree provisions in relation to the treatment of Northern Ireland.

applicable international nuclear laws, which would have remained binding on both parties. The UK's withdrawal from Euratom in the event of a 'no deal' Brexit, however, would also have left the UK without critical nuclear safeguards agreements[28] with the IAEA that underpinned its well-developed programmes of international nuclear trade and cooperation. The UK would also no longer have access to the suite of nuclear cooperation agreements that Euratom had agreed with third states on behalf of its members, which prior to Brexit had provided much of the framework for its international nuclear trade and collaboration. Whilst the UK could continue existing programmes of international nuclear trade and collaboration with many of its international partners without replacing these agreements, several key partners such as the USA, Canada, and Australia had adopted domestic law or policy requiring such agreements to be in place as a prerequisite for the continuation of trade and collaboration with another state.

Whilst the UK government continued its efforts to negotiate the Withdrawal Agreement and secure the necessary approval from the UK Parliament, it also began to implement contingency measures designed to mitigate the impacts of a 'no deal' Brexit on the UK nuclear sector. As part of this programme, the UK government published a series of technical notices setting out information to allow businesses and citizens to understand the implications of a 'no deal' Brexit, which were subsequently replaced by updated guidance.[29]

During the negotiations, the UK government was successful in securing the following contingency measures:

(a) a new bilateral Voluntary Offer Safeguards Agreement (VOSA) and Additional Protocol (AP)[30] with the IAEA to underpin its international nuclear trade and collaboration with other states after Brexit;
(b) the development of a domestic safeguards regime to allow the UK to comply with its obligations in its new VOSA and AP with the IAEA and relevant international agreements with other states; and
(c) new, bilateral nuclear cooperation agreements with the USA,[31] Canada,[32] and Australia,[33] and an extension of an existing agreement with Japan. Euratom also has other nuclear cooperation agreements in place,[34] but the UK

28 Such as a Voluntary Offer Safeguards Agreement pursuant to the UK's status as a nuclear weapons state under the UN Treaty on the Non-Proliferation of Nuclear Weapons and the associated Additional Protocol to that agreement.

29 Department for Business, Energy and Industrial Strategy, 'Civil Nuclear regulation if there's no Brexit deal' (*GOV.UK*, August 2019) <www.gov.uk/government/publications/civil-nuclear-regulation-if-theres-no-brexit-deal/civil-nuclear-regulation-if-theres-no-brexit-deal#reporting-and-notification-obligations-under-article-37-of-the-euratom-treaty> accessed 3 December 2021.

30 During the UK's membership of Euratom, these agreements were tripartite, including the Euratom Community.

31 Concluded on 4 May 2018.

32 Concluded on 2 November 2018.

33 Concluded on 21 August 2018.

34 With Argentina, Kazakhstan, South Africa, Ukraine, and Uzbekistan.

government did not prioritise agreeing replacements for these given that the countries signed up to these had no legal or policy requirement for a nuclear cooperation agreement to be in place as a prerequisite for the continuation of nuclear trade or collaboration with the UK after Brexit.

Although potentially necessary irrespective of any deal reached between the UK and the EU and Euratom, the possibility of a 'no deal' Brexit rendered the contingency measures above vital for the UK to mitigate the associated risks.

9.5 The Withdrawal Agreement

On 31 January 2020, the UK entered into the Withdrawal Agreement and formally left both the EU and Euratom. Despite having formally left, however, the UK retained unfettered access to the EU Single Market (including the nuclear common market) during the Transition Period until 31 December 2020, on the condition that it remained in compliance with EU law, including the Euratom Treaty and its subordinate legislation.

Title IX of the Withdrawal Agreement (Euratom Related Issues) provided that at the end of the Transition Period:

(a) The UK would inherit sole responsibility for ensuring that ores, source materials, and special fissile materials covered by the Euratom Treaty present within the UK would be handled in accordance with international law;
(b) The UK would have sole responsibility for ensuring its compliance with international obligations, such as its new bilateral VOSA and AP with the IAEA, which would include implementing its own domestic nuclear safeguards regime;
(c) The UK would ensure that any specific obligations under Euratom agreements with 'third states' or international organisations in relation to nuclear equipment, nuclear material, or other nuclear items present in the UK were fulfilled or alternative arrangements made;
(d) Special fissile materials owned by Euratom under Article 86 of the Euratom Treaty present in the UK would become the property of the persons or undertakings that previously enjoyed the unlimited rights of use and consumption of those materials under Article 87 of the Euratom Treaty. Where these Article 87 rights of use were with Euratom Member States:
    (i) Euratom could require such materials to be deposited with the Euratom Supply Agency or in other stores supervised by the Commission;
    (ii) The Euratom Supply Agency would have the exclusive rights to conclude supply contracts for such materials;
    (iii) The export and shipment of such material from the UK would remain subject to EU law;[35]

35 Commission Regulation (Euratom) 302/2005 of 8 February 2005 on the application of Euratom safeguards [2008] OJ L54/81, art 20.

(iv) The export of such materials from the UK to a 'third state' would be subject to authorisation from the competent authorities of the Euratom Member State where the person or undertaking with Article 87 rights was established;

(v) Euratom would have the right to exert any other rights under the Euratom Treaty which flow from Euratom ownership of materials under Article 86;

(vi) Euratom equipment and other property related to the enforcement of Euratom Safeguards that is in the UK would be sold to the UK; and

(vii) The UK would remain responsible for safe management of spent fuel and radioactive waste generated in the UK but present in another Euratom Member State.[36]

9.6 The negotiation of the Free Trade Agreement

Article 184 of the Withdrawal Agreement obliged the EU and the UK to use their best endeavours to take the necessary steps to negotiate the agreements governing their future relationship referred to in a 'political declaration' of 17 October 2019 and to conclude those agreements where possible by the end of the Transition Period on 31 December 2020.

The intention of the parties in relation to the nuclear sector were set out in Part B of Chapter XI of the 'political declaration'. This provided that the future relationship between the parties should include:

> a wide-ranging Nuclear Cooperation Agreement between the European Atomic Energy Community (Euratom) and the United Kingdom on peaceful uses of nuclear energy, underpinned by commitments to their existing high standards of nuclear safety. The agreement should enable cooperation between Euratom and the United Kingdom and its national authorities. This should include exchange of information in areas of mutual interest such as safeguards, safety and cooperation with the International Atomic Energy Agency (IAEA). It should facilitate trade in nuclear materials and equipment, and provide for the participation of the United Kingdom as a third country in Union systems for monitoring and exchanging information on levels of radioactivity in the environment, namely the European Community Urgent Radiological Information Exchange and the European Radiological Data Exchange Platform.[37]

36 Directive 2011/70/Euratom of 19 July 2011 establishing a Community framework for the responsible and safe management of spent fuel and radioactive waste [2011] OJ L199/48, arts 4(1)–(2),(4).

37 HM Government, 'Political Declaration setting out the framework for the future relationship between the European Union and the United Kingdom' (October 2019) <https://www.gov.uk/government/publications/new-withdrawal-agreement-and-political-declaration> accessed 2 December 2021, para 66.

A nuclear cooperation agreement was chosen as the form of the future relationship between the UK and Euratom on the basis that it was a familiar format to both parties.[38] Also of considerable benefit was that the Commission was able to enter into such an agreement with the approval of the European Council acting by a qualified majority,[39] leaving less leverage for anti-nuclear states to block ratification. By way of comparison, an alternative would have been an Association Agreement under Article 206 of the Euratom Treaty, which had never been used before and would require the unanimous consent of the European Council.

The other provisions relevant to the nuclear sector in the 'political declaration' included:

(a) confirmation the UK intended to seek continued participation in the Euratom Research and Training Programme as an 'associated' state after the end of the Transition Period;
(b) confirmation that the Euratom Supply Agency would consider the need to reapprove ongoing contracts for the supply of materials which it had co-signed before Brexit;[40] and
(c) a commitment for the parties to cooperate through the exchange of information on the supply of medical radioisotopes.

On 29 March 2019, the UK government announced it had agreed a new contract with the EU to continue the operation of the Joint European Torus facility at the Culham Centre for Fusion Energy, which had secured at least €100m in additional funding until the end of the Transition Period on 31 December 2020.

In early 2020, it was widely expected that the UK government's main focus would be on negotiating a free trade agreement with the EU before the end of the Transition Period on 31 December 2020. Whilst the Coronavirus pandemic understandably dominated the UK government's agenda in 2020, work continued on Brexit, with the UK government resisting calls from the EU and UK political parties to extend the end of the Transition Period into 2021.

During the negotiations over future trading arrangements, there was never any indication that negotiation of the nuclear cooperation agreement between Euratom and the UK was proving problematic.

On 24 December 2020, just 7 days before the end of the Transition Period, the parties announced agreement of the Trade and Cooperation Agreement (TCA)

38 Department for Business, Energy and Industrial Strategy, 'UK–Euratom nuclear cooperation agreement – notice' (*GOV.UK*, 24 December 2020) <https://www.gov.uk/government/publications/nuclear-cooperation-agreements-implementation-guidelines-for-operators/uk-euratom-nuclear-cooperation-agreement> accessed 31 January 2022.

39 Euratom Treaty (n 6) art 101.

40 In early 2019, the UK government confirmed there was no need for such contracts to be reapproved.

and a Nuclear Cooperation Agreement (NCA)[41] between the EU, Euratom, and the UK.[42] The TCA was subsequently updated on 30 April 2021.[43]

Given that Euratom and the UK were entering a separate NCA, the TCA did not contain many provisions of direct relevance to the nuclear sector, with the exception of:

(a) Article 29 Part Two, Title I (Trade) – which specifically reserves the rights of the parties to establish export controls in order to meet the requirements of UN Security Council Resolutions[44] and a number of multinational non-proliferation regimes, including the Wassenaar Arrangement on Export Controls for Conventional Arms and Dual-Use Goods and Technologies and the Nuclear Suppliers' Group;[45] and
(b) Article 710 of Part V (Participation in Union programmes) which confirms the UK's ongoing participation in, and contribution to, the EU programmes and activities listed in Protocol I.

9.7 The Joint Declaration on Participation in Union Programmes and Access to Programme Services

The parties could not finalise Protocol I in the limited time available to negotiate the TCA, so instead a Joint Declaration on Participation in Union programmes and Access to Programme Services was adopted. The Joint Declaration included draft text for Protocol I[46] which, although agreed in principle between the parties,

41 'Agreement between the Government of the United Kingdom of Great Britain and Northern Ireland and the European Atomic Energy Community for cooperation on the safe and peaceful uses of nuclear energy' (December 2020) <https://assets.publishing.service.gov.uk/government/uploads/system/uploads/attachment_data/file/948106/EU_UK_Civil_Nuclear_Agreement_24.12.2020.pdf> accessed 2 December 2021.

42 'EU–UK Agreement for cooperation on the safe and peaceful uses of nuclear energy' (December 2020) <https://ec.europa.eu/info/strategy/relations-non-eu-countries/relations-united-kingdom/eu-uk-trade-and-cooperation-agreement/eu-uk-agreement-cooperation-safe-and-peaceful-uses-nuclear-energy_en> accessed 2 December 2021.

43 'Trade and cooperation agreement between the European Union and the European Atomic Energy Community, of the one part, and the United Kingdom of Great Britain and Northern Ireland, of the other part' (April 2021) <https://www.gov.uk/government/publications/agreements-reached-between-the-united-kingdom-of-great-britain-and-northern-ireland-and-the-european-union> accessed 2 December 2021.

44 Particularly United Nations Security Council Resolution 1373 of 28 September 2001 in relation to threats to international peace and security caused by terrorist acts and United Nations Security Council Resolution 1540 of 28 April 2004 relating to the non-proliferation of weapons of mass destruction.

45 'The Wassenaar Arrangement on Export Controls for Conventional Arms and Dual-use Goods and Technologies' <https://www.wassenaar.org/> accessed 2 December 2021.

46 See 'Joint Declaration on Participation in Union Programmes and Access to Programme Services' <https://assets.publishing.service.gov.uk/government/uploads/system/uploads/attachment_data/file/948105/EU-UK_Declarations_24.12.2020.pdf> accessed 31 January 2022, 15.

remains (at the time of writing) subject to discussion and formal adoption by the Specialised Committee on Participation in EU Programmes.[47] The delay to the adoption of Protocol 1 appears to have been caused by the delay in implementing the associated legislation in the EU and the UK until 1 May 2021 and the more recent disputes over the UK's implementation of the Northern Ireland Protocol.[48]

As set out in the Joint Declaration, the draft Protocol I provides the UK with continuing access to a number of EU programmes, including the Euratom Research and Training Programme and the ITER Project in return for financial contributions.[49] In both cases, the draft Protocol I provides for the UK's continued participation in these programmes, on the same basis as other Euratom legal entities, from 1 January 2021 (pending the formal adoption of the draft protocol) until the earlier of either the expiry of the programmes, or the end of the current EU multiannual framework in 2027.[50]

The key conditions of the UK's participation in the Euratom Research and Training Programme are set out in Article 7 of the draft Protocol I, which confirms that:

(a) the UK would participate as an 'associated country'; and
(b) UK entities would be able to continue to participate in direct actions of the Joint Research Centre.

The key conditions of the UK's participation in Fusion for Energy and hence the ITER Project are set out in Article 8 of the draft protocol, which confirms that:

(a) the UK would continue to participate in Fusion for Energy under the pre-existing Fusion for Energy Council Decision and its statutes;
(b) UK representatives will continue to participate in Fusion for Energy meetings; and
(c) The Agreement on the Establishment of the ITER International Fusion Energy Organization for the joint implementation of the ITER project[51] and associated agreements applies to the UK.

47 Established as one of eight specialized Committees under the TCA Partnership Council.
48 House of Commons Library "Is the UK still participating in EU programmes" November 2021 <https://commonslibrary.parliament.uk/is-the-uk-still-participating-in-eu-programmes/> accessed on 24 February 2022.
49 The contributions required from the UK to be subject to adjustment depending on the amount of funding apportioned to UK entities.
50 This reflects the fact that the current Euratom Research and Training Programme, despite being part of Horizon Europe, is due to expire on 31 December 2025. Previous programmes have been extended so they end on the same date as Horizon Europe and the EU's wider multiannual framework.
51 Agreement on the Establishment of the ITER International Fusion Energy Organization for the joint implementation of the ITER project <https://www.europarl.europa.eu/document/activities/cont/201105/20110506ATT18844/20110506ATT18844EN.pdf> accessed on 2 December 2021.

In relation to the formal adoption of the draft Protocol I, the UK minister for the Cabinet Office, Michael Gove,[52] confirmed that the UK's further participation remained subject to certain financial, constitutional, legal. and public policy questions, namely whether each programme provides value for money; whether such participation involves a surrender of sovereignty, Court of Justice of the European Union (CJEU) jurisdiction, and the application of EU law in the UK; and the broader concept of public judgment as to whether the programme in question works.[53]

At the time of writing, the UK is pushing for the EU to formally adopt Protocol I and is finalising negotiations to extend the Joint European Torus contract until 2023.

9.8 An agreement for cooperation on the safe and peaceful uses of nuclear energy

As set out in Part B of Chapter XI of the 'political declaration' in the Withdrawal Agreement, the UK and Euratom also entered into an NCA relating to the safe and peaceful uses of nuclear energy, which the UK government describes as legally underpinning future civil nuclear cooperation between the parties.

The NCA between the UK and the Euratom broadly follows the conventional format of such agreements, but unsurprisingly, the recitals refer to Brexit and particular UK specific matters, such as recognising the agreement, is without prejudice to the Amelo Treaty between the UK, Germany, and the Netherlands founding Urenco.[54]

The NCA's overriding object is set out in Article 1 as:

> to provide a framework for cooperation between the parties in the peaceful uses of nuclear energy on the basis of mutual benefit and reciprocity and without prejudice to the respective competencies of each Party.

The intended scope of the NCA is broad. It includes the facilitation of trade and commercial cooperation; the supply of certain materials, equipment, and technology; and the procurement of certain equipment and devices.[55] Whilst it remains the responsibility of UK and Euratom entities to enter into their own legal

52 Interim UK co-chair of the TCA Partnership Council until 1 March 2021, when the role was taken over by Lord Frost CMG.

53 House of Lords European Union Committee 'Beyond Brexit: the institutional framework' (March 2021) (HL Paper 246) <https://publications.parliament.uk/pa/ld5801/ldselect/ldeucom/246/24602.htm> accessed 2 December 2021, para 141.

54 'Agreement between the United Kingdom of Great Britain and Northern Ireland, the Federal Republic of Germany, and the Kingdom of the Netherlands on Collaboration in the Development and Exploitation of the Gas Centrifuge Process for Producing Enriched Uranium', <https://fissilematerials.org/library/urenco70.pdf> accessed 2 December 2021.

55 Nuclear Cooperation Agreement 2020 (NCA), art 3.

arrangements,[56] the NCA lists forms of potential cooperation, such as the transfer of materials, equipment, and technology; the exchange of information, training, and experts; and commercial cooperation relating to the nuclear fuel cycle.[57]

The NCA applies to the following items across all Euratom Member States,[58] unless the parties agree otherwise or a Euratom Member State has applied for a particular technology to be excluded from the framework:[59]

(a) transfers of nuclear material,[60] non-nuclear material,[61] equipment,[62] and technology[63] between the parties;
(b) any such materials, equipment, or technology produced through the use of items subject to the agreement;
(c) any such materials, equipment, or technology as determined in accordance with the administrative arrangements established under the NCA; and
(d) any other items agreed by the parties following consultation in the Joint Committee established under Article 19 of the NCA.

A key function of any nuclear cooperation agreement is to establish a framework for nuclear safeguards, including a robust and effective system of nuclear material accountancy and control. This is especially pertinent in this agreement following the UK's withdrawal from the Euratom Safeguards regime, the establishment of its own domestic nuclear safeguards regime, and the entry into force of a new, bilateral VOSA and AP between the UK and the IAEA.

Other key areas covered by the NCA include the physical protection of nuclear materials[64] and nuclear safety,[65] which includes continued access for the UK to established Community systems for monitoring and exchanging information

56 Ibid, art 3(2).
57 Ibid, art 4.
58 Ibid, art 5(1).
59 Ibid, art 5(4).
60 Defined in the NCA as any 'source material' of 'special fissionable material' as those terms are defined in Article XX of the Statute of the IAEA 1956.
61 Defined by reference to Annex B of Part I of the Nuclear Suppliers' Group Guidelines as including deuterium and heavy water and nuclear grade graphite.
62 Defined by reference to Sections 1 (nuclear reactors and related equipment); 3 (plants for the reprocessing of irradiated fuel elements and related equipment); 4 (plant for the fabrication of nuclear reactor fuel elements and related equipment); 5 (plant for the separation of isotopes of natural uranium, depleted uranium, or special fissionable material and related equipment [excluding analytical instruments]); 6 (plant for the production of heavy water, deuterium, and deuterium compounds and related equipment); and 7 (plant for the conversion of uranium and plutonium for use in the fabrication of fuel elements and the separation of uranium isotopes and related equipment) of Annex B of Part I of the Nuclear Suppliers' Group Guidelines.
63 Defined by reference to Annex A of Part I of the Nuclear Suppliers' Group Guidelines as specific information required for the 'development', 'production', or 'use' of any item contained in the List. This information may take the form of 'technical data' or 'technical assistance'.
64 NCA (n 53) art 7.
65 Ibid art 8.

on levels of radioactivity in the environment, such as the European Community Urgent Radiological Information Exchange (ECURIE) and the European Radiological Data Exchange Platform (EURDEP).

The parties have also agreed that any transfers of materials, equipment, or technology must be made on fair commercial terms[66] in accordance with the applicable international commitments of both parties including nuclear safeguards, physical protection measures, and any applicable guidelines of the Nuclear Suppliers' Group.[67]

Continued cooperation under the NCA is stated to be contingent on the mutually satisfactory application of nuclear safeguards by each party and a lack of interference with the integrity and smooth operation of the Community's nuclear common market.[68]

The NCA also contains relatively common[69] provisions prohibiting the enrichment of any nuclear material to more than 20% in the isotope Uranium-235 without the other party's consent and an agreement for each party to reprocess nuclear fuel in accordance with the provisions in a dedicated annex to the NCA.

The parties also agree to cooperate on research and development for peaceful purposes in areas of common interests but only where those interests are covered by respective research and development programmes and activities. The NCA sets out examples of cooperation in research and development, which includes the UK's participation in the Euratom Research and Training Programme and membership of Fusion for Energy on the terms set out in the TCA.[70]

The NCA establishes a Joint Committee to oversee the implementation of the agreement, co-ordinate action for cooperation in non-power uses of nuclear energy such as the supply of medical radioisotopes and settling any disputes which arise.[71]

9.9 Nuclear cooperation agreements with other third states

Once the UK left Euratom, it was unable to make use of a suite of NCAs Euratom had entered into with its key trading partners such as China and the USA.

Whilst the UK is likely to replace all of these agreements over time with its own bilateral nuclear cooperation agreements based on its status as a third state, prior to leaving Euratom, it prioritised securing its own bilateral agreements with the United States, Japan, Canada, and Australia, all of which made the existence of an NCA a requirement for ongoing civil nuclear trade.

These agreements were categorised as 'relevant international agreements' for the purposes of Section 112(1A) of the Energy Act 2013,[72] which in turn brought

66 Ibid art 9(6).

67 Ibid art 9(1).

68 Ibid art 9(4).

69 For two parties that already possess enrichment and reprocessing capability.

70 NCA (n 53) art 12.

71 Ibid art 19.

72 Through the Nuclear Safeguards (Fissionable Material and Relevant International Agreements) (EU Exit) Regulations 2019.

them within the 'nuclear safeguards purposes' of the Office for Nuclear Regulation (ONR)[73] and empowered the Secretary of State to give effect to their provisions through the adoption of nuclear safeguards regulations.[74]

9.10 Nuclear safeguards in the UK

On leaving Euratom, it was necessary for the UK to establish its own domestic safeguards regime in order to meet its international obligations to the IAEA under the VOSA and AP and to trading partners under the relevant international agreements referenced above.

To implement its new domestic safeguards regime, the UK has adopted a number of domestic laws, including:

(a) The Nuclear Safeguards Act 2018 – which creates the legal framework for a new UK domestic nuclear safeguards regime, extends the regulatory purposes of the ONR to include nuclear safeguards,[75] and empowers the Secretary of State to make regulations relating to nuclear safeguards; and
(b) The Nuclear Safeguards (EU Exit) Regulations 2019 – made under the Nuclear Safeguards Act 2018, which set out the UK's domestic nuclear safeguards regime in more detail.

To minimise the impact on UK nuclear operators and maintain continuity for international trading partners, the new UK safeguards regime is broadly similar in content to the requirements that applied to UK nuclear operators under the Euratom Safeguards regime[76] with necessary changes to reflect the UK's withdrawal from the EU and Euratom, such as the appointment of the ONR as the safeguards regulator in place of the Commission.

The new UK nuclear safeguards regime does, however, impose additional obligations[77] on UK nuclear operators to facilitate the UK's compliance with the 'relevant international agreements' referenced above. By way of example, if a UK nuclear operator were to be advised by the Secretary of State that it holds tritium or tritium-related equipment covered by the UK–Canada agreement, that operator would have to provide certain information to the Secretary of State. In other instances, UK nuclear operators are required to provide the Secretary of State with certain information when they export, ship, import, receive, produce, process, derive, or fabricate certain items specified in each international agreement.

73 Energy Act 2013, s 2(b).
74 Energy Act 2013, s 76(A)(1)(b).
75 By amending the ONR's 'purposes' in the Energy Act 2013.
76 Governed by Euratom Treaty (n 6) Chapter 7, Commission Regulation (Euratom) No 302/2005 (n 35) and Commission Recommendation of 11 February 2009 on the implementation of a nuclear material accountancy and control system by operators of nuclear installations [2009] OJ L54/1.
77 Nuclear Safeguards (Fissionable Material and Relevant International Agreements) (EU Exit) Regulations 2019, Part 13.

9.11 Medical radioisotopes in the UK

The potential impact of a 'no deal' Brexit on the supply of medical radioisotopes for UK cancer patients was the subject of dramatic headlines in the national press during Brexit negotiations.[78]

The most commonly used medical radioisotope, technetium-99m (^{99m}Tc),[79] is produced from the radioactive decay of molybdenum-99 (^{99}Mo), which is generally produced by nuclear research reactors in Euratom,[80] South Africa, or Australia.[81]

Despite assurances from the UK government that the supply of medical radioisotopes, such as ^{99}Mo, would not be affected by Brexit, concern grew that wider Brexit-related disruption at the UK border could impact supplies. These concerns arose because neither ^{99}Mo nor ^{99m}Tc can be stockpiled because of their rapid radioactive decay. Generally, ^{99}Mo is loaded into dispensers called generators, which are then shipped to radio-pharmacies in hospitals where ^{99m}Tc doses are extracted. The yield of ^{99m}Tc from these ^{99}Mo generators halves every 66 hours, making them extremely vulnerable to any delays.[82]

In the NCA, cooperation to minimise the risk of shortage of supply of medical radioisotopes was specifically included in the scope of the agreement,[83] whilst the exchange of information regarding the supply of radioisotopes was also specifically included as a possible form of that cooperation under Article 3.[84] Finally, the functions of the Joint Committee established by the NCA included coordinating action to minimise the risks of shortage of supply of medical radioisotopes.[85]

Outside its ongoing relationship with Euratom, the UK also remains part of the OECD/NEA High Level Group on Medical Radioisotopes.[86] This group recently concluded its fourth mandate in which it continued its efforts to help ensure the global security of supply of ^{99}Mo/^{99m}Tc through the implementation of its six policy principles. These principles include the promotion of full-cost recovery for supply chain participants, the establishment of reserve capacity, the need for

78 Deborah Cohen and Marianna Spring, 'Brexit: Warning over cancer treatment supplies after no deal' (*BBC News*, 1 August 2019) <https://www.bbc.co.uk/news/education-49153073> accessed 2 December 2021; 'EU officials warn UK over radioactive isotopes' (*Financial Times*, 17 July 2017) <https://www.ft.com/content/f146cd86-6714-11e7-8526-7b38dcaef614> accessed 2 December 2021.

79 Which accounts for over 80% of diagnostic nuclear medicine procedures.

80 Particularly the Netherlands, France, and Belgium.

81 Although future research reactors are planned in Argentina and South Korea.

82 Parliamentary Office of Science and Technology, 'Supply of Medical Radioisotopes' (July 2017) <https://researchbriefings.files.parliament.uk/documents/POST-PN-0558/POST-PN-0558.pdf> accessed 2 December 2021.

83 NCA (n 53) art 3(1)(i).

84 NCA (n 53) art 4(b).

85 NCA (n 53) art 19(4)(f).

86 'High-level Group on the Security of Supply of Medical Radioisotopes (HLG-MR)' (Nuclear Energy Agency) <https://www.oecd-nea.org/jcms/pl_26152/high-level-group-on-the-security-of-supply-of-medical-radioisotopes-hlg-mr> accessed on 2 December 2021.

national governments to establish the necessary national infrastructure, and the need for ongoing international collaboration.[87]

9.12 The future of UK nuclear law

Brexit was never specifically about leaving Euratom. There was no indication from those supporting Brexit that continued membership of Euratom was something they vehemently opposed, beyond the fact that it involved ceding sovereignty to Euratom and the CJEU.

It appeared that the UK government almost begrudgingly accepted that it had no choice but to leave Euratom given the degree to which the EU treaties had become intertwined. As the UK nuclear sector grappled with the potential implications of leaving Euratom in relation to its future trade and collaboration with Euratom and the rest of the world, questions began to arise as to whether, and to what extent, UK nuclear law and regulation would change after leaving Euratom.

Since midnight on 31 December 2020, when the Transition Period formally ended, the UK has been under no legal obligation to comply with the Euratom Treaty. To avoid potentially harmful cliff-edge effects following the end of the Transition Period, the UK adopted the European Union (Withdrawal) Act 2018[88] which simply transposed the majority of direct EU/Euratom law[89] directly into the UK legal system. As a result, the majority of UK nuclear law reflects the requirements of Euratom, although the UK government is currently reviewing retained EU/Euratom legislation with a view to either amending, retaining, or revoking it.

UK government guidance issued after Brexit has indicated the following changes to UK nuclear law and practice, which have taken effect from 1 January 2021:

(a) UK operators are no longer be required to secure the approval of the European Commission that any plan for the disposal of radioactive waste would not be liable to result in the radioactive contamination of the water, soil, or airspace of another Member State, under Article 37 of the Euratom Treaty.[90] The Transboundary Radioactive Contamination (England)

87 Nuclear Energy Agency, Steering Committee for Nuclear Energy, 'High-Level Group on the Security of Supply of Medical Radioisotopes – Final Report of the Fourth Mandate of the HLG-MR' (February 2021) <https://www.oecd-nea.org/upload/docs/application/pdf/2021-02/nea_sen_hlgmr_2019_2_approved.pdf> accessed 2 December 2021.

88 As amended by the European Union (Withdrawal Agreement) Act 2020.

89 Such as EU/Euratom regulations and EU/Euratom decisions.

90 Department of Business, Energy & Industrial Strategy, 'Guidance: Transboundary impacts of Radioactive Waste Disposal: reporting and notification obligations' <https://www.gov.uk/guidance/transboundary-impacts-of-radioactive-waste-disposal-reporting-and-notification-obligations-euratom-article-37> accessed 2 December 2021.

Direction 2020[91] now requires the Environment Agency to consider the potential for transboundary radioactive contamination before granting an environmental permit for the disposal of radioactive waste to ensure the UK remains in compliance with other relevant international law, such as the UNECE Convention on Environmental Impact Assessment in a Transboundary Context;[92]

(b) UK entities will no longer be required to report details of certain nuclear investments to the European Commission under Article 41 of the Euratom Treaty and its associated Euratom regulations;[93]

(c) The use of UK rather than EU documentation in relation to trans-frontier shipments of radioactive waste and spent nuclear fuel;[94]

(d) Changes to the requirements for the shipment of radioactive sources between the UK and the EU;[95]

(e) The introduction of a new Open General Export Licence for the export of dual-use nuclear items from the UK to the EU or the Channel Islands to replace the previous licence issued by the UK pursuant to the EU Dual-Use Regulation;[96]

(f) A new, legal requirement for an Open General Import Licence for certain nuclear materials[97] under the Import of Goods (Control) Order 1954;[98] and

(g) Obligations on UK nuclear operators to ensure compliance with the UK's obligations in its bilateral nuclear cooperation agreements including those it has entered as a result of Brexit and those which it entered before or during its membership of Euratom.[99]

91 Transboundary Radioactive Contamination (England) Direction 2020 (December 2020) <https://www.legislation.gov.uk/uksi/2016/1154/pdfs/uksiod_20161154_en_001.pdf> accessed 2 December 2021.

92 Convention on Environmental Impact Assessment in a Transboundary Context (adopted 25 February 1991, entered into force 10 September 1997) 1989 UNTS 309.

93 Communication of Investments (Revocation) (EU Exit) Regulations 2018.

94 Department for Business, Energy and Industrial Strategy, 'Guidance: Shipping radioactive waste and spent fuel' (*GOV.UK*, 31 December 2020) <https://www.gov.uk/guidance/shipping-radioactive-waste-and-spent-fuel> accessed 2 December 2021.

95 Department of Business, Energy & Industrial Strategy, 'Guidance: Shipping radioactive sources between the UK and EU' (*GOV.UK*, 31 December 2020) <https://www.gov.uk/guidance/shipping-radioactive-sources-between-the-uk-and-eu> accessed 2 December 2021.

96 The Department of Business, Energy & Industrial Strategy, 'Guidance: Exporting nuclear-related items' (*GOV.UK*, 31 December 2020) <https://www.gov.uk/guidance/exporting-nuclear-related-items> accessed 2 December 2021.

97 Uranium ore and concentrates, plutonium, uranium-233, enriched uranium and mixtures, compounds and alloys containing such substances.

98 Department for Business, Energy and Industrial Strategy, 'Guidance: Import Controls' (*GOV.UK*, 9 August 2021) <https://www.gov.uk/guidance/import-controls> accessed 2 December 2021.

99 Department of Business, Energy and Industrial Strategy and the Office for Nuclear Regulation, 'Nuclear Cooperation Agreement between the United Kingdom and International Partners: Implementation Guidelines for Nuclear Operators' (*GOV.UK*, 24 December 2020) <https://www.gov.uk/government/publications/nuclear-cooperation-agreements-implementation-guidelines-for-operators> accessed 2 December 2021.

9.13 Conclusion

In the medium to long term, there would seem to be relatively little scope for significant divergence of UK nuclear law from the Euratom regime given that the UK will remain bound by the same international nuclear laws and good practice which underpin the current Euratom legislative and regulatory framework. By way of example, although the Euratom Basic Safety Standards Directive is no longer legally binding on the UK, the UK legislation implementing it, which includes the Ionising Radiations Regulations 2017, is unlikely to change given that the UK must continue to implement the IAEA International Basic Safety Standards, on which the Basic Safety Standards Directive is based.

10 Brexit and Energy Disputes

Challenges and Opportunities

Ana Stanič and Wendy Miles

In the post-Brexit world, UK and EU energy sector business and industry have experienced delay and disruption in supply chains, difficulty in accessing migrant labour, and increased costs on imported materials and equipment. This is compounded by the impact of COVID-19, UK and EU net zero commitments, and associated energy systems transition. Disruption creates risk, uncertainty, and, ultimately, an increase in disputes. The Brexit changes to trading relations between the EU and the UK impact aspects of existing dispute resolution mechanisms that parties choose for resolving energy sector disputes. It is prudent to examine whether or not pre-Brexit contractual dispute resolution mechanisms are still fit for purpose.

Post-Brexit, the UK is no longer part of the EU framework for civil justice and judicial cooperation. As part of the TCA, no agreement has been reached between the UK and the EU regarding a possible framework for civil justice and judicial cooperation. This Chapter discusses the implications of Brexit on resolving energy cross-border EU-related disputes (for example, where one of the parties is domiciled in the UK and the counterparty is domiciled in an EU Member State or where a party needs to enforce an English judgment in the EU Member State). It considers the implications of Brexit on English-seated arbitration, English court jurisdiction and English choice of law clauses in energy contracts. It also looks at the impact of Brexit on EU-related investment treaty arbitration.

The Chapter, however, does not discuss the dispute resolution and enforcement mechanism for resolving disputes as between the UK and the EU for, inter alia, failure to appropriately or properly implement the Trade and Cooperation Agreement (TCA) into domestic law and/or for the adoption of subsequent legislation, executive actions, or decisions which are incompatible with their respective obligations under the TCA as concern energy or more generally.

In particular, this Chapter will discuss in turn the implications of Brexit on (i) international commercial arbitration, (ii) governing law clauses, (iii) choice of jurisdiction clauses, (iv) service, (v) anti-suit injunctions, (vi) taking of evidence, and (vii) investment treaty arbitration.

DOI: 10.4324/9781003364337-11

10.1 Background

One of the aims of the UK government's Brexit strategy was to end direct jurisdiction in the UK of the Court of Justice of the European Union (CJEU).[1] Although the UK left the EU on 31 January 2020, during the Transition Period established by the Withdrawal Agreement, EU law continued to apply to it and in the UK, the UK was treated by the EU as an EU Member State for the purposes of international agreements to which the EU was a party, and the UK was under the direct jurisdiction of the CJEU.

However, this all changed post-Brexit. The practical effect of Brexit is that EU–UK agreements no longer automatically form part of the legal orders of England and Wales, Scotland, or Northern Ireland, and instead domestic legislation will need to be enacted to give effect to them. Although '[t]he CJEU will continue to interpret EU law and be the ultimate arbiter of EU law within the EU and its Member States',[2] it no longer has direct jurisdiction in the UK.

10.2 Brexit and international commercial arbitration

This Section explores the implications of Brexit on international commercial arbitration. The international instrument that governs recognition and enforcement of international arbitration agreements and awards is the 1958 New York Convention.[3] As the UK was party to the New York Convention in its own right, its status in English and Welsh, Scottish, and Northern Irish law is unaffected by Brexit or the Withdrawal Agreement.

Post-Brexit, this Convention continues to apply and requires both UK and EU Member States to treat arbitration agreements as valid and to recognise and enforce arbitral awards seated in each other's jurisdictions except in a few expressly and exhaustively defined circumstances. With over 165 countries in the world being parties to this Convention, arbitration has been the preferred mechanism for resolving cross-border energy disputes even before Brexit.[4] The reasons for this include that (i) arbitration offers a neutral forum for disputes between international counterparties that would otherwise be resolved in the courts of one party's home state; (ii) arbitration awards are final and binding and can only be

1 UK Parliament European Union Committee, Dispute resolution and enforcement after Brexit, '15th Report of Session 2017-19' (HL Paper 130, 3 May 2018) <https://publications.parliament.uk/pa/ld201719/ldselect/ldeucom/130/13003.htm> accessed 6 November 2022.

2 Department for Exiting the European Union, 'Enforcement and dispute resolution: a future partnership paper' (2017) <https://www.gov.uk/government/publications/enforcement-and-dispute-resolution-a-future-partnership-paper> accessed 6 November 2022, 18.

3 The United Nations Convention on the Recognition and Enforcement of Foreign Arbitral Awards (New York, signed 10 June 1958, entered into force 7 June 1959) (the 'New York Convention').

4 International Centre for Energy Arbitration, 'Dispute Resolution in the Energy Sector – Initial Report' (2015) <http://scottisharbitrationcentre-org.stackstaging.com/wp-content/uploads/2015/05/ICEA-Dispute-Resolution-in-the-Energy-Sector-Initial-Report-Square-Booklet-Web-version.pdf> accessed 6 November 2022.

challenged on limited grounds; (iii) they are more easily enforceable than court judgments; (iv) parties can agree to keep the arbitration confidential and the hearings are private; (v) parties are able to choose their own arbitrator(s) and agree to appoint a technical expert to the panel where appropriate – such as an engineer, quantity surveyor, or architect; and (vi) the arbitral proceedings can be tailor-made by the parties.

Brexit arguably reinforces the independence of international arbitration from national courts in the UK and its efficacy by removing the application of EU law in relation to (i) court proceedings in support of cross-border arbitration and (ii) enforcement of cross-border arbitral awards. First, although in relation to cross-border court proceedings the Brussels Recast Regulation sought to clarify that international arbitration remains outside the reach of EU law,[5] the position in respect of court proceedings in support of international arbitration in EU courts (e.g., enforcement, interim relief (including anti-suit injunctions, challenge to arbitrators) remained unclear. By way of example, in an English High Court decision that followed the adoption of the Brussels Recast Regulation,[6] the court held that the ECJ decision in *West Tankers Inc.*[7] remained binding. The court rejected the reasoning of Advocate General Wathelet in *Proceedings concerning Gazprom OAO* (Case C-536/13) [2015] 1 WLR 4937 and held that the *West Tankers* decision reflected EU law on this point. Accordingly, the court held that it had no power to grant relief in respect of proceedings pending before the courts of another EU Member State. Post-Brexit, the UK is no longer part of the EU framework for civil justice and judicial cooperation. As part of the TCA, no agreement has been reached between the UK and the EU regarding a possible framework for civil justice and judicial cooperation. Therefore, English courts are now able to grant anti-suit injunctions in support of England-seated arbitration proceedings in appropriate cases to stop proceedings pending in the courts of an EU Member State (it will have an equivalent power to stop proceedings commenced in breach of an exclusive English court jurisdiction clause).

Secondly, in relation to enforcement of arbitral awards, the New York Convention provides for grounds for challenging an arbitral award, which include public policy of the place of enforcement. In the case of enforcement of English-seated arbitral awards, or indeed EU-seated awards, the English courts no longer need to take into account EU law in relation to arbitrability, enforceability, and/or public policy. These questions are now governed by the English Arbitration Act 1996 and English law, without regard to EU law. Importantly, English courts are no longer required to set aside arbitral awards on account of breach of EU law concerning competition

5 See: Regulation (EU) 1215/2012 of the European Parliament and of the Council on jurisdiction and the recognition and enforcement of judgments in civil and commercial matters (recast) (Recast Brussels Regulation), Article 1(2)(d).

6 *Nori Holdings Ltd & others* v. *Public Joint-Stock Company Bank Otkritie Financial Corporation* [2018] EWHC 1343 (Comm).

7 *West Tankers Inc.* v. *Allianz SpA* (Case C-185/07) [2009] Ac 1138.

law, State aid, or another ground of EU public policy.[8] That EU public policy is a very broad concept is revealed by a review of CJEU case law. By way of example, in *Eco Swiss*,[9] the ECJ (as the CJEU was known at the time) held that Articles 101 and 102 Treaty on the Functioning of the European Union (TFEU), which prohibit cartel agreements and abuses of dominant position, are fundamental provisions of EU law and form part of its *ordre public*.[10] In *Mostaza Claro*, the ECJ held that provisions in a directive protecting consumers from unfair terms were fundamental for the 'accomplishment of the tasks entrusted to the Community and, in particular, to raising the standard of living and the quality of life in its territory'.[11] In *Ingmar*, the ECJ held that indemnity provisions in a directive concerning commercial agents were mandatory.[12] In *Klausner*, the ECJ further held that State aid is also a fundamental principle of EU law.[13] In this regard, it is important to bear in mind that the European Commission has repeatedly argued that arbitral awards can *per se* amount to State aid, thus requiring the courts of EU Member States to set them aside. Recently, CJEU held in *Federal Republic of Germany v European Commission* that energy solidarity as a specific expression in the field of energy of the principle of solidarity was a fundamental principle of EU law.[14]

Post-Brexit, the grounds for challenging arbitral award under English law are much more limited. This was reinforced in *Betamax Ltd v State Trading Corporation (Mauritius)*,[15] a 2021 Privy Council decision (albeit dealing with a Mauritius-seated arbitration). In this case, the Privy Council found that the Supreme Court of Mauritius was wrong to set aside an international arbitration award on the basis that

8 Ana Stanič, 'Enforcement of Awards and Other Implications of Achmea' in Crina Baltag and Ana Stanič (eds), *The Future of Investment Treaty Arbitration in the EU - Intra-EU BITs, the Energy Charter Treaty, and the Multilateral Investment Court* (Wolters Kluwer, 2020) 149.

9 Case C-126/97 *Eco Swiss China Time Ltd v Benetton International NV* [1999] ECR I-03055 ('*Eco Swiss*').

10 In particular, the ECJ noted in para 36 that '… Article 85 … constitutes a fundamental provision which is essential … for the functioning of the internal market' and concluded in para 39 that consequently it was 'a matter of public policy within the meaning of the New York Convention'.

11 See para 37 of Case C-168/05 *Elisa María Mostaza Claro v Centro Móvil Milenium SL* [2006] ECR I-10421 ('*Mostaza Claro*'). See also Case C-40/08 *Asturcom Telecomunicaciones SL v Cristina Rodríguez Nogueira* [2009] ECR I-09579.

12 Case C-381/98 *Ingmar GB Ltd v Eaton Leonard Technologies Inc* [2000] ECR I-09305 ('*Ingmar*').

13 Case C-505/14 *Klausner Holz Niedersachsen v Land Nordrhein-Westfalen* [2015], not published ('*Klausner*'). In particular, see para 45 in which the ECJ held that 'it must be concluded that a national rule which prevents the national court from drawing all the consequences of a breach of the third sentence of Article 108(3) TFEU because of a decision of a national court, which is res judicata, given in a dispute which does not have the same subject-matter and which did not concern the State aid characteristics of the contracts at issue must be regarded as being incompatible with the principle of effectiveness. A significant obstacle to the effective application of EU law and, in particular, a principle as fundamental as that of the control of State aid cannot be justified either by the principle of res judicata or by the principle of legal certainty'.

14 Case C848/19 P Federal Republic of Germany v European Commission [Mitja rest of citation] <https://eur-lex.europa.eu/legal-content/EN/TXT/HTML/?uri=CELEX:62019CJ0848&from=en>, para. 38.

15 [2021] UKPC 14.

it was contrary to Mauritius public policy, in circumstances where the tribunal had found that the underlying contract was not illegal and had the jurisdiction to do so. The Privy Council determined that, when considering whether an award conflicts with public policy, the supervisory court is only entitled to apply public policy to the findings made in the award. It may not, 'under the guise of public policy … reopen issues relating to the meaning and effect of the contract or whether it complies with a regulatory or legislative scheme'.

At the time of writing this Chapter, there has been no case before the English courts post-Brexit in which an arbitral award has been challenged for breach of EU public policy. It therefore cannot be said with certainty how the English courts will approach the issue. However, given the reasoning of the Supreme Court in the *Micula & Ors v Romania*,[16] it is most likely that the English courts will not consider a decision of European Commission declaring an arbitral award as amounting to State aid as forming part of international public policy and thus part of English public policy. It is also very unlikely that an English court will set aside or vary an arbitral award rendered in London on the grounds of breach of EU State aid or public policy, as defined in the aforementioned CJEU cases. Similarly, when it comes to the enforcement of an arbitral award rendered outside England, the English courts will no longer be bound to *ex officio* uphold EU public policy. The rules governing the enforcement will be governed by national law and the provisions of the New York Convention.

So, while Brexit has had, and will continue to have, a significant impact on many areas of business, it has had a limited effect on international arbitration as a form of dispute resolution. In fact, international arbitration is likely to be a more attractive alternative to litigation of commercial EU/UK cross-border contracts, especially given the uncertainties involving service of process discussed below and increased costs and risks concerning enforcement of court judgments. International arbitration is also likely to be a better option in respect of contracts entered into by UK companies which do not have an EU nexus but where enforcement may be necessary in an EU Member State, and similarly in respect of contracts entered into by an EU company which does not have a UK nexus but where enforcement may be sought in the UK. Moreover, for parties trying to insulate their disputes from EU law, the UK, and in particular London, may, post-Brexit, become a more attractive seat for arbitral proceedings. It may also become a more attractive place for the enforcement of arbitral awards compared to enforcement in EU Member States.[17]

10.3 Brexit and governing law clauses

This Section discusses the implications of Brexit on governing law of commercial contracts in general and energy contracts in particular. Governing law, also

16 See para 148 of *Micula & Ors v. Romania* [2018] EWCA Civ 1801.

17 Ana Stanič, 'Enforcement of Intra-EU BIT and ECT Awards in the UK Post Micula' (*Kluwer Arbitration Blog*, 25 April 2020) <http://arbitrationblog.kluwerarbitration.com/2020/04/25/enforcement-of-intra-eu-bit-and-ect-awards-in-the-uk-post-micula/> accessed 6 November 2022.

known as the applicable or substantive law, is the law that governs the parties' rights and obligations under contracts and/or tortious acts.

10.3.1 Conflict of law concerns

Most energy contracts contain an express clause concerning the governing law. In circumstances where they do not, both UK and EU laws contain conflict of law provisions in order to work out what law should apply. Under EU law, these rules are set out in the Rome I[18] and the Rome II Regulations.[19]

With effect from 1 January 2021, Rome I, Rome II, and EU-derived domestic legislation dealing with the law applicable to contractual and non-contractual obligations became part of retained EU law.[20] In addition, Article 66 of the Withdrawal Agreement provided that the EU version of Rome I Regulation continued to apply in the UK to contracts concluded before the end of the Transition Period and that the EU version of Rome II Regulation continued to apply in the UK to events giving rise to damage, where such events occurred before the end of the Transition Period.

As a consequence, at present, Brexit has not led to a change in choice of law rules in the UK in contractual and non-contractual matters. A choice of law is likely to continue to be respected in the UK and across EU Member States given that the provisions of their laws are materially the same and require courts to generally respect a choice of law.

Going forward, there is a possibility of divergence between the manner in which the UK government will apply and UK courts will interpret retained law and that of the CJEU. The fact that the UK will not be required to mirror in its laws any amendments made to Rome I Regulation and Rome II Regulation going forward is another reason for divergence between UK and EU regarding choice of law.

10.3.2 English law as the governing law of energy contracts

An important implication of Brexit concerns the scope of English law as the governing law of energy contracts. Since 1 January 2021, EU law no longer forms part of the substantive law of England and Wales, Scotland, or Northern Ireland. The adoption of the European Union (Withdrawal) Act 2018[21] transposed directly

18 Regulation (EC) 593/2008 of 17 June 2008 on the law applicable to contractual obligations [2008] OJ L 177 (the 'Rome I Regulation').

19 Regulation (EC) 864/2007 of 11 July 2007 on the law applicable to non-contractual obligations [2007] OJ L 199 (the 'Rome II Regulation').

20 The Law Applicable to Contractual Obligations and Non-Contractual Obligations (Amendment etc.) (UK Exit) Regulations 2019, 2019 No. 834.

21 An Act to Repeal the European Communities Act 1972 and make other provision in connection with the withdrawal of the United Kingdom from the EU, 2018 c. 16. See in particular Sections 3 to 7 thereof.

applicable, pre-existing EU law into UK law and so created a new category of domestic law in the United Kingdom known as 'retained EU law'. It also made clear that the EU law doctrine of direct effect, the principle of supremacy of EU law over national law, and the doctrine of sincere cooperation ceased to apply in the UK after the Brexit date.[22] Section 7 provides the procedure whereby retained EU law can be modified going forward, and Section 8 sets out the circumstances in which the government has the power to remove or amend EU retained law.

Accordingly, going forward, it is possible that there will be a divergence between the rules that apply in the EU and in the UK, and between the approach of the CJEU and the approach of UK courts when interpreting EU law. However, since historically EU law has had little impact on the substance of English law as it relates to commercial transactions, little should change going forward as concerns contract and tort law. English law was a popular choice of substantive law for energy contracts, and commercial contracts more generally, for the duration of the UK's membership of the EU. Energy companies choose English law for contracts with no nexus to England because of its well-developed body of English contract law principles, its flexibility, and its respect for the parties' bargain. These benefits are unaffected by the UK's departure from the EU. The express choice of the parties to choose English law to govern their commercial contracts is expected to be upheld by national courts of EU Member States post-Brexit, pursuant to the provisions of Rome I and Rome II Regulations.

It has been argued that for parties wanting to insulate their energy contracts from EU law, English law has become an even more attractive option post-Brexit, especially if combined with arbitration as a mechanism for resolving disputes which may arise thereunder.

10.4 Brexit and jurisdiction clauses and enforcement of judgments

Although energy contracts typically contain international arbitration clauses, this Section discusses the implications of Brexit regarding exclusive or non-exclusive jurisdiction of UK or EU Member State courts, including enforcement thereof.

Post-Brexit, the UK has ceased to be subject to the application of the Brussels Recast Regulation.[23] Pursuant to this regulation, EU Member States' courts are obliged to uphold jurisdiction clauses contained in commercial contracts that confer exclusive or non-exclusive jurisdiction on courts in other EU Member States.

22 Ibid s 5.

23 Regulation (EU) 1215/2012 of 12 December 2012 on jurisdiction and the recognition and enforcement of judgments in civil and commercial matters (recast) as amended by Commission Delegated Regulation 2015/281 of 26 November 2014 replacing Annexes I and II of Regulation (EU) No 1215/2012 of the European Parliament and of the Council on jurisdiction and the recognition and enforcement of judgments in civil and commercial matters [2015] OJ L 54 (the Recast Brussels Regulation), unofficial consolidated version available at <https://eur-lex.europa.eu/legal-content/en/TXT/?uri=CELEX%3A32012R1215> accessed 6 November 2022.

Furthermore, it prevents parallel proceedings in EU Member State courts by requiring any EU court, other than the court first seized, to stay proceedings on its own motion until such time as its jurisdiction is established.[24] It further provides for automatic enforceability of civil judgments of EU Member State courts within the EU via a relatively quick and user-friendly process.

The Withdrawal Agreement provides that the provisions of the Brussels Recast Regulation apply to claims commenced in UK and EU Member State courts prior to and including 31 December 2020. In particular, Articles 1(a) and (2)(a) of the Withdrawal Agreement provide that the Brussels Recast Regulation applies to proceedings instituted before the end of the Transition Period and to the recognition and enforcement of judgments given in legal proceedings instituted before the end of the Transition Period. Article 67(1)(d) provides that Regulation (EC) No 805/2005 creating a European Enforcement Order for uncontested claims[25] applies to judgments given in legal proceedings instituted before the end of the Transition Period, and to court settlements concluded before the end of the Transition Period.[26]

Post-Brexit, the UK has also ceased being a party to the Lugano Convention.[27] The Lugano Convention mirrors the Brussels Recast Regulations regarding jurisdiction and enforcement, and extends their application to EFTA states, excluding Liechtenstein, that is to Iceland, Switzerland, and Norway. The UK sought to re-join the Lugano Convention in its own right on 8 April 2020, with effect from 1 January 2021.[28] Pursuant to Article 72(3) of the Convention, unanimous agreement of all contracting parties is required. Iceland, Norway, and Switzerland indicated support.[29]

24 This rule is known as the *lis alibi pendens* rule.

25 Regulation (EC) No 805/2004 of the European Parliament and of the Council of 21 April 2004 creating a European Enforcement Order for uncontested claims [2004] OJ L 143.

26 Judgments from courts in EFTA states in proceedings instituted before the end of the transition period continue to be enforceable in the UK on a unilateral basis under the Civil Jurisdiction and Judgements (Amendment) (EU Exit) Regulations 2019 (SI 2019/479) as amended by the Civil, Criminal and Family Justice (Amendment) (EU Exit) Regulations 2020 (SI 2020/1493).

27 Convention on jurisdiction and the recognition and enforcement of judgments in civil and commercial matters [2007] OJ L 339 (the 'Lugano Convention').

28 Anna Pingen, 'Commission Rejects UK Application to Join Lugano Convention' (*Eucrim*, 5 June 2021) <https://eucrim.eu/news/commission-rejects-uk-application-to-join-lugano-convention> accessed 6 November 2022.

29 Switzerland formally consented on 25 February 2021 to the UK being invited to deposit its instrument of accession to the 2007 Lugano Convention; see Swiss Federal Department of Foreign Affairs, 'Notification to the Parties of the Convention on Jurisdiction and the Recognition and Enforcement of Judgements in Civil and Commercial Matters, concluded at Lugano on 30 October 2007' (25 February 2021) <https://www.eda.admin.ch/dam/eda/fr/documents/aussenpolitik/voelkerrecht/autres-conventions/Lugano2/20210225-LUG_en.pdf> accessed 6 November 2022. Iceland confirmed its consent on 18 March 2021; see Thomson Reuters, 'Brexit: Iceland consents to UK being invited to deposit instrument of accession to 2007 Lugano Convention' (23 March 2021) <https://uk.practicallaw.thomsonreuters.com/w-030-2563?transitionType=Default&contextData=(sc.Default)> accessed 6 November 2022. The Federal Department of For-

However, on 4 May 2021, the European Commission recommended that the EU reject the UK's application to re-join. Despite Article 71(1)(c) of the Convention expressly envisaging non-European Free Trade Association (EFTA) states becoming parties, the EU submitted that the Lugano Convention is 'a flanking measure of the internal market [which] relates to the EU-EFTA/EEA context'.[30] The EU argued that, as the UK is 'a third country with an "ordinary" Free Trade Agreement facilitating trade but not including any fundamental freedoms and policies of the internal market', post-Brexit, it could not support its accession.[31] On 28 June 2021, the European Commission further deposited a Note Verbale at the Swiss Federal Department of Foreign Affairs stating that it is not in a position to give its consent to the UK's accession to the Lugano Convention. As of December 2022, the European Council has not voted on the matter, but it is not expected that the Council will take a different view from that taken by the Commission.

In view of the position taken by the EU in relation to the Lugano Convention, and with effect from 1 January 2021, the UK acceded to the Hague Choice of Court Convention[32] in its own right. The Hague Convention offers similar protection to commercial contracts containing exclusive court jurisdiction agreements as between UK and EU/EFTA companies as do the Recast Brussels Regulation and Lugano Convention. Where the Hague Convention applies, there is some protection against parallel proceedings, as courts other than the named court (whether in England or in an EU Member State) generally have to stay their proceedings in favour of the chosen court.

It does not, however, offer the same protection for EU/UK commercial contracts (i) containing an asymmetric or non-exclusive clause[33] or (ii) not containing any choice of court clause. As a matter of English common law, the commencement of foreign proceedings in breach of the non-exclusive jurisdiction clause is unlikely to be regarded as a breach of contract, and an anti-suit injunction will only be granted if the pursuit of the foreign proceedings is vexatious or oppressive.

---

eign Affairs of Switzerland published a letter confirming Norway's consent on 28 April 2021, see Thomson Reuters, 'Brexit: Norway consents to UK being invited to deposit instrument of accession to 2007 Lugano Convention, EU yet to decide' (12 May 2021) <https://uk.practicallaw.thomsonreuters.com/w-030-9519?transitionType=Default&contextData=(sc.Default)> accessed 6 November 2022. For further information, see ibid.

30 European Commission, 'Communication from the Commission to the European Parliament and the Council: Assessment on the application of the United Kingdom of Great Britain and Northern Ireland to accede to the 2007 Lugano Convention' (4 May 2021, COM(2021) 222 final) <https://eur-lex.europa.eu/legal-content/EN/TXT/HTML/?uri=CELEX:52021DC0222&from=EN> accessed on 15 December 2022.

31 Ibid 3.

32 Convention on Choice of Court Agreements (The Hague, concluded 30 June 2005, entered into force 1 October 2015) (the 'Hague Convention').

33 Neither the EU nor the UK have made a declaration under Article 22 of the Hague Convention to extend the recognition and enforcement provisions of the Hague Convention to non-exclusive choice of court agreements.

It is also currently uncertain whether courts in EU Member States will apply the Hague Convention to EU/UK contracts entered into before 1 January 2021. This is because the EU Commission has taken the view that the Hague Convention does not apply to exclusive jurisdiction agreements entered into before 1 January 2021.[34] The UK takes the position that the Hague Convention entered into force for the UK on 1 October 2015, when the EU acceded to it, and that the provisions thereof have applied to it ever since. Since the EU's declaration under Article 30 of the Hague Convention expressly provided that EU Member States were individually bound by its provisions and that the UK was an EU Member State until 31 December 2020, this so called 'change of status' risk is small.

In view of the above, the position regarding the enforcement of exclusive UK court jurisdiction clauses agreed on or after 1 January 2021 will be the same as before Brexit. In other words, EU Member State courts will respect exclusive English jurisdiction clauses and enforce the resulting judgments pursuant to the terms of the Hague Convention. The same respect will be accorded by English courts to EU exclusive jurisdiction clauses and resulting judgments of courts of EU Member States.

In its Communication calling for the UK's accession to the Lugano Convention to be rejected, the EU Commission suggested that it would propose to the EU to become a signatory to the Hague Judgements Convention[35] 'in the near future' and suggested that should the UK become a party to the same 'that Convention … would apply to the future judicial cooperation with the EU'.[36] At the time of writing, there are no signs that either side is actively pursuing this avenue for future judicial cooperation. To the extent that the Hague Convention is found not to apply to a specific cross-border EU/UK energy contract (e.g., because of a change of status risk, the jurisdiction clause being non-exclusive or unilateral or agreed before 1 October 2015, or absent any jurisdiction clause), UK and EU Member State courts will apply their domestic rules to questions of jurisdiction clauses and enforcement of judgments. This in practice means that post-Brexit, fresh court proceedings will need to be commenced in the UK courts to enforce as a debt a judgment issued by a court in an EU Member State.

In England in particular, the statutory regimes under the Administration of Justice Act 1920 and the Foreign Judgements (Reciprocal Enforcement) Act 1933 may be applicable in respect of certain EU countries with equivalent

34 European Commission, 'Notice to Stakeholders regarding the withdrawal of the United Kingdom and EU Rules in the field of civil justice and private international law' (Brussels, 27 August 2020, REV2) <https://ec.europa.eu/info/sites/info/files/brexit_files/info_site/civil_justice_en.pdf> accessed 6 November 2022.

35 Convention on the Recognition and Enforcement of Foreign Judgements in Civil or Commercial Matters (The Hague, concluded 2 July 2019, not yet in force).

36 European Commission, 'Communication from the Commission to the European Parliament and the Council: Assessment on the application of the United Kingdom of Great Britain and Northern Ireland to accede to the 2007 Lugano Convention' (4 May 2021, COM(2021) 222 final) <https://ec.europa.eu/info/sites/default/files/1_en_act_en.pdf> accessed 6 November 2022, 4.

provisions in their own law to ensure reciprocal recognition and enforcement. Although many countries participate in this system, 'the coverage of EU Member States and 2007 Lugano Convention states is limited'.[37] In order to ensure the continued enforcement of judgments as between the UK and Norway post-Brexit, a treaty was signed between the UK and Norway on 13 October 2020 to continue to apply the 1961 Mutual Enforcement Agreement.[38]

In other words, it is clear that Brexit has had a significant impact on the enforcement of jurisdiction clauses and judgments. The Civil Jurisdiction and Judgements (Amendment) (EU Exit) Regulations 2019 Explanatory Memorandum identified two primary impacts of the European regime ceasing to apply:[39] firstly, the increased risk of parallel proceedings due to the absence of the operation of *lis alibi pendens* rule as set out in the Recast Brussels Regulation;[40] and secondly, increased costs, time, and risks for those seeking to enforce their judgments in the UK, since common law rules involve a less efficient mechanism for recognising and enforcing judgments, including because the grounds on which enforcement can be resisted under the statutory regime and the common law are wider than under the European regime.[41]

One way to ensure that UK courts have jurisdiction in post-Brexit scenarios discussed above is for the non-UK party to nominate an agent for service of process in England. This will also eliminate the need to seek the UK court's permission to serve proceedings outside jurisdiction in such cases.

10.5 Brexit and service of proceedings

Prior to Brexit, in circumstances where the Recast Brussels Regulation conferred jurisdiction on English courts, the claimant was able to serve process on the defendant domiciled in an EU Member State without having to obtain permission from the court, provided certain conditions in the Civil Procedure Rules were met. At the end of the Transition Period, the EU Service Regulation[42] ceased to apply to the UK, except in the circumstances set out in Article 68(a) of the Withdrawal Agreement.

37 Explanatory Memorandum to the Civil Jurisdiction and Judgements (Amendment) (EU Exit), Regulations 2019, 2019 No. 479 (the 'Explanatory Memorandum') <www.legislation.gov.uk/uksi/2019/479/pdfs/uksiem_20190479_en.pdf> accessed 6 November 2022, para 7.8.

38 The terms of the agreement are available at <https://assets.publishing.service.gov.uk/government/uploads/system/uploads/attachment_data/file/932354/CS_Norway_2.2020_UK_Norway_Agreement_Enforcement_Judgement_Civil_Matters.pdf> accessed 6 November 2022.

39 The Civil Jurisdiction and Judgements (Amendment) (EU Exit) Regulations 2019, SI 2019 No. 479.

40 Explanatory Memorandum para 7.5.

41 Explanatory Memorandum para 7.8.

42 Regulation (EC) No 1393/2007 of the European Parliament and of the Council of 13 November 2007 on the service in the Member States of judicial and extrajudicial documents in civil or commercial matters (service of documents), and repealing Council Regulation (EC) No 1348/2000 [2007] OJ L 324, unofficial consolidated version available at <https://eur-lex.europa.eu/eli/reg/2007/1393/2013-07-01> accessed 6 November 2022.

Article 68(a) provides that in the UK, and in EU Member States in situations involving the UK, the EU Service Regulation continues to apply to judicial and extra-judicial documents which were received for the purposes of service before the end of the Transition Period by one of the following: (i) a receiving agency; (ii) a central body of the Member State where service is to be effected; and (iii) diplomatic or consular agents, postal services, or judicial officers, officials, or other competent persons of the Member State addressed, as referred to in Articles 13, 14, and 15 of the EU Service Regulation.

As a consequence, unless the Hague Convention applies, English court permission is required to serve proceedings in the EU. The UK is a party to the Hague Service Convention, as are all EU Member States. Following the Transition Period, the Hague Service Convention[43] applies to most new requests for service of judicial and extra-judicial documents as between the UK and EU Member States. The Hague Service Convention is similar in many respects to the EU Service Regulation.[44] However, service under it is considered to be less efficient and more expensive, not least because the EU Service Regulation, adopted on 25 November 2020, enables increased use of electronic methods of cross-border service and collection of evidence. Accordingly, post-Brexit, the procedure for service of process between the UK and EU Member States will be less efficient and more expensive. One way for a UK party negotiating a contract with a counterparty in the EU (and vice versa) to reduce the risk and costs associated with service of process outside the UK is to consider appointing an agent for service of process and inserting a clause to this effect in the contract.

Jurisdiction under English common law is generally founded on service of process or submission to the jurisdiction by the defendant. In particular, in order for English courts to exercise jurisdiction over foreign defendants, the claimant must serve proceedings outside the jurisdiction, either without permission if allowed under the Civil Procedure Rules, or with the court's permission if the claimant can demonstrate that the subject matter of the dispute has a sufficient connection with England and Wales and that England and Wales is the most appropriate place to hear the dispute. Most importantly, a claim form can be served without the permission of the court if it contains a jurisdiction clause in favour of the English courts.[45] Court permission to serve out of jurisdiction is discretionary and subject to the court's ability to decline jurisdiction on a *forum non conveniens* basis if satisfied that the courts of another country would be a manifestly more appropriate place for the case to be heard. This is another important contrast with the Recast Brussels Regulation regime where the 'first come first served'

43 The Convention on the Service Abroad of Judicial and Extrajudicial Documents in Civil or Commercial Matters (The Hague, signed 15 November 1965, entered into force 10 February 1969).

44 Regulation (EU) 2020/1784 of the European Parliament and of the Council of 25 November 2020 on the service in the Member States of judicial and extrajudicial documents in civil or commercial matters (service of documents) (recast) [2020] OJ L 405.

45 Rule 6.33(2B) was introduced pursuant to Article 6 of Civil Procedure (Amendment) Rules 2021, 2021 No. 117 (L. 2).

approach of *lis alibi pendens* rule applies as described above. In Scotland, the relevant jurisdictional rules are those set out in Schedule 8 to the Civil Jurisdiction and Judgements Act 1982. The general jurisdictional rule in these cases more closely replicates the Recast Brussels Regulation rules and provides that, subject to certain exceptions, persons shall be sued in the courts of the place where they are domiciled. As discussed above, one way to minimise the impact of Brexit as concerns service of proceedings is to include a provision nominating an agent for service of process in England.

10.6 Brexit and anti-suit injunctions

As discussed above in relation to arbitration, post-Brexit, UK courts will be able to grant anti-suit injunctions to try to limit the ability of a party to pursue competing proceedings in EU Member States in certain circumstances, such as where an action has been brought in breach of an exclusive English jurisdiction clause. These were not permitted under the Recast Brussels Regulation because they were said to interfere with the application of the Brussels rules of jurisdiction by the other court.

10.7 Brexit and the taking of evidence

Pre-Brexit, parties to UK court proceedings were able to take advantage of the Regulation (EC) 1206/2001)[46] to obtain assistance of EU Member State courts in obtaining evidence. During the Transition Period, Article 68 of the Withdrawal Agreement provided that the Evidence Regulation continued to apply. In relation to requests for evidence made after the end of the Transition Period, the Evidence Regulation no longer applies.

Post-Brexit, the provisions of the 1970 Convention on the Taking of Evidence Abroad in Civil or Commercial Matters[47] will govern most requests for the taking of evidence as between the UK and all EU Member States, except Austria, Belgium, and Ireland. The 1970 Hague Evidence Convention is similar to the Evidence Regulation in many respects, but it is not as modern and is likely to be less efficient (and therefore more expensive). One way to reduce risks and costs going forward is to opt for arbitration.

46 Council Regulation (EC) No 1206/2001 of 28 May 2001 on cooperation between the courts of the Member States in the taking of evidence in civil or commercial matters [2001] OJ L 174, unofficial consolidated version available at < https://eur-lex.europa.eu/eli/reg/2001/1206/2008-12-04> accessed 6 November 2022 (the 'Evidence Regulation).

47 Convention on the Taking of Evidence Abroad in Civil or Commercial Matters (The Hague, signed 18 March 1970, entered into force 7 October 1972) (the 'Hague Evidence Convention').

10.8 Brexit and investment treaty arbitration

This Section discusses the implications of Brexit on investment treaty arbitration as a mechanism for resolving disputes as between UK investors investing in EU Member States and investors from EU Member States investing in the UK. First, it should be noted that the TCA contains provisions on investment protection. In terms of substantive protections, it guarantees non-discrimination, thus importing national and most favoured nation treatments and ensuring that investors between the UK and EU are treated no less favourably than local or third-party investors. In stark contrast to other recently signed treaties, the TCA contains no provisions on fair and equitable treatment, full protection, and security or expropriation. Access to the TCA's substantive protections is further restricted by the TCA's narrow definition of 'investor', which requires substantive business operations in the investor's home State and therefore creates an additional jurisdictional hurdle for investors to meet. The TCA does not provide for any form of investor–State dispute settlement (ISDS), and the 'most favoured nation' clause explicitly excludes ISDS from its scope. Accordingly, an investor whose rights under the TCA have been breached will have to convince its government to commence arbitral proceedings against the State in which it had made the investment. While investors will have the possibility to file *amicus curiae* submissions once an arbitration is instituted, the arbitral tribunal is not obliged to address these submissions.

At the time of writing, the status of the UK's bilateral investment treaties (UK BITs) with 11[48] EU Member States is not clear as they are not specifically mentioned in the TCA. It is clear from the *Achmea* case that the CJEU takes the view that ISDS provisions in intra-EU BITs are incompatible with EU law.[49] The UK did not sign the Agreement for the Termination of Bilateral Investment Treaties Between the Member States of the European Union,[50] and the European Commission started infringement proceedings against it before it left the EU.[51] Nevertheless, post-Brexit, these continuing BITs are no longer intra-EU. Whatever uncertainty there may be about their validity as a matter of EU law, there is no such uncertainty as a matter of international law.[52]

48 These countries are: Bulgaria, Czech Republic, Croatia, Estonia, Hungary, Latvia, Lithuania, Poland, Romania, Slovakia, and Slovenia.

49 Case C284/16 *Slowakische Republik (Slovak Republic) v Achmea BV* [2018] EU:C:2018:158 ('*Achmea*').

50 Agreement for the termination of Bilateral Investment Treaties between the Member States of the European Union (SN/4656/2019/INIT) OJ L 169 <https://eur-lex.europa.eu/legal-content/EN/TXT/?uri=CELEX:22020A0529(01)> accessed 6 November 2022.

51 European Commission, 'May infringements package: key decisions' (14 May 2020) <https://ec.europa.eu/commission/presscorner/detail/EN/INF_20_859> accessed 6 November 2022.

52 As discussed in detail in Stanič, 'Enforcement of Awards and Other Implications of Achmea' (n 38) 143–162, there has to date been no arbitral tribunal who has refused jurisdiction over an investor–State intra-EU dispute on the grounds of the ISDS clause being invalid as a matter of EU law.

Following the recent CJEU judgment in *Komstroy*,[53] there is uncertainty as to whether or not *Achmea* will also apply to arbitration pursuant to the Energy Charter Treaty (ECT),[54] to which the EU, EU Member States, and other third parties are signatories. Pursuant to the ECT, investors of UK and/or EU Member States are able to commence arbitral proceedings against the host State of the investment for breach of rights accorded to them in respect of investments in the energy sector under the ECT. The rights accorded to investors under the ECT are in principle substantively the same as those accorded to investors under the UK BITs.

Post-Brexit, UK investors investing in EU Member States and vice versa are able to enjoy continued investment protection under both the ECT and other BITs between the UK and EU Member States.[55] The UK may also be favoured over EU Member States including Sweden for the enforcement of intra-EU BITs and intra-EU ECT arbitral awards, especially those rendered under the auspices of the International Centre for Investment Disputes (ICSID) Convention.[56]

10.9 Conclusion

Notwithstanding the uncertainty caused by Brexit, London is likely to remain a major hub for the resolution of cross-border energy disputes. This Chapter has explained why the choice of English law and use of English courts (through English-seated arbitration or English choice of courts) remain attractive. By inserting a service of process agent clause in a contract as well as an exclusive English jurisdiction clause, the risks associated with Brexit are significantly reduced, albeit not eliminated. Arbitration, English-seated or otherwise, remains the best option for resolving cross-border energy disputes. It is likely that London will, post-Brexit, be preferred as a seat for resolving energy disputes even those who have no nexus with England.

53 Case C741/19 *Republic of Moldova v Komstroy LLC* [2021] ECLI:EU:C:2021:655.

54 Energy Charter Treaty (The Hague, signed 17 December 1991, entered into force 16 April 1998) 2080 UNTS 100, 10 ICSID Rev—Foreign Investment L J 258.

55 By the end of November 2022, seven EU Member States had announced their withdrawal from the ECT. Due to the sunset clauses in the ECT, its provisions will remain in force for another 20 years.

56 Stanič, 'Enforcement of Awards and Other Implications of Achmea' (n 38) 144.

11 The Impact of Brexit on Ireland

The Energy Perspective

Garret Farrelly and Owen Collins

11.1 Background

In order to understand Brexit's impact on Ireland from an energy perspective, it is important to understand first why Brexit should impact on Ireland at all in this area. There are two main reasons: (1) the shared land border between Ireland and Northern Ireland and (2) various geographical and practical complications.

11.1.1 Shared land border

First, the island of Ireland contains two separate and distinct jurisdictions – Ireland and Northern Ireland. While Ireland has full legislative autonomy as a country in its own right, Northern Ireland is a part of the UK and operates a devolved administration with London as the ultimate source of legislative authority. Energy, with the exception of nuclear energy and installations, is a devolved matter in Northern Ireland. The Department for the Economy (a Northern Irish government body) is responsible for energy policy in Northern Ireland.

Despite Ireland and Northern Ireland being separate and distinct jurisdictions, their laws, policies, and standards have become increasingly aligned in recent decades. In particular, due to both Ireland and the UK being EU Member States up until Brexit, the majority of recent energy legislation and regulation has derived from EU legislation. In addition, laws, policies, and standards have become increasingly aligned due to the development of an all-island wholesale electricity market (discussed in further detail below), which is regulated jointly by the Commission for Regulation of Utilities (CRU) in Ireland and the Utilities Regulator (UR) in Northern Ireland.

It seems inevitable then that Brexit and the principles enshrined in the Withdrawal Agreement,[1] together with the Northern Ireland Protocol[2] and the

1 Agreement on the withdrawal of the United Kingdom of Great Britain and Northern Ireland from the European Union and the European Atomic Energy Community [2019] OJ C384I/1 (Withdrawal Agreement).

2 Protocol on Ireland/Northern Ireland to the Agreement on the withdrawal of the United Kingdom of Great Britain and Northern Ireland from the European Union and the European Atomic Energy Community [2019] OJ C384I/1 (Protocol on Ireland/Northern Ireland).

DOI: 10.4324/9781003364337-12

Trade and Cooperation Agreement (TCA),[3] will cause the alignment of laws, policies, and standards between both Ireland and Northern Ireland and Ireland and Great Britain to diverge – the only questions are exactly when and to what extent.

11.1.2 Geographical and practical complications

Second, Ireland and Northern Ireland have historically been reliant on Great Britain from an energy perspective due to the island's geographical position at the periphery of Europe. For example, all of Ireland's existing gas and electricity interconnectors connect to Great Britain. Ireland, therefore, has no direct physical energy connections with the EU (albeit that a new electricity interconnector between Ireland and France is currently being developed, as considered further below).

Any possible future legal and regulatory divergence between Ireland and the UK due to Brexit will not change these geographical realities. Northern Ireland will continue to share a land border with Ireland and be separated from the rest of the UK by the Irish Sea. Similarly, Ireland will itself remain isolated geographically from the rest of the EU now that the UK is no longer an EU Member State.

What this means is that Ireland and the UK will have to work together in spite of diverging laws and regulations to ensure that existing cross-border energy trading and the all-island wholesale electricity market remain intact post-Brexit.

In the lead up to Brexit, and in light of the political importance of the all-island electricity market for both jurisdictions, both Ireland and the UK emphasised in particular their support for the preservation of the current all-island electricity market notwithstanding Brexit. This support has now been enshrined in the Withdrawal Agreement[4] (including the Northern Ireland Protocol).[5] The Withdrawal Agreement was agreed on 17 October 2019 and entered into force on 1 February 2020. Aspects of energy trading between the EU and the UK are also covered in the TCA.[6]

11.2 Impact of Brexit on Ireland's energy market

11.2.1 Gas

Ireland relies heavily on energy imports and, as a result, is one of the most vulnerable EU countries in terms of security of energy supply. The Irish government has stated that Ireland is expected to be dependent on over 80% gas imports by the mid-2020s and over 90% by 2030. As over 50% of Ireland's electricity is generated from gas, there is a critical interdependence between electricity and gas security.[7]

3 Trade and Cooperation Agreement between the European Union and the European Atomic Energy Community, of the one part, and the United Kingdom of Great Britain and Northern Ireland, of the other part [2020] OJ L444/1 (TCA).

4 Withdrawal Agreement (n 2).

5 Protocol on Ireland/Northern Ireland (n 3).

6 TCA (n 4).

7 Department of the Environment, Climate and Communications, 'Gas' (*GOV.IE*, 12 June 2020) <www.gov.ie/en/policy-information/f1ecf1-gas/> accessed 9 December 2021.

The Irish government has also noted that 'Brexit poses a particular risk as Ireland imports the vast majority of its energy requirements, oil, gas and transport fuels, from or via the UK'.[8] Thus, Ireland's vulnerability in terms of import dependency is increased by the UK's withdrawal from the EU due to its lack of physical connection with the EU energy network.

In addition, the UK is no longer bound by EU security of supply legislation, including the rules in relation to solidarity in a supply disruption scenario.[9] This means that Ireland's energy network is even more reliant on the cooperation of the UK than it was pre-Brexit (see detailed discussion under 'Regulatory challenges' below).

Thus, the prospect of the reliance on gas supply through the UK in a post-Brexit scenario is an area of concern for Ireland from a security of supply perspective. Ireland's vulnerability in this context is exacerbated by recent bans on new oil and natural gas exploration licences, as well as opposition to and general uncertainty regarding LNG terminals in Ireland, both of which are discussed further below. This vulnerability has also become more evident in light of the threats to gas supply resulting from the war in Ukraine.

11.2.1.1 Gas interconnection

As outlined above, Ireland's reliance on the UK for gas imports is a key area of concern post-Brexit and also from a security of supply perspective generally. There are currently two sub-sea gas interconnectors between Ireland and Scotland,[10] and there are no current plans for further gas interconnection between Ireland and the UK nor the EU.

Supply from the Corrib gas field off the west coast of Ireland is Ireland's only producing indigenous gas supply. It was anticipated to meet 27% of Ireland's gas demand in 2021–2022[11] and the source is expected to decline in the coming years. Assuming no alternative supplies of gas are found, it is likely that Ireland will have to rely on these sub-sea gas interconnectors (and therefore the UK) to an even greater extent than today.

11.2.1.2 Potential alternative gas sources

It does not appear likely that Ireland will establish alternative domestic supplies of gas, given the Irish government's current energy policy to ban the issue of new oil

8 Government of Ireland, 'National Risk Assessment 2019' (*GOV.IE,* July 2019) <https://merrionstreet.ie/en/news-room/20190804_national_risk_assessment.pdf> accessed 9 December 2021.

9 Regulation (EU) 2017/1938 of the European Parliament and of the Council of 25 October 2017 concerning measures to safeguard the security of gas supply and repealing Regulation (EU) 994/2010 [2017] OJ L280/1.

10 GNI, 'Gas Networks Ireland confirms completion of twinning of Ireland to Scotland interconnector' (*GNI,* 19 December 2018) <www.gasnetworks.ie/corporate/news/active-news-articles/twinning-ireland-scotland-interconnector/> accessed 17 November 2021.

11 Source: GNI, Winter Outlook 2021/22 <https://www.gasnetworks.ie/docs/corporate/gas-regulation/GNI_Winter_Outlook_2021.pdf>

and natural gas exploration licences. Indeed, the Climate Action and Low Carbon Development (Amendment) Act 2021 has repealed previous statutory powers held by the relevant government minister to grant new exploration licences for 'petroleum' (which, for the purposes of this legislation, includes both oil and natural gas).

A number of developers in Ireland have explored the possibility of liquefied natural gas (LNG) terminals in recent years. At least three LNG projects have been planned in Ireland, one in the Shannon Estuary (Shannon LNG)[12] and two in Cork (Predator LNG and Port of Cork LNG), with Port of Cork LNG having been abandoned in January 2021.[13] Predator LNG is a proposed offshore floating LNG terminal located in the former Kinsale gas field, which Predator Oil & Gas plc, a UK-listed exploration company, plans to deliver in 2024.[14] However, there is currently no further information on the Predator LNG project in the public domain. The Shannon LNG project received planning permission in 2008 (extended in 2018) to build an LNG plant and power station. Media reports have claimed that the Shannon LNG project will cost €650 million and will include a 600 MW gas-fired power plant, an LNG terminal, and 120 MW of batteries, a combination which would be a significant addition to the Irish electricity system.[15]

It remains to be seen if and when the Shannon LNG project will be built. This uncertainty is mainly due to LNG projects in Ireland having faced some public resistance, and the Shannon LNG project in particular has recently been subject to a number of legal permitting challenges.[16] In addition, the Department of Environment, Climate and Communications stated in its May 2021 policy statement that 'it would not be appropriate for the development of any LNG terminals in Ireland to be permitted or proceeded with' until an ongoing review is concluded which should assess whether it would be appropriate, or not, to develop LNG terminals in Ireland and, if any such terminals were to be developed, whether they should only be in order to provide a contingency supply in the event of failure of existing natural gas supply infrastructure.[17]

12 Shannon LNG <www.shannonlng.ie/>; Predator Oil & Gas Holdings plc <www.predatoroilandgas.com/> accessed 2 December 2021.

13 Barry Roche, 'Plans to import fracked gas through Cork shelved' (*Irish Times*, 18 January 2021) <www.irishtimes.com/news/ireland/irish-news/plans-to-import-fracked-gas-through-cork-shelved-1.4461032> accessed 2 December 2021.

14 Sean Pollock, 'Predator has 2024 LNG delivery in sight' (*Independent.ie*, 11 October 2020) <www.independent.ie/business/irish/predator-has-2024-lng-delivery-in-sight-39606150.html> accessed 2 December 2021.

15 Barry O'Halloran, 'Shannon LNG to seek approval to build €650m gas plant in Kerry' (*Irish Times*, 24 August 2021) <www.irishtimes.com/business/energy-and-resources/shannon-lng-to-seek-approval-to-build-650m-gas-plant-in-kerry-1.4654412> accessed 2 December 2021.

16 Aideen O'Dochartaigh, 'Shannon gas plan would make mockery of Irish climate goals' (*Irish Times*, 3 September 2021) <www.irishtimes.com/opinion/shannon-gas-plan-would-make-mockery-of-irish-climate-goals-1.4663349> accessed 9 December 2021.

17 Department of the Environment, Climate and Communications, 'Policy Statement on the Importation of Fracked Gas' (*GOV.IE*, 18 May 2021) <www.gov.ie/en/publication/f3774-policy-statement-on-the-importation-of-fracked-gas/> accessed 9 December 2021.

It remains to be seen whether the Shannon LNG project (or indeed other LNG projects) will be developed in Ireland.

While these LNG terminals would in theory strengthen Ireland's gas supply and reduce its reliance on the UK for gas imports, the global nature of the LNG market means that this situation in reality is not always so straightforward. For example, LNG exporters cancelled cargoes in 2020 due to less demand and low spot prices in Asian and European markets. As the global economy began recovering from the COVID pandemic in 2021, demand in Asia increased and spot prices soared, leaving Europe with limited cargoes.[18] The Irish government is aware of these possible issues with LNG supply. In a debate of the Joint Oireachtas Committee on Environment and Climate Action, it was stated that 'energy security does not become more guaranteed by putting in an LNG import terminal'.[19]

In September 2022, the Irish government published its consultation on security of supply of Ireland's electricity and natural gas systems together with supporting economic analysis from consultants, CEPA.[20]

While, as at the date of writing, the consultation process is ongoing it is worth noting that the option of a Fixed LNG terminal (commercially operated or operated as a back-up facility) and the option of a Floating LNG terminal (commercially operated) were not shortlisted by CEPA. However, the Floating LNG (operated as a back-up facility) was shortlisted.

Other options to improve Ireland's gas security of supply which were shortlisted by CEPA include an onshore gas storage facility (operated as a back-up facility), indigenous renewable gas production and green hydrogen, and demand response in the gas sector.

11.2.1.3 Regulatory challenges

The possible future divergence of laws with regard to gas trading between Ireland and Great Britain in a post-Brexit scenario is a further cause of concern from an economic and practical perspective. While the Irish government does not anticipate any disruption to gas supplies as a result of Brexit, the legal position is that EU Regulation 2017/1938,[21] a regulation which aims to strengthen EU energy security by helping prevent potential supply disruptions (and to respond to them

18 Anna Shiryaevskaya, 'Here's Why Europe, Desperate for Gas, Isn't Buying LNG' (*Bloomberg*, 20 September 2021) <www.bloomberg.com/news/articles/2021-09-20/here-s-why-europe-desperate-for-gas-isn-t-buying-lng> accessed 9 December 2021.

19 Joint Committee on Environment and Climate Action debate – Tuesday 28 Sep 2021 (*Houses of the Oireachtas*) <www.oireachtas.ie/en/debates/debate/joint_committee_on_environment_and_climate_action/2021-09-28/2/> accessed 9 December 2021.

20 <https://www.gov.ie/en/consultation/dbe14-review-of-the-security-of-energy-supply-of-irelands-electricity-and-natural-gas-systems/>

21 Regulation (EU) 2017/1938 of the European Parliament and of the Council of 25 October 2017 concerning measures to safeguard the security of gas supply and repealing Regulation (EU) 994/201 [2017] OJ L280/1.

when they occur) to ensure that households and other vulnerable consumers are always supplied, no longer applies to the UK. Consequently, the UK is no longer legally obliged to provide solidarity to Ireland in a gas supply disruption scenario. Ireland's gas supply vulnerability has therefore increased post-Brexit.

The Irish government stated in its 2019 Contingency Plan[22] that contingency plans have been prepared for the gas wholesale and network sectors following Brexit. GNI published an updated Natural Gas Emergency Plan[23] in April 2021 to minimise supply disruption in Ireland in the event that gas interconnectors cease flowing (noting, however, that such a scenario is not anticipated). In Irish parliament debates in November 2020,[24] the Minister for the Environment, Climate and Communication, Eamon Ryan, noted this position and that no bilateral cooperation agreement existed between Ireland and the UK. He confirmed, however, that Ireland would continue to work with the UK to 'ensure continued future cooperation on natural gas security of supply'. The TCA provides in Article 315 that the EU and the UK 'shall cooperate with respect to the security of supply of electricity and natural gas'.

While the Irish government has stated that it does not expect any disruptions in gas supply due to Brexit, this scenario cannot be entirely ruled out given Ireland's reliance on gas supply from the UK and the non-existence of a solidarity obligation imposed on the UK in a security of supply situation. It remains to be seen in the long term how gas imports and gas interconnection will operate between Ireland and the UK.

11.2.2 Electricity

Similarly to the gas market, Ireland's electricity market is closely connected to that of the UK. However, unlike in the case of gas, Ireland has a strong indigenous electricity generation sector. The sector is expected to continue to grow due to the Irish government's commitment in its National Development Plan 2021–2030 that up to 80% of electricity consumed will come from renewable sources by 2030.[25] However, in its November 2021 policy statement, the Irish government noted that 'these sources of renewable energy are variable in nature and therefore will require other technologies to both support their operation and provide electric-

22 Government of Ireland, 'Preparing for the withdrawal of the United Kingdom from the European Union – Contingency Action Plan Update' (*Government of Ireland*, July 2019) <www.dfa.ie/media/dfa/eu/brexit/keydocuments/Contingency-Action-Plan-Update.-July-2019.pdf> accessed 2 December 2021.

23 GNI, 'Natural Gas Emergency Plan' (*GNI*, April 2021) <www.gasnetworks.ie/corporate/company/our-network/Natural-Gas-Emergency-Plan-V5-April-2021.pdf> accessed 2 December 2021.

24 Energy Policy Dáil Éireann Debate (*Houses of the Oireachtas*, 4 November 2020) <www.oireachtas.ie/en/debates/question/2020-11-04/26/> accessed 17 November 2021.

25 Department of Public Expenditure and Reform, 'National Development Plan 2021-2030' (*GOV.IE*, 4 October 2021) <www.gov.ie/en/publication/774e2-national-development-plan-2021-2030/> accessed 9 December 2021.

ity supplies when they are not generating'. It noted further that 'this will require a combination of conventional generation …, interconnection to other jurisdictions, demand flexibility and other technologies such as energy storage … and generation from renewable gases'.[26] Thus, the fact that all of Ireland's existing electricity interconnectors connect to the UK (until a new interconnection to the EU is built) is of concern post-Brexit in terms of security of supply and market efficiency.

In addition, Ireland and Northern Ireland are closely connected via an all-island wholesale electricity market, the Single Electricity Market (SEM), which pre-Brexit was governed by EU legislation but which post-Brexit is now governed by EU legislation, the Northern Ireland Protocol, and the TCA. Throughout Brexit negotiations the continued operation of the SEM was one of relatively few topics on which the negotiating parties were in agreement. Even with the prospect at various stages of a 'no deal' Brexit, the EU and the UK were clear that the SEM would continue to function.[27] The all-island SEM Committee has stated that:

> '[t]he SEM allows generators and suppliers to trade electricity in a single market across the island of Ireland. Being part of an all-island market brings benefits to electricity customers in both Northern Ireland and Ireland by reducing electricity prices and by increasing security of electricity supply'.[28]

However, even with the necessary political will, the question remained how the SEM, a wholesale electricity market which is inextricably linked to EU electricity market standards and regulations, would continue to apply in both Northern Ireland, a non-EU jurisdiction, and in Ireland, an EU jurisdiction.

Before moving on to assess the impact of Brexit on the Irish electricity market, it is important to clarify the applicable legislation and agreements. Post-Brexit, the Withdrawal Agreement, including the Northern Ireland Protocol and the TCA, provide the legal basis for the continued operation of the electricity market in general and the SEM in particular.

The Northern Ireland Protocol applies initially for a period of 4 years from 1 January 2021. Its continued application is then subject to democratic consent (i.e., approval by the Northern Ireland Legislative Assembly), and it remains to be seen whether it will be replaced by any multilateral or bilateral agreements between the UK and the EU/Ireland.

26 Department of the Environment, Climate and Communications, 'Policy Statement on Security of Electricity Supply' (*GOV.IE*, 30 November 2021) <www.gov.ie/en/publication/a4757-policy-statement-on-security-of-electricity-supply/> accessed 9 December 2021.

27 SEMC, 'Notice to Industry in the event of a "no deal" Brexit' (*SEMC*, 28 March 2019) <www.sem-committee.com/sites/semc/files/media-files/SEM%20Committee%20Statement%20-%20Notice%20to%20Industry%20on%20a%20%27no-deal%27%20Brexit.pdf> accessed 9 December 2021.

28 SEMC, 'SEM Committee Statement – Operation of the SEM after the End of the Brexit Transition Period' (*SEMC*, 27 November 2020) <www.semcommittee.com/publications/sem-committee-statement-operation-sem-after-end-brexit-transition-period> accessed 9 December 2021.

Article 9 of the Northern Ireland Protocol[29] notes as follows:

> The provisions of Union law governing wholesale electricity markets listed in Annex 4 to this Protocol shall apply, under the conditions set out in that Annex, to and in the United Kingdom in respect of Northern Ireland.

Article 12 of the Northern Ireland Protocol[30] requires the authorities of the UK to be responsible for implementing and applying the provisions of EU law.

Annex 4 of the Northern Ireland Protocol[31] provides as follows:

> The following acts shall apply to and in the United Kingdom in respect of Northern Ireland insofar as they apply to the generation, transmission, distribution, and supply of electricity, trading in wholesale electricity or cross-border exchanges in electricity.
>
> Provisions relating to retail markets and consumer protection shall not apply. References to a provision of another Union act in the acts listed in this Annex shall not render the provision referred to applicable where it does not otherwise apply to and in the United Kingdom in respect of Northern Ireland, unless it is a provision governing wholesale electricity markets which applies in Ireland and is necessary for the joint operation of the single wholesale electricity market in Ireland and Northern Ireland.

Annex 4 then lists a number of key EU energy-related directives and regulations which will continue to apply in respect of Northern Ireland post-Brexit. This list references a number of directives and regulations which have, in fact, been replaced by newer directives and regulations as part of the Clean Energy Package. For example, Directive 2009/72/EC has been replaced by Directive (EU) 2019/944. However, Article 13(3) of the Northern Ireland Protocol makes it clear that unless otherwise stated, any references to a Union Act 'shall be read as referring to that Union Act as amended or replaced' and, in this way, directives and regulations replacing those listed in Annex 4 should apply in respect of Northern Ireland, notwithstanding that they are not expressly listed in Annex 4.

The following phrase in Annex 4 merits further consideration: 'unless it is a provision governing wholesale electricity markets which applies in Ireland and is necessary for the joint operation of the single wholesale electricity market in Ireland and Northern Ireland'. It effectively states that provisions of EU legislation not listed in Annex 4 but referred to in the EU legislation listed in Annex 4 may also apply in respect of Northern Ireland if (1) they are provisions which govern wholesale electricity markets and these provisions apply in Ireland; and (2) they are necessary for the joint operation of the SEM. The scope of this provision is clearly open to interpretation but will presumably be the basis on which

29 Protocol on Ireland / Northern Ireland (n 3) art 9.

30 Ibid art 12.

31 Ibid annex 4.

certain EU electricity legislation will apply in Northern Ireland (see, e.g., discussion on the scope and application of REMIT further below). However, it remains to be seen over time whether there are any disagreements between the EU and the UK as to the exact scope of this provision.

In addition to the possible issues of identifying the exact scope of EU directives and regulations which fall within the scope of Annex 4, the actual practicalities of how these directives and regulations will continue to apply and be implemented in respect of Northern Ireland will require further work and development.

11.2.2.1 Electricity interconnection

There is currently one direct electricity sub-sea interconnector between Ireland and Wales, the East West Interconnector (EWIC), with a capacity of 500 MW. Northern Ireland is connected to Great Britain by the 500 MW Moyle Interconnector to Scotland.

In addition to Moyle and EWIC, there are three further electricity interconnectors planned on the island of Ireland: the 500 MW private Greenlink Interconnector between Ireland and Wales, the 700 MW Celtic Interconnector between Ireland and France (which is being developed in a joint venture between the Irish transmission system operator, EirGrid, and the French transmission system operator, RTE) and the 750MW private MaresConnect Interconnector between Ireland and Wales. There are currently no further plans for new interconnectors between Ireland and the EU, except for the Celtic Interconnector.

Both the Greenlink Interconnector and the Celtic Interconnector had been designated as 'Projects of Common Interest' by the EU – a status which has recently been removed from the Greenlink Interconnector.[32] This means that the Greenlink Interconnector will no longer be eligible for financial assistance in the form of grants and other financial instruments under the Connecting Europe Facility.[33]

Nonetheless, the Greenlink Interconnector continues to be developed and is currently at pre-construction stage, with the intention that it will become operational in 2024. The Greenlink Interconnector has also in the meantime received a regulatory determination from both the CRU and Ofgem that they will apply a 'cap and floor' financial model in respect of project costs and project revenues and has also received other consents such as an interconnector licence from Ofgem. The developers of the Greenlink Interconnector have stated that '[t]he construction of Greenlink will deliver increased security of supply for electricity

32 The change in status of the UK from a EU Member State to a third country led to the ineligibility of 12 projects from the list of Projects of Common Interest; EU Commission, 'Questions and Answers on the fifth list of energy Projects of Common Interest (PCIs)' (*European Commission*, 19 November 2021) <https://ec.europa.eu/commission/presscorner/detail/en/qanda_21_6093> accessed 9 December 2021.

33 Ibid.

consumers, by diversifying energy sources and providing additional import and export capacity in both countries'.[34]

The Celtic Interconnector is also at pre-construction stage. The Celtic Interconnector has received a grant of planning permission and a foreshore licence. Most recently, the construction and finance agreements were signed by the Irish and French governments. The stated intention is that the Celtic Interconnector will become operational in 2026.[35] In contrast to the Greenlink Interconnector, the Celtic Interconnector is a public project co-funded by EirGrid, RTE, and the EU (including €530.7 million of funding from the EU Commission's Connecting Europe Facility).

The Celtic Interconnector is of particular interest in the context of Brexit as, when completed, it will be Ireland's only direct electricity connection to the EU and the Internal Energy Market. It will, therefore, also be the only electricity interconnector which will count towards Ireland's electricity 2030 interconnection targets set by the EU as part of its 2030 Climate & Energy Framework.[36] However, in practice, Ireland will struggle to meet any EU interconnection targets in circumstances where interconnection with the UK no longer counts towards such targets and for so long as there are no new interconnectors connected with the EU.

11.2.2.2 Regulatory challenges

11.2.2.2.1 SINGLE ELECTRICITY MARKET

Increased legal and regulatory alignment between Ireland and Northern Ireland in recent decades paved the way for the development of an all-island wholesale electricity market known as the Single Electricity Market (SEM), covering both Ireland and Northern Ireland, which went live on 1 November 2007. It is worth noting that, in contrast to the SEM, the Irish and Northern Irish gas grids are physically connected but operated separately. The Commission for the Regulation of Utilities (CRU), together with its counterpart in Northern Ireland, the Utilities Regulator (UR), regulates the SEM through an all-island executive for the SEM, the Singe Electricity Market Committee (SEMC). The SEMC consists of three representatives from the CRU, three representatives from the UR, and two independent representatives.[37] It recently underwent significant redevelopment as part of the 'integrated single electricity market' project, I-SEM, to facilitate integration with the EU's Internal Energy Market and to align the SEM's energy and

34 Greenlink <www.greenlink.ie/summary> accessed 9 December 2021.

35 EirGrid, 'Celtic Interconnector' (*EirGrid*) <www.eirgridgroup.com/the-grid/projects/celtic-interconnector/the-project/> accessed 2 December 2021.

36 European Commission, '2030 Climate & Energy Policy Framework' (*European Council*, 24 October 2014) <https://data.consilium.europa.eu/doc/document/ST-169-2014-INIT/en/pdf> accessed 17 November 2021.

37 SEMC, 'About us' (*SEMC*) <https://www.semcommittee.com/about-us> accessed 9 December 2021.

capacity markets with the European Target Model, a common set of rules and regulations including the introduction of day-ahead, intraday, and balancing markets (participants may also trade financially and hedge in a forwards market).[38]

The SEM has widely been acknowledged as a success. In its first annual report, the SEMC stated that the SEM promoted competition as the market structures have encouraged the entry of generators, reduced electricity prices through a mandatory pool market, and improved security of supply for both Ireland and Northern Ireland by attracting new generators and building new stations.[39] The continued operation of the SEM was confirmed by the SEMC in an information note issued to the market on 27 November 2020,[40] and on the basis of the Northern Ireland Protocol, EU law will effectively govern the SEM. This will lead to a diversion from the laws applying in the rest of the UK.

However, while trade between the SEM and the market in Great Britain (through the Moyle and EWIC interconnectors, as set out above) has continued post-Brexit, it has become less efficient. This is because it is no longer possible for some platforms to be used (such as the platform for forward interconnection capacity, the European balancing platform, and the single day-ahead and intraday coupling of EU electricity markets[41] – see further discussions below) on the basis that these platforms currently operate under EU rules.[42]

Acknowledging this new inefficiency, the SEMC also stated in their information note:

> The SEM Committee has to date taken a number of steps to facilitate future trade between the SEM and the market in Great Britain so as to address this potential loss of efficiency:
>
> 1. New arrangements have been put in place, which facilitate greater access for GB participants to the SEM. These arrangements went live

38 EirGrid, 'Quick Guide to the Integrated Single Electricity Market' (*EirGrid*, 2016) <www.eirgridgroup.com/__uuid/f110639e-9e21-4d28-b193-ed56ee372362/EirGrid-Group-I-SEM-Quick-Guide.pdf> accessed 9 December 2021.

39 UR, 'Single electricity market is "successfully delivering consumer benefits"' (*UR*, 16 April 2009) <www.uregni.gov.uk/news-centre/single-electricity-market-successfully-delivering-consumer-benefits> accessed 9 December 2021.

40 SEM Committee Statement, 'Information Note on the Operation of the SEM after the End of the Brexit Transition Period' (*SEMC*, 27 November 2020) <www.semcommittee.com/news-centre/sem-committee-statement-operation-sem-after-end-brexit-transition-period> accessed 17 November 2021.

41 European Commission, 'Notice to Stakeholders: Withdrawal of the United Kingdom and EU Rules in the Field of the Internal Energy Market' (*European Commission*, 12 February 2021) <https://ec.europa.eu/info/sites/default/files/notice-to-stakeholders-brexit-energy-market_en.pdf> accessed 17 November 2021 (EC Notice to Stakeholders).

42 SEM Committee Statement, 'Information Note on the Operation of the SEM after the End of the Brexit Transition Period' (*SEMC*, 27 November 2020) <www.semcommittee.com/news-centre/sem-committee-statement-operation-sem-after-end-brexit-transition-period> accessed 17 November 2021 (SEMC Information Note).

in the Intraday Market between the SEM and Great Britain on 4 August 2020.

2. New, more flexible order types have been added to the Intraday Markets between the SEM and Great Britain. These 'complex order' types went live on the 29 September 2020.

In addition, due to Brexit (and the rules under the EU Network Codes),[43] the SEM day-ahead market (DAM) is now a local market only, and day-ahead cross-border trading with Great Britain is no longer possible. This has resulted in a more volatile DAM. Volatility in the DAM is an issue because it is one of the fundamental markets in the SEM and is the market by reference to which various renewable support schemes and other items are indexed. Trading in the intraday market between SEM and Great Britain has however continued and is in fact facilitated in order to move focus from the DAM to the intraday market. Thus, potentially, it could going forward become the reference market rather than the DAM.[44]

In terms of enforcement, it remains to be seen how the UK authorities will, in practice, implement and apply EU law with respect to the SEM in light of Article 12 of the Northern Ireland Protocol[45] – in particular, whether the UK will implement and apply EU law consistent with implementation and application by Ireland and the EU and, if not, how this issue will be resolved.

This arrangement also gives rise to an interesting question as to what would happen if a dispute arose in respect of the SEM generally – affecting both Ireland and Northern Ireland. The Northern Ireland Protocol charges the UK courts and authorities with responsibility for applying EU law with respect to the SEM insofar as it relates to Northern Ireland. The governing law of a number of the key SEM market and industry codes (e.g., the Trading and Settlement Code and the Capacity Market Code)[46] is Northern Irish law. but both the courts of Ireland and Northern Ireland have jurisdiction in relation to any disputes under those codes. However, the Court of Justice of the European Union (CJEU) ultimately has jurisdiction over the SEM insofar as it applies to Ireland.[47] If an issue affects the entirety of the SEM (i.e., both Ireland and Northern Ireland), it is not immediately

43 Commission Regulation (EU) 2015/1222 of 24 July 2015 establishing a guideline on capacity allocation and congestion management [2015] OJ L197/24. Article 1(2) provides: 'This Regulation shall apply to all transmission systems and interconnections in the Union except the transmission systems on islands which are not connected with other transmission systems via interconnections'. As a result of Brexit, Ireland's transmission system is only connected to the UK, and as such Ireland's transmission system is no longer connected with other EU transmission systems following Brexit.

44 SEMC Information Note (n 43).

45 Protocol on Ireland / Northern Ireland (n 3) art 12.

46 Single Electricity Market Operator, 'Trading and Settlement Code' (*SEMO*) <www.sem-o.com/rules-and-modifications/balancing-market-modifications/market-rules/> accessed 17 November 2021; Single Electricity Market Operator, 'Capacity Market Code' (*SEMO*) <www.sem-o.com/rules-and-modifications/capacity-market-modifications/market-rules/> accessed 17 November 2021.

47 Protocol on Ireland / Northern Ireland (n 3) art 12.

clear whether it will fall within the jurisdiction of the UK courts or the Northern Irish, Irish, and EU courts. However, the UK government's stated position has been that the 'starting point should be to return to a normal treaty framework, similar to other international agreements including our Trade and Cooperation Agreement, in which governance and disputes are managed collectively and ultimately through international arbitration'.[48]

11.2.2.2.2 REMIT

Another regulatory challenge arises in the context of the REMIT.[49] REMIT established common standards of transparency and stability in the EU energy market to prevent market abuse and insider trading. REMIT is one of the pieces of legislation referenced in Annex 4 of the Northern Ireland Protocol and continues to apply to SEM market participants in Northern Ireland. However, discussions between the UK, the EU, and the Agency for Cooperation of Energy Regulators (ACER) have been ongoing as to how exactly REMIT would apply to Northern Ireland in practice.[50]

For example, the UK government issued a policy paper in which it states that market participants in Northern Ireland will need to be registered with the National Regulatory Authority in the Member State in which they are established, resident, or active, i.e., the UR in Northern Ireland. It maintains that 'market participants in Northern Ireland can stay registered with UR' while the EU 'has set out its consideration that all Northern Ireland market participants should be registered with the [CRU]' (i.e., the National Regulatory Authority in Ireland).[51]

In particular, the EU Commission issued a 'Notice to Stakeholders' on Brexit and the Internal Energy Market,[52] which highlighted that (i) Northern Ireland will not, among other things, have the ability to participate in the decision-making of the EU, nor can the UR participate in ACER and (ii) a registration with the UR is not valid in the EU, and market participants must register with a member state of the EU. This means in practice that Northern Irish market participants will be required to register with the CRU.

The UK government noted that it is seeking to resolve this issue with the EU.[53]

48 HM Government, 'Northern Ireland Protocol: the way forward' (*GOV.UK*, July 2021) <https://assets.publishing.service.gov.uk/government/uploads/system/uploads/attachment_data/file/1008451/CCS207_CCS0721914902-005_Northern_Ireland_Protocol_Web_Accessible__1_.pdf> accessed 9 December 2021.

49 Regulation (EU) 1227/2011 of the European Parliament and of the Council of 25 October 2011 on wholesale energy market integrity and transparency [2011] OJ L326/1.

50 Protocol on Ireland/Northern Ireland (n 3) annex 4.

51 Department for Business, Energy & Industrial Strategy, 'Policy Paper – Trading electricity with the EU' (*GOV.UK*, 3 February 2021) <www.gov.uk/government/publications/trading-electricity-with-the-eu/trading-electricity-with-the-eu> accessed 9 December 2021 (BEIS Policy Paper).

52 EC Notice to Stakeholders (n 42).

53 BEIS Policy Paper (n 52).

Similarly, on 12 February 2021, the SEMC released a statement on the application of REMIT in Northern Ireland post-Brexit.[54] An extract from that statement is as follows:

> [T]he UK Government and the European Commission (along with ACER) have been discussing the issue of registration of market participants under REMIT in the context of Brexit. The SEM Committee notes that these discussions are ongoing as to a common interpretation as regards how the Northern Ireland Protocol and the Protocol apply to this issue.

In that statement, the SEMC emphasises that REMIT continues to apply to all market participants and that the SEM Market Monitoring Unit will actively monitor the market.

The outcome of the discussions as to how exactly REMIT would apply to Northern Ireland in practice remains unclear. While ACER published the sixth edition of its guidance on REMIT in which it seems to maintain the position that it 'requires persons not established or resident in the EU entering into transactions which are required to be reported to the Agency … to register in the EU Member State in which they are active',[55] it is unclear whether this is a position agreed with the UK government. In light of this updated guidance, however, it seems likely that the EU will not change its position that market participants in Northern Ireland must re-register with the CRU in Ireland.

11.2.2.2.3 GUARANTEES OF ORIGIN

A further regulatory challenge arises in the context of guarantees of origin post-Brexit. While the continued operation of the SEM is complicated by the fact that it is an all-island market between an EU and non-EU jurisdiction, other areas are complicated by the fact that certain EU laws simply no longer apply with respect to Northern Ireland.

One such example are the EU laws with respect to the Guarantee of Origin scheme, a creature of EU directives.[56] According to these directives, EU Member

54 SEM Committee, 'SEM Committee Statement on REMIT' (*SEMC*, 12 February 2021) <www.semcommittee.com/news-centre/sem-committee-statement-remit-0> accessed 17 November 2021.

55 ACER, 'ACER Guidance on the application of Regulation (EU) No 1227/2011 of the European Parliament and of the Council of 25 October 2011 on wholesale energy market integrity and transparency' (*ACER*, 22 July 2021) <https://documents.acer.europa.eu/en/remit/Documents/ACER_Guidance_on_REMIT_application_6th_Edition_Final.pdf> accessed 9 December 2021.

56 Directive 2009/28/EC of the European Parliament and of the Council of 23 April 2009 on the promotion of the use of energy from renewable sources and amending and subsequently repealing Directives 2001/77/EC and 2003/30/EC [2009] OJ L140/16; and Directive (EU) 2018/2001 of the European Parliament and of the Council of 11 December 2018 on the promotion of the use of energy from renewable sources [2018] OJ L328/82 – as implemented by the relevant national authorities.

States are required to have a scheme to issue and accept guarantees of origin. The UK scheme is the Renewable Energy Guarantees of Origin (REGO) scheme, under which Ofgem issues generators of renewable electricity in the UK with one REGO certificate per megawatt hour (MWh) of eligible renewable output. With effect from 1 January 2021, EU Member States no longer recognise REGOs issued by Ofgem. This applies to REGOs generated in Great Britain and in Northern Ireland – notwithstanding Northern Ireland's continued participation in the SEM and the continued application of a number of EU energy-related laws in respect of Northern Ireland. The UK government and Ofgem have both also confirmed this position. Ofgem stated that it will continue to issue REGOs and will continue to accept guarantees of origin from EU Member States (including Ireland) despite the current lack of a reciprocal arrangement but indicated 'its intention to review this in 2021 so that, longer term, domestic recognition of Guarantees of Origin issued in EU countries will take place only on a reciprocal basis'.[57]

Non-recognition of REGOs by EU Member States will be of particular concern to Northern Irish renewable energy projects that are heading into a post-subsidy phase, or projects that are looking to agree PPAs with corporate offtakers, as the value of the REGOs generated by those projects will likely be lower on account of their lack of recognition by EU Member States.

11.3 Conclusion

It is quite clear that Brexit has already had a significant impact on Ireland from an energy perspective, raising significant issues with regard to electricity policy, market efficiency, regulatory oversight, cross-border energy trading, and security of supply – to name just a few.

What is less clear is exactly how Brexit will continue to impact on Ireland from an energy perspective in the medium to long term due to the unique circumstances and challenges facing Northern Ireland in the context of Brexit and the controversy and political instability around the Northern Ireland Protocol. It seems inevitable that increasing divergence between the laws of Ireland and the EU on one hand and the laws of Great Britain and Northern Ireland on the other hand will cause further complications for the continued operation of the SEM, cross-border energy trading, and other matters as it pushes the boundaries for domestic territorial self-determination in the UK and leads to the selective application of the four freedoms and unclear enforcement rules in the EU.

In addition, while the Northern Ireland Protocol provides a solution to many of the immediate Brexit-related concerns, it is untested from a practical and legal perspective. The Northern Ireland Protocol has also proved divisive from a political perspective, with certain politicians calling for it to be rejected. Most recently,

57 Ofgem, 'Renewable Energy Guarantees of Origin (REGO)' (*Ofgem*) <www.ofgem.gov.uk/environmental-and-social-schemes/renewable-energy-guarantees-origin-rego> accessed 8 December 2021.

the EU and the UK have disagreed on the UK's new proposals for post-Brexit trade with Northern Ireland and the related amendment of the Northern Ireland Protocol.[58] The UK prime minister, Boris Johnson, stated that 'the protocol is not working in the way that it needs to in order to guarantee the Belfast-Good Friday agreement', and that while the UK intends to continue working with the EU to resolve the issue, the UK does 'not remove the possibility of invoking Article 16 to protect trade between Great Britain and Northern Ireland'.[59] Invoking Article 16 of the Northern Ireland Protocol would allow either party to undertake unilateral safeguarding measures if the Northern Ireland Protocol leads to 'serious economic, societal or environmental difficulties that are liable to persist, or to diversion of trade', effectively suspending the Northern Ireland Protocol for a certain period of time. It is not, therefore, inconceivable that the energy markets of Ireland, Northern Ireland, and Great Britain could be unintended victims if the Northern Ireland Protocol is abandoned.

However, in spite of the very real challenges posed by Brexit, it remains the case that there is strong political support in Ireland, Northern Ireland, and Great Britain for the continued operation of the SEM and other cross-border energy initiatives. The Northern Ireland Protocol is evidence that as long as this strong political support remains in place, it should be possible to mitigate the negative consequences of Brexit on Ireland from an energy perspective.

58 Rob Merrick, 'EU rejects UK's demand to rip up Brexit deal for Northern Ireland after less than three hours' (*Independent*, 21 July 2021) <https://www.independent.co.uk/news/uk/politics/brexit-northern-ireland-protocol-eu-b1888015.html> accessed 16 February 2022.

59 House of Commons, Commons Hansard for 8 December 2021 (Volume 705), <https://hansard.parliament.uk/commons/2021-12-08/debates/45C3B261-14F7-4DDC-A7D8-EB8A76097CFB/Engagements> accessed 16 February 2022.

12 Swiss–EU Energy Relations and Insights for Brexit

Jean-Christophe Füeg

12.1 Introduction

This Chapter discusses the energy relations between Switzerland and the EU and analyses their likely path of development post-Brexit. It deals primarily with electricity, as electricity is by far the most dominant facet of Swiss–EU energy relations. Section 12.13 at the end of this Chapter considers natural gas, emissions trading, and other energy issues.

12.2 The Swiss paradox

Switzerland faces a paradox. On the one hand, with the first cross-border interconnection with Germany and France in 1958, it laid the foundation of what was to become the Internal Energy Market (IEM), and has ever since played a pivotal role in electricity exchanges on the continent. On the other hand, this physical reality is not grounded in an international agreement between Switzerland and the EU. To address this, negotiations on an electricity agreement were launched in 2007. In 2012, the EU made the outcome of the electricity negotiations contingent on the conclusion of an Institutional Framework Agreement (IFA). The IFA aimed at resolving issues related to dispute settlement and the transposition of future EU acquis by Switzerland for existing and future internal market access agreements. On 26 May 2021, Switzerland concluded that no agreement could be reached and ended the IFA negotiations. Consequently, no electricity agreement is expected in the foreseeable future.

Without an electricity agreement, the legal gap between Switzerland and the evolving EU acquis in the field of electricity continues to widen. The EU argues that, without an IFA and an electricity agreement, there are no control and dispute settlement mechanisms to ensure a level playing field in the electricity market. The crux of electricity is that it is difficult to draw a clear limit between market and technical matters. The Directorate-General for Energy (DG Energy) interprets market matters very broadly, leaving little room for technical matters.

EU electricity legislation has progressively expanded to processes and institutions which were previously governed by private agreements. Some of these were initiated or co-founded by the Swiss transmission system operator (TSO),

DOI: 10.4324/9781003364337-13

Swissgrid. As processes and institutions fall under EU jurisdiction, Swissgrid is either being displaced or risks being displaced from these processes and institutions.

Since 2015, the Commission has denied Switzerland access to its electricity trading platforms. It has stepped up its ostracism by blocking Switzerland's participation in new balancing platforms, which are crucial for grid security, and by pressing for the exclusion of Switzerland from various bodies, such as Regional Coordination Centres (see Section 12.12) or the European Network of Transmission System Operators for Electricity (ENTSO-E). The Clean Energy Package and its implementation bring new uncertainties. Comitology processes, in which Switzerland is not able to partake, such as the revision of the Capacity Allocation and Congestion Management (CACM) Regulation,[1] impact Switzerland. Only where grid security is strained by new EU trading practice has DG Energy conceded an avenue to Swissgrid for arrangements between TSOs. These arrangements under private law are not yet finalised and are no substitute for an intergovernmental agreement (see Section 12.10).

Swissgrid is seeking alternative forms of involvement in bodies from which it is being expelled. Swiss market participants, who are barred from market coupling, continue to use less efficient explicit trading, whereby power sales and booking of cross-border capacity are carried out separately. This is a handicap, especially for highly flexible hydropower, which cannot be optimally offered in neighbouring markets, where it presents a high value and contributes to integrating growing volumes of variable solar and wind.

Large Swiss utilities have EU-based subsidiaries to conduct long-established trading, and their intra-EU business is not affected by the missing electricity agreement. By late 2019, Swiss utilities and investment funds had invested in capacities generating 11.5 TWh of renewable electricity in the EU and Norway.[2] Swiss utilities also own some conventional power plants in EU countries. By contrast, there is practically no EU ownership in Swiss generation assets since Electricité de France sold its 25% stake in Switzerland's second largest utility, Alpiq, in 2019.[3]

Potential welfare gains from electricity not being traded from high-price to low-price areas are estimated at some 39 million EUR by the Agency for the Cooperation of Energy Regulators (ACER).[4]

1 Commission Regulation (EU) 1222/2015 of 24 July 2015 establishing a guideline on capacity allocation and congestion management [2015] OJ L197/24 (CACM).

2 Energie Zukunft Schweiz, 'Investments in renewable energy production outside Switzerland by Swiss energy providers and institutional investors, Update 2019' (20 February 2020) <https://energiezukunftschweiz.ch/wAssets/docs/hkn-neue-energie/EZS-Update-Investitionen-Erneuerbare-2019.pdf>

3 Alpiq, 'EOS and Primeo Energie acquire block of Alpiq shares from EDF' (4 May 2019) <www.alpiq.com/alpiq-group/media-relations/media-releases/media-release-detail/eos-and-primeo-energie-acquire-block-of-alpiq-shares-from-edf> accessed 8 November 2021.

4 ACER, 'ACER Market Monitoring Report 2020 – Electricity Wholesale Market Volume' (30 October 2021), Fig 25, p. 55 <ACER Market Monitoring Report 2020 – Electricity Wholesale Market

On 13 October 2021, the Swiss government released a study on the impact of the missing electricity agreement.[5] Three scenarios up to 2025 are examined. The welfare effects of the different scenarios range from a yearly loss of 150 million EUR (with no inter-TSO arrangements) to a yearly gain of 150 million EUR (with an electricity agreement). By 2025, EU Member States must implement a rule to avail 70% of their cross-border capacity for trade.[6] Depending on how this rule will be applied to Switzerland's borders, it may have significant consequences. If the negotiations between Swissgrid and TSOs are successful, EU Member States will account for Switzerland when implementing the 70% rule, and trade with Switzerland will not be restricted. In January 2022, an agreement between Swissgrid, the Italian TSO, and TSOs of other countries bordering Italy was signed,[7] while negotiations with TSOs of the Core region were still ongoing. Security of supply will be endangered only if the worst-case scenario (i.e., failure to reach inter-TSO agreements) is further exacerbated by the shutdown of two nuclear plants in Switzerland and one-third of the French nuclear fleet (as occurred in the winter of 2016–2017). This could lead to Switzerland facing up to 47 hours of shortages in late winter. The study has triggered a wide debate in Switzerland about the need to rapidly ramp up domestic production capacity.

An earlier study of the Swiss National Research Programme estimated that Switzerland's annual electricity trade deficit could increase by a few hundred million CHF (Swiss francs) to up to 1 billion CHF by 2030 because lucrative flexible Swiss hydropower could not be optimally commercialised, given that Switzerland has no access to implicit trading on EU trading platforms. Swiss electricity prices could be 15–20 CHF/MWh higher than in neighbouring states because the Swiss market would remain protected from EU competition. Re-dispatch would become costlier because it would need to be increasingly sourced domestically.[8]

12.3 Commonalities and differences in Switzerland's and the UK's energy relations with the EU

Switzerland watched the Brexit process closely, as it has grappled with many similar political issues as the UK: sovereign lawmaking versus chosen or imposed adoption of EU legislation; the role of the Court of Justice of the European Union

Volume.pdf (europa.eu) ACER Market Monitoring Report 2020 – Electricity Wholesale Market Volume.pdf (europa.eu)> accessed 27 November 2021.

5 Frontier Economics, 'Analyse Stromzusammenarbeit CH-EU' (September 2021) <www.newsd.admin.ch/newsd/message/attachments/68518.pdf> accessed 8 November 2021.

6 Regulation (EU) 2019/943 of the European Parliament and of the Council of 5 June 2019 on the internal market for electricity [2019] OJ L158/54, Art. 16.8. (Electricity Market Regulation).

7 Swissgrid, 'Swissgrid signs contract with the capacity calculation region Italy North' (7 January 2022) <https://www.swissgrid.ch/en/home/newsroom/newsfeed/20220107-01.html>

8 70 NRP Energy Tournaround National Research Programme, 'Switzerland's influence on European energy policy continues to decline' (10 December 2019) <www.nfp70.ch/en/News/Pages/191210-news-nfp70-switzerland-influence-in-europe-continues-to-decline.aspx> accessed 8 November 2021.

(CJEU); and immigration and access to social benefits for EU residents. In the field of energy, however, Switzerland and the UK do not share many common features in their relations with the EU.

Politically, the two countries are moving in opposite directions: whereas the UK has left the EU, Switzerland remains committed to consolidating the system of sectoral bilateral agreements, which has proved a success since the 1990s. When signing the Trade and Cooperation Agreement (TCA), UK energy policy was fully EU-compatible, and should remain so by virtue of the no-regression clause. By contrast, Switzerland's energy policy features many hiatuses with the EU acquis. The now stalled electricity negotiations were aimed at bridging these hiatuses. The most salient differences are the as yet incomplete opening of the retail electricity market, the pending unbundling of large distribution companies, and missing state aid rules.

Post-Brexit, the UK lost access to EU day-ahead market coupling, while Switzerland was never granted such access. The effect is very different on both countries: the UK is asynchronously connected to the continent with merely five direct-current cables, whereas Switzerland pursues a highly dynamic trade through its 41 synchronous interconnectors. Switzerland seeks not only access to the EU day-ahead trading platform, but also to intraday and balancing platforms. Both countries currently trade by way of less efficient explicit auctions. Although the details of the future Multi-Region Loose Volume Coupling between the UK and the EU have yet to emerge, it is likely to be less efficient than full market coupling and could hardly serve as a model for Switzerland.

Furthermore, Switzerland's electricity grid is strained by increasing volumes of unscheduled flows from its neighbours. Unscheduled flows require costly measures to stabilise the grid (e.g., re-dispatch) and increase the risk of grid failures. In the longer term, the grid may need costly adaptations such as grid reinforcement or additional substations. In comparison, sea cables allow the UK to shelter itself from such unscheduled flows.

The departure of the UK National Grid from ENTSO-E further undermines Swissgrid's fragile position within ENTSO-E. Swissgrid cannot discount the possibility of full exclusion from ENTSO-E in future. DG Energy refuses to treat Swissgrid differently from the National Grid. Because of Swissgrid's more central role in the European system, ENTSO-E and TSOs from Switzerland's neighbouring states have been reluctant to bow to DG Energy's pressure.

On 26 August 2021, ACER terminated a memorandum of understanding which it had signed with Swiss NRA ElCom in 2016, and which admitted ElCom as an observer to the ACER Electricity Working Group.

12.4 Switzerland: an electricity hub in the European system

Switzerland is one of the most interconnected countries in Europe. Some 13% of European electricity trade and 41 of Europe's 420 interconnectors cross Swiss borders. Legally, however, Switzerland finds itself excluded from the IEM. Increasingly, the legal vacuum between Switzerland and the EU impinges on electricity trade, grid operations, and security of both the EU and Switzerland.

In 2020, cross-border electricity flows between the EU and Switzerland reached 59.5 TWh, corresponding to 90% of domestic production (65.5 TWh). Of the 59.5 TWh, 21.5 TWh was electricity transit, predominantly from Germany and France to Italy. Switzerland exports its excess hydropower in summer but relies on imports in winter to cover its higher demand. Its yearly electricity trade balance has been positive with the exception of a few years.

Swiss hydropower, including pumped storage, plays a key role in the surrounding EU markets. Historically, Switzerland imported cheap nuclear energy from France at night to pump water up into its reservoirs, and exported power, mainly to Italy, during high-price day time. Italy imports some 7% of its electricity demand from and through Switzerland. Swiss pumped storage plants were not designed for the Swiss market alone, but for the wider European market. With the onset of solar and wind power development and dwindling mid-day prices, particularly in Germany, the former trade model was replaced by more dynamic trading. Highly flexible hydropower – both reservoirs and pumped storage – contributes to integrating ever growing volumes of variable wind and solar. Hydropower can be activated in less than a minute if needed and provides valuable ancillary services to help stabilise the grid. Pumped storage can absorb and store excess wind or solar. Unfortunately, absent an electricity agreement and access to the EU electricity market platforms, these assets cannot be optimally used.

12.5 The impact of the missing electricity agreement on Switzerland's energy and climate targets

Switzerland decided after the Fukushima catastrophe to phase out nuclear power. This decision was endorsed in a referendum in 2017 by 58.2% of voters.[9] Existing nuclear plants, which currently account for about 35% of production, have no set closure dates. Instead, they can run as long as they comply with safety standards. Assuming a 50-year lifespan, the last plant will close in 2034. Operators are pondering extending the lifetime of the more recent plants to 60 years.[10] Switzerland's Energy Strategy and its Net Zero Emissions Target by 2050 bank on nuclear power being replaced by new renewables (mostly solar) and hydropower.[11]

However, because of permitting delays, nimbyism, and utilities' preference to invest in Europe where returns are more attractive than in Switzerland, new capacity is being commissioned at a slow rate. Legislation is being prepared to prolong investment aid for new renewables and large hydro until 2035 to boost

9 Swissinfo.ch, 'Swiss give green light for renewables and nuclear phase out' (21 May 2017) <www.swissinfo.ch/eng/vote-opener/43190762> accessed 8 November 2021.

10 Energate Messenger.ch, 'Laufzeitverlängerung der Kernkraftwerke sorgt für Diskussionen' (5 July 2021) <www.energate-messenger.ch/news/213514/laufzeitverlaengerung-der-kernkraftwerke-sorgt-fuer-diskussionen> accessed 8 November 2021.

11 Swiss Federal Office of Energy, 'Energy perspectives 2050+' <www.bfe.admin.ch/bfe/en/home/policy/energy-perspectives-2050-plus.html> accessed 8 November 2021.

investment. According to projections, new renewables and additional hydropower will only be able to fully supplant nuclear closures and cover some 11% of incremental demand stemming from electric mobility and heat pumps towards the middle of the century. As a result, Switzerland's import dependence will increase in coming years, particularly during winter months. Various policies are currently being considered to incentivise dispatchable capacity in winter.

The increasing import dependence is causing growing concern, given that the export capacity of traditional exporters to Switzerland will decrease: Germany is phasing out nuclear and coal, while France may reduce the size of its nuclear fleet. Various generation adequacy studies,[12] including by the Pentalateral Forum[13] or ENTSO-E's Mid-Term Adequacy Forecast,[14] do not anticipate significant disruptions by 2025–2030, provided electricity trade is efficient and unimpeded. This latter condition could be jeopardised by recent developments in Swiss–EU electricity relations.

Electricity was conspicuously absent in the public debate about the institutional framework agreement (IFA) (see Section 12.8). The debate was dominated by the remaining sticking points of the IFA (sovereignty, social benefits for EU residents, wage protection) and ignored wider economic consequences. Swissgrid was the most vocal about the risks, in particular with regard to the impact on its relations with the EU should the IFA negotiations fail. Other players, and notably the electricity industry, began to plead for the electricity agreement only once the failure of the IFA became a realistic possibility. Economic arguments related to electricity, such as welfare losses or opportunity costs resulting from non-implicit trading, went unnoticed.

12.6 A brief history of Swiss–EU relations: from first interconnections in 1958 to launch of electricity negotiations in 2007

In 1951, Switzerland, along with seven other European countries,[15] founded the Union for the Coordination of the Production and Transmission of Electricity.[16] It grouped vertically integrated electricity companies, which defined common standards for grid operations. In 1958, the first electricity grid interconnection was

12 Pentalateral Energy Forum Support Group 2, 'Generation Adequacy Assessment' (April 2020) <www.swissgrid.ch/dam/swissgrid/about-us/newsroom/newsfeed/2020/2020-PLEF-GAA-3-0-report.pdf> accessed 8 November 2021.

13 The Pentalateral Energy Forum was established in 2009 by the governments of the Benelux states, France and Germany to facilitate the implementation of the EU energy acquis and initial price coupling. Participants in working groups include ministries, TSOs and NRAs. In 2011 Austria and Switzerland joined (the latter as an observer).

14 ENTSO-E, 'Mid-term Adequacy Forecast 2020, Executive Summary', <www.entsoe.eu/outlooks/midterm/> accessed 8 November 2021.

15 Austria, Belgium, France, Germany, Italy, Luxemburg, Netherlands.

16 UCPTE was the precursor of ENTSO-E.

established between Switzerland, France, and Germany through a transformer station at Laufenburg (in Switzerland). The transformer station became known as the 'Star of Laufenburg' and can be considered as the embryo of today's pan-European electricity system. As the system expanded to more countries, Swissgrid and Laufenburg maintained their role as the central control centres.

The year 1992 marked a hiatus in Swiss–EU relations, as Swiss voters rejected the accession of Switzerland to the EEA in a referendum. In the following years, Switzerland concluded two packages of bilateral agreements with the EU.[17]

In the second half of the 1990s, Switzerland prepared the Electricity Market Act,[18] which was broadly aligned with the EU's First Energy Package.[19] There were informal contacts between Switzerland and the Commission, notably at the Florence Forum,[20] to which Switzerland was invited. However, an electricity agreement was not a priority for either side. In 2002, the Electricity Market Act, after having been adopted by Parliament, was rejected by 52.5% of voters in a referendum.[21] Opponents included the Social Democrats, Greens, and the unions, who campaigned on fears of dismantlement of public service and job losses. The derelict state of British rail and the Enron scandal in California fuelled opposition.[22]

On 28 September 2003, the tripping of a high-voltage line in Switzerland plunged 56 million Italians into a blackout for 19 hours. The subsequent investigation[23] by the Union for the Coordination of the Transmission of Electricity (UCTE) diagnosed that a lack of coordination among TSOs was the cause. The Commission suddenly became aware of the need to integrate Switzerland more closely in common EU technical rules. Pressure mounted on the seven largest owners of Swiss transmission lines to create a joint grid company, ETRANS AG, in 1999.

17 Swiss Federal Department of Foreign Affairs, 'The main bilateral agreements between Switzerland and the EU' <www.eda.admin.ch/dam/europa/en/documents/folien/Folien-Abkommen_en.pdf.> accessed 8 November 2021. The first package in 1999 covered Free movement of persons, Technical barriers to trade, Public procurement markets, Agriculture, Research, civil aviation, and overland transport. The second package in 2004 covered Schengen/Dublin, automatic exchange of information related to taxation, fight against fraud, creative Europe, environment, statistics, pensions, and education, vocational training and youth.

18 Swiss Federal Chancellery FCh, 'Elektrizitätsmarktgesetz (EMG)' <www.bk.admin.ch/ch/d/pore/rf/cr/1999/19994295.html> accessed 7 November 2021.

19 This refers to Directives 96/92/EC (electricity) and 98/30/EC (gas).

20 The Florence Electricity Regulatory Forum discusses developments of the IEM. It was established in 1998. Switzerland was not invited to the latest meeting in June 2021 after the failure of the IFA.

21 SWI swissinfo.ch, 'Elektrizitätsmarktgesetz abgelehnt' (22 September 2002) <www.swissinfo.ch/ger/elektrizitaetsmarktgesetz-abgelehnt/2941468> accessed 7 November 2021.

22 Bundesamt für Energie, 'Analyse des Meinungsbildungs- und Entscheidungsprozesses zum Elektrizitätsmarktgesetz' (April 2003), p. 12 <https://pubdb.bfe.admin.ch/de/publication/download/476> accessed 27 November 2021.

23 UCTE, 'Final Report of the Investigation Committee on the 28 September 2003 Blackout in Italy' (April 2004) <https://eepublicdownloads.entsoe.eu/clean-documents/pre2015/publications/ce/otherreports/20040427_UCTE_IC_Final_report.pdf> accessed 7 November 2021.

12.7 A brief history (continued): electricity negotiations until linkage with the IFA (2012)

In 2005, Switzerland and the EU announced their intention to launch negotiations on an electricity agreement,[24] and formal negotiations began in 2007.

Meanwhile, after the demise of the Electricity Market Act, a new Electricity Supply Act was drafted. A ruling by the Swiss Federal Tribunal, upholding a large electricity consumer's claim for third-party access, impelled legislators to act. The new Act differed from the failed Electricity Market Act in that it foresaw a two-step market opening, i.e., an initial opening for eligible consumers with an annual demand of more than 100 MWh, with a full opening after a period of at least 5 years and subject to a facultative referendum. Today, some three-quarters of country-wide demand is sold on the free market. In 2006, ETRANS, which was much-criticised after the blackout, converted into Swissgrid.[25] Its governance became more EU-compatible, but unbundling was still incomplete. Except for the different timeline, the new Act was in line with the two-step liberalisation set out in the EU's Second Energy Package. The Electricity Supply Act entered into force in 2007.

One particular bone of contention from the onset of negotiations between the EU and Switzerland were the long-term contracts of Swiss utilities for French nuclear power. After Chernobyl, new nuclear plants became unacceptable in Switzerland. As an alternative, Swiss utilities invested in French nuclear and secured long-term supply contracts. These were granted priority in case of congestion at the French–Swiss border. Some of these contracts last well into the 2030s. In a case between Belgium and the Netherlands, the CJEU ruled that such prioritisation was incompatible with EU law.[26] An EU-compatible solution consists in converting the physical prioritisation into financial rights. Contract holders participate in congestion auctions but are compensated with some congestion management revenue.

The EU's Third Energy Package of 2009 required an adjustment of the Swiss negotiation mandate. The EU demanded that the electricity agreement, which had previously focused on electricity issues in a narrow sense, be expanded with elements of EU's energy acquis with an indirect bearing on electricity This included the Renewables Directive,[27] and some in Switzerland were consequently

24 The Federal Department of the Environment, Transport, Energy and Communications, 'Schweiz und EU streben ein bilaterales Abkommen im Strombereich an' (29 September 2005) <www.admin.ch/gov/de/start/dokumentation/medienmitteilungen.msg-id-643.html> accessed on 7 November 2021.

25 Swissgrid AG, 'Operational launch of national transmission system operator Swissgrid' (*Presse-portal*, 17 November 2006) <www.presseportal.ch/de/pm/100011338/100519945> accessed on 7 November 2021.

26 Case C-17/03 *Vereniging voor Energie, Milieu en Water, Amsterdam Power Exchange Spotmarket, Eneco NV v Directeur van de Dienst uitvoering en toezicht energie* [2005] ECR I-5016 <https://eur-lex.europa.eu/legal-content/EN/TXT/PDF/?uri=ecli:ECLI%3AEU%3AC%3A2005%3A362> accessed on 7 November 2021.

27 Directive 2009/28/EC of the European Parliament and of the Council of 23 April 2009 on the promotion of the use of energy from renewable sources and amending and subsequently repealing Directives 2001/77/EC and 2003/30/EC [2009] OJ L140/16.

concerned about the prospect of having to reach a renewable target imposed by the EU. If calculated according to the EU methodology, Switzerland's target for 2020 was out of reach.[28] Moreover, the Renewables Directive did not set a discrete target for electricity; this was seen as a first breach of Switzerland's effort to circumscribe the scope of the electricity agreement to electricity only.

'Horizontal' issues were another new item which the EU imposed. These included environmental aspects related to electricity, competition, and state aid. It was feared that the 'horizontal' issues could not be confined to the electricity sector and would eventually spill over to other sectors. Among such sensitive sectors was taxation, where the EU had pressured Switzerland on previous occasions. The EU insisted on environmental issues to ensure equal treatment between Switzerland and the Energy Community Treaty.[29]

State aid is a particularly thorny issue in Switzerland. The country lacks relevant legislation, and the cantons are circumspect of any interference in what they consider their domain. Concrete state aids were discussed with the Directorate-General for Competition. Some, like the support for renewables or a planned strategic winter reserve, were deemed unproblematic. But questions remained open, such as the tax exemption of cantonally (municipally) owned utilities which, instead of being taxed, transfer profits to their owners. A market premium for large hydropower to partly cover losses, which generators incur by selling at loss in times of depressed wholesale prices, would qualify as illegal state aid under EU law. However, the premium is seen as vital for Swiss hydropower, notably to compensate for very high 'water royalties' paid to mountain jurisdictions.

Switzerland adopted its new negotiation mandate in 2010. Unfortunately, the new contentious issues, in addition to the controversial opening of the full electricity market, were complicating factors in negotiations with the EU.

Moreover, Switzerland observed some developments in the EU with caution. Among these were letters of formal notice, which the Commission sent in 2019 to eight EU Member States about the award of hydropower concessions.[30] Although these had no direct incidence on the negotiations, they exacerbated Swiss fears about potential EU interference in Switzerland's hydropower concession award procedures, which is a sensitive political matter.

Negotiations also dealt with Switzerland's relations with ACER and dispute resolution in case an ACER decision impacted Switzerland. Without an electricity agreement, the Swiss national regulatory authority (NRA) ElCom cannot be a member of ACER.

28 Switzerland should have reached a renewable share of 34% by 2020 according to the EU methodology, which factors in GDP. In 2019, its share was 28.6%.

29 Treaty establishing the Energy Community of 25 October 2005 <www.energy-community.org/aboutus/whoweare.html> accessed on 7 November 2021.

30 Commission, 'Hydroelectric power concessions: Commission calls on 8 Member States to comply with EU law', Press release, 7 March 2019 <https://ec.europa.eu/commission/presscorner/detail/en/IP_19_1477> accessed 27 November 2021.

The Third Energy Package saw the institutionalisation and placement under EU law of ENTSO-E. Swissgrid remained a member, but its rights, including voting rights, have been progressively curtailed. Later, non-controversial items were added to the electricity negotiations, such as REMIT[31] and infrastructure.[32] With the latter, Switzerland would have introduced measures for the timely permitting and development of priority electricity corridors with neighbouring countries.

12.8 2012: Electricity agreement conditioned on Institutional Framework Agreement (IFA)

A paradigm shift occurred in 2012, when the EU declared that it would not conclude any new market access agreement in the absence of an IFA. As the electricity agreement was the first new market access agreement, it became inextricably tied to the IFA.

The EU had grown increasingly impatient over the years as disputes arising from bilateral agreements remained unresolved for lack of a dispute settlement mechanism. With the IFA, the EU wanted to institute a dispute settlement mechanism and to lay down rules for the control of agreements, the future transposition of the relevant EU acquis by Switzerland, and the interpretation of EU law.[33]

Switzerland adopted its negotiation mandate for the IFA in 2013.[34] The negotiations had a bumpy start, because in February 2014 Swiss voters accepted a new constitutional proposition to limit immigration. The EU considered that the implementation of the proposition would breach the Agreement on Free Movement of Persons and temporarily froze contact.[35]

Negotiations on the IFA and the electricity agreement resumed after several months. The electricity agreement became a test case for institutional issues, which made negotiations more intricate. The last round of electricity negotiations took place in July 2018, as the outcome of the IFA negotiations was awaited. At that time, the EU's Clean Energy Package was being finalised and it became evident that it would eventually replace the Third Energy Package as a basis for

31 Regulation (EU) No 1227/2011 of the European Parliament and of the Council of 25 October 2011 on wholesale energy market integrity and transparency [2011] OJ L326/1.

32 Regulation (EU) No 347/2013 of the European Parliament and of the Council of 17 April 2013 on guidelines for trans-European energy infrastructure and repealing Decision No 1364/2006/EC and amending Regulations (EC) No 713/2009, (EC) No 714/2009 and (EC) No 715/2009 [2013] OJ L115/39.

33 Swiss Federal Department of Foreign Affairs, 'Institutional agreement between Switzerland and the EU: key points in brief' (7 December 2018) <www.eda.admin.ch/dam/europa/en/documents/abkommen/InstA-Wichtigste-in-Kuerze_en.pdf> accessed 8 November 2021.

34 Swiss Federal Council, 'Swiss–EU relations: strengthening the bilateral approach through negotiations on institutional issues' (18 December 2013) <www.admin.ch/gov/en/start/documentation/media-releases.msg-id-51490.html> accessed 8 November 2021.

35 Commission, 'Declaration of the European Commission following the popular vote in Switzerland on the "mass immigration" initiative' (9 February 2014) <https://ec.europa.eu/commission/presscorner/detail/en/MEMO_14_96> accessed 8 November 2021.

the electricity agreement, requiring yet another adjustment to the negotiation mandate.

Such considerations have become moot after Switzerland decided on 26 May 2021 to end negotiations on the IFA as no compromise was found on politically highly controversial issues such as the application of the EU's Citizens' Rights Directive,[36] wage protection, and state aid issues.

12.9 EU Network Codes exclude Switzerland from market coupling

The Third Energy Package mandated the elaboration of eight Network Codes to implement the Single Market Model. The Network Codes are legally binding implementing regulation. There are three types of Network Codes:

- Codes for Grid Connections: Requirements for Generators and Demand Connection, HVDC Connection. These are of technical nature.
- Operational Network Codes: System Operation (SOGL[37]) and Emergency & Restoration.[38]
- Market Network Codes: CACM,[39] Energy Balancing,[40] and Forward Capacity Allocation.[41]

The CACM explicitly excludes Switzerland from the Market Network Codes[42] and hence from market coupling.[43] The SOGL instead calls for cooperation

36 Directive 2004/38/EC [2004] OJ L158/77 of the European Parliament and of the Council of 29 April 2004 on the right of citizens of the Union and their family members to move and reside freely within the territory of the Member States amending Regulation (EEC) No 1612/68 and repealing Directives 64/221/EEC, 68/360/EEC, 72/194/EEC, 73/148/EEC, 75/34/EEC, 75/35/EEC, 90/364/EEC, 90/365/EEC and 93/96/EEC.

37 Commission Regulation (EU) 2017/1485 of 2 August 2017 establishing a guideline on electricity transmission system operation [2017] OJ L220/1.

38 Commission Regulation (EU) 2017/2196 of 24 November 2017 establishing a network code on electricity emergency and restoration [2017] OJ L312/54.

39 CACM, see footnote 1.

40 Commission Regulation (EU) 2017/2195 of 23 November 2017 establishing a guideline on electricity balancing [2017] OJ L 312/6.

41 Commission Regulation (EU) 2016/1719 of 26 September 2016 establishing a guideline on forward capacity allocation [2016] OJ L259/42.

42 Art. 1.4: 'The Union single day-ahead and intraday coupling may be opened to market operators and TSOs operating in Switzerland on the condition that the national law in that country implements the main provisions of Union electricity market legislation and that there is an intergovernmental agreement on electricity cooperation between the Union and Switzerland'. Art. 1.5: 'Subject to the conditions in paragraph 4 above being fulfilled, participation by Switzerland in day-ahead coupling and single intraday coupling shall be decided by the Commission based on an opinion given by the Agency'.

43 Market coupling links control areas (including cross-border management) and market areas. Market participants trade electricity and book cross-border capacity in a single operation on dedicated platforms. Trade becomes more efficient and prices converge.

with synchronous non-EU TSOs.[44] This sets the base for the Synchronous Area Framework Agreement (SAFA; see Section 12.10). The Network Codes replaced the 2005 Operations Handbook, a multilateral inter-TSO agreement. Ironically, Swissgrid participated in much of the preparatory work for the Single Market Model. Along with the Swiss government and NRA ElCom, it was involved in work of the Pentalateral Energy Forum, which functioned as a test ground for the rollout of market coupling and the flow-based capacity calculation in the Central Western European Region (CWE).[45] It was part of the European Cross-Border Intraday project before being excluded in 2017. In 2016, CWE was merged with the Central Eastern European Region into the European Core Capacity Calculation Region.[46]

Flow-based market coupling (FBMC) was introduced in 2015 for day-ahead in the CWE region and is being expanded to other countries of the Core region. Switzerland's northern neighbours are part of the Core region.

In 2018, intraday trading was introduced in CWE and the Nordic, Baltic, and Iberian regions, and later to the Central Eastern Europe (CEE) region. A pre-existing flexible intraday trading at Switzerland's borders with France and Germany was discontinued. As a result, Swiss intraday trade came almost to a standstill.

Flow-based day-ahead market coupling went live on 8 June 2022, to go live for the entire Core region in 2022, to be followed by flow-based intraday in 2023. Electricity trade with Switzerland's northern neighbours (France, Germany, Austria) and with Italy will be handled differently.

Italy is part of the Italy North[47] capacity calculation region (CCR). Its heavy reliance on electricity imports and network configuration required the formation of a region with its EU neighbours. Capacity allocation and congestion management (CACM) dispensed Italy from adopting flow-based methodology.[48] Implicit intraday auctions were introduced at the Swiss–Italian border in April 2019. In September 2021, as Italy joined EU Single Intraday Coupling, implicit intraday auctions at the Swiss border had to be replaced by less efficient explicit auctions.[49] With the planned revision of the CACM, Italy may have to introduce FBMC. With

44 Art. 13: 'Where a synchronous area encompasses both Union and third country TSOs, … all Union TSOs in that synchronous area shall endeavour to conclude with the third country TSOs not bound by this Regulation an agreement setting the basis for their cooperation concerning secure system operation and setting out arrangements for the compliance of the third country TSOs with the obligations set in this Regulation'.

45 CWE encompassed the same countries as the Pentalateral Energy Forum, except for Switzerland.

46 Austria, Belgium, Croatia, Czech Republic, France, Germany, Hungary, Luxemburg, Netherlands, Poland, Romania, Slovakia, Slovenia.

47 Austria, France, Italy, Slovenia.

48 Art. 20.3.: 'The TSOs from the capacity calculation region where Italy … is included, may extend the deadline … for submitting the proposal for a common coordinated capacity calculation methodology using flow-based approach for the respective region … up to six months after Switzerland joins the single day-ahead coupling'.

49 Joint Allocation Office JAO, Intraday Auctions on Italy-Switzerland border' (5 August 2021) <www.jao.eu/news/intraday-auctions-italy-switzerland-border> accessed 27 November 2021.

additional interconnectors and grid reinforcements, Italy is readying for FBMC. The adoption by Italy of FBMC risks significantly impacting Swiss–Italian trade.

In late 2020, ACER laid down the rules for cross-border participation in capacity mechanisms in EU Member States.[50] With increasing shares of variable renewables, many Member States are procuring back-up generation capacity. The ACER rules have dashed hopes of Swiss suppliers to offer such capacity to neighbouring countries.

The Commission contends that there is no level playing field between the EU and Switzerland as long as the Swiss retail market remains shut. Still, this does not prevent numerous EU market participants from being active on the Epex Spot Switzerland exchange.[51] Well over half of the some 70 participants are foreigners.

12.10 Unscheduled flows, SAFA, negotiations on system operations

The introduction of day-ahead market coupling in CWE in 2015 increased unscheduled flows through Switzerland (while they decreased in CWE). Switzerland's northern neighbours, when calculating their cross-border capacity, ignored the congestion of the Swiss grid, implying that the Swiss grid had no capacity limits. Their booked trade volumes exceeded their interconnection capacity, congesting interconnectors and diverting excess flow through Switzerland. Thus, about one-third of incremental German–French trade transited through the Swiss grid. This violates N-1 grid security rules, causes critical grid situations at times, and restricts Switzerland's own imports. Swissgrid has to resort to more re-dispatch and other remedial actions. In 2020, unscheduled flows through Switzerland amounted to 28 TWh, a quarter of total unscheduled flows in the Core and Italy North regions.[52] The full implementation of day-ahead FBMC in 2022 is expected to generate additional unscheduled flows.

Independently of Swiss–EU relations, as from the winter 2018–2019, trilateral re-dispatch solutions were introduced between Switzerland, Germany, and France to ease the most critical winter congestions.

In March 2019, all continental European TSOs signed SAFA in accordance with SOGL Art. 13, which calls for the cooperation with non-EU TSOs to ensure

50 ACER, 'ACER decides on common rules for cross-border participation in electricity capacity mechanisms' (22 December 2020) <https://documents.acer.europa.eu/Media/News/Pages/ACER-decides-on-common-rules-for-cross-border-participation-in-electricity-capacity-mechanisms-.aspx>

51 EpexSpot: figures provided on 12 November 2021: CH Day-Ahead: total 69 participants, incl. 44 foreigners. CH Intraday: 64 participants, incl. 40 foreigners. Less recent data available: EpexSpot, 'Stromhandel in der Schweiz -gestern, heute und morgen' (6 March 2019) <www.strom.ch/system/files/media/documents/EPEXSPOT_Stromhandel_gestern_heute_morgen_20190306.pdf>, Slide 7.

52 ACER, 'Evolution of unscheduled flows in continental Europe: their lasting negative impact on electricity cross-border capacity' (7 July 2021) <www.acer.europa.eu/events-and-engagement/news/evolution-unscheduled-flows-continental-europe-their-lasting-negative> accessed 8 November 2021.

secure system operations. SAFA contains a Swiss clause whereby the TSOs commit themselves to find a common approach to include Switzerland in certain issues covered in the CACM, such as capacity calculations and other pertinent methodologies, by the end of 2020. Conversely, SOGL and ER became binding on Swissgrid.

DG Energy has realised that unscheduled flows pose a security risk for the whole region. In July 2019, it allowed Swissgrid to negotiate bilateral private agreements respectively with its 16 TSO counterparts of the Core region and with its 4 counterparts in the Italy North region. The letter also clarified that, with these agreements, Swiss cross-border elements would be accounted for in EU Member States' obligation to make 70% of their border capacity available for market participants by 2025.[53] Without such a clause, it was feared that some neighbouring states, especially Germany, would have to restrict their export capacity to Switzerland to comply with the rule, thereby causing possible supply shortages for Switzerland in winter.

The hurdles for the inter-TSO agreement with the Core region are high: it must be unanimously accepted by all TSOs and their 13 NRAs. Negotiations have been slow. While Switzerland's neighbours are keen on concluding it, TSOs from more distant countries do not regard these negotiations as a priority. Some TSOs are reluctant, because accounting for Switzerland in capacity calculations will limit their own cross-border trading capacity. Arduous technical issues and financial interests, including cost-sharing for remedial actions, pose challenges. The anchoring of a private inter-TSO agreement within EU and international law and finding a dispute settlement mechanism remain open. Many issues can only be solved after FBMC goes live in 2022. The Commission has followed these negotiations benevolently, but its attitude after the failure of the IFA has cooled. Overall, chances for the agreement with the Core region remain uncertain.

A similar agreement with the Italy North region was signed in January 2022.[54] Negotiations were easier because of the fewer parties and Italy's high interest in such an agreement. For reasons specific to Italy, border capacity at its borders has been calculated on Net Transfer Capacity (NTC) basis.[55] Until recently, the Italian TSO Terna considered the introduction of FBMC technically unfeasible because of its grid characteristics. This is changing, and Italy could switch to FBMC by 2025.

53 Electricity Market Regulation, Art. 16.8.

54 See footnote 7.

55 NTC is determined by TSOs from reference data as the maximum commercial exchange between two areas consistent with security standards. Neighbouring TSOs align the NTC values on their common border. By contrast, Flow-Based Market Coupling (FBMC) is not agreed bilaterally, but regionally by all TSOs of a region, determining the commercial flows for each network branch (instead of only for the direction along a given border). As a result, FBMC allows for a more efficient market-based cross-border capacity allocation based on bids and offers. It is less challenging to find solutions for NTC than for flow-based.

12.11 Balancing energy and Platform TERRE

Balancing energy[56] is yet another challenge. Balancing arrangements existed before the Electricity Balancing Guideline (EBGL) came into force. In 2010, Swissgrid initiated the first international cooperation for primary control power with Germany and Austria. This cooperation developed into the FCR Cooperation[57] for the procurement and exchange frequency containment reserves, launched in 2019 with 11 TSOs from eight countries, including Switzerland.

Also in 2010, the International Grid Control Cooperation (IGCC) was launched, initially by 14 TSOs, including Swissgrid.[58] In November 2021, the ACER Electricity Working Group initiated the exclusion of Swissgrid from the IGCC (renamed Inbalance Netting, IN), which is the implementation project for the imbalance netting process as defined by EBGL Art. 22.

Furthermore, there are regional balancing arrangements, such as the French *mécanisme d'ajustement*, which is open to Swiss and German participants.

New balancing platforms, such as TERRE,[59] MARI, and PICASSO,[60] are being established under the EBGL by varying groupings of TSOs.

The EBGL sets out the conditions for Switzerland to join balancing platforms.[61] In September 2017 and April 2018 respectively, ENTSO-E and ACER issued favourable opinions as foreseen in Art. 1.7 of the EBGL.[62]

56 Balancing energy is called for on short notice for grid stabilisation. Primary energy is available within 30 seconds, which makes hydropower well-suited. Secondary energy (available within 5 minutes) is provided for by IGCC and the future PICASSO platform. Tertiary energy (available within 15 minutes) is provided for by the TERRE platform (activation within 30 minutes) and the future MARI platform (activation within 12.5 minutes).

57 The FCR Cooperation participating countries are Austria, Belgium, Denmark, France, Germany, the Netherlands, Slovenia, and Switzerland.

58 Meantime, it has grown to 27 TSOs from 24 countries.

59 TERRE: Trans European Replacement Reserves Exchange.

60 MARI (Manual Reserves Initiative) and PICASSO (Platform for the International Coordination of Automated Frequency Restoration and Stable System Operation) platforms will become operational by 2022.

61 Art. 1.6: 'The European platforms for the exchange of standard products for balancing energy may be opened to TSOs operating in Switzerland on the condition that its national law implements the main provisions of Union electricity market legislation and that there is an intergovernmental agreement on electricity cooperation between the Union and Switzerland, or if the exclusion of Switzerland may lead to unscheduled physical power flows via Switzerland endangering the system security of the region'. Art. 1.7: 'Subject to the conditions of paragraph 6, the participation of Switzerland in the European platforms for the exchange of standard products for balancing energy shall be decided by the Commission based on an opinion given by the Agency and all TSOs … The rights and responsibilities of Swiss TSOs shall be consistent with the rights and responsibilities of TSOs operating in the Union, allowing for a smooth functioning of balancing market at Union level and a level-playing field for all stakeholders'.

62 ACER stated that 'The Agency agrees with the all TSOs' assessment that the full participation of Switzerland in the European platforms for the exchange of standard products for balancing energy could be an efficient solution to help remove possible congestion problems in the Swiss network and increase the efficiency of the Swiss cross-zonal capacity calculation and allocation, as well as the overall operational security in the region'.

Regardless of these two opinions, DG Energy has not taken a decision on the participation of Swissgrid. Together with seven other TSOs,[63] Swissgrid established the TERRE platform and started operations on 8 October 2020. On 17 December 2020, DG Energy requested, in a letter to the TERRE TSOs, that they exclude Swissgrid by 1 March 2021. On 26 February 2021, Swissgrid lodged a case (Case T-127/21) with the General Court of the EU for annulment of DG Energy's request of 17 December 2020. The case is currently pending. As this Chapter is written, Swissgrid is still participating in TERRE.

12.12 Other pending electricity issues

In the absence of an electricity agreement, the Clean Energy Package and other developments bring additional disadvantages and uncertainties for Switzerland. These include the following:

- One setback was that the EU Member States no longer recognise guarantees of origin (GOs) by virtue of Art. 19.11 of the Renewables Directive.[64] Previously, EU legislation had left a loophole open, allowing Switzerland to conclude a number of bilateral agreements for the recognition of GOs. Switzerland, however, continues to recognise GOs from EU Member States and Norway.
- In April 2020, ACER, when defining the System Operations Regions (SORs), deleted all reference to the Swiss borders. Each SOR is to be served by a Regional Coordination Center (RCC). These will replace the Regional Security Coordinators (RSC) with enhanced prerogatives for grid planning, operation, and critical grid situation management on 1 July 2022. The planned RCC for the Core region will substitute TSCNet, a RSC founded in 2008 by Swissgrid, among others. Swissgrid will not be admitted to the new RCC and is negotiating a service-level agreement to secure access to information, which is relevant for grid security. Another process is the Regional Operational Security Coordination, whereby Swissgrid continues to be involved in the elaboration of methodologies, based on the consent given by TSOs in the SAFA.
- The Risk Preparedness Regulation[65] does not explicitly foresee arrangements with third countries. Switzerland is associated with related works of the Pentalateral Forum. In December 2021, Pentaforum ministers signed a memorandum of understanding on emergency planning and crisis management in the power sector.[66]

63 TSOs from Czech Republic, France, Italy, Poland, Portugal, Spain, UK (National Grid was originally part of the project).

64 Directive (EU) 2018/2001 of the European Parliament and of the Council of 11 December 2018 on the promotion of the use of energy from renewable sources [2018] OJ L328/82.

65 Regulation (EU) 2019/941 of the European Parliament and of the Council of 5 June 2019 on risk-preparedness in the electricity sector and repealing Directive 2005/89/EC [2019] OJ L158/1.

66 Pentalateral Energy Forum: 'Penta countries discuss measures to make the clean energy transition secure and resilient' (2 December 2021) <https://www.benelux.int/nl/kernthemas/holder/energie/pentalateral-energy-forum/>

- The revision of the TEN-E Regulation,[67] which is currently underway, risks restricting the eligibility of energy projects involving third countries. In the past, several electricity interconnector projects from Switzerland to Germany and Italy and the reverse flow of the Transitgas pipeline were listed as Projects of Common Interests.

After the failure of the IFA in May 2021, DG Energy put Switzerland on a par with other third countries like the UK and Russia. Such a stance ignores Switzerland's fundamentally different integration level and interconnectivity. The EU had hitherto denied Switzerland access to the IEM, which was consistent with a certain logic. Furthermore, DG Energy stated that Switzerland 'risks losing its privileged connection with EU electricity system'.[68] The rationale for this change in terminology – qualifying more than 60 years of connections and cooperation as a privilege and suggesting that not only market access, but also system access is at risk – is more elusive.

12.13 Other energy and climate matters

Electricity is the only energy field in respect of which Switzerland and the EU have pursued an agreement. In the early negotiations on an electricity agreement, some thought was given to eventually expanding the agreement to other energy domains, but this never materialised.

The Clean Energy Package covers both energy and climate policies. The Governance Regulation[69] is intended to ensure the implementation of the Energy Union. The EU never requested Switzerland to adopt the Governance Regulation in the late phase of the electricity negotiations as the Clean Energy Package was shaping up. This would not have been acceptable, because it would have widened the scope of the electricity agreement to other domains.

A bilateral agreement was never considered necessary for natural gas, since gas trade between Switzerland and its neighbours has functioned smoothly. Switzerland has a small natural gas market (about 3 billion cubic metres per year,

67 Regulation (EU) No 347/2013 of the European Parliament and of the Council of 17 April 2013 on guidelines for trans-European energy infrastructure and repealing Decision No 1364/2006/EC and amending Regulations (EC) No 713/2009, (EC) No 714/2009 and (EC) No 715/2009 [2013] OJ L115/39.

68 European External Action Service (EEAS), 'What if there is no Institutional Framework Agreement (IFA)?' (May 2021) <https://eeas.europa.eu/sites/default/files/str_ifa_eu-switzerlandrelations_factsheet_final.pdf> accessed 9 November 2021.

69 Regulation (EU) No 2018/1999 of the European Parliament and of the Council of 11 December 2018 on the Governance of the Energy Union and Climate Action, amending Regulations (EC) No 663/2009 and (EC) No 715/2009 of the European Parliament and of the Council, Directives 94/22/EC, 98/70/EC, 2009/31/EC, 2009/73/EC, 2010/31/EU, 2012/27/EU and 2013/30/EU of the European Parliament and of the Council, Council Directives 2009/119/EC and (EU) 2015/652 and repealing Regulation (EU) No 525/2013 of the European Parliament and of the Council [2018] OJ L328/1.

representing 13% of the energy mix). The Y-shaped Transitgas trunk line passing through Switzerland from Germany and France to Italy is a major European artery. Its transportation volume to Italy exceeds domestic demand fivefold, with Italy importing about 3% of its gas demand through Switzerland. In 2010, a landslide interrupted the Transitgas pipeline and put Italy's gas supplies under stress. Consequently, at the request of Italy, Switzerland was invited to a number of meetings of the EU Gas Coordination Group. Switzerland coordinated its risk assessment, preventive action, and emergency plans with its neighbours, without adopting the relevant EU regulation.[70] The Swiss gas market is dominated by regional or local utilities. Large consumers have secured third-party access to the gas market through an industry covenant. In 2020, the Competition Authority ruled that small consumers had to be afforded access to the free market. A Gas Market Act is therefore being prepared, mandating regulated third-party access.

A bilateral agreement is also not considered necessary for energy efficiency. The level of ambition of Switzerland's energy efficiency policy is regarded as equivalent with that of the most advanced EU Member States. Policy instruments may differ, including as concerns target-setting. Building efficiency lies within the remit of the cantons, which are wary of too much centralised prescription. Switzerland typically aligns its standards for energy-using products and vehicles with those of the EU on account of the substantial trade.

Switzerland pursues its own climate policy, with its target set under the UNFCCC, aiming for a -50% reduction of emissions by 2030 compared to 1990 levels under the Paris Agreement, of which up to 16.6% is to be achieved via international offsets. It has its own policy instruments, such as a CO_2 levy on heating and process fuels (120 CHF/tonCO_2). Transport fuel importers must offset 10% of their induced emissions. Switzerland has also committed to net zero by 2050.

The Swiss Emissions Trading Scheme (ETS) and the EU ETS were linked in 2020. This was an important agreement for both parties. It brought liquidity to the tiny Swiss market (about 5 million tons of CO_2 as opposed to 2000 million tons of CO_{2eq} in the EU) and was welcomed by the EU as the first linking world-wide of its ETS. A joint committee manages the agreement. Since the agreement is not intended to provide access to the internal market through the adoption of EU law, it was not made contingent on the IFA. Climate-related proposals under the 'Fit for 55' Package will need to be examined in light of the ETS linking.[71] Because of the linking, Switzerland will not be subjected to the EU's proposed Carbon Border Adjustment Mechanism.

70 Regulation (EU) No 994/2010 of the European Parliament and of the Council of 20 October 2010 concerning measures to safeguard security of gas supply and repealing Council Directive 2004/67/EC [2010] OJ L295/1.

71 Swiss Federal Office of the Environment, 'Fourth meeting of the Joint Committee on linking emissions trading systems' (21 October 2021) <www.bafu.admin.ch/bafu/en/home/topics/climate/info-specialists/reduction-measures/ets/linking-swiss-eu/fourth-meeting-joint-committee.html> accessed 9 November 2021.

Switzerland has participated in the EU Framework Programme for Research and Innovation, including in energy, as an associated country since 2004 by virtue of a bilateral agreement. On 13 July 2021, the EU Commission decided that Switzerland will be treated as a non-associated third country in Horizon Europe and the European Atomic Energy Community (Euratom) Programme. It added that this status can be changed at any time. Switzerland was temporarily excluded from Horizon 2020 in 2014 after the vote on 'mass immigration'. This renewed exclusion is to be placed in the context of the end of the IFA.

In the field of nuclear energy, Switzerland is not confronted with the same issues as the UK. It participates only in the research and development (R&D) programme of Euratom (subject to the EU's announcement on 13 July 2021). The Swiss Nuclear Safety Inspectorate, ENSI, is a member of ENSREG (the European Nuclear Safety Regulators Group).

12.14 Conclusions

On 15 November 2021, after his first meeting with Swiss foreign minister Ignazio Cassis, Maroš Šefčovič, the vice-president of the European Commission for Interinstitutional Relations, reaffirmed that a bilateral electricity agreement between Switzerland and the EU requires an IFA.[72] It will take much time to craft a new institutional solution between Switzerland and the EU in light of how controversial the issue is. As this Chapter went to press, Switzerland and the EU were holding exploratory talks on how to resume negotiations on institutional issues, which, in turn, could lead to resuming electricity negotiations. The outcome of these exploratory talks remain uncertain. In the meantime, Swiss–EU electricity relations will continue to erode. Pressure is likely to mount gradually, depending on the evolution of the EU energy acquis and electricity sector developments in Switzerland and the EU, with no set milestones. Russia's attack on Ukraine and the energy crisis in Europe have not induced the EU to adopt a more pragmatic stance towards Switzerland. Gas has caught more attention. Swiss suppliers have secured gas storage in EU states and Switzerland is pursuing talks on so-called gas solidarity agreements with neighbouring states with no EU involvement. The winter outlooks of ENTSO-E and ENTSO-G do not diagnose stress factors for Switzerland, which could be specifically imputed to the lack of electricity or gas agreements with the EU. By contrast, the greatest challenge facing the UK energy sector is the termination of Title VIII Energy of the TCA in 2026.

72 Tages-Anzeiger, 'EU-Kommissions-Vize im Interview «Ich möchte schnelle Ergebnisse. In einem Jahr können wir viel erreichen»' (17 November 2021) <www.tagesanzeiger.ch/wir-brauchen-ein-signal-dass-die-schweiz-es-ernst-meint-749949623387> accessed 27 November 2021.

13 Brexit

The Challenges Ahead for the UK Energy Sector

Dorothy Smith

13.1 Introduction

During the 2016 Brexit campaign, issues concerning the energy sector barely featured in the debates about 'sovereignty' and EU membership. Soon after the UK entered its second year outside of the EU, however, with prices rising following the pandemic, security of supply fears exacerbated by the war in Ukraine, and mounting pressure to achieve net zero by 2050, energy-related concerns rose to the top of the political agenda.

Although Brexit has meant that the UK is no longer part of the EU's Internal Energy Market (IEM), it remains dependent upon imports coming largely from mainland Europe for roughly 35% of its overall energy supplies.[1]

The debate on how to reduce direct or indirect dependence on Russian fossil fuel supplies has been taking place within the EU and the UK (despite the UK being less dependent than the EU on Russian imports) post Russia's invasion of Ukraine. In 2021, Russia was supplying between 10% and 25% of the world's fossil fuels, including more than 40% of the EU's gas and coal imports, and a quarter of its crude oil.[2] Tensions have now emerged between the price and supply pressures on fossil fuels (prompting calls for developing new fields in the North Sea) and the binding decarbonisation commitments made by both the UK and the EU at the United Nations Conference of the Parties (COP26) in 2021.[3] The net zero transition remains vital, and, to be effective, must be so fundamental that it alters entire economies. It will require substantial investment in 'green' technologies, as

1 N Sönnichsen, 'Energy imports in the UK – statistics & facts' (*Statista*, 1 July 2021) <https://www.statista.com/topics/4938/energy-imports-in-the-united-kingdom-uk/#topicHeader__wrapper> accessed 4 May 2022.

2 N Sönnichsen, 'Energy imports in the UK – statistics & facts' (*Statista*, 1 July 2021) <https://www.statista.com/topics/4938/energy-imports-in-the-united-kingdom-uk/#topicHeader__wrapper> accessed 4 May 2022.

3 The Law Society, 'Reflecting on COP26: what were the key outcomes?' (*The Law Society: Climate Change*, 19 November 2021) <https://www.lawsociety.org.uk/topics/climate-change/reflecting-on-cop26-what-were-the-key-outcomes> accessed 4 May 2022.

DOI: 10.4324/9781003364337-14

well as active demand management through changes in behaviour and increased energy efficiency.[4]

As the impact of exclusion from the EU policy and regulatory structures which previously underpinned UK's international and domestic energy relationships finally begins to take hold on its energy sector, many uncertainties remain:

- Will Brexit create more opportunities for the UK to 'take back control' of energy policy? Arguably this could have been the case if measures such as the cut in VAT on domestic fuel bills, promised in 2016 but yet to be seen, had in fact been delivered?[5] Or alternatively, given its proximity and interconnection to European markets, is the UK's (and, in particular, Northern Ireland's) position in relation to security of price and supply of energy, post-Brexit, now more fragile?
- What leverage, if any, does the UK have on a market six times greater than itself? And how will the impact of the energy crisis engulfing the UK and EU, heightened by events in Ukraine, be felt by policy makers, investors, operators, and consumers?[6]
- How will the UK, a medium-sized market no longer party to EU energy solidarity mechanisms, fare in a bidding war for liquefied natural gas (LNG) supplies against giants such as the EU IEM and competing Asian markets?
- Are the UK's new nuclear ambitions potentially compromised by its departure from the European Atomic Energy Community (Euratom) Treaty?
- Last but not least, is the UK government's wish to promote energy self-sufficiency compatible with its own net zero commitments?

This Chapter discusses in turn the implications of Brexit on the ability of the UK energy sector to (i) meet net zero and decarbonisation challenges and (ii) address the new security of supply challenges.

13.2 Implications of Brexit for achieving net zero targets

New policy tools are urgently required to deliver the commitments to net zero. Ambitious targets such as 'Net Zero by 2050' had already been adopted by the UK government in 2019, in anticipation of the UK's high-profile joint presidency as co-chair of COP26. The UK Department for Business, Energy and Industrial

4 Camilla Hodgson & others, 'Boris Johnson under Pressure to set out UK's route to net zero emissions' *Financial Times* (London, 29 September 2021).

5 Oliver Wright, 'EU referendum: Boris Johnson and Michael Gove claim Brexit would allow UK to scrap VAT on energy bills' *The Independent* (London, 01 June 2016) <https://www.independent.co.uk/news/uk/politics/we-can-scrap-vat-on-energy-bills-if-we-leave-eu-say-johnson-and-gove-a7057146.html> accessed 4 May 2022.

6 'The Observer view on Britain's energy crisis' *The Guardian* (London, 30 January, 2022). <https://www.theguardian.com/commentisfree/2022/jan/30/observer-view-britains-energy-crisis>. Accessed 21 May 2022.

Strategy (BEIS) published a White Paper titled 'Powering our Net Zero Future' on 14 December 2020.[7] In the run up to COP26 in Glasgow in November 2021, BEIS went on to publish a further policy paper, 'Build Back Greener'.[8] These papers demonstrate that the government, or at least BEIS, clearly understands the dangerous implications of the relentless onset of climate change.[9]

Under the Paris Agreement of 2015, 169 countries committed to trying to limit warming to 'well below 2 degrees Celsius above pre-industrial levels and to pursue efforts to limit the temperature increase even further to 1.5 degrees Celsius'.[10] The main focus of the joint presidency of COP26 was to keep the 1.5 degrees Celsius limit alive by securing more robust 'nationally determined contributions' on greenhouse gas emissions from participating countries, reducing emissions by half by 2030 compared to 2010 levels. However, the Paris Agreement is too weak on this. One estimate, published by Climate Action Tracker on 9 November 2021, claims the national climate pledges made at COP26 are likely to deliver a median of 2.4 °C warming by 2100, with catastrophic consequences.[11]

To keep their COP26 commitments and achieve net zero emissions by 2050, both the UK and the EU will need to phase out fossil fuels in the short to medium term and replace them with carbon-free alternatives, including by greatly expanded renewable electricity capacity. By spring of 2022, however, the essential focus on decarbonisation was already in danger of being overshadowed by concerns about the security of price and supply of fossil fuel.

Whilst the UK was a leading advocate of action against climate change when a member of the EU, post-Brexit 'the UK … lacks a convincing strategy to match its rhetoric at COP on net zero',[12] despite its ambitious pledges and targets.[13] This view is shared by the House of Lords Industry and Regulators' Committee, whose report 'The net zero transformation: delivery, regulation and

7 Department for Business, Energy & Industrial Strategy, '*Powering Our Net Zero Future*' (Energy White Paper, 2020) <https://www.gov.uk/government/publications/energy-white-paper-powering-our-net-zero-future/energy-white-paper-powering-our-net-zero-future-accessible-html-version> accessed 4 May 2022.

8 Department for Business, Energy & Industrial Strategy. '*Net Zero Strategy: Build Back Greener*'. Policy Paper, 2021 < https://assets.publishing.service.gov.uk/government/uploads/system/uploads/attachment_data/file/1033990/net-zero-strategy-beis.pdf> accessed 4 May 2022.

9 Ibid.

10 United Nations (UN), 'Adoption of the Paris Agreement'. Framework for Convention on Climate Change. U.N. Doc. FCCC/CP/2015/L.9/Rev/1 (Dec. 12, 2015) <https://documents-dds-ny.un.org/doc/UNDOC/LTD/G15/283/19/PDF/G1528319.pdf?> OpenElement. Accessed 4 May 2022.

11 Climate Analytics and New Climate Institute. 'What do governments need to deliver in 2022?' (*Climate Action Tracker*, 1 December 2021. Berlin. <https://climateactiontracker.org/blog/what-do-governments-need-to-deliver-in-2022/> accessed 4 May 2022.

12 See *Financial Times* (2021). FT Editorial Board: 'UK needs a rapid plan to hit its green power goal'. 5 October, 2021. <https://www.ft.com/content/3b9d5f02-7085-4c55-a9a8-489e5314b2ff> accessed 22 May 2022.

13 See *Financial Times* (2021). FT Editorial Board: 'UK needs a rapid plan to hit its green power goal'. 5 October, 2021. <https://www.ft.com/content/3b9d5f02-7085-4c55-a9a8-489e5314b2ff> accessed 22 May 2022.

the consumer' concluded that the UK did not in fact have a credible plan to implement net zero.[14] On 1 April 2022, energy economist Sir Dieter Helm criticised the UK pledge to reach net zero by 2050 at minimal cost for being 'hopelessly unrealistic'.[15]

To support its target of quadrupling offshore wind capacity by the same date, the UK regulator committed in December 2021 to more than doubling the country's existing electricity interconnector capacity by 2030.[16] As discussed in Chapter 6, this should not only allow offshore wind farms to provide surplus electricity to both UK and the EU as required but should also enable the UK to import electricity from the EU when the wind is not blowing in the North Sea, addressing the challenge of the intermittency of renewable supply.[17]

As Goldberg explains in Chapter 2, post-Brexit trade in electricity between the UK and the EU IEM is, however, much less efficient and more costly since the UK is no longer party to the price market coupling arrangements that apply in the IEM. Although the Trade and Cooperation Agreement (TCA) foresees alternative market mechanisms via multi-region low-volume coupling, these are less efficient. Furthermore, there has been little progress in developing mechanisms to date due to the lack of political cooperation between the EU and the UK.

Even before the rise in fossil fuel prices at the end of 2021, the 27 countries of the post-Brexit EU had already set out a new strategy to expand renewable energy and reduce energy use quicker in the 'Fit For 55' Package.[18] This will require reliable back-up sources of supply to cope with the intermittency of renewables. Ideally these will be low or carbon-free alternatives such as hydro-electricity (an important source of energy in Switzerland), solar, or 'green' or 'blue' hydrogen abated by carbon capture and storage (CCS) technology. A number of Member States are also advocating for renewed investment in nuclear. Such policies, if

14 House of Lords Industry and Regulators Committee, *'The net zero transformation: delivery, regulation and the consumer'* <https://committees.parliament.uk/committee/517/industry-and-regulators-committee/news/161468/uk-will-miss-net-zero-target-without-urgent-action-warns-lords-committee/> accessed 4 May 2022.

15 Jim Pickard and Nathalie Thomas, 'Energy Expert slams UK's net-zero strategy as |"hopelessly unrealistic"' *Financial Times* (London 2 April 2022) <https://www.ft.com/content/18ed12e9-30c5-49ce-8543-549930a552c3?bingParse> accessed 22 May 2022.

16 Department for Business, Energy & Industrial Strategy, 'Powering Our Net Zero Future' (Energy White Paper, 2020) <https://www.gov.uk/government/publications/energy-white-paper-powering-our-net-zero-future/energy-white-paper-powering-our-net-zero-future-accessible-html-version> accessed 4 May 2022.

17 Department for Business, Energy & Industrial Strategy. 'Net Zero Strategy: Build Back Greener'. Policy Paper, 2021 <https://assets.publishing.service.gov.uk/government/uploads/system/uploads/attachment_data/file/1033990/net-zero-strategy-beis.pdf> accessed 4 May 2022.

18 Publication Office of the European Union 'Communication from the Commission to the European Parliament, the European Council, the Council, the European Economic and Social Committee and the Committee of the Regions – The European Green Deal' COM (2019) 640 Final 11.12.2019 Communication from the Commission on The European Green Deal [2019] COM(2019) 640 final accessed 4 May 2022

adopted more widely, could potentially secure long-term energy and climate security around the world, albeit (particularly in the case of new nuclear production) bringing with them corresponding significant environmental concerns. It remains to be seen how resilient the EU's commitment to decarbonisation remains in the face of the security of price and supply crisis it now faces.

13.3 New challenges and impact of Brexit: divergence or dependence?

As time passes, specific consequences of Brexit will be subsumed as part of the overwhelming dominance of the energy crisis associated with Russia's behaviour leading up to and culminating in the Ukraine war, and the (now distinct) responses to this of the UK and the EU.

In 2021–2022, soaring global wholesale oil and gas prices in the UK accompanied by Ofgem's 'price cap' forced nearly 30 'new entrant' energy suppliers to cease trading. This demonstrated that competition in and of itself does not deliver price security. As observed by Dieter Helm, 'officials and regulators forgot that … security of supply is a public and not a private good'.[19] This led to an interrogation of the concept of 'competition for competition's sake'.

Governments have become more interventionist both in the UK and the EU. The UK government announced a package of grants and loans to try to mitigate the impact of price rises on consumers.[20] Chancellor Rishi Sunak's 'Energy Bills Rebate', which offered consumers £200 off energy bills in October 2022, to be paid back over five years, was described by consumer campaigner Martin Lewis as a 'negative compulsory levy on all bills for one year, then a compulsory levy on all bills for five years'.[21] There was no help, however, for the 4.5m UK households with prepayment meters, which pay higher prices for their energy, despite being more likely to be considered 'vulnerable'.[22] Meanwhile in the EU, France announced a 4% 'price cap' by limiting energy bills and forcing state controlled Électricité de France (EDF), at an estimated cost of €8.4bn (£7bn), to sell wholesale electricity at well below market prices. Spain introduced a windfall tax on electricity generators

19 Dieter Helm, 'The gas and electricity crisis – causes, consequences'. (*Dietr Helm Blog*, 4 October 2021) <http://www.dieterhelm.co.uk/energy/energy/the-gas-and-electricity-crisis-causes-and-consequences/ > accessed 4 May 2022.

20 HM Treasury, 'Energy Bill Rebate'. Press Release. <https://www.gov.uk/government/news/millions-to-receive-350-boost-to-help-with-rising-energy-costs>

21 M. Lewis, 'How the new flat rate £200 energy bill loan really works'. Money Saving Expert. '<https://www.moneysavingexpert.com/news/2022/02/martin-lewis--how-the-flat-rate-p200-energy-bill-loan-really-wor/> accessed 21 May 2022.

22 Clare Barrett, 'Sunak's energy rebate leaves the poorest out in the cold' *Financial Times* (London, 10 February 2022) <https://www.ft.com/content/14a4ff41-68f5-4361-aed1-603d1a16bef9> accessed 4 May 2022.

and gas producers, and Germany decided to replace green levies on bills with state subsidies.[23]

This trend towards state intervention runs counter to the EU tradition of liberalising the IEM and is indicative of the future drivers of energy policy. In the UK, the legitimacy of state aid or subsidies of various forms is yet another area of uncertainty created for the energy sector, amongst others, by Brexit, as, at the time of writing, the post-Brexit UK subsidy control (state aid) regime is still not in place.[24] The notable shift towards using state subsidies to cushion the impact of higher energy prices on consumers is criticised by economists as lowering the incentive for households and businesses to reduce their consumption of energy, while making it harder to wean countries off Russian fossil fuels.[25]

In the EU, Member States were free to choose how they would respond to the urgent need to provide support for consumers in the face of the energy crisis. The EU's response to the threat to security of supply, however, whether as a result of unilateral action by Russia[26] or sanctions on Russia by the West, had to be made collectively, in the context of the policies of the integrated IEM as a whole. On 4 April 2022, with the agreement of Member States, the EU Commission announced that Member States would have up to 4 months (180 days) to terminate existing coal supply contracts with Russian providers. Agreeing measures relating to the supply of oil and gas, however, would prove more difficult. Member States have different degrees of dependency on these key fuels, making it harder to reach a consensus.[27]

Following Brexit, the UK must follow its own path in relation to its response to the crisis, as its policies are no longer determined by the EU IEM rules and associated policy decisions. In 2021, the UK imported roughly half its gas from Europe (with the other half coming from the North Sea), and only around 4%[28] of its

23 See Jillian Ambrose, 'France to force EDF to take €8.4bn hit with energy bill cap'. *The Guardian* (London, 14 February 2022) <https://www.theguardian.com/business/2022/jan/14/france-edf-cap-household-energy-bills> accessed 5 May 2022.

24 See P. Foster, 'Rethinking State Aid Rules After Brexit' *Financial Times* (London, 2 December 2021) <https://www.ft.com/content/716dd066-2ebc-4a06-996b-27ab7bc47d66>

25 See Martin Arnold, 'Shielding EU energy users from high prices may backfire, warn economists' *Financial Times* 17 April 2022 <https://www.ft.com/search?q=Shielding+EU+energy+users+from+high+prices+may+backfire%2C+warn+economists>

26 At time of writing, Russia has already taken unilateral action in relation to gas supplies to EU members Poland, Bulgaria, and Finland.

27 See Jorge Liboreiro and Pedro Sacadua. 'Coal, trucks, vodka and Putin's daughters' Euronews 8 April 2022 (Updated) <https://www.euronews.com/my-europe/2022/04/08/coal-trucks-vodka-and-putin-s-daughters-here-s-what-s-in-the-latest-round-of-eu-sanctions> accessed 4 May 2022.

28 See Oliver Wright, Emily Gosden, Kat Lay: 'Britain to spend more than £2bn on Russian gas imports'. *The Times* (2022). 3 March 2022. <https://www.thetimes.co.uk/article/britain-to-spend-more-than-2bn-on-russian-gas-imports-mb76tj5k9#:~:text=Britain%20is%20on%20track%20to,shipments%20arriving%20in%20the%20country>

supply came directly from Russia, in the form of LNG.[29] On 6 April 2022, the UK government announced that 'by the end of 2022, the UK will end all dependency on Russian coal and oil, and end imports of gas as soon as possible thereafter'.[30]

Whilst the UK is therefore less dependent on Russian gas than the EU, which prior to Russia's invasion of Ukraine relied on Russia to provide 35%–40% of its gas supplies,[31] it remains one of the biggest users of gas in Europe. Not only does gas heat an estimated 85% of UK homes,[32] but gas-fired plants also still account for over 35% of total UK power generation. As the UK market is closely connected to markets in mainland Europe, price rises on the continent are inevitably passed on to UK consumers,[33] and serious supply shortages in Europe could result in the UK having to compete with the EU and others on world markets for supplies of LNG.

The UK's economy is roughly one sixth the size of that of the EU, and it is no longer party to EU energy solidarity treaties. If Russian gas supplies were to be cut off, whether by Russia or by the EU through sanctions, the UK may be forced to bid for gas on the world market, against much larger markets in both the EU and Asia.[34] Bilateral relationships with EU and European Economic Area (EEA) partners such as Norway, an important supplier, and with the Republic of Ireland (which, conversely, is heavily dependent upon energy imports from the UK), could become even more important going forward in ensuring reciprocal supply security in relation to gas.

Furthermore, there are very specific ongoing Brexit consequences, e.g., in Northern Ireland/the Republic of Ireland, and in relation to the exclusion of the UK from protocols etc. relating to getting the most from efficient electricity interconnection. The future trajectory of these consequences remains unclear, as

29 See Ambrose, J: 'How vulnerable is the UK energy system as tensions rise between Russia and the Ukraine', *The Guardian*: 2022. 24 January 2022 <https://www.theguardian.com/business/2022/jan/24/how-vulnerable-is-uk-energy-system-as-tensions-rise-between-russia-and-ukraine>

30 FCDO, 'UK imposes sweeping new sanctions to starve Putin's war machine. Foreign Commonwealth and Development Office: Press release. 6 April 2022. <https://www.gov.uk/government/news/uk-imposes-sweeping-new-sanctions-to-starve-putins-war-machine#:~:text=In%202020%20UK%20investment%20in,as%20soon%20as%20possible%20thereafter>. accessed 21 May 2021.

31 Se Kate Abnett. 'Europe's plans to wean itself off Russian gas'. Reuters Fact Box. 8 March 2022 <https://www.reuters.com/business/energy/europes-plan-wean-itself-off-russian-gas-faster-2022-03-02/#:~:text=The%2027%2Dcountry%20EU%20imports,or%20Moscow%20could%20curb%20supply>. Accessed 21 May 2021.

32 Energy Savings Trust (2021) 'The Future of Heating in the UK Heat Pump or Hydrogen' blog post 28 May 2021 <https://energysavingtrust.org.uk/the-future-of-heating-in-the-uk-heat-pumps-or-hydrogen/> accessed 31 May 2021.

33 OpCit (24).

34 See Michael Grubb: 'The UK energy strategy is both cowardly and incoherent' *Financial Times* 10 April 2022 <https://www.ft.com/content/3fe73617-5f8f-4b70-8856-ca53e2ec92b3> accessed 21 May 2022.

they will, in turn, depend on political developments. These include, for example, whether or not Article 16 of the Northern Ireland Protocol is triggered unilaterally by the UK, thereby undermining the TCA, with potential consequences for the Single Electricity Market of Northern Ireland and the Republic and possibly for ongoing cooperation with EU countries in relation to the interconnectors from the UK to the continent of Europe.

13.4 A new British Energy Security Strategy

Post-Brexit, there had been mounting pressure on the UK government to announce a new energy security strategy. The BEIS finally announced the 'British Energy Security Strategy' on 7 April 2022 (the Strategy). It claims to be 'accelerating our move towards cleaner home-grown energy'. It has, however, been widely criticised for a lack of ambition around developing onshore wind and solar, the most cost-effective and speedily available sources of renewable energy. The Strategy prioritises instead less strategic, more costly options, such as nuclear power (which will take years to deliver results and has a history of underperformance in both the UK and Europe) and offshore wind (which requires expensive and complex infrastructure and will take several years to become operative).

The Strategy includes investment in a new generation of nuclear power stations. The UK Climate Change Committee's (CCC) sixth carbon budget, published in 2020, identified nuclear as playing a key role in the UK's transition to net zero, with nuclear and power generation abated by CCS providing 10%–25% of electricity by 2050. Building on this, the Strategy set the goal of up to eight more nuclear reactors and up to 24GW of deployed nuclear power by 2050. However, there is scepticism about the likelihood of this level of commitment to nuclear in the UK in the long term. Under the 'regulated asset base' model that the government now proposes, many of the costs would be reflected in consumers' bills years before they begin operating, exacerbating the problem of high energy costs. As *The Economist* commented about the new Strategy: 'By favouring expensive technologies it may end up with nothing'.

The Strategy increases the target for offshore wind from 40GW to 50GW by 2030. The Strategy also aims to 'double our UK ambition for hydrogen production to up to 10GW by 2030, with at least half of this from electrolytic [green] hydrogen' (made by passing electricity through water to separate out the hydrogen and oxygen). This target, at least, seems relatively unambitious when one considers the potential to use existing (retrofitted) natural gas infrastructure to transport offshore green energy to shore more efficiently as hydrogen (electrolysed at sea) rather than as electricity.

Aspects of the Strategy notably differ from EU policies. The lack of commitment to onshore wind, for example, is at odds with the approach of the German Green party, now part of the governing coalition, who have committed to up to 10GW of new annual onshore wind by 2025. This implies that, unlike the UK, Germany plans to base its future electricity mix around wind and solar, with hydrogen as back-up. Similarly, whilst plans to improve energy efficiency in buildings are an integral part of the EU's energy strategy, the UK Strategy is notably devoid of any such plans, apparently reflecting the reluctance of the Treasury to make any new energy efficiency commitments. This ignores both the CCC's warning in the sixth carbon budget that the UK's existing plans were inadequate and the reality that the UK has many poorly insulated homes.

The Strategy also affirms the UK's 'commitment to a strong and evolving North Sea industry', and also leaves the door open to 'fracking'. Despite protestations to the contrary by the UK government, further exploitation of new fossil fuel sources is undoubtedly inconsistent with the legally binding commitment to 'net zero by 2050' made in 2019, as well as the UK's enhanced climate commitments pledged at COP26 in Glasgow in November 2021. If the UK cannot move away from continued exploitation of fossil fuels in favour of renewable sources, it looks likely to fail to implement both net zero and decarbonisation targets.

If the UK had remained a member of the EU, it would have had to align with the EU's policies about how to respond to both the energy security crisis and the price shock caused both by the Ukraine war and the ongoing climate crisis. Post-Brexit, however, it is free to choose its own response and corresponding policies. The main legacy of Brexit, therefore, is increased isolation and uncertainty in an already dangerously unstable environment. This isolation, in turn, is leading to questionable choices on national energy security which both fail to address the short-term energy price crisis and potentially undermine 'net zero' commitments. Instead of further integration with the EU's IEM, the attempts to create more self-sufficiency as a form of nationalistic protectionism are leading to misguided choices which will deliver nothing to struggling consumers and also undermine the UK's climate change credentials in the longer term.

Beyond Brexit – In Lieu of a Conclusion

Ana Stanič and Silke Goldberg

Introduction

'Get Brexit Done' was the slogan for Boris Johnson's winning electoral campaign in December 2019, which provided the political platform to negotiate the Trade and Cooperation Agreement (TCA), the legal and institutional framework for the cooperation between the UK and the EU post-Brexit.

The implications of Brexit on the energy sector barely featured in the debates about sovereignty and EU membership in the run up to the Brexit referendum and thereafter during the Brexit negotiations. Yet, as the provisions of the TCA show, the energy sector has by operation of law been swept up in the political consequences of Brexit, which makes the search for practical solutions (e.g., in relation to market coupling) harder.

Although the UK left the EU on 1 January 2021, it has been in near constant negotiations with the EU ever since – be it over the status of Northern Ireland, financial services, fisheries, or energy trading. Following the end of the Transition Period, the UK is now a third country in relation to the EU, and is beginning to feel the impact of this status. A recent study by the Centre for European Reform has shown a significant shortfall in the UK's GDP by the last quarter of 2021, which is attributable to Brexit rather than other factors such as the COVID-19 pandemic.[1]

While the TCA avoids the imposition of tariffs on electricity, on gas, and on equipment necessary to generate electricity given their classification as goods, as this book shows, Brexit has brought about changes that have and will invariably continue to have an impact on the GB, Irish, and EU energy markets. As discussed in Chapters 2 and 4, the impact of Brexit on the energy sector has already been felt keenly, in particular in relation to electricity trading and the creation of new interconnectors.

This final Chapter of the book identifies and summarises in turn the main post-Brexit challenges facing the energy sectors of both the UK and the EU:

1 John Springford, 'What can we know about Brexit so far?', Center for European Reform, 9 June 2022, available at <https://www.cer.eu/publications/archive/policy-brief/2022/cost-brexit-so-far>

DOI: 10.4324/9781003364337-15

uncertainty, regulatory divergency, and the return to political economy. In view of the impact of the war in Ukraine and the sanctions imposed on Russia's energy flows and energy sector, the ongoing tensions between UK and EU pertaining to Northern Ireland unleashed by Brexit, the energy transition challenges facing the energy sector, it calls for pragmatic cooperation between the UK and the EU, at the very least in relation to the energy sector, to be made a priority.

The key terms of the TCA and the ensuing uncertainty

As evidenced in this book, the provisions of the TCA concerning energy are expressed by reference to general principles and are vaguely worded. Specifically, obligations to cooperate are imposed without providing concrete detail as to the framework for such cooperation or any timeframe for implementation.

Whilst the TCA proclaims, in relation to the energy sector, as its aim (i) the facilitation of trade and investment in energy and raw materials between the EU and the UK; and (ii) 'support security of supply and environmental sustainability, notably in contributing to the fight against climate change'[2] this does not mask the following:

First, that its overall scope and architecture is narrower and does not cover the same range of energy sector regulation as the EU's Internal Energy Market (IEM) framework.

Second, that it merely enshrines a number of core principles which are to underpin energy relations between the UK and EU going forward, such as non-discrimination, third party access (TPA) in relation to transmission and distribution networks, and unbundling of Transmission System Operators (TSOs) as well as competition and market principles as the governing principles for the operation of their energy markets.

Third, that in doing so, the TCA mirrors the principles which underpinned the regime introduced in the EU as part of the liberalisation of the energy market in the late 1990s and early 2000s whilst falling short of requiring the UK to commit to the EU's unbundling and target model to achieve these principles.

Fourth, that it does not contain a detailed implementation framework for achieving cooperation in practice. As the ongoing negotiations since the signature of the TCA already demonstrate, this means that the UK and the EU will have to negotiate various aspects of their energy relations on a near-permanent basis in future. The ongoing negotiations concerning the future electricity trading and market-coupling arrangements, as discussed in Chapter 2, are evidence of this.

Fifth, that the energy framework as agreed in the energy Chapter of the TCA is provisional in nature. As per Article 331, the entire energy Chapter is set to

2 See Article 299 of the TCA.

automatically expire in June 2026 unless both sides agree to extend it. This creates considerable structural uncertainty which cannot easily be addressed.

The ongoing negotiations between UK and the EU concerning the nature and scope of the cooperation, given the temporary nature of the energy relations agreed under the TCA, are a major source of uncertainty for the energy markets. Regulatory certainty is a key precondition for large investments to be made in both jurisdictions to achieve energy transition and decarbonisation goals.

It remains to be seen if and how the UK and the EU will cooperate in relation to the regulatory framework for hydrogen and carbon capture respectively, as neither is covered by the TCA, and both jurisdictions are currently developing the relevant legislation for this nascent industry. In order to enable the required investments, UK and EU legislators should be wary of instituting rule changes or tolerating regulatory uncertainty as a default by failing to cooperate.

The TCA and ensuing regulatory divergence

Importantly, the TCA differs from trade agreements entered to date around the world. It is the first such agreement that places the management of future divergences between signatories at its core. Typically, trade agreements provide for regulatory alignment and deepening cooperation. As discussed in Chapter 6, the TCA, instead, (i) circumscribes the right of the signatories to regulate in order to achieve legitimate public policy goals to those based on objective and non-discriminatory criteria;[3] (ii) imposes a non-regression obligation from climate and environmental levels of protection below the levels that were in place at the end of the Transition Period;[4] and (iii) accords a right to adopt strictly necessary and proportionate rebalancing measures in circumstances where there is a significant divergence in the signatories' future policies and priorities in respect of labour and social and environmental or climate protection and including subsidy control which materially impacts on trade or investment between them.[5]

In other words, going forward, divergence in the way the energy sectors of the UK and the EU are regulated will only be tempered to the extent it triggers the aforementioned provisions of the TCA. Accordingly, over time, divergence between the UK and EU regulatory frameworks will grow and this in turn will only increase uncertainty for the sector and hamper investment.

Return to political economy

Another important implication brought about by Brexit highlighted in this book is the return of politics as the driving force in energy relations as between the

3 Article 303(4) TCA.
4 Article 391 TCA.
5 Article 411 TCA.

UK and the EU. After decades of liberalisation, market integration, and the depoliticisation of regulatory decisions, the TCA has regressed and put politics back at the core of the energy sector. The implementation of many provisions of the TCA depends on political agreement being reached by the parties to translate the general principles proclaimed therein into a precise framework for the sector. The energy Chapter of the TCA resembles the provisions of bilateral pipeline treaties of the 1970s and 1980s, with general diplomatic declarations of intent and little in the way of practical implementation.

This new 'era of political economy' in the energy sector has a number of practical consequences for the energy sector, including:

1. The designation of the relevant EU authority for granting exemptions to new cross-border infrastructure pursuant to the TCA is subject to the prior political agreement of the Specialised Committee on Energy, whose members are appointed by the UK Government and the EU Commission, respectively.
2. On more than one occasion in 2021 disagreements including regarding fisheries between France and the UK have threatened to affect the cross-border flow of electricity.[6]

The Swiss experience, as discussed in Chapter 12 of this book, shows that the primacy of politics and the insistence on politically and institutionally 'pure' decisions and outcomes create difficulties both at macro levels (in relation to the design of the energy market and the cross-border cooperation of institutions) and at more micro levels (e.g., balancing of transmission systems). As discussed here, this has implications for the ability of both the UK and the EU to meet objectives such as decarbonisation and security of supply going forward.

Brexit and the ability to meet climate change and energy transition challenges

The TCA is the first foreign trade agreement which elevates climate change commitments and standards to an 'essential element' for a 'level playing field' between the parties. Not only does it require the UK and the EU to 'respect the Paris Agreement and the process set up by the UNFCCC and refrain from acts or omissions that would materially defeat the object and purpose of the Paris Agreement', it also introduces sanction mechanisms should either fall behind on its commitments.

While the positioning of climate change as a key element in the future cooperation between the parties has won plaudits, the obligation to cooperate in relation to climate change remains entirely theoretical as at the time of writing this book. The newly introduced UK emission trading system (UK ETS) is designed in a way to make linking to the EU ETS straightforward since key technical design

6 <https://www.theguardian.com/world/2021/oct/05/france-uk-jersey-eu-energy-supply-fishing-row-channel>, 5 October 2021.

features of the two systems match. However, and as discussed in Chapters 6 and 7, respectively, for political reasons, no real effort has been made to link the two regimes as at the date of this book.

Importantly, and as highlighted in Chapters 3 and 6, the ongoing uncertainty regarding the regulatory framework governing the UK's energy sector post-Brexit and the likely regulatory divergence between the UK and EU energy sectors has increased costs for new energy investments. This could jeopardise the UK's ability to achieve its 'net-zero by 2050' targets. This is particularly the case as the supply chains in renewable energy are dominated by foreign manufacturers of equipment.[7] The Offshore Wind Energy Council noted in 2019 that Ørsted (a Danish company) currently has the largest UK offshore wind portfolio by owner share (~24%). Other companies who own a significant proportion of the current offshore capacity deployed offshore include Vattenfall (~13%), SSE (~12%), Iberdrola (~11%) and Innogy (8%). In the market for foundations for offshore wind projects, German, Danish, and Dutch companies were found, in the same study, to have the majority of the market share in the UK and the EU.[8] As supply chains are already under strain as a result of measures taken in response to COVID-19, Brexit has added to the challenges facing energy sector in transition.

Brexit and geopolitical challenges

The new geopolitical realities of the war in Ukraine have raised fundamental questions regarding Europe's energy security. In response to Russia's invasion of Ukraine on 24 February 2022, broad sanctions have been introduced by the US, UK, and EU against Russia and Belarus including in respect of trade and investment in energy resources. Steps have also been taken by the UK and the EU to reassess their energy strategies.

Supply security is not a new concern for the EU, and the war in Ukraine has only exacerbated the situation. Already in 2014, the European Commission stated that '[i]n the long term, the Union's energy security is inseparable from and significantly fostered by its need to move to a competitive, low-carbon economy which reduces the use of imported fossil fuels'.[9] In light of the war in Ukraine, the European Commission has called for energy security policies of the EU to undergo a paradigm shift[10] and contribute to the acceleration of investment in renewable energies and the accompanying infrastructure. As outlined in Chapters 2 and 6, respectively, even before the war in Ukraine, the ability to meet energy transition

7 Offshore Wind Energy Council: 'The UK Offshore Wind Industry: Supply Chain Review', January 2019 <https://cdn.ymaws.com/www.renewableuk.com/resource/resmgr/publications/supply_chain_review_31.01.20.pdf>

8 Ibid, page 7.

9 Commission, 'European Energy Strategy' COM (2014) 330 final.

10 Nikolaus J. Kurmayer, 'EU ministers brace for future without Russian energy', Euractiv, 1 March 2022 <https://www.euractiv.com/section/energy/news/eu-ministers-brace-for-future-without-russian-energy/>

and decarbonisation targets required more interconnectors to be built to address the increase in intermittent load. As the stalled interconnector projects reveal, closer cooperation between the EU and the UK as well as Switzerland is key to the construction of such projects.

In its REPower EU paper of 8 March 2022, the European Commission called for a reduction in the EU's demand for Russian gas by two thirds before the end of 2022 and for complete independence from Russian gas well before 2030.[11] Although this first objective has now been quietly dropped by the Commission, Kadri Simson, the European Commissioner for Energy, has recently confirmed that liquefied natural gas (LNG) terminals and new interconnectors will play a key role in reducing dependence on Russian gas.[12] Whilst she did not specifically reference the role of the UK in achieving this objective, there is no doubt that British LNG terminals and the Fluxys/IUK gas interconnector represent important infrastructure for energy imports into the EU and are therefore key to enhancing EU's security of gas supply.

As Gazprom stopped deliveries, the EU, is deliberating ways to enlarge its sanction regime to include an embargo on Russian oil and gas, the effects of the war in Ukraine will be felt in the energy sector and beyond as established energy supply chains need to be replaced at higher costs in Europe – including from the UK.

It goes without saying that in light of likely further sanctions on Russian fossil fuel imports into the EU or the UK and the ensuing disruption to the gas market, closer cooperation between the EU and the UK will be needed. Yet, in spite of the political alignment of the UK and the EU against Russia, there is little evidence of any such cooperation at present.

The newly proposed British energy security strategy seems to ignore the regional energy interdependence with the EU.[13] Whilst the Strategy reiterates existing renewable energy targets and includes new commitments to phase out Russian oil and coal by the end of 2022 and imports of Russian LNG as soon as possible thereafter, it does not include a long-term strategy for regional or international engagement. In this context, proximity matters, and having good cooperation mechanisms with immediate neighbours matters – otherwise Global Britain may turn out to be isolated Britain.

11 COM(2022) 108 final: Communication from the Commission to the European Parliament, the European Council, the European Economic and Social Committee and the Committee of the Regions: 'REPowerEU: Joint European Action for more affordable, secure and sustainable energy'

12 REPowerEU: A plan to rapidly reduce dependence on Russian fossil fuels and fast forward the green transition, <https://ec.europa.eu/commission/presscorner/detail/en/IP_22_3131>. For the statement by Commissioner Simson, see: 'How Europe can cut natural gas imports from Russia significantly within a year', <https://www.iea.org/news/how-europe-can-cut-natural-gas-imports-from-russia-significantly-within-a-year>.

13 <https://www.gov.uk/government/publications/british-energy-security-strategy/british-energy-security-strategy#international-delivery>

Brexit and the challenges facing Ireland and Northern Ireland

As discussed in Chapter 11, Brexit has already had a significant impact on Ireland from an energy perspective. There are significant issues with regard to electricity policy, market efficiency, regulatory oversight, cross-border energy trading, and security of supply, to name just a few.

In addition, the continuous disagreements between the UK government and the EU as to the status of the Northern Ireland Protocol as well as the UK's government threat to unilaterally disapply the same create further uncertainty for the energy market of Ireland and Northern Ireland as well as for the GB energy market and the EU IEM. Should the UK government decide to walk away from the Northern Ireland Protocol, the entire TCA could be suspended.

Pragmatic cooperation is needed in the decade ahead

As this book evidences, the challenges the GB energy sector is experiencing at present might only be the beginning of its difficulties unless the UK and the EU manage to set aside their differences in favour of outcome-based solutions.

It is unlikely that the UK will re-join the EU, the European Economic Area (EEA), or the European Free Trade Association (EFTA) any time soon. Yet there is no place for British isolation at a time when the whole of Europe has to re-think its energy policy and supply security strategy and achieve decarbonisation targets.

In light of the challenges ahead, pragmatic cooperation between the EU and the UK must be the way ahead. Article 33 of the TCA envisages a more detailed agreement on energy matters to be made. Now is the time to take steps to do so in earnest.

Index

**Page numbers in bold reference tables.

For Product Safety Concerns and Information please contact our EU representative GPSR@taylorandfrancis.com
Taylor & Francis Verlag GmbH, Kaufingerstraße 24, 80331 München, Germany

www.ingramcontent.com/pod-product-compliance
Lightning Source LLC
LaVergne TN
LVHW021122300926
849160LV00010B/819
9781032427713